THE
LETTERBOOK OF
SIR GEORGE
ETHEREGE

Schöner PROSPECT der Steinern Brucken zu Regensburg.

Regensburg.

Statt am Hof.

THE
LETTERBOOK OF
SIR GEORGE
ETHEREGE

Edited with an Introduction
and Notes by
SYBIL ROSENFELD
M.A. (*Lond.*)

BENJAMIN BLOM, INC.
Publishers New York 1971

First published London, 1928
Reissued 1971 by
Benjamin Blom, Inc.
New York, N.Y. 10025

Library of Congress
Catalog Card Number 79-173181

Printed in the
United States of America

CONTENTS

vii

INTRODUCTION

I. SIR GEORGE ETHEREGE

S IR George Etherege[1] takes a prominent place
in the category of authors whose biography
when regarded from the point of view of dates
and facts is but barren ground, but of whose
character and habits we have nevertheless an
intimate knowledge. The dates of the dramatist's
birth, marriage, and death are all uncertain, but the
Letterbook can more than compensate us for these
lamentable missing links by revealing to us the
personality of one of whom it has been well said:
'He is the perfect man of his particular world'.[2]

Our chief sources of information for the life of
Etherege are Oldys's article in the *Biographia
Britannica* (1750), which is unreliable, and various
contemporary references, which are more often
than not contradictory. One of the biographer's
principal difficulties lies therefore in the necessity
for discriminating between legendary and authori-
tative material.

Until quite recently Oldys's assertion that Etherege
was descended from, or allied to, an ancient Oxford-
shire family, whereof the scholar Dr. George
Etherege was a scion, passed unchallenged. The
antiquarian also noted the existence of an Etherege
in the town of Thame before the Reformation, but
opined that the dramatist was born near London
from a branch of the family that had settled in
Middlesex. Successive biographers mechanically
copied Oldys's statements until Miss D. Foster,[3]

[1] Etherege invariably spells his name this way; contemporaries use Etheredge, Etheridge, or Etheridg.

[2] Palmer's *Comedy of Manners*, p. 35.

[3] *Times Literary Supplement*, Feb. 16, 1922; *Notes and Queries*,
May 6, 13, 27, 1922.

following up Sir Edmund Gosse's[1] suggestion that Captain George Etherege, a planter in Bermuda, may have been the author's father, together with an allusion to 'my cousin Middleton' in the Letterbook, evolved a plausible theory of descent, accompanied by the following genealogical tree:

Richard Powney				George Etherege, gent., of Maidenhead	
John Powney	daughter, m. John Whitfield, Esq., of Maidenhead, Berks.	Mary Powney	George Etherege, resident in Bermuda	Martha, m. Willm. Canning of Elsenham, Essex[2]	John Etherege, clerk, of Tangmer

George Etherege 'the younger', the dramatist   Five other children

Captain Etherege's father, according to Miss Foster, was one George Etherege of Maidenhead, Berks., who later became a vintner in London,[3] to whom she alludes for the sake of convenience as George Etherege the elder. He was born in 1576, was a pioneer in the Bermuda settlement, one of the 118 original adventurers in the Bermuda Company, and a subscriber to the Virginia Company of London (dissolved in 1625). He lived until after 1656, in which year he is referred to as being about 80 years of age. In 1625 George Etherege the elder and one William Middleton entered into possession of a lease of the manor or farm of Ives. Three years later Etherege purchased the farm of Hollenden and six parcels of land called Oldwood in Kent, but, finding the land encumbered with obligations amounting to

[1] *Seventeenth Century Studies*, p. 261.

[2] On Feb. 19, 1627, the Bishop of London issued a marriage licence for William Canning, Gent., of Elsenham, Essex, bachelor, 22, and Martha Etherege, of St. Clement Danes, spinster, 18, daughter of George Etherege of same, vintner (Harleian Society Publications, 26, p. 192).

[3] See note 2, also *Colonial Records, Bermuda*, 1622–76, where he is described as a vintner in a transfer of land.

£650, he took the conveyance of inheritance in the names of his sons George, then a married man of about 21 years of age, resident in Bermuda, and John, clerk, of Tangmer, Sussex. John had been placed first with a glass seller and subsequently with a proctor in Arches Court, but 'being idle or constrained in his resolution [he] did not continue with the said proctor'. Of 'unsettled and improvident courses' he refused, on the death of his elder brother, to transfer the property that he held in trust to his nephews, asserting that the farm was now solely his and bringing a law-suit[1] to prevent the six children of Captain Etherege from inheriting. The orphans, however, were helped by their grandfather, who transferred to them in trust the use of the property in Kent.

Captain George married Mary Powney, daughter of Richard Powney, of Berks., and was already in Bermuda in 1628, where presumably he took over his father's property and where he was much esteemed by his fellow-colonists. He died in 'parts beyond the seas' in 1651, leaving the administration of his property to his wife, who, we may assume, returned to England with her six children to claim the manor which her brother-in-law was supposed to be holding in trust for them.

The identification of the dramatist with George Etherege the younger, eldest of the Captain's children, rests principally on the connexion of the family with the family of Middleton.[2] If indeed he was the son of Captain Etherege, he was in all probability born in Bermuda. Oldys gives the date of his birth as about 1636, but a poem addressed to him by Dryden early in 1686 contains the couplet:

And do not much for cold atone
By bringing thither [to Ratisbon] fifty-one,

[1] P.R.O. Hamilton, C. 7/428/43; Collins, 133/83, Chancery Proceedings.   [2] See p. 313, 'my cousin Middleton'.

3   B 2

which points to his being fifty-one at the time of its composition, in which case the year of his birth would be either 1634 or 1635. A. W. Verity[1] has pointed out that 'bringing' might be taken to imply that Etherege was fifty-one on his arrival in Ratisbon in late 1685, so that he may possibly have been born as early as 1632 or 1633. There remains the third possibility that the exigency of rhyme compelled Dryden to stretch a point. Between an unreliable authority and an ambiguous rhymed couplet there is little to choose.

If Etherege was born in Bermuda, he probably came to England with his mother on the death of his father when he was in his teens. It is somewhat strange then that neither he himself nor any contemporary, in lampoon, poem, or letter, appears to have made any reference to those early years in a far distant colony.

With regard to the dramatist's education, authorities are equally vague and unsatisfactory. Cibber in his *Lives of the Poets*[2] states that he travelled in France in his younger years, and therefore could have made no long stay at the University, whilst Oldys tentatively lets slip the remark: "'Tis thought he had some education at the University of Cambridge', and agrees that he afterwards travelled into France and then to Flanders. In the absence of any sort of proof, these statements carry but little weight, and it seems unlikely, taking into consideration his private circumstances and the unfavourable political situation, that Etherege ever attended either University. Internal evidence from his plays and letters, on the other hand, combined with a consideration of the necessarily anomalous position of any Royalist family during the Commonwealth, make easily

[1] *Works of Sir George Etherege.*
[2] Compiled from MS. notes of Thomas Coxeter, 1753, vol. iii, p. 33.

credible the story of a sojourn in France. Sir Edmund Gosse[1] suggests that Etherege resided abroad from 1658 to 1663, and believes that those years were spent principally in Paris: 'His French, in prose and verse, is as fluent as his English; and his plays are full of allusions that show him to be intimately at home in Parisian matters'. The French of the Letterbook is certainly idiomatic, though the grammar is by no means unimpeachable, but Etherege had had twenty years in which to forget, and we may blame the secretary for mistakes in orthography. What is of more importance is that his first play exhibits clearly the influence of the new school of French comedy, which found its consummation in Molière, whose early productions Etherege may quite well have seen in the French capital. Of other languages Etherege appears to have had little or no knowledge. Dennis[2] affirms: 'to my certain knowledge he understood neither Greek nor Latin', whilst the Letterbook is witness to his poverty of German.

We re-enter the realm of mere gossip with Gildon's[3] phrase: 'His first applications were to the law', to which Oldys added the details: 'he studied for a while the Municipal Laws at one of the Inns of Court in London', and the *Biographica Dramatica* the embroidery: 'but finding that kind of study too heavy for his volatile and airy disposition, and consequently making but little progress in it, he soon quitted it for pleasure and the pursuit of gayer accomplishments'.

It is pleasant at last to stand on firm ground with the date 1664, the year of the production and publication of our author's first play, *The Comical Revenge, or Love in a Tub*, acted at the Lincoln's Inn Fields

[1] *Op. cit.*, p. 262.
[2] *Defence of Sir Fopling Flutter*, p. 16.
[3] Followed by Giles Jacob, Cibber, and Whincop.

Theatre in March by the Duke's Company,[1] and printed twice within nine months. Its production marked an important era, not only in the life of Etherege, but also in the history of English comedy, for it was the first full-fledged Restoration comedy of manners to be seen on our stage, the model for all those licentious, debonair, witty plays for which the latter half of the seventeenth century is so notorious. The indefatigable Pepys[2] records on January 4, 1664/5: 'Saw *Love in a Tub*, which is very merry, but only so by gesture, not wit at all, which methinks is beneath the house', a verdict with which the majority of the gallants and ladies who patronized the theatre would certainly not have agreed. On October 29, 1666, Pepys saw the comedy given at court in the presence of the King and Queen, Duke and Duchess of York, and court ladies, but still thought it 'a silly play, and though done by the Duke's people yet having neither Betterton nor his wife, and the whole thing ill done'. Nevertheless, Downes records that the play brought £1,000 to the company in a month, and gained more reputation than any preceding comedy.

In the dedication of the play to Charles, Lord Buckhurst (afterwards Earl of Dorset), the author remarks: 'The Writing of it was a Means to make me known to your Lordship: The Acting of it has lost me no Reputation'; indeed, from this time on-

[1] Downes gives the following cast (*Roscius Anglicanus*, 1711, pp. 24–5):

Lord Beaufort = Betterton.	Wheadle = Sandford.
Colonel Bruce = Smith.	Graciana = Mrs. Betterton.
Lovis = Norris.	Aurelia = Mrs. Davies.
Sir Nicholas Cully = Nokes.	Widow = Mrs. Long.
Palmer = Underhill.	Sir Frederick Frollick =
Dufoy = Price.	Harris.

[2] Evelyn saw this 'facetious comedy' on April 27, 1664, and Pepys went again on April 29, 1668; Anthony à Wood witnessed a performance at the Guildhall July 8, 1669.

6

wards we find Etherege the boon companion of Sedley, Rochester, Dorset, and the gay rakes and vicious profligates of their circle. He had gained his spurs as a man of wit, and likewise his entrée into the society of the court gallants, among whom such a title was the surest claim to esteem.

Etherege's second comedy, *She Wou'd If She Cou'd*, was staged at Lincoln's Inn Fields in February 1667/8, and printed in 1668. It appears to have been a failure, in spite of Edward Phillips's[1] assertion that it and the former work 'for pleasant Wit and no bad Œconomy are judged not unworthy the applause they have met with', and Shadwell's[2] eulogy of it as: 'the best Comedy that has been written since the Restoration of the Stage'. It is at the first performance of this play that we get from the hand of Pepys the first glimpse of Etherege. The diarist, arriving at the Duke's playhouse at 2 o'clock on February 6th, saw '1000 people put back that could not have room in the pit', and adds the following details of the performance: 'But Lord! how full was the house, and how silly the play, there being nothing in the world good in it, and few people pleased in it. The King was there . . . and among the rest here was the Duke of Buckingham to-day openly sat in the pit; and there I found him with my Lord Buckhurst and Sedley and Etherege the poet; the last of whom I did hear mightily find fault with the actors, that they were out of humour, and had not their parts perfect, and that Harris did do nothing, nor could so much as sing a ketch in it; and so was mightily concerned: while all the rest did, through the whole pit, blame the play as a silly, dull thing, though there was something very roguish and witty, but the design of the play and end mightily insipid.'

[1] *Theatrum Poetarum*, 1675, p. 215, followed by Winstanley, *Lives of the Poets*, 1687. The untrustworthy Downes says 'it took well' (*op. cit.*, p. 29).   [2] Preface, *The Humourists*.

7

That Etherege was justified in his complaints about the acting[1] is confirmed in the following reference to *She Wou'd If She Cou'd* in Shadwell's Preface to *The Humourists*: 'And even that, for the imperfect representation of it at first received such prejudice, that had it not been for the favour of the court in all probability it had never got up again'.[2] It is evident from Pepys's remarks that Etherege was vexed and, being unable to adopt the superior attitude of a Congreve towards his literary labours, was so far discouraged as to refrain from giving the theatre another play for eight years.

Six months after the production of *She Wou'd If She Cou'd* Etherege was appointed secretary to the embassy in Turkey. We may conjecture that the failure of his play induced him to accept this post in order to earn a little money; for the embassy at Constantinople was far from being a garden of roses, and must have been too far from his beloved London to suit the new secretary's tastes. However that may be, Thomas Rugge announces in his Diary[3] under 1668: 'In the month of August the Right Worshipful Sir Daniel Harvey went Ambassador Extraordinary for his Majesty into Turkey . . . and took along with him for his secretary Mr. George Etheridg'. Harvey landed on December 23rd, and Sir Joseph Williamson, secretary of state, received a letter[4] from Etherege on May 3, 1670, containing a masterly and entertaining description

[1] Downes gives the following cast:

Courtall = Smith.	Freeman = Young.
Sir Joslin = Harris.	Sir Oliver = Nokes.
Ariana = Mrs. Jennings.	Gatty = Mrs. Davies.
Lady Cockwood = Mrs. Shadwell.	

[2] It was performed before Royalty on February 25th, March 7th, April 20th, and at court on May 29th (Professor Nicoll's *Restoration Drama*, p. 309).

[3] See *Gentleman's Magazine*, July 1852.

[4] P.R.O. State Papers, Turkey, 19.

of events and personalities. Of this document Mr. G. F. Abbot,[1] an authority on the subject, says: 'a better informed or better written document does not exist in all the Turkey state papers', a verdict upon which we may place more reliance than upon that of a contemporary lampoon:[2]

> Ovid to Pontus sent for too much Wit;
> Eth'rege to Turkey, for the want of it.

Yet Etherege was bored: 'Here seldome happens anything worthy remark', and boredom was followed by sickness, for Harvey writes to Williamson from Belgrade in July 1670: 'I have severall times spoken to Mr. Etherege to give you a particular account of this place, wch I suppose hee has not bin wanting in, tho his present sicknes may in part excuse him'. Whether or no this was the cause of his recall we do not know, but 'gentle George' was back in London[3] by September 1671, when John Muddyman sends the following items of news to Rochester: 'This side [of the page] shall carry you within the rayles of Covent Garden where you shall behold the furious combat of Ashton and Etheridg, which ended happily in a fall on Ashton's part—company interposing and not suffering um to renew fight'.[4] The following month[5] Etherege's prologue for the opening of the new playhouse of the Duke's Company was spoken to Dryden's *Sir Martin Mar-all* on the stage of the

[1] *Under the Turk in Constantinople*, p. 385.

[2] Quoted by Oldys.

[3] According to an extract from a letter dated May 1, 1671, that W. Perwick wrote from Paris to Blathwayt at the Hague 'Etheridge that made Love in a Tub is here and contributes extremely to our divertisement' (Brett-Smith, *Works of Sir George Etherege*, vol. i, p. xx).

[4] *Historical MSS. Commission: Calendar of MSS. of Marquess of Bath*, vol. ii, pp. 152–3.

[5] Nov. 9th. The prologue was printed in 1672 in *A Collection of Poems* (Kemp), but was first attributed to Etherege in a *Collection of Poems* printed in 1673.

sumptuous Dorset Garden Theatre. Nothing could prove more surely the esteem in which the author was held as a wit than his being chosen to compose the prologue for such an important occasion.

For four years we lose sight of Etherege except for a curt manuscript note by Oldys,[1] to the effect that 'In 1673 Geo. Etherege Esqr. was a Witness of Sr. Willm Pawle's Knighthood in 1671'. The chief interest of this entry lies in the fact that Sir William Paul, knighted at Windsor on July 6, 1671, was of Bray in Berkshire, and therefore an additional link in connecting Etherege's name with that county.

It was now seven years since the dramatist had given a play to the stage, and his friend Rochester by no means gently hinted that it was about time he set to work and produced another comedy:

But Apollo had got gentle George in his eye
And frankly confess'd, of all men that writ,
There's none had more fancy, sense, judgment and wit:
That his long seven years silence was not to be pardon'd.
                    A Trial of the Poets for the Bays.

Rochester was answered by *The Man of Mode, or Sir Fopling Flutter*, the most famous and the wittiest of all the author's comedies, produced at Dorset Garden in March 1675/6.[2] Etherege here presented English literature with an immortal character—the quintessinal fop, and never wrote another play. *The Man of Mode* was a tremendous success,[3] and was greeted

---

[1] In a copy, now in the British Museum, of Langbaine's *Lives of the Dramatick Poets.*

[2] Downes gives the following cast (*op. cit.*, p. 36):

Dorimant = Betterton.	Medley = Harris.
Sir Fopling = Smith.	Old Bellair = Leigh.
Young Bellair = Jevon.	Mrs. Lovit = Mrs. Barry.
Belinda = Mrs. Betterton.	Lady Woodvil = Mrs. Leigh.
Emilia = Mrs. Twiford.	

[3] Downes says: 'This comedy being well cloath'd and well acted got a great deal of money'.

10

with a chorus of applause, a fact borne witness to by Shadwell in the prologue to his *Bury Fair* in 1689:

> Sir Fopling you
> Have seen and justly have applauded too.

The play is further of interest because of the statements of contemporaries that the principal characters are portraits. St. Evremond[1] avers that Etherege depicted Wilmot, Earl of Rochester, in Dorimant, and Dennis[2] even enumerates the 'several qualities' in which this character resembles Rochester, though Tom Davies[3] had it from Thomas Sheridan that Dorimant was drawn from two originals—Rochester and Dorset. Lockier told Spence:[4] 'Sir George Etherege was as thorough a fop as ever I saw; he was exactly his own Sir Fopling Flutter. And yet he designed Dorimant, the genteel rake of wit, for his own picture'. On the other hand, Oldys[5] notes: 'Himself he has also set forth therein under the character of Young Bevil [*sic*] or Medley'; whilst Dennis[6] sees in Medley Sir Fleetwood Sheppherd. Unfortunately the identifications are too conflicting to be of any value.

The next recorded incident is the most famous of Etherege's career and one which caused much stir in contemporary circles. The fullest account of the escapade is to be found in the Hatton Correspondence,[7] in a letter dated June 29 [1676]: 'Mr Downs is dead. Ye Ld Rochester doth abscond, and so doth Etheredge, and Capt Bridges who occasioned ye riot Sunday sennight. They were tossing some fidlers in a blanket for refusing to play, and a barber, upon

[1] *The Works of Rochester and Roscommon*, 1709, Introduction. See also Giles Jacob, *The Poetical Register*, 1719.
[2] *Defence of Sir Fopling Flutter*.
[3] *Dramatic Miscellanies*, 1784, vol. iii, p. 169.
[4] *Anecdotes*, edited Singer, 1822, p. 63.
[5] MS. notes in Langbaine and *Biographia Britannica*.
[6] *Defence of Sir Fopling Flutter*.   [7] Vol. i, p. 133.

ye noise, going to see what ye matter [*sic*] they seized upon him, and to free himself from them, he offered to carry them to ye handsomest woman in Epsom, and directed them to the constables' house, who demanding what they came for, they told him a wh—, and, he refusing to let them in, they broke open his doores and broke his head, and beate him very severely. At last, he made his escape, called his watch, and Etheredge made a submissive oration to them and soe far appeased them that ye constable dismissed his watch. But presently after, ye Ld Rochester drew upon ye constable. Mr Downs, to prevent his pass, seized on him, ye constable cryed out murther, and, the watch returning, one came behind Mr Downs and with a sprittle staff cleft his scull. Ye Ld Rochester and ye rest run away, and Downs, having noe sword, snatched up a sticke, and striking at them, they run him into ye side with a half pike, and soe bruised his arm yt he wase never able to stirr it after.'

John Verney, writing to Edmund Verney[1] on the same day, gives a more succinct account: 'Mr Downes who (with Lord Rochester, Mr William Jepson, and Geo. Etheridge) skirmisht the watch at Epsom 12 days since, died last Tuesday of his hurts received from the rustics'. Attempts were made to bring the offenders to justice, for the Earl of Anglesey writes to the Earl of Essex on June 27, 1676,[2] 'Its said also that Mr Downes is dead of his wounds in a late assault of a Constable and that the Earl of Rochester who was in company at the disaster is to be tryed also'; whilst William Harbord, who announced to the Earl of Essex[3] the following

¹ *Historical MSS. Commission, Report VII*, p. 467.
² *Selections from the Correspondence of Arthur Capel, Earl of Essex*, p. 59.
³ *Ibid.*, p. 61. I am indebted for these two references to Miss D. Foster.

month that Lord Cornwallis was to be indicted for murder, adds: 'My Ld Rochester's turne wilbe next, Mr Downes being dead, and I am informed another was wounded occasioned by a fraye at Epsom'. Etherege probably retired from public view for a little while, though he was in trouble again in December 1677, as we gather from a letter of Henry Savile to Rochester:[1] 'There is not one sinner in England now out of London but your selfe. . . . Sheaperd[2] has been overturned in a coach att Matt Cliffords'[3] funerall and broake his head, and a little before was runn with a sword under the eye endeavouring to part Buckly and Etheridge squabbling in a taverne.'

It will be convenient whilst chronicling this 'small beer' to include here two incidents of indefinite date preserved on a scrap of paper in a collection of biographical anecdotes in the British Museum:[4] 'Sr George Etheridge us'd to frequent Lockets the famous Ordinary, I think at Charing Cross. Once with some Company those who were highly incensed at some ill management of their entertainment or attendance were all in violent Passion with the Waiters so that Mrs Locket came up, when Sir Geo: told her they were so provok'd that he cou'd find in his Heart to pull the Nosegay out of her Bosom and throw the flowers in her Face wch turn'd all their Rage to a Jest. This Mr Otway had from W. Clark[5] of Grays Inn some year since dead, who knew more of Sr Geo: than anybody perhaps now alive.' 'Some say of Sr Geo:

---

[1] *Hist. MSS. Com.: Calendar of MSS. of Marquess of Bath*, vol. iv, p. 160.   [2] Probably Fleetwood Shepphered.

[3] Martin Clifford, Master of Charterhouse and part author of *The Rehearsal*, was buried in St. Margaret's, Westminster, Dec. 13, 1677.   [4] Sloane 4221.

[5] A William Clarke, son of John Clarke of Hereford, was admitted to Grays Inn on Aug. 12, 1631. The next of that name registered is William, of Cuckfield, Sussex, admitted May 31, 1686.

others that it was of an Officer in the Guards that having run up a Score with her and grown a Stranger at the House she sent a Man to dun him and he wou'd not pay him, threatened to go herself to him. He sent word back if she did he wou'd kiss her. She fell into such a rage that She call'd for her Hood and Scarf. Her Husband came in, asked the Matter: She plainly told him but she'd see if any Fellow alive cou'd have the Impudence. Prithee my dear don't be too rash you don't know what a Man may do in his Passion.'

Of Etherege's knighthood and marriage, which took place between 1677 and 1680,[1] we know next to nothing, but the two events have been connected together by Gildon with the words 'for Marrying a Fortune he was Knighted', and by a contemporary lampoon entitled *The Present State of Matrimony*,[2] in the verses:

What then can Etheridge urge in his Defence:
What reason bring unless 'tis want of Sence?
For all he pleads beside is meer pretence . . .
Merit with Honour joyn'd 's a Crown to Life,
But he got Honour for to get a Wife.
Prepost'rous Knighthood! in yr gift severe,
For never was a Knighthood bought so dear.

Whether the knighthood begot the wife or the wife the knighthood seems to be a matter of disagreement, but satirists were busy about the marriage, for Lady Mary Etherege was well known for a shrew, as Sir George was to experience later:

'Tis said when George did Dragon slay,
He sav'd a Maid from cruel fray.
But our Sir George (whom knaves do brag on)
Miss'd of the Maid and caught the Dragon.[3]

Others are too coarse for quotation, but Bucking-

[1] *A Westminster Wedding* is dated 1679 (Old Style?); Mary Etherege is described as being 'sole' in November 1677.
[2] B.M. Harleian MS. 162.
[3] *A Westminster Wedding*, Harleian MS. 162.

ham's reference in his *A Consolatory Epistle to Captain Julian* is noticeable because of its imputation that Etherege married for money:

E'en gentle George (flux'd both in tongue and purse)
Shunning one Snare yet fell into a worse.
A Man may be reliev'd once in his life,
But who can be reliev'd that has a Wife.[1]

The lady is described as 'Mary Arnold of London widow';[2] Giles Jacob[3] speaks of her as 'a considerable Fortune', Oldys as 'a rich old widow'. We hear of no children of this union, though Bowman the actor told Oldys that Etherege had a daughter by Mrs. Barry who died young, and on whom he settled £5,000 or £6,000. Probably shortly after his marriage Etherege met with an unfortunate accident, for a letter dated Jan. 15 (16)79/80[4] mentions that 'ye roof of ye Tennis Cote in ye Haymarket fell down. Sr Charles Sidley being ther had his skull broke, and it is thought it will be mortall. Sr George Etheridge and severall others were very dangerously hurt.'

After this misfortune we hear nothing more of Sir George until in March 1685 he is suddenly appointed envoy to the Diet in Ratisbon in succession to Edmund Poley. According to Gildon,[5] he owed the appointment to his being in the good graces of the Queen, who admired his courtly address and accomplishments, but in the Letterbook Etherege attributes his position to Lord Sunderland: 'You preferred me to his Majesty's service',

[1] *Miscellaneous Works of the Duke of Buckingham*, 1704.
[2] P.R.O. Chancery Proceedings, Wittington, 274/36.
[3] *Op. cit.* Also Whincop.
[4] *Hatton Correspondence*, vol. i, p. 216. The court was in Peters Street, near Clare Market (*True Domestic Intelligence*, Jan. 16th). The accident occurred on Wednesday, Jan. 14th, and 'Sir Charles Sidley, George Etheridg, and others' are mentioned as victims in Anthony à Wood's *Life and Times*, ii. 477. The omission of Etherege's title would suggest a recent conferment.
[5] Gildon gives the place as Hamburg.

and later: 'I do not doubt but your Lordship will be careful of the work of your own hands, and secure me a friend in the treasury'. That Etherege, however, had been in some capacity attached to the Queen when she was still Duchess of York is evident from his dedication to her of *The Man of Mode*: ''Tis the first thing I have produced in your service'; and the bounty of £100 entered to his name in 'The Book of the Establishment of H.R.H. the Duke of York',[1] a book described as 'An Establishment of the Wages, Fees, Pencions and Allowances yearly made and allowed by me unto my Officers and Servants of my Chamber, of my Household and of my Revenue, and unto others beginning at Michaelmas 1682 and to continue during my Pleasure'.

The envoy's salary was £3 a day paid quarterly, the first quarter being paid in advance: 'And further . . . such summes for Intelligence etc. as shall bee allowed by one of the principall Secretaries of State'.[2] Records of payments to the envoy are to be found scattered throughout the Treasury Books,[3] and besides these a bounty of £200 was granted him on Sept. 29, 1685, from the secret service expenses.[4]

[1] *Hist. MSS. Com.*, *15th Report*, Appendix, Part II, p. 18 (MSS. of Eliot Hodgkin, Esq.).

[2] P.R.O. Signet Office Doquets, 6817.

[3] April 14, 1685: £273.
August 20, 1686: £546 for Nov. 1685—May 1686.
November 9, 1686, for letters to England: £8 4.
Feb. 23, 1686/7: £546.
June 7, 1687: £273 to Feb. 1686/7.
Nov. 1, 1687: £546 to Aug. 1687.
Nov. 17, 1687, for letters 'as well from England to the Hague as from thence to Ratisbon' : £9 10.
March 1688: £273 from Aug. to Nov. 1687.
May 1688: £550 'in his extraordinaries'.
June 1688: £273 for Nov. 1687—Feb. 1687/8.
Aug. 1688, remaining due for post of letters received for and sent to Etherege: £3.

[4] *Moneys Received and Paid for Secret Services of Charles II and James II*, 1851 (Camden Society).

Poley left Ratisbon on April 15th;[1] Etherege 'took leave of his Majesty before he went as his Majesty's minister to Ratisbonne on the 30th of August 1685'.[2] He lingered, as we learn from the Letterbook,[3] some time in Holland, and his first extant letter from Germany is dated 19/29 November. He was lucky in being able to obtain the house formerly inhabited by Poley in St. James's Square, which was both commodious and convenient, and had the additional advantage of a large garden. It is of these years at Ratisbon that the Letterbook provides us with so detailed and vivid an account.

During Etherege's sojourn in Ratisbon he and his wife became involved in a law-suit at home in an attempt to recover two pieces of land, parcel of a long slip of ground of about $3\frac{1}{2}$ acres in extent in the parishes of St. Martin-in-the-Fields and St. Anne's, Westminster.[4] Dame Mary, when a widow in November 1677, had been given the land as security for £300 lent to one John Rowley.[5] Rowley having died in 1680 without redeeming his pledge, it was purchased by Sir Anthony Deane, who in his turn sold his interest in it to one Richard Bourne. Dame Mary complained that the deeds of assignment and the mortgages were being concealed from her in order to prevent her enjoying the lands and the profits accruing therefrom. Deane denied all knowledge of the mortgage, and protested that he had handed over the documents to Bourne. Anne

---

[1] Treasury Books, 1685–9, vol. ii, p. 731.   [2] Ibid., p. 876.

[3] From these references many modern biographers have carelessly alleged that Etherege was envoy at the Hague.

[4] P.R.O. Chancery Proceedings, Mitford, C. 8/510/40; Hamilton, C. 7/573/66; Wittington, 274/36. I am indebted to Miss Foster for the first two references.

[5] John West and Dr. Nicholas Barebone, mentioned in the Letterbook, had purchased part of the land from the Earl of St. Albans, and Rowley held it in trust for them. West afterwards sold his share to Anne Rowley.

Rowley declared that her husband had paid the interest up to the time of his death, but had not left enough to pay the initial debt; she likewise denied knowledge of the whereabouts of the missing papers. Of the result of this suit we are left in ignorance.

The Letterbook finally dispels Oldys's picturesque story that Etherege met his death by falling downstairs and breaking his neck whilst, in an intoxicated condition, he was showing his guests off the premises. The last extant letter from Ratisbon bears the date Jan. 28, 1689, nine months later than the last dispatch in the Letterbook, and Etherege must have left his post between that time and April 25th, on which day his successor, Hugh Hughes, sent his first letter to England. James II fled from England at the close of December 1688, and William III was made King on February 13, 1689. This decisive event probably decided Etherege to escape to France, where he may have joined the exiled King in St. Germains. According to Gildon 'he went for France to his Master and dyed there, or very soon after his arrival in England from thence', but we owe to Luttrell[1] the more precise information, dated Feb. 1690/1: 'Those from France say . . . that Sir George Etherege, the late King James' ambassador to Vienna, died lately at Paris'. A. W. Verity points out that this date is inconsistent with Southerne's lines to Congreve written in 1693, which speak of Etherege as still alive:

Loose wand'ring Etherege, in wild pleasures tost,
In foreign interests to his hopes long lost.
Poor Lee and Otway dead, Congreve appears,
The darling and last comfort of his years,[2]

[1] *A Brief Historical Relation of State Affairs from Sept. 1678 to April 1714*, vol. ii, p. 171. Vienna is probably a mistake for Ratisbon, though it is possible that Etherege was sent to Vienna by James II to ask for assistance.

[2] Cf. Langbaine in 1691: 'I heartily wish for the publick

but at the same time suggests that this was a mistake on Southerne's part occasioned by the fact that people had lost sight of and interest in the absent envoy. We have also to take into consideration Dennis's statement in 1722 that Etherege had been dead 'nearly thirty years'—that is to say, he died in 1693; but little reliance can be placed on a vague phrase penned so many years after the event. Dame Mary died soon after, for Sir Edmund Gosse records the discovery of an administration to her estate dated February 1, 1692.

Oldys speaks of a brother of Sir George's, a courtier of strict honour, who was twice married, and who lived and died in Westminster. It is this brother's son by his first wife to whom Luttrell[1] refers as Captain, later Colonel, Etherege. He was wounded before Namur in July 1695, was one of the commanders of six hundred men drawn out of the 1st and 2nd regiments of footguards who embarked for Lisbon in July 1704, and died in January 1708.[2] Oldys adds that he lost his right eye and suffered a contusion in his side at the battle of Landen, that he died in Ealing, and was buried in Kensington Church. The register of St. Mary Abbot's, Kensington, records the interment of Colonel George Etherege on January 8, 1708, and of Mrs. Margaret Etherege, who was most likely his widow, on September 1, 1716.[3]

satisfaction, that this great Master would oblige the world with more of his performances' (*Account of the English Dramatick Poets*).

[1] *Op. cit.* The *Dictionary of National Biography* wrongly states that the Colonel was Sir George's brother.

[2] From Dalton's Army Lists we learn that Etherege was promoted to be 2nd-lieutenant to Captain Villiers in the 1st regiment of footguards in June 1690; that he served in Flanders; was appointed quarter-master in August 1693, and promoted to a captaincy in 1700.

[3] I am indebted to the kindness of Captain Feilden, church

Concerning Sir George Etherege's appearance we have only the actor Bowman's testimony transmitted by Oldys: 'that Sir George was, in his person, a fair, slender, genteel man; and in his deportment very affable and courteous, of a sprightly and generous temper', or according to the version in the MS. notes, he 'was a Man of mighty courtesy and delicate address . . . a fair man but spoil'd his Face with Drinking'.

Like most of the rakes of his or any other age he freely indulged in wine, women, and gambling. Unfortunately he was not capable of draining his glass with the best of them—a weakness that seriously handicapped him at Ratisbon, where the popularity of a man depended to a great extent on his capacity for imbibing intoxicating liquors. Etherege resorted to stratagems such as mixing his wine with water, but even then found the next morning that, though other ministers had only a headache, he was suffering from an attack of the ague. It is to his credit that, knowing his fatal facility to insobriety, Etherege tried to avoid toping —though not always, if we are to believe his secretary, with success. Dryden in his *Letter to Sir George Etherege* is emphatic when speaking of drinking orgies among the envoys:

> These Dutch Delights I mention'd last,
> Suit not I know your English taste:
> For Wine to leave a Whore or Play
> Was ne'er your Excellency's way. . . .[1]
> Now if you tope in form, and treat,
> 'Tis the sour Sauce to the sweet Meat,
> The fine you pay for being great.

secretary, for this information. According to Oldys, Colonel Etherege's son was given an ensign's commission under Marlborough but died young, whilst his daughter married Aaron Hill, of Faversham, Kent.

[1] Cf. Etherege's own statement, Appendix, p. 414.

It cannot be said that Etherege endeavoured to exercise the same continence with regard to women. Even if we discount the secretary's more lurid stories, we have Etherege's own testimony. The life which he led in London he desired to continue in Ratisbon, but he found the Bavarians unattractive and 'insensibles à tout hormis le tonnerre', and sighed regretfully after the 'kind Nymphs of gentle Thames' or 'the lily at the bar of the Rose Tavern'. Not only did he find the women in Ratisbon 'un-attend'd by the graces', of 'brawny limb and martial face', but he missed in them the coquetry, the allure, the wit to which he had been accustomed in London. However, he made the best of it, and wrote to Corbet: 'I have only a plain Bavarian with her sandy locks, brawny limbs and a brick complexion, and yet I find myself often very hearty'.

As a diversion he would flirt with the Countess of Crécy over ombre, feign a *belle passion,* or exercise his wit on the turning of a neat compliment. Then Julia, the comedian from Nuremberg, arrived, and even the Puritanical secretary had to concede that she 'seemed to have something of grace in her face, though', he hastily adds, 'none in her manners'. It is idle to affirm, as some biographers have done, basing their affirmation on Etherege's remark that she was as *fière* as she was fair, that there was nothing more than a platonic friendship between the envoy and the actress. We need not be ashamed to record an act of which Sir George himself was but too brazenly proud. He expressly avers that 'the best adventure I have had here has been with a comedian no less handsome and no less kind in Dutchland than Mrs. Johnson was in England', and even compares her with his erstwhile mistress: 'The best fortune I have had here has been a player, something hand-somer and as much a jilt as Mrs. Barry'. At last he had found some one who could play the game of love, could be 'effeminate, changeable, longing and liking; proud, fantastical, apish, shallow, inconstant, full of tears, full of smiles', and withal beautiful.

The scandal caused by this connexion proceeded not so much from outraged morality as from outraged formality; as Mr. Palmer[1] has well said: 'The offence of Etherege in the eyes of Ratisbon was his open entertainment, innocent or otherwise, of a player, his obvious good fellowship and delight in her company'. Etherege was no doubt well aware that players were considered the scum of the earth in Germany, and probably took all the more delight in flaunting before the eyes of his colleagues his defiance of their prejudices. He mistook brazenness for dignity, professed contempt for the scandal that he was causing, and put Julia 'into his coach before all the company, notwithstanding all the giggling and hishing of the Austrian ladies and of the ministers' wives and daughters, himself humbly walking home on foot'. Such a course of action would not only have appealed to his sense of humour, but would have enabled him to fancy himself the dashing and gallant hero of some comedy of manners. The gusto of the adventure at least relieved the tedium of life at Ratisbon—for which relief no price could be too high.

With regard to Etherege's moral conduct in general it must be borne in mind that, licence being the fashion of the age, only contempt would fall upon the gallant, courtier, or man of the world who did not indulge in it. In the eyes of a society that had dethroned morality from among the angels and cast it among the devils, debauchery was not only excusable but commendable, and the open parade of it was welcomed as a challenge to hypocrisy, the detested vice of the Puritans—a point of view expressed by Etherege himself in the phrase: 'it would

[1] *Op. cit.*

22

be very hard to be excommunicated for fornication, it being a point all the differing churches agree in'. Though we cannot escape from the fact that Etherege's exploits as related in the Letterbook are to us often nauseating, we must admit that many of them are informed by the comic spirit, and of these none more so than his escapade with the Nuremberg actress.

To his fondness for cards Etherege frequently alludes in his letters. He was able to play ombre with the Countess of Crécy, but he missed the high stakes and the fine society: 'I have not played at anything but 6 penny ombre these 13 months'; and again: 'la bassette a ses charmes en certains endroits et j'aimerais mieux y perdre mon argent en voyant Madame Mazarine que de gagner les bonnes grâces de toutes les dames et même de demoiselles d'ici'. The secretary's tales of his master's falling into the hands of sharpers are most likely true, for Etherege himself admits the loss of £200 on his first arrival in Ratisbon. But gullibility is often accompanied by good nature, and Etherege's good nature was a pleasant weakness: he pawned his watch to buy Julia clothes, he entertained in his house a French outcast, and lent 100 florins to a shabby, fugitive count, all of which was foolish and tactless in a responsible official, but at least betokened an open-handedness bordering upon generosity.

Gaming was not Etherege's only diversion in Ratisbon; the secretary numbers among his household a fencing and a dancing master, the invariable companions of a Restoration gallant. Music, too, occupied some of his leisure hours: 'I have three now in my family who now and then give me a little music, they play very well and at sight. We have all the operas and I have a correspondent at Paris who sends me what is new there.' Nevertheless, he asks Betterton the actor to procure him 'some of the best composition with the several parts'.

In London Etherege had been an ardent theatre-goer, though perhaps with an eye to the actresses rather than to the plays. Exiled in Ratisbon, he can only thank his friend Jephson 'for leading me behind the scenes: you put me in mind of the time I have well employed there'; ask him to send Shadwell's latest comedy, 'that I may know what follies are in fashion', and lament to Corbet: 'We have a theatre too, but not only our plays but our actors would be hissed in a country fair'.

As for writing, in spite of Dryden's exhortations and Middleton's encouraging assertion that 'The King was pleased to tell me that he expected you should put on your socks', the atmosphere was not conducive to it. Some occasional verses and lampoons are all Etherege produced. Specimens of the former are scattered throughout the Letterbook; of the existence of the latter we know from a letter from James Vernon to Matthew Prior[1] on Prior's being appointed envoy at Ratisbon: 'I have heard how two of your predecessors spent their time there, Mr. Poley in making love to the fräuleins and Sir George Etherege in making lampoons upon them'. Etherege himself wearily confesses, 'I have lost for want of exercise the use of fancy and imagination'; in truth he had never been a prolific writer, and lacking the stimulus of a refined, elegant, and witty society, soon sank into sterility.

Of outdoor sports Sir George's favourite appears to have been hunting: 'I have good horses and often go a hunting'; or again, 'I have good greyhounds and coursing is one of my greatest recreations. We have such plenty of game that now and then I start 6 brace of hares in a day.' He also indulged in tennis, 'bungling away', as he puts it, 'now and then a morning at tennis', and in the winter joined in the sleighing, which he seems to have enjoyed rather

[1] *Hist. MSS. Com.: Marquess of Bath*, vol. iii, p. 52.

for the sake of the opportunity it gave him to kiss the ladies than for the sport. Yet ironically, in a moment of depression, he writes to Barillon: 'Je ne veux pas plus dire sur cet chapitre de peur de ne vous degoûter des plaisirs de Londres'.

Far removed from such pleasures Etherege had much ado to find some one to laugh with or something to laugh at. 'I am so glad of an occasion of laughing here;' he exclaims, 'it is no wonder the ridicule gets the better of the heroic.' He looks forward with glee to the arrival of Prince Herman of Baden, whose temper he has heard is as violent as the Count de Windischgrätz's, the Imperial envoy, which 'will doubtless hereafter occasion some pleasant scenes which may help to divert us'. Old age, too, was creeping on him like a thief in the night, and he reproaches Mulgrave for reminding him: 'I have always by my way of living taken care to banish age from my thoughts—you should quietly have let me alone till age had surprised me and not have wounded my imagination with your raillery'. He dreads the time, which he knows cannot be long in coming, when he will have to take his leave 'of the pleasures of this world', and urges Guy to 'take care our years do not sour us with any of the common vices of age, let us still preserve our good humour and our good nature to make us welcome near those young people who possess that plentiful estate we have pretty well run out of'. Yet Etherege was remarkably lucky in being vigorous at over fifty when Rochester had died worn out at thirty-three, and Mulgrave at thirty-nine spoke of himself as among the 'grave, decayed people', and in escaping that empty and early old age which was the penalty the Restoration rakes called down upon themselves for a prodigal and incontinent youth.

As an envoy Etherege's most admirable quality was undoubtedly loyalty. His expressions of respect and devotion to James II ring true amidst a crowd of hollow compliments to courtiers: 'The passion which has most power over me is faithfully to serve his Majesty'. He continually expresses admiration for the King's moral honesty and integrity: 'All who are not blind see that his Majesty's word is sacred and unviolable, never prince was so firm to his promise'. 'What prince', he exclaims, 'is more merciful, more bountiful, and takes more particular care to advance all those who have any merit?' Etherege may have had a false conception of James's qualities, but he was true to his master, and did not in his hour of need compromise with his successor like so many of his subjects.

On the other hand, Sir George did not hesitate to flatter his superiors to the top of their bent; the secretaries of state and lords of the treasury were the recipients of the most fulsome compliments in true Restoration style. How hollow these professions were may be judged by a phrase in a letter to an anonymous friend: 'You may without jealousy let me keep my compliments for those whom I know not how to entertain without'. Etherege could be tactful, too, as is evident from his letter to Laurence Hyde, Earl of Rochester, on the latter's dismissal from office, a model of neat insinuation. Yet in Ratisbon he never troubled to exercise any tact. The incident of Schnolsky's coach and his remark on the capture of Buda, 'that he neither believed it nor hoped it to be true', evince an open and aggressive disregard for the feelings of the Imperialists most reprehensible in an envoy. His mode of life, too, was eminently unsuited not only to his position but to the town in which he resided, yet he declared he would 'not omit any company or indeed anything which can give me any sort of pleasure'. Irritated by the formality of the Diet and the ministers, he does not appear ever to have attempted to adapt himself to his circumstances, but was content to remain the queerest of anomalies—an English man of fashion in a typical German city. Though his careless and inconsiderate behaviour caused many disagreeable incidents in which his dignity suffered, he could, when he so desired, bear himself with distinction: 'His Majesty did not send me hither to make my court to the proud and fantastic humour of any man, but to live well with all, and to give an impartial account of affairs'. If only he had more constantly remembered that 'civility and moderation' were the necessary equipment of an envoy, he would not have been so unpopular, or perhaps so unhappy in his work. At times, indeed, he expresses content at being 'a man of business', and even asserts that he was beginning to 'be more vain of making a good dispatch than of writing a witty letter'; at others he is only too sensible of his inadequacy: 'Nature no more intended me for a politician than she did you for a courtier'; whilst even more frequently disgust prevails, and he dreads that he may 'return into England well enough accomplished to walk with Mr. Spicer and Mr. Vandebendy and the rest of that wise company who never talk of any affairs but such as do not concern them'.

It remains to speak of Etherege's favourite vice— laziness, 'that darling sin' on which he so much prided himself; not, indeed, a physical, but 'a noble laziness of the mind', a contempt of mental effort, an exquisite affectation. Just as Congreve disdained the title of author and desired only that of gentleman, so Etherege wished to be reputed an 'idle fellow', superior to any mundane activity except pleasure. He would not be thought to stoop to ambition, though 'necessity now forces me to set up for a fop of business', but sums up his pose of coxcombry, his delight in urbane courtliness, with the words: 'I must confess I am a fop in my heart;

ill customs influence my very senses, and I have been so used to affectation that without the help of the air of the court what is natural cannot touch me. You see what we get by being polished as we call it.' No more concise or pregnant phrase could depict the state of English society in the latter half of the seventeenth century.

Curiously enough, Etherege, dubbed an atheist by the secretary, makes many references to religion. As might be expected, he poses as giving little thought to religious or speculative matters: 'Par la grâce de Dieu je sais où mon esprit est borné et je ne me mets guère en peine de savoir de quelle manière ce monde ici a été fait ou comment on se divert dans l'autre'. He did not always maintain this frivolous tone, and the following passage is written in a more serious mood: 'I have ever enjoyed a liberty of opinion in matters of religion; 'tis indifferent to me whether there be any other in the world who thinks as I do; this makes me have no temptation to talk of the business, but quietly following the light within me I leave that to them who were born with the ambition of becoming prophets or legislators'. Etherege at least acknowledged a 'light within', and, if he had not the courage to lay himself open to the ridicule of his friends by discussing it, he had enough conviction to attempt to follow it in isolation.

A strange character this 'easy Etherege', stepping out of the centuries: generous, loyal, and gay; affectionate to his friends, adulatory to his superiors, contemptuous of his enemies; affecting supercilious indifference, indulging in any pleasure that offered itself; quick-tempered at times, at times depressed and disillusioned; a less wooden figure than Congreve, and one whose outward pose may be more easily penetrated, revealing to the inquiring eyes of a curious posterity the humanity which lay beneath the artificial gallant of Restoration society.

II. THE EUROPEAN SITUATION, 1685–9

(i)

The years during which Etherege was envoy in Ratisbon—years of preparation, expectation, and intrigue—were crucial ones in the history of Europe. On August 15, 1684, the Emperor Leopold I, unable to combat Louis XIV of France and resist the Turks at one and the same time, signed the Truce of Ratisbon, by which he agreed to hand over to the French for the term of twenty years Strassburg and the lands assigned to Louis by the Chambers of Reunion before August 1, 1681, whilst Louis promised protection to the Protestants in these territories, and stipulated that a definitive peace should at once be put under consideration.

Such a truce possessed obvious elements of instability. In the first place, the Imperialists considered that they had not surrendered any rights but that after twenty years had elapsed the lands would be restored without further question, whilst the French chose rather to regard the armistice as a diplomatic prelude to a final cession of the territories. Secondly, it was only natural that Louis should be continually suspicious that the Empire would seize the earliest opportunity of breaking so unfavourable an agreement, and would try to create that opportunity by concluding a peace with the Turks. On the other hand, the Empire must have realized that the ambitious Louis would move heaven and earth to try to convert the Truce into a peace, by which the territories provisionally assigned to him should come into his permanent possession. This note of mutual mistrust occurs constantly in the dispatches. The Imperialist successes in Hungary added to Louis's alarm: 'his Christian Majesty urges that he has sat still and looked on while the Emperor has conquered a whole kingdom and perfectly secured himself against his ancient enemy the Turk'. Rumours that the Emperor was about to make peace with the Turks and turn his arms westwards were countered by rumours that Louis XIV had made an alliance with the Grand Signor to attack the Empire: 'Monsieur Scherer, the second minister for Austria, has read an Italian paper to the Diet which makes much noise here; the business of it is to persuade them there is a good understanding between the French and the Turks'. Hostility was further increased by preparations on both sides. Thus the Emperor attempted to consolidate his Empire by the Alliance of Augsburg,[1] signed on July 6, 1686, by which the circles of Franconia, Swabia, and Bavaria, and the kings of Spain and Sweden,[2] bound themselves together for mutual defence, with the determination not to suffer any infraction of the rights of the Empire. The overt aim of the alliance was to preserve the treaties of Münster and Nimeguen and the Truce of Ratisbon, its real object to form the nucleus of an opposition to French aggrandisement. Its weakness lay in the fact that the important military states of Saxony, Brunswick, and Brandenburg remained outside it, whilst, as regards the European allies, Spain was far away and powerless, and Sweden was busy with her own affairs in the north. Crécy, the French envoy at Ratisbon, however, exaggerated its importance and its possibilities in his letters home, thus causing Louis—who was well aware that the alliance was due to a fear of his

[1] The circle of Franconia had already in December 1685 discussed at a conference the necessity for a new organization for the defence of the Empire to replace the expired Luxemburg alliance.

[2] It appears from the Letterbook that the Elector Palatine and the Duke of Holstein-Gottorp were admitted during a further conference at Nuremberg, though this fact is not generally known. See p. 103.

attacking the Palatinate or infringing the privileges of the Empire and that it represented a certain amount of public spirit in the ill-coordinated states —more disquiet than was strictly necessary.

Meanwhile the French, taking advantage of the vague phrasing of the Truce, were securing themselves by the erection of fortresses along the Rhine on the territory provisionally allotted to them. Hüningen, Fort Louis, Trarbach, followed one another with alarming rapidity; whilst the Diet protested and argued, the French built and fortified. The reservation made by the Truce stated ambiguously that the French were not to innovate or alter anything which related to the spiritual or temporal concerns of the places handed over to them. The question of prohibition to build had been raised and expressly rejected, so that the French claimed that the Empire had yielded the point in their favour, whilst the Imperialists urged that such permission would have to be justified by positive articles, and that the Empire had not yielded the point but had only left it undetermined. The pros and cons, the memorials, letters, precedents, are set forth in the Letterbook. These and other contraventions detailed in Etherege's correspondence served to delay the execution of the armistice, the determining of the limits, and the conclusion of the peace. The Emperor demanded that these 'griefs' should first be treated of, whilst the French pressed, though but half-heartedly, the limits and the peace. In January 1687 the Electoral College proposed a mutual guarantee whilst the griefs were being prepared, a proposal opposed by the College of Princes, who were 'more inclined to treat of the armament for the public security'. The French prescribed a time-limit (the following March) for the execution of the armistice, but the Emperor's ministers declared it impossible to settle affairs in such a short time. The situation at this juncture was summarized by Etherege: 'The Empire would willingly treat of the execution of the Truce as far as concerns the redressing of the griefs, but cannot find in their hearts to conclude a peace with the French upon such hard terms as they made the truce. The French will have the peace treated of according to the eleventh article of the armistitia, and if it be not they do not think it reasonable to wait till the Empire be at leisure to attack them.' Councils in Paris were divided: Croissy and the peace party expressed themselves contented with a general guarantee from the Emperor and the States, or a mutual guarantee referring the griefs to amicable discussion and prohibiting further infringement on either side; Louvois and the war party demanded a one-sided guarantee, refused to give up the forts, and desired the Diet should speak no more of the griefs. The Royal Council vacillated between the two parties, declared at last for Louvois, and thus finally put an end to all hope of a settlement.

The situation was further complicated by the intervention of the Pope at the suggestion of Croissy. Louis, however, would submit to nothing less than that the truce should be converted into a peace without modification of terms—a demand which evoked a remark from Etherege: 'It seems a little hard for the Empire to grant by a peace not only what they have given but for twenty years by the truce, but likewise all the French are now in possession of'. The Emperor's answer to these high demands was a declaration of the pacific intentions of the Alliance of Augsburg and renewed protests against the contraventions. Meanwhile Crécy aggravated Louis by suggesting that the Empire, far from desiring peace, had set on foot these negotiations only in order to discover Louis's designs. At length the Emperor consented to renounce the griefs, and Louis declared himself well satisfied. The Diet, however, delayed communicating the French King's reply, 'being unwilling the contraventions should die without being examined', and Etherege opined that 'they may think fit to let them sleep till they see the success of the next campaign, and accordingly wake them when they please by pretending the Emperor can only answer for himself and not for the States of the Empire who pretend to be grieved'. After another exchange of letters between Lobkowitz, the Emperor's representative in Paris, and Croissy, in which both monarchs engaged to keep the Truce and to give no cause for complaint, the way seemed open for an amicable discussion of the limits and execution of the armistice. James II of England was asked to be guarantor but refused, whereupon dissensions again broke out. Henceforth Crécy and Windischgrätz bombarded each other with memorials about the rights of fortification, and they were still wrangling when Louis XIV suddenly invaded Germany in the autumn of 1688.

Both sides, in fact, had been eager to delay the final conclusion of a peace. Louis's ambition prompted him to postpone a definition of limits which would set bounds to his aspirations; whilst Leopold, apart from the fact that he knew a peace would be unfavourable to him, understood that it would also mean the disarmament of the princes who were supporting him in Hungary. Both the Imperial and French ministers, then, were glad of pretexts which would serve to postpone the execution of the Truce, and which would at the same time leave open a loophole for a rupture. Etherege realized the truth when he remarked: 'I know not how the treaty for the execution of the Truce will go. It seems to me the Imperial commission have no mind to facilitate that business', and summarized the situation with the words: 'His hope of being in a condition ere long to be able to dispute with his Christian Majesty that branch of the Empire which is lopped off makes them [the Imperialists] with more impatience see him endeavour to secure himself the possession of it. . . . This has made me think the Emperor's intention to let the French peaceably possess what they have by the Truce during the time prescribed is conformable to theirs of restoring it after that time is elapsed.' But the growing sense of power engendered by the victories in Hungary was not the sole reason for the Emperor's attitude. The French throughout had acted in an aggressive manner little calculated to conciliate the Empire, and never more so than in the Orleans affair, which was occupying everybody's thoughts on Etherege's arrival in Ratisbon. Louis XIV's brother, Philippe, Duke of Orleans, had married Charlotte Elizabeth, sister of the Elector Palatine Charles. On the death of Charles, last of the line of Simmern, his inheritance passed to Philip William of Neuburg, a Catholic prince warmly attached to the Austrian interests. Louis XIV claimed on behalf of his sister-in-law, the Duchess of Orleans, lands which were not an integral part of the electorate, that is to say, all territories acquired either by marriage or inheritance since the Golden Bull. Such were Simmern, Lautern, a section of Sponheim, and the district of Germersheim. Philip William replied that Louis's claims must be proved according to the customs and laws of the Empire, and that the Elector himself could not dispose of any fiefs of the Empire without the Emperor's consent; that a woman could never inherit and that anyway the Duchess had renounced her rights in her marriage-contract. Louis and the Elector at last submitted their case to the Pope, an unprecedented step of which neither the Emperor nor the Elector of

Brandenburg approved since the affair was one which the German laws were perfectly adequate to settle. There ensued discussions and arguments as to what lands were included in the French King's claim, and as to what precedents could be cited for or against female succession. Etherege regaled Middleton with specimens of the controversies[1] and documents.[2] A provisionary settlement made in May was followed by the agreement of July 12, 1686, and the affair fizzled out, Louis temporarily contenting himself with the transference of some of the late Elector's furniture to St. Cloud. The matter sprang once more into prominence when the French King made it the pretext for his invasion of the Palatinate in 1688, and was finally settled by the Treaty of Ryswick in 1697, when Louis abandoned his claim in return for a sum of money.

(ii)

Whilst the Empire and France were haggling, Brandenburg under its Elector Frederick William was growing in strength and importance. The Elector had since his succession cleared his country of Swedish troops, increased his territories by the Peace of Westphalia, and disciplined his army. Nominally he was in alliance with France, with whom he had renewed friendly relations by the Treaty of St. Germain in 1677, but, perceiving the danger of French aggression, he gradually drifted away from his ally. In August 1685 he signed a treaty with Holland as a preliminary step to an alliance of Protestant princes. The Revocation of the Edict of Nantes rendered inevitable a break between His Most Christian Majesty and the champion of Protestantism. The Elector replied with the Edict of Potsdam (October 1685), condemning the Revocation and offering protection to the Huguenot

[1] pp. 67–8, 69–70. [2] p. 76.

refugees. He made a secret alliance with Sweden in February 1686, and an alliance containing secret clauses with Austria for twenty years in March. By the latter the Elector received Schweibus and renounced his claims to Jägerndorf,[1] and was granted a subsidy of 100,000 florins in peace and 100,000 thalers in war, together with the cession of a right to part of East Friesland. On his side, Frederick William promised to oppose any new dismemberment of the Empire, to protect the Palatinate, to give his voice for the Archduke Joseph in case of an Imperial election, to guarantee to the house of Austria all its rights, especially the Spanish heritage, to defend the Spanish Netherlands, and, in case of a war between France and the Empire, to help the Duke of Lorraine to regain his estates. As yet there had been no open rupture with France, although by this time that country was well aware that she could not hope for any support from her so-called ally and was projecting an alliance with Brunswick.[2] Meanwhile the Jena affair had added another grievance to the long list that France held against Brandenburg. The Imperial ministers disliked Jena, Brandenburg's envoy in Ratisbon, as he passed for a partisan of France, and they accused him of being pensioned by the French, though he had done nothing more than accept the usual gratifications, support the claims of the Duchess of Orleans, and, in conjunction with the three ecclesiastical Electors, reserve his approval of one of the Emperor's letters until the latter would declare himself ready to negotiate the execution of the armistice and treating of the limits. Hereupon Leopold complained to the Elector. Meanwhile Frederick William had ordered Jena to support the project for the mutual guarantee, but before the envoy had received the orders the Elector was

[1] See p. 92, notes 2 and 3.
[2] A treaty was concluded February 1688.

advised from Ratisbon that the Electoral College was engaged in discussing a one-sided guarantee. Schoenbeck, the second minister, who hoped to have Jena's place, hinted that the envoy had proposed the one-sided guarantee, with the consequence that the Elector addressed to him a letter of reproach for having made such a proposal without instructions. Another letter followed, announcing the minister's dismissal, a decision which was equivalent to a denunciation of Brandenburg's treaty with France. Louis protested, and the Great Elector, not yet prepared for an irrevocable breach, recoiled, accepted Jena's apologies, and actually excused himself to the French King on the plea that he thought Jena was endangering his relations with that country by his actions. The truth was that the Elector also had reasons for delaying a war with France. The occasion was not yet favourable: Brandenburg was politically isolated, the Empire was hesitant, Sweden could not be depended upon, and there was always the hope that soon William of Orange would ascend the English throne and throw in her forces against the enemy. So the Elector waited, and died before the crisis came.

(iii)

The energy of the Northern powers at this period was principally expended on the Holstein-Gottorp question.

By the Peace of Roeskilde, 1658, Denmark had been compelled to share her suzerainty over Schleswig with the Duke of Holstein-Gottorp. Later Duke Christian Albert urged his claim to sole sovereignty and obtained ratification thereof in 1663. Mutual dissatisfaction followed; the Duke complained of the building of a fortress in Kiel harbour; the King of Denmark was incensed because Lübeck had engaged to choose six Gottorp princes in succession as bishops. Differences were temporarily reconciled in 1667 by the marriage of Christian Albert with the daughter of Frederick III of Denmark, but on the accession of Christian V the question of succession in Oldenburg and Delmenhorst rekindled the old enmity. The ruling line of Oldenburg princes having died out the lands were left divided between Frederick III and Duke Christian Albert. The Count of Holstein-Ploen protested and allied himself with Denmark, to whom he offered to relinquish half of Oldenburg and Delmenhorst in exchange for possessions in Holstein and other concessions. The law decided against Duke Christian, who was compelled to yield his share of Oldenburg and Delmenhorst, which Ploen immediately transferred to Denmark, and also to pay an indemnity for the revenues from these lands which he had up till that time enjoyed.

In 1675 the Duke of Holstein-Gottorp, held prisoner by the Danes, who had entrapped him at Rendsburg, was compelled to sign a renunciation of Schleswig, whilst Sweden, pressed by Brandenburg and Denmark, was unable to come to his assistance. By the Treaty of Nimeguen, however, the Emperor's protection was secured for the Duke, and Denmark by the Treaties of Fontainebleau and Lund, 1679, was compelled to restore to him his possessions according to the Treaty of Roeskilde and recognize his sovereignty over a portion of Schleswig. In May 1684 the Danes, taking the law into their own hands, seized that part of Schleswig which belonged to Christian Albert, whereupon the Duke sought protection from the Emperor and the Diet, and found it in the person of the Elector of Brandenburg, who espoused his cause in the face of a Franco-Danish alliance.

War was narrowly averted in 1686. The town of

Hamburg refused to recognize the right of the Duke of Zell to take winter-quarters in its territory, whilst Zell excused himself on the plea that it had disobeyed the Emperor's orders with respect to the re-installation of the ex-burgomaster Meurer and had prohibited commerce with Zell. Denmark and Brandenburg were ready to assist Hamburg, and Danish troops entered Holstein territory. On his arrival outside Hamburg King Christian demanded homage and 400,000 crowns, whereupon the burghers called upon Brandenburg and Lüneburg for assistance. Troops were thrown into the town, and the Elector of Brandenburg wrote to the King of Denmark warning him that he would regard any attack on Hamburg as an attack on himself. This resulted in a cessation of hostilities followed by negotiations. The difficulty lay in the fact that Denmark's check had to be covered, yet Hamburg left independent. An accommodation was reached in November, whereby King Christian consented to leave all *in statu quo ante* and to restore the ships that he had seized in return for 300,000 thalers.

Already in March 1686 the Emperor together with the Electors of Saxony and Brandenburg had offered their mediation in the affairs of Holstein-Gottorp, an offer which led to a conference at Altona. Holstein demanded complete restitution, whilst Denmark offered an equivalent in Oldenburg and Delmenhorst. Sweden pressed Denmark to grant the Holstein demands, whilst Louis XIV urged Holstein to be content with the equivalent. The sympathies of Brandenburg were with Holstein, but the Elector agreed with the French King to try to avoid a settlement by force at all costs; Louis, however, reproached the Great Elector with supporting the obstinacy of Duke Christian Albert, whilst Frederick William accused the French King of favouritism to Denmark. The obduracy of the principals and the dissensions of the mediators caused the prolongation of negotiations until April 1688, when the Duke was granted his demands by the Treaty of Altona.

(iv)

Perhaps, however, the chief historical interest of the Letterbook lies not so much in its relation of and comments on these well-known facts as on the vivid picture it presents of the effeteness of the Diet and the disordered condition of the Empire. When the Diet met at Ratisbon in 1663 it had ceased to be an assembly of electors and princes, and had degenerated into a congress of envoys, who had to refer everything to their masters; the Emperor was represented by two commissioners, the electors, princes, towns, and foreign powers by agents. It is clear that little or no important business could be transacted by means of such a clumsy Parliament, and disputes about ceremonials and precedents became its chief concern. Since, however, the real authority of the Empire was vested in the Diet rather than the Emperor, Leopold I found himself considerably hampered by the dilatory methods and petty contentions of this body. We have only to trace the progress of the demand for 'Roman months' through Etherege's correspondence to realize the truth of this statement. After having with great difficulty obtained a grant of fifty Roman months, Leopold in March 1687 required a further tax of one hundred Roman months 'to enable him to carry on the war against the Turks'. The following month the ministers at Ratisbon received instructions from their masters which were 'so various, some of their principals limiting them to twenty, others to thirty, none exceeding fifty, that the Imperial commission do not think it fit this matter should be yet deliberated on in the Diet'. The circle of Swabia having refused the Emperor's request the matter was postponed; even the Electors whose business it was to persuade the others to comply would 'not shew their good inclinations but upon conditions which are very hard to the Emperor'. In May, in view of the opposition, it was decided to defer discussion once more: 'In the mean time the Imperial commission, who think it would look ill if they should get nothing, would be glad if they could compass half'. By this time Etherege was heartily sick of the whole matter: 'This tax by the number of months and the noise it makes one would think, should it be granted, would bring in millions'; whereas the last concession of fifty Roman months, he tells us, had realized only 100,000 crowns. One by one the various circles desired to be excused on the grounds that they had already assisted with troops. The matter was still dragging on in September, when it had reached the stage of word-quibbling: 'the dissenters not allowing the word unanimous to be inserted'. A week later Etherege was able to announce: 'The Electoral and Princes College have granted the Emperor the 100 Roman months which have long lain dormant. The Towns make some difficulty in giving their consent but this day the general conclusion will be passed.' This is but an example of the difficulties with which the Emperor had to contend. A perusal of the Letterbook leaves us marvelling how he ever managed to keep an army in the field and drive the Turks out of Hungary.

The Hungarians themselves were a thorn in his side. Leopold had already persecuted the Hungarian Protestants, and they were rightly afraid that under pretence of protecting them from the Turks the Emperor intended to deprive them of their freedom. Under Tökölyi many revolted and aided the Turks, but the Pasha of Grosswardein betrayed the

Hungarian leader and sent him to imprisonment in Adrianople, though his wife Helen Zrinyi held the fortress of Munkács for over two years against the Imperial army. General Caraffa was appointed head of a Court of Justice in Eperies to deal with the rebels—an office which he carried out with great severity, whilst on Oct. 31, 1687, a Diet was convened at Pressburg to discuss the Habsburg claims to the Hungarian crown. The nobility were forced to submit to the Emperor's propositions, as Etherege writes: 'The States of Hungary will struggle at the meeting at Pressburg to preserve the right of election but as the case stands they will be fain to submit to the Emperor's will'. The clause in the Golden Bull granting Hungary right of rebellion in defence of her liberties was annulled, the Hungarian crown was made hereditary in the male Habsburg line, and Leopold's son, the Archduke Joseph, was crowned King on December 9, 1687.

In spite of opposition in Hungary itself, of jealousy fostered by France between his two generals —the Duke of Lorraine and the Elector of Bavaria— and of tardy assistance from the States of the Empire in the matter both of men and money, the Emperor's army regained in five years what it had taken the Turks two centuries to conquer. The chief event of the campaign of 1686 was the fall of Buda, long the centre of the Ottoman power in Hungary. After this the Turks appear to have lost courage and confidence, with the result that the Margrave of Baden was able to seize one town after another in the autumn campaign. The following year the enemy, after having repulsed the Imperialists from Esseck, met with a crushing defeat at Mohács (Aug. 1687), a battle which gave Hungary to the Christian forces, and was the cause of a mutiny in the Turkish army which led to the deposition of the Sultan in favour of his brother Solyman II.

In 1688 the Elector of Bavaria, owing to the illness of the Duke of Lorraine, was given supreme command, and succeeded in capturing Belgrade in September. But Leopold looked in vain towards Constantinople, for Louis, jealously watching the Imperial army's progress, realized that it was time to strike.

Indeed, it was too late. The capture of Philippsburg by the French on October 29, 1688, caused the German princes to rally to the Emperor, whilst on the same day William of Orange set sail for England. The overthrow of James II, upon which Louis had hardly reckoned, ruined the French chances. In May 1689 Leopold and William signed the Grand Alliance, by which each undertook to defend the territories of the other, and, after a severe and prolonged struggle, the French were compelled by the Peace of Ryswick in 1697 to surrender, with the exception of Strassburg and Landen, all the territories occupied by them since the Peace of Nimeguen. Thus ended Louis's ambitious schemes and France's preponderance of power in Europe.

III. THE LETTERBOOK

The Letterbook of Sir George Etherege was acquired by the British Museum on December 3, 1838, of Wilkes the bookseller. It was quoted by Macaulay in his *History of England,*[1] and thereafter sank into oblivion until Sir Edmund Gosse, through the offices of Mr. Edward Scott, rediscovered the volume and utilized its information in an essay

[1] The Letter to Dryden had been printed in the *European Magazine,* June 1795, p. 397, but probably from the original manuscript, as it follows an extract from a letter of Wigmore's to Etherege speaking of the death of Nell Gwyn, which is not contained in the Letterbook. Peter Cunningham in his life of the actress refers the letter, which he dates Nov. 18, 1687, to Seward's *Anecdotes,* but I am unable to trace it.

published in 1883. Following Sir Edmund Gosse, extensive quotations were made by A. W. Verity in his *Works of Sir George Etherege*, Mr. Palmer in *The Comedy of Manners*, and Mr. Dobrée in his *Essays in Biography*. Sir Leslie Stephen, in his unsympathetic article in the *Dictionary of National Biography*, dismissed the Letterbook with the words: 'Most of the dispatches are political, but others are sufficient to show that he [Etherege] continued his habits of squalid debauchery and disgusted the Germans by worse things than breaches of etiquette'; but other critics have done full justice to the value of its historical, social, and literary material.

In order fully to appreciate these remarkable letters it is necessary to understand Etherege's position in Ratisbon. In the first place, it must be realized that not only Etherege himself, but also the statesmen to whom he was responsible in London, were courtiers rather than politicians, men therefore who expected and desired entertainment as well as information from the dispatches of a wit with whom they were on intimate terms. Thus the envoy writes to the Secretary of State: 'I have had the honour to know your Lordship long; and when you were not so great I loved you no less than I do now'; whilst the Secretary encourages the newly arrived envoy with the words: 'I hope in a little time we may hear something of your diversions as well as your business, which would be much pleasanter and perhaps as instructive'. Etherege abstains from writing to Godolphin on the plea that 'The business of the Diet for the most part is only fit to entertain those insects in politics which crawl under the trees in St. James' Park and I am not so vain as to think my dull imagination capable of making his good nature receive them well'; but, on the other hand, he is afraid of being too free for fear his former companions should have altered their

44

attitude in their official capacity: 'I know you are Mr. Secretary still, but I know not whether you are still the same Lord Middleton I left you'. He was equally suspicious of Mulgrave, who tried to allay his scruples: 'This is a little revenge for your suspicion of my being altered, as well as a vindication of my innocency in that particular'. The fact, then, that Etherege met his employers on equal terms accounts for the frivolity and flippancy of these official communications, and therefore for that entertaining quality which places them in a unique position among the correspondence of envoys of the time.

For the comedy revealed by the Letterbook we have in part to thank those men who sent Etherege to Ratisbon curiously failing to realize how hopelessly out of place he would be in such an environment. From the very first the envoy was dumbfounded by the ceremoniousness of the ministers of the Diet. They never unbent: 'Car les messieurs de la Diète sont toujours vêtus de leur caractère, et à peine s'en dépouillent-ils, à ce que je crois, quand ils s'approchent de leurs femmes ou de leurs maîtresses'. At times Etherege was in the mood to find diversion in this formality, but more often he expressed only contempt and weariness. But it was not only their stiffness but their pettiness and inertia that irritated him. They spent their time in quarrelling over points of precedence, in amusing themselves with garden parties and comedies, and in taking holidays: 'Generally once a week or a fortnight here uses to blow a trade wind which makes us see the Diet under sail though she suddenly casts anchor again'. This cumbrous and incapable body took weeks to resolve on anything, and would probably end by forgetting the main object in view, and expending any energy they had on a trifling dispute that had in the meantime arisen.

45

The hypocrisy and Puritanism of the German burghers likewise got on the envoy's nerves:

> In such an idle, sneaking place
> Where vice and folly hide their face,
> And in a troublesome disguise
> The wife seems modest, husband wise,

and he regretted the 'liberty of speech and passion' to which he had been accustomed in England. How often in his correspondence does he sigh for London society and diversions: 'There is not a day but my thoughts dog you from the coffee house to the play, from thence to Marylebone'; or again: 'A letter from you so fires me with the thought of the life I have led I can hardly forbear to rail at that I am condemned to'. He felt he was losing hold on his friends, and—dread fear of the modish fop—was becoming old-fashioned and out of date. So eager was he to hear news from his beloved city that he would write again and again to correspondents from whom he received no answer. In July 1687 he laments to Corbet: 'I begin to think I wear out of the memory of my acquaintance in England since I have not had a letter from any particular friend these three months'; and a month later he is forced to reflect cynically that 'neither the idle nor the busy are much given to think of a friend so far off as I am'. There is pathos in his humble and grateful acknowledgements of letters: 'I am very sensible of the trouble the correspondence you have with me gives you'; and in his tormenting doubts of the sincerity of friends: 'I know not whether there be any such thing as love or good fellowship stirring'. The self-sufficiency of the gallant breaks down before isolation from his kind and he becomes timid, appealing, and disillusioned.

To add to his difficulties Etherege's position in Ratisbon was none too pleasant. Owing to the

French sympathies of James II the envoy was from the first looked on with suspicion as a friend of France—a suspicion fostered by Etherege's intimacy at the house of the French envoy, where he found congenial, refined society and a game of cards awaiting him. The Englishman complains that the Austrian and German ministers 'put no confidence in me, esteeming his Majesty to have too strict an alliance with France', and that 'some of the ministers of the Empire cannot forgive a man who does not live in open hostility with the French'. In another letter he defends himself from partiality: 'all the account I have given of affairs into England . . . shew that I have behaved myself according to my instructions with all the impartiality imaginable', and indeed his dispatches do not reveal any very remarkable French bias.

The unrelenting malice of the villain of the piece, the Count de Windischgrätz, was the chief factor in Etherege's discomfiture. As a jealous husband and an ambitious diplomat the former exposed himself to the ridicule of the comic dramatist who has given a brilliant and witty character of him[1] worthy of the creator of Sir Fopling Flutter. The story of the Count's pretensions to be the Emperor's first commissioner in the teeth of obstinate opposition from the College of Electors gradually unfolds itself in the Letterbook until it became 'the only business of the Diet', who simply revelled in all such intricacies and intrigues. Fascinated, they let the affairs of Europe slide whilst they argued as to whether the Count, who was not a prince of the Empire, was entitled to hold this position; finally they agreed to disappoint his hopes by appointing Prince Herman of Baden to the post.

Etherege could not bear the airs Windischgrätz gave himself: 'Nobody can imagine the pride and

[1] pp. 103-4.

malice of that man who esteems himself the emperor of the place, and cannot suffer any one who will not neglect all besides to cringe to him. . . . The only pique he has to me is because I would not play the fool to please him.' Since Etherege would not cringe to him but only loaded him with opprobrium the Austrian determined to humble his adversary and caused letters to be written to England, France, Holland, and Vienna complaining of his conduct. By his tactless behaviour Etherege laid himself open to this kind of attack, and though he indignantly repudiates the charges as falsehoods they seem to have gained some credence. In Ratisbon Windisch-grätz made things as disagreeable as he could, and tried, Etherege complains, 'to hinder me from the liberty of coursing to make my footmen be enrolled by officers who have made levies here'. He even dared to accuse the English envoy of revealing an important secret that had been entrusted to him. Poor Etherege, though he had a certain shrewdness in managing affairs and was not easily to be bluffed, was not able to stand up against this sort of diplomacy, and could only anticipate with glee, when it was rumoured that his enemy was to be sent on a mission to Turkey, his meeting 'his match if he comes to treat about ceremonials with the Grand Vizier'.

The Austrian's ungovernable temper, underhand methods, and unscrupulous ambition, made him everywhere detested, and Etherege's testimony is borne out by Lord Galway in a letter to Lord Lexington, 1696:[1] 'You are right in believing this Court does not much regret the loss of the Count de Windischgrätz. The Abbé Grimani had no great regard for him.'

But Etherege had to contend with a covert as well as an overt enemy. His vicious secretary, Hugh

[1] Lexington Papers.

Hughes,[1] was writing home a farrago of scandal about his master, and carefully preserving among official dispatches in the Letterbook all 'expressions' that might do Sir George disservice in the future. Windischgrätz naturally looked on such an ally with a favourable eye, witness Hughes's statement in the 'List of some of the Lords and others who have done me good offices with his Majesty'[2] that 'The Count de Windischgrätz offered me a pension from ye Empr and writ in my behalf'; whilst in a letter written after the Revolution he says: 'During the last reign I did endeavour to support His Majesty's interest in the Empire and particularly at Ratisbon against the insolence and venomous libels of the French ambassador and his partisans who so persecuted me upon that account that I was often forced to flee to the Count de Windischgrätz and to Mr. Valkenier [the Dutch envoy] and to other ministers for their protection'. Hughes continues: 'Upon the happy Revolution in England I refused to go for France, tho' much solicited, and continued my zeal and duty to his present Majesty tho' without either character or allowance as it is well known to the whole Diet at Ratisbon'. He was rewarded by Etherege's place, in which he did not give much satisfaction, for in September 1692 he appealed against a command to return, accused Abbot Fleming, Etherege's friend at the Scotch monastery, of maligning him, and begged favour for a post in Berlin. In 1695 a warrant[3] was issued to pay Hughes,

[1] That the cryptic initials H.H. in the Letterbook stand for Hugh Hughes is proved by an entry in the State papers dated from Whitehall, April 1689: 'Pass for Hugh Hughes late English Secretary to the Imperial Courts resident at Ratisbon', and also by the fact that the handwriting of Hughes's autograph dispatches in the Record Office corresponds with that of the Letterbook.

[2] P.R.O. State Papers, Germany (States), 33.

[3] State Papers Domestic, 39.

'late His Majesty's agent in Ratisbon', £200 for removing his goods and family from Ratisbon to England. His subsequent career is buried in obscurity.

Hughes's account of his master's life in the Letterbook conveys an impression of an unpleasant personality. His melodramatic accusations, malicious interpretations, pompous parade of learning, cringing servility to superiors, and shocked sanctimoniousness, would be enough to condemn him apart from the knowledge of his betrayal. A cynical malice which could find no good in anything, much less in Sir George's intentions, pervades the letters; his account is more than 'an essay in misunderstanding',[1] it is an essay in deliberate malignancy.

These, then, are the principal protagonists of a comedy of which the Letterbook is the text. With regard to style Etherege is frequently clumsy and involved in his more official moments, but when he likes he can be both lucid and succinct, as witness his account of the quarrel between Brandenburg and Saxony.[2] His comments on the situation have a shrewdness approaching brilliance, as in his curt summary: 'It seems to me to be very natural for the Imperialists to be daily more sensible of the loss of what they have yielded to the French after their late great and unexpected success in the war against the Turk'—an aside which goes to the root of the matter in one pregnant sentence.

When he had not occasion to be fulsome Etherege could turn as neat and pretty a compliment as the best courtier of the age—a gift which he did not hesitate to employ to his own advantage, though his sense of humour prompted him to exclaim: 'You see what a fine courtier I am like to make, if ever I come back to England!' But it is in his letters to

[1] Palmer, *op. cit.*   [2] p. 94.

50

his friends and acquaintance[1] in London that the envoy allowed full rein to personality, expressing himself in a delicate, easy, simple style, infused with wit, raillery, and grace. His sensual similes and impertinent sallies are of the stuff of which his comic dialogue is made—a welcome relief from the careless phrasing and loose periods of his dispatches. His sketches of Windischgrätz, Cooke, and Duheron[2] make excellent reading, the entertaining qualities of which may be equalled by his vivid description of such an incident as the Countess of Windischgrätz's inquisitiveness and his own revenge.[3]

If Etherege does not deserve Dryden's eulogy— 'I will never enter the lists in prose with the undoubted best author of it which our nation has produced'—yet in his most characteristic moments his exquisite phrasing and delicate cadences, falling gently on the ear like the plash of a fountain, entitle him to a place of honour among the noble company of authors whose letters are an adornment to English literature.

For many of the notes on the text I am indebted to the *Dictionary of National Biography*, the *Encyclopaedia Britannica*, the *Cambridge Modern History*, *Allgemeine Deutsche Biographie*, *Nouvelle Biographie Générale*, B. Erdmannsdörffer's *Deutsche Geschichte vom Westfälischen Frieden*, Page's *Le Grand Électeur et Louis XIV*, and A. Waddington's *Le Grand Électeur Frédéric Guillaume*.

I have modernized the spelling and expanded the abbreviations of the Letterbook, with the exception of some proper names, both in the English and French letters, but have left uncorrected the grammatical errors in the latter.

[1] See letter to Corbet, p. 189, or to Dryden, p. 167.
[2] pp. 61, 103-4, 115-16, 311.   [3] p. 232.

THE LETTERBOOK

begun Saturday 5/15 Mar. 86/7.

... They are a people pamper'd up in ease
That no King can govern nor no god can please.[1]

A Ratisbonne ce 19/29ᵉ Nov. 85.

Monsieur·

Je ne fais que d'arriver ici, et j'ai été si embarrassé
pour m'établir, que je n'ai pas eu le loisir de vaguer
ni pour moimême ni pour mes amis. J'ai fait tout
ce que je pouvais pour m'informer sur le sujet dont
nous avons parlé, et je trouve que toute l'Empire est
épuisée, et la Bôheme plus que tous les autres pays
hormis l'Autriche. J'ai eu[2] beaucoup de déplaisir
de ces nouvelles que vous aviez reçues lors que nous
nous disions adieu. J'espère que c'était plutôt la
crainte que vos veritables amis avaient pour vous,
qu'aucune chose réelle. J'ai déjà une fort jolie
maison, une carosse, et des bons chevaux, des valets,
et un cuisinier; mais je ne me puis pas vanter d'être
bien servi dans ma cuisine—tout le reste est passable.
Je ne manquerai pas de vous donner les nouvelles
que je vous ai promises quand le temps servira. Si
les choses ne vont pas à votre gré, et que vous avez
envie de changer de climat vous pourrez vivre tout
doucement, et serez toujours le mieux venu du
monde chez un Homme qui est sincèrement

Monsieur,
votre très humble et très obéissant serviteur
G.E.

à Monsieur Germain à la Haye.

[1] Cf. Dryden's *Absalom and Achitophel*:
'God's pamper'd People, whom, debauch'd with ease,
No King could govern nor no God could please'.

Mr. Dobrée suggests that these lines may refer to Etherege
under the disguise of the plural (*Essays in Biography*). Mr.
Brett-Smith suggests that the letters included in the Letterbook dated before 5/15 March 1686/7 may have been copied
into it from existing transcripts.   [2] MS. Je eu.

1685

Monsieur (Barrillon):[1]

Je vous dois tout ce qui m'est agréable ici: la faveur, et la bonne opinion de Monsieur de Crécy,[2] et le privilège d'être chez lui sans cérémonie, est un meuble qui ne se trouve pas dans aucune autre maison de la ville. Car les messieurs de la Diète sont toujours vêtus de leur caractère, et à peine s'en dépouillent-ils, à ce que je crois, quand ils s'approchent de leurs femmes, ou de leur maîtresses. On ne rend jamais des visites qu'à une heure assignée et si vous manquez un peu de votre temps vous courez risque de morfondre un pauvre ministre qui se tient en sentinelle pour vous reçevoir à la portière

[1] Paul Barillon d'Amoncourt, Marquis de Branges (1630–91), French Ambassador in England, whither he arrived on Aug. 30, 1677. He helped to bring about the fall of Lord Rochester and, sure of a civil war in England, encouraged Louis XIV to pursue his designs against the Empire. By order of William III he left the country, Dec. 24, 1688. He returned to France out of favour with Louis, and his health became affected (Burnet, *History of My own Time*, 1753, vol. ii, p. 500). Macaulay says he 'was not without parts, and possessed in large measure the graces and accomplishments which then distinguished the French gentry. But his capacity was scarcely equal to what his great place required. He had become sluggish and self-indulgent, liked the pleasures of society and of the table better than business, and in great emergencies generally waited for admonitions, and even for a reprimand from Versailles before he showed much activity' (*History of England*, 1867, vol. i, pp. 561–2).

[2] Louis Verjus Comte de Crécy (1629–1709). Appointed French plenipotentiary to the Diet 1679, he retained that post until December 1688, when the Emperor, then at war with France, ordered him to leave, he having tried 'everywhere to attaint the Emperor's honour and fame'. St. Simon gives him the following character: 'C'était un petit homme accort, doux, poli, respectueux, adroit, qui avait passé toute sa vie dans les emploies étrangers, et qui en avait pris toutes les manières. . . . Il avait beaucoup d'insinuation, l'art de redire cent fois la même chose, toujours en différentes façons, et une patience qui, à force de ne se rebuter point, réussissait très souvent.'

de votre carrosse. Il est vrai que la bassette[1] nous manquent, mais nous nous consolons d'un peu de l'hombre,[2] et la comette[3] commence à s'établir. Le divertissement le plus galant du pays cet hiver c'est le traîneau[4] où l'on se met en croupe de quelque belle Allemande, en manièr(e) que vous ne pouvez ni la voir, ni lui parler à cause d'un diable de tintamarre des sonnettes dont les harnais sont tous garnis. Le droit néanmoins du traîneau est quelque chose de considérable. Vous pouvez prétendre un baiser dans tous les carrefours de la belle que vous menez. Et la faveur n'est pas méprisable, puisque le baiser ne se donne pas en cérémonie comme chez nous; si par bonheur vous renversez la belle vous lui pouvez faire présent d'une nouvelle jupe, et elle ne la peut refuser. Je ne veux pas plus dire sur cet chapitre, de peur de ne vous degoûter des plaisirs de Londres. Quoique je ne mérite pas ce que vous avez écrit en ma faveur je tâcherai de m'a(c)quiter en sorte qu'on vous excusera la bonté que vous avez eu pour moi; et je ne manquerai jamais en toute occasion de reconnaître les obligations que j'ai à votre Excellence d'être

Monsieur
votre très humble et très obéissant serviteur
G.E.

A Monsieur Barrillon ambassadeur de France en Angleterre.

[1] A French game of cards for five players, popular at this period. Etherege wrote a song called 'Basset', in which he complained that the ladies neglected his society for the card table.

[2] A Spanish card-game for three players, which rivalled picquet in popularity among the ladies.

[3] A now obsolete card-game.

[4] cf. Burnet, *op. cit.* iii. 302: 'while he was driving the Princess upon the snow in a Traineau, according to the German manner.'

Ditto.

My Lord (Rochester):[1]

I have only ventured to trouble you with one letter since my being here, the season of the year affording nothing worth the interrupting you one moment from the great business you are perpetually employed in. Your Lordship knows this country and this place; they are not apt to change; women keep their own longest who are not over handsome. I dare say no more of them; 'tis hard to be pleasant, when we are afraid of being impertinent. The Imperial army has some time since taken up their winter quarters in Transylvania,[2] and I expect no news from Hungary worth your knowledge till the campaign begins to open. The Princess of Ragotzi[3] keeps her fortress of Mongatz still, and the Imperialists have been so civil to draw from the town at

---

[1] Lawrence Hyde, Earl of Rochester (1641–1711) second son of Edward Hyde, Earl of Clarendon, was made Lord of the Treasury in Nov. 1679 and was virtually principal adviser to Charles II. He was connected with the royal family by the marriage of his sister Anne to James, Duke of York. His removal in August 1684 from the Treasury to the more dignified but less influential post of Prince of the Council evoked from Halifax the famous expression 'kicked upstairs'. On the accession of James II Rochester regained the office of Lord Treasurer, but was dismissed on his refusal to become a Roman Catholic in 1687. Although at first opposing the election of William and Mary, he afterwards held several posts under them. Dryden has praised his qualities of honesty, economy, and generosity as Hushai in *Absalom and Achitophel*. He was nevertheless of a weak character, and would endorse opinions of which he disapproved for the sake of remaining in power and favour.

[2] The envoy at Vienna complained about the quartering of troops in Transylvania and even threatened to dislodge them by force.

[3] Helen Zrini, widow of Francis Rákóczy, or Ragotski, married in 1682 Prince Tököly, the Hungarian rebel. When her husband was seized by the Turks General Caprara required her to surrender Munkács, and on her refusal invested the castle, which he was not able to capture until 1688.

her request. Caprara[1] nevertheless has blocked up the avenues with three regiments. The Count de Windisgratz[2] is returned hither from Vienna, and there is like to be more disputes about ceremonials, but I reserve them to entertain my Lord Middleton,[3] as my duty obliges me. I shall be very diligent to serve His Majesty as well as I am able, in what can be expected from me here; if in doing that your goodness will afford me any mark of your favour, I shall not regret whatever I have lost in London. I wish your Lordship a long enjoyment, and daily increase of your happiness, and myself the good fortune to have an opportunity to shew how warmly I am,

My Lord

Your Lordship's most faithful and most humble servant.

To my Lord Rochester, Lord High Treasurer.

[1] Ænius Sylvius, Count of Caprara (1631–1701), Austrian Field Marshal, Vice-president of the Imperial Council of War, and Knight of the Golden Fleece, was born at Bologna. In the wars against the Turks he succeeded in putting both them and the Hungarian rebels to flight. He died in Vienna, having seen forty-four campaigns.

[2] Gottlieb Amadeus, Count of Windischgrätz (1630–95), Austrian statesman, was born at Ratisbon. At the age of 28 he became an aulic councillor, and was later sent on several missions as envoy extraordinary. Thus from 1663–4 he was in Sweden, in 1676 in France, from 1673–4 in Brandenburg and Denmark, in 1674 at Hamburg, and in 1691–3 at the Hague. From 1683–8 he assisted the Bishop of Passau as imperial commissioner to the Diet. In 1682 he became a Catholic, and in 1684 received a seat and vote on the Counts' bench (Grafenbank). He attained the position of Vice-Chancellor of the Empire and died in Vienna. See Introduction, pp. 47–8.

[3] Charles, 2nd Earl of Middleton (1640–1719), was appointed in 1684 an English Secretary of State. He remained loyal to James at the Revolution, and tried to bring about his Restoration by peaceful means. Born a Protestant, he joined the Roman Catholic Church in 1701, in pursuance of the dying wish of James II. Burnet says he was 'a man of great parts and a generous temper, but of loose principles in religion' (*op. cit.* ii. 381).

1685

My Lord:

Since my coming hither I have had a little fever, which has been the reason I have not paid my duty so regularly as I ought to do to your Lordship. I am now pretty well recovered, and hope I am quit at a reasonable price for what I was to pay on the change of climates, and a greater change in my manner of living. Is it not enough to breed an ill habit of body in a man who was used to sit up till morning, to be forced, for want of knowing what to do with himself, to go to bed in the evening; one who has been used to see his friends with all freedom never to approach anybody but with ceremony; instead of rattling about the streets to seek variety of company, to sit at home and entertain himself with solitude and silence? The pleasures of play and women are not so much as talk[ed] of, and one would think the Diet had made a *Reichsgutachten* to banish them the city. Here was the Countess of Nostitz, but malice, that always persecutes the good, has made her lately remove to Prague. Company met nightly at her house and had a little ombre to entertain 'em. An abler woman, by what I hear, never kept a basset in London. If I do well after all this you must allow me to be a philosopher, and I dare affirm Cato left not the world with more firmness of soul than I did England. The disputes that happen about ceremonials in the Diet I shall only torment my Lord Middleton with as a tax due from his province; when anything of moment is debated I shall acquaint you with it. But that which I shall be most careful to inform you of is what is done when the campaign opens, knowing the King loves to hear of these matters. The best acknowledgement I can make to your Lordship for all I owe you, which is indeed all I have, is to be industrious in my station. You preferred me to his Majesty's service and in gratitude

I shall daily study to acquit myself well in it. I have no better way here of letting your Lordship know how truly sensible I am of your favour; wherever I am hereafter all the actions of my life shall still show with how much sincerity and humility I am

My Lord

Your Lordship's most faithful and most obedient servant.

To the Earl of Sunderland.[1]

Ratisbon . . . Dec. 85.

My Lord (Middleton):

The Count de Windisgratz pretends a commission to be of equal power in the Diet with the Prince of Passau, and chief Commissioner for all foreign affairs here and all over the Empire. He sent his commission by the Chancellor of the Commission Decrees to be showed the French Plenipotentiary[2] but he excused himself from seeing it, saying it would come to his knowledge more properly from the Diet, and intends to send his secretary to return the compliment, and defers his visit till the Diet give their opinion of the commission. He has sent to all other ministers to acquaint them of his arrival. His commission, as 'tis thought, will be disputed by the College of Electors, for the letter from the Emperor

[1] Robert Spencer, 2nd Earl of Sunderland (1640–1702), only son of Henry Spencer and Dorothy Sidney, the Sacharissa of Waller's poems, held posts as ambassador successively at Madrid, Paris, and Cologne. On the accession of James he was appointed Lord President of the Council and one of the members of the Commission for ecclesiastical causes. Meanwhile he was both receiving a pension from France and corresponding with William of Orange. In 1687 he became a Roman Catholic, but was dismissed by James in October 1688, with the remark, ' I hope you will be more faithful to your next master than you have been to me '. Macaulay wholeheartedly condemns him, but Burnet speaks of his 'clear and ready apprehension' and his 'quick decision in business'.

[2] Crécy.

is highly resented by the masters, and the deputies. The Elector of Cologne[1] sent a letter to protest against the Emperor's proceeding, that it is a violation of the right of the Electors, whose ministers ought not to be chid, or receive any instructions but from themselves. The Elector of Saxony[2] writ himself to the Emperor in answer to the circular letter he received, inveighing against the Count de Windisgratz as much as the Emperor does against the deputies of the College of Electors, and saying it is only his vanity and ambition which have occasioned all the delays and disputes. The Elector of Brandenburg[3] is warm in the business. The Elector of Bavaria[4] meddles not in it. Mayence[5] and

[1] Maximilian Henry, brother to the Elector of Bavaria, born 1621, was sent to study in Cologne in 1673 along with the Count of Fürstenburg, who exercised a lifelong influence over him. He succeeded his uncle as Elector and Archbishop of Cologne in 1649. In 1684 he lived for some time as a monk and sought comfort in alchemy. He sent troops to aid the Emperor against the Turks, and died at Bonn after a long illness in 1688. He was pious and moderate, but too weak and dependent.

[2] John George III, Elector of Saxony (1647–91), forsook the vacillating policy of his father by joining the alliance against France in 1683. He helped to drive the Turks from Vienna, and sent aid to Leopold I in 1685.

[3] Frederick William, the Great Elector (1620–88). See Introduction.

[4] Maximilian Emanuel II, Elector of Bavaria (1662-1726), took over the reins of government from the Regent in 1680. Both Louis and the Emperor were anxious to gain his support; he favoured the latter, and led 12,000 men to the rescue of Vienna in 1683. In the spring of 1685 he married the Emperor's daughter, Maria Antonia, and gained much fame in the following campaigns against the Turks, which culminated in his capture of Belgrade, 1688. He defended the Empire when it was invaded by Louis in the same year, and was given the chief command of the Imperial army on the death of the Duke of Lorraine.

[5] The archbishopric of Mayence was one of the seven electorates of the Empire. Its archbishop was President or

Treves[1] have sent back the letter, made sharper in some places by reason of the general dissatisfaction of the Electors, &c.

Ratisbon, 20/30 Dec. 1685.

My Lord (Middleton):

The Prince of Passau[2] is a quiet, good man, and meddles little in affairs (only in the forms his commission obliges him to); he is, as I judge by his person, near three score years of age. The Count de Windisgratz is about five and fifty, as I am told, hot, and of a busy insulting temper, which has lost him the goodwill of most of the ministers of the Diet, especially of the whole Electoral College, who still oppose him in all his designs, and pretensions. The clashing of these two factions has been the reason why matters of moment have been deliberated on with so much delay. The Directors of the Princes College are of the Count de Windisgratz his faction, and will never propose anything to their College which comes to them from the College of Electors if they judge their party is not strong enough to carry it as they would. This made them keep the acts lately made for congratulating the Emperor on his victory, &c. from the 1st of September (which date the *Reichsgutachtens* bear), till the Emperor sent lately a commission decree not to name the Count de Windisgratz in such acts of the Diet as passed in his absence, and never read them in the College till the point was yielded. The deputies of the towns serve only for form's sake, and have never

Director of the Electoral College, Arch-Chancellor of the Empire, and Primate of Germany. From p. 113 it is evident that he vested his directorship in a deputy.

[1] Treves or Trier was an archbishopric and electorate of the Empire.

[2] Sebastian, Count of Poetting, became Bishop of Passau in 1673. He died in 1689.

any business transmitted to them till the other two
Colleges have agreed. I have enclosed with this all
the news we have here, and am &c.

Ratisbon, 9/19 Jan. 1685/6.

To my Lord Middleton with the following copy
of verses:[1]
From hunting Whores, and haunting play,
And minding nothing else all day
And all the night too, you will say;
To make grave legs in formal fetters,
Converse with fops,[2] and write dull letters;
To go to bed 'twixt eight and nine,
And sleep away my precious time
In such an idle, sneaking[3] place,
Where vice and folly hide their face,
And in a troublesome disguise
The wife seems modest,[4] husband wise.
For pleasure here has the same fate
Which does attend affairs of state,
The plague of ceremony infects,
Ev'n in love, the softer sex;
Who an essential will neglect
Rather than lose the least respect.
With regular approach we storm,
And never visit but in form;
That is, sending to know before
At what o'clock they'll[5] play the whore.

[1] These verses seem first to have been printed in 'The
History of Adolphus, Prince of Prussia and the Princess
Fidelity by a Person of Quality. With a Collection of Songs
and Love verses by several hands. To which is added two
letters in verse from Sir G[eorge] E[therege] to the E[arl] of
M[iddleton] with Mr. D[ryden]'s answer to them' (Term
Catalogues ii. 392) and were reprinted in Rochester's *Familiar
Letters*, 1697, and in *The Works of Sir George Etherege*, 1704.
[2] 1704 'fools'.   [3] 1697 'sneaking, idle'.
[4] 1704 'honest'.   [5] 1704 'she'll'.

The nymphs are constant, gallants private,
One scarce can guess who[1] 'tis they drive at.
This seems to me a scurvy fashion, ⎫
Who have been bred in a free nation ⎬
With liberty of speech, and passion. ⎭
Yet I cannot forbear to spark it,
And make the best of a bad market.
Meeting with one, by chance, kind-hearted,
Who no preliminaries started,
I enter'd, beyond expectation,
Into a close negotiation:
Of which hereafter a relation.
Humble to fortune, not her slave,
I still was pleas'd with what she gave;
And, with a firm, and cheerful mind, ⎫
I steer my course with every wind, ⎬
To all the ports she has design'd. ⎭

Monsieur: Ratisbonne ce 17/27 fevrier 85/6.

Nous avons été employés ici plus que d'ordinaire le temps de ce carnaval. Autrement je n'aurais pas manqué *devant*[2] de vous faire mes reconnaissances. Vous m'accablez d'une telle manière de compliments, et de tabac, que je manque des paroles, et des moyens en ce misérable endroit pour faire le retour que votre générosité mérite, et pour tout ce que je vous dois je vous puis seulement assurer que je suis avec beaucoup de sincérité,

A Monsieur Purpurat[3] à Vienne. Monsieur, &c.

Ratisbon, 22 Feb./4 March, 1685/6.
My Lord (Middleton):

The Diet sleeps still, and when they will awake I know not. In my last I told you what I had reason

---

[1] 1704 'what'.　　[2] Bad French underlined by the secretary.
[3] See *post*, p. 380.

to think kept them from deliberating on those affairs they have had so long before them. Ease and quiet, the common breeders of discord and mutiny, have[1] revived the quarrel which was made up between the Count de Windisgratz and the Electoral College. The Emperor's Concommissary is recalled for not behaving himself to the liking of his superior officers, and the Count de Windisgratz has writ a letter to Monsieur de Scherers, the first minister of Austria, and one of the directors of the Princes College, in which is given the detail of the whole business. He, as Monsieur de Windisgratz's friend, acquaints the rest of the ministers with the contents, but will not part with a copy. I have heard some part of it, which is pleasant on that subject, and, if I had the whole, I would send it to your Lordship that you might have a share in our diversions here.

The last post from Vienna brings no news; it only says that Tekely[2] labours in vain to make the Hungarians rebel again, who have anew sworn allegiance to the Emperor.[3]

---

[1] MS. 'has'.

[2] Emerich Prince Tököly (1657–1705), born at Késmark, led the Magyars in revolt against the Emperor and compelled him to grant an armistice (1681). He became Prince of Upper Hungary, but shared the fate of the Turkish army in the Vienna campaign of 1683. Unable to come to terms with Leopold, Tököly renewed the war in 1685, but was seized by his former allies, the Turks, and sent to Adrianople in chains. He was soon released and sent with a small army into Transylvania in 1686, but this and another expedition in 1688 failed and the leader was again imprisoned. He is said to have possessed personal charm, courage, eloquence, constancy, and ambition; the ruling passion of his life was hatred of Austria.

[3] Tököly sent circular letters to several counties of Upper Hungary requiring them to send deputies for orders and styling himself Prince of Hungary and Transylvania. In February 1686 he was with the Turkish army at Lippa trying to regain, without success, the Hungarians, who had abandoned him since his imprisonment.

Mr. Wynne[1] talks of a circular letter the Elector Palatine[2] should write to the States of the Empire, signifying the apprehensions he has of the French King's marching that way. We know here of no such letter; only before his minister gave in his memorial he sent a copy of it, together with a letter, to the Elector of Brandenburg to desire his opinion.

Monsieur Schnolsky, the King of Sweden's deputy in the Diet, is still at Heidelberg negotiating some affairs with the Elector.[3] We expect to know the effects of his journey when the meeting is at Nuremberg about renewing the alliances. Besides the near relation which makes that King concern himself so much for the Elector, he would fain recover his duchy of Deuxponts,[4] which his minister mentioned in the Diet, when they were hot upon the King of France's contraventions.

[1] Dr. Owen Wynne, Secretary to Lord Middleton.

[2] Philip William of Neuburg, a zealous Catholic (1615–1690), succeeded Charles as Elector Palatine in 1685. He married (1) Anne, daughter of Sigismund III of Poland, (2) Elisabeth-Amelia of Hesse-Darmstadt.

[3] The Elector Palatine.

[4] The following genealogical tree explains Charles XI's claim. On the death of Frederick Louis, according to family compacts and will, Deuxponts descended to Charles XI of Sweden. Adolf John claimed the inheritance and sought to gain the support of Louis XIV by promising to hold Deuxponts as a fief. Louis refused his protection. The territory of Deuxponts came under French sovereignty by the decree of the Chambers of Reunion 1680. Charles made abortive efforts to get his claims recognized at Frankfurt (1682) and Ratisbon (1684).

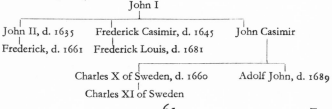

John I

John II, d. 1635   Frederick Casimir, d. 1645   John Casimir

Frederick, d. 1661   Frederick Louis, d. 1681

Charles X of Sweden, d. 1660   Adolf John, d. 1689

Charles XI of Sweden

F

1685/6

The Duke of Zell's [1] forces in the land belonging to Hamburg are grown more moderate, and keep themselves cantoned together, since the marching of the King of Denmark's troops into Holstein. The Duke upon his making that invasion sent two letters, one to the King of Denmark, another to the Elector of Brandenburg, to acquaint them with the motives which induced him to it. The King of Denmark has sent a copy of the Duke's letter to Monsieur de Schenbeck, one of the deputies of the Elector of Brandenburg, together with the answer he sent upon the marching of his forces into Holstein. The Duke of Zell pretends he did it as the Emperor's commissioner for the protection of that town: they having refused to restore to his place and possessions Monsieur Meurer, [2] one of their burgomasters, whom they formerly expelled for being of the Duke's faction, and branded him with a design

[1] George William, Duke of Zell (1624–1705), supported the Emperor and personally led his troops against the French in 1674 and 1675, and in support of Brandenburg undertook a campaign against Sweden in conjunction with Denmark. For the Hamburg incident see Introduction, p. 39.

[2] Henry Meurer (1643–90), an eminent Hamburg statesman, was elected mayor of that free town in 1678. He was *persona grata* at the courts of Zell and Vienna, but was looked upon with coldness at Berlin and open hostility at Copenhagen owing to his efforts to frustrate Denmark's designs on Hamburg. In the town he was opposed by an unscrupulous, democratic party, and was but weakly supported by the council. In 1684 his enemies succeeded in having him arrested as a traitor, and though their accusations were both petty and unproven, he was compelled to resign. His place was taken by a committee of thirty. Two years later his opponents' plot to hand over Hamburg to the Danes came to light when the latter appeared with a besieging army before the city. Hamburg, strengthened by reinforcements from neighbouring countries, held out until a peace was arranged. The despotic rule of the committee of thirty came to an end, the council was reinstated, and Meurer was restored to his offices and honours in November 1686.

of betraying their privileges. Monsieur Meurer resides still in the Duke's court, but he is lately made Reichshofrat or conciliarius Imperii aulicus [1] by the Emperor. His other pretence is that they have affronted him by forbidding all manner of commerce with any of his subjects and refusing to disannul the decree at his request. The King of Denmark's answer to the Duke, with which he desired Monsieur de Schenbeck to acquaint the Diet, was: that he did not intend anything against the armistitia concluded, but only designed to defend his own frontiers from the incursions and insolences they are liable to, by reason of their neighbourhood. The Elector of Brandenburg offered the Hamburgers 2,000 foot, but they refused them. They are jealous not without cause; all their neighbours have a mind to swallow them, and it is happy for them there are so many long for the morsel. The number of the rivals only hinder the rape. It is generally believed here the Luneburgers will draw off, as soon as honourably they can.

Pray continue me always in your favour, and when you are in any of those leisure places where idle fellows are admitted let me intrude sometimes into your memory. I am, &c.

Ratisbon, 4/14 March, 85/6.

My Lord (Middleton):

I send you enclosed a copy of the memorial Monsieur de Crécy delivered to the Diet yesterday; by that you will judge what his Christian Majesty designs against the Elector Palatine. It seems to me a protestation that what he undertakes in that business is not against the armistitia. The substance is: that he will accept of the Pope's mediation, which is what the Elector Palatine offered when he would

---

[1] The aulic council was the Emperor's supreme court.

not submit to the arbitration,[1] in case the States of the Empire will engage forthwith that the Duchess of Orleans[2] shall receive no damage by the possession the Elector will have had of the things in dispute, till the year is elapsed; it being a law of the Empire that after a year's peaceable possession, no plea lies to recover the possession or the profits, and the possessor is esteemed legally possessed till the title be tried, and judgement given against him. I find the reason cleared in the memorial, and by discourse with some ministers here why the Elector waived the arbitration, and would yield to the mediation of the Pope; the arbitration giving him power immediately to dispossess the Elector, which the mediation does not. When I send your Lordship the resolution of the Diet on this memorial I will also venture to trouble you with the diverse opinions of the learned of this place as to the right in question.

Yesterday the fifty Roman months[3] were voted to the Emperor, and this day the conclusion is to be put in form.

This evening the post comes in from Vienna, and, if I have time enough after I receive the news, I will transcribe it, and send it to Mr. Wynne for your Lordship.

[1] Louis had already referred his pretensions to the Palatinate to the arbitration of the Pope in November 1685.

[2] Charlotte Elisabeth, Duchess of Orleans (1652–1722), sister of the Elector Palatine Charles, married Philippe, Duke of Orleans, brother of Louis XIV, 1670. Her sympathies were with the Empire, and when her claims to the Palatinate were made the pretext for the French invasion of her country in 1688 she writes pathetically: 'If they were to kill me for it, I should still find it impossible not to regret—or, rather, deplore—being made the pretext for my country's destruction' (*Letters of Madame*, i. 83). See Introduction, p. 34.

[3] German *Römermonate*, a war-tax so called because the Princes and States of the Empire had to pay their contributions monthly.

Mr. John Cooke[1] in a letter I lately had the favour to receive from him, gave me a pleasant account of the adventures of a marriage which I hope is happily consummated by this time, and numps[2] is now in the stocks in earnest. I am, &c.

Ratisbon, 8/18 March, 86/7 [*sic*].

My Lord [Middleton]:

With my last of the fourth instant I sent you a copy of the memorial Monsieur de Crécy delivered to the Diet. I find upon a better examination I was misinformed, and that the law here is much like ours in England. The elapsing of the year will do Madame d'Orleans no other prejudice than that she already receives by being kept out of possession, and being forced to be plaintiff. If she recovers the lands in dispute, she will recover the mean profits also, and, admit it were disputable, the claim made for her by Monsieur de Crécy in his first memorial concerning this business secures her right. Nevertheless most of the deputies of the Diet talk as if they thought it reasonable something should be done towards the satisfying of his most Christian Majesty, and I find this affair has been communicated to some of the Princes of the Empire beforehand, since many of their deputies (amongst the rest those of Cologne and Brandenburg) own they have already received instructions therein. Many are of opinion the Elector has done himself a prejudice by possessing himself of the personal estate, which undoubtedly belongs to Madame d'Orleans, and especially that the Elector was in the wrong to take possession of it before it was priced, though he offers to be

[1] Probably the clerk in the Secretary of State's office to whom the letter is addressed (p. 293).

[2] numps = fool (Wright's *Provincial Dictionary*). Cf. 'There is a certain creature called a Grave Hobby-Horse, a kind of she-numps' (Marquis of Halifax's *Advice to a Daughter*).

responsible, it giving his adversaries a just occasion to say the true value can never be known, it chiefly consisting in corn and wine, of which there is a daily consumption. The moderate affirm that the county of *Sponheim*[1] came into the family by the marriage of an heiress, and is allodial, but that Simmern and Lautern[2] came by purchase and are fiefs male, which are (not unlike our entails) made by compacts in several families of the Empire, but have been never ratified by the Diet. The Germans say it is not necessary and the French urge it is. It is certain the duchy of Simmern is not a member of the electorship since the branch of Charles the late Elector[3] were dukes of Simmern, when that dignity fell to them. Besides, it hath been bequeathed to younger brother[s] of the family, who have enjoyed it, among the rest Edward, brother to Charles Lewis,[4] who died not many years since; but still upon failure of issue male it has come back to the family. What the Diet will propose to satisfy his most Christian Majesty is not discoursed of yet. Many look on this memorial to be no other than a manifest that his Majesty will not do anything against the common peace, and intends suddenly to seize on these lands in Madame d'Orleans name, and so remove the wrong the Elector does her by withholding the possession, and making him plaintiff in his turn.

The Electoral College and that of the Princes being agreed on the conclusion about the fifty Roman months on Saturday last, they communicated

---

[1] The Electors Palatine had been Counts of Sponheim since the marriage of Anna, heiress of Sponheim, with the Palatine of Simmern.

[2] MS. 'Zimeren' and 'Lauteren'.

[3] Charles II, Elector Palatine (1651—May 1685), eldest son of Elector Charles Louis and Charlotte of Hesse.

[4] Charles Louis, Elector Palatine (b. 1617, d. Aug. 1680).

it to the College of the Towns, who differ with them in their conclusion: desiring there may be an abatement be made in the payment of the tax proportionable to the forces they have assisted the Emperor with in his war against the Turks, and likewise that the winter quarters they have furnished may be considered, meaning the money which the Lüneburg troops exacted from the towns of Nordhausen and Mühlhausen in their return from the last campaign. This is thought very reasonable, since the Emperor has by his letters privately assured the princes who have assisted him with their troops that, in consideration thereof, he will excuse them.

This day 'tis hoped that notwithstanding this difficulty the matter will be unanimously resolved. It is thought there will be more delays before this act is presented to the Emperor's commissioners. Disputes about the deputation and ceremonials are to be adjusted, since the quarrel is renewed between the Count de Windisgratz and the Electoral College. But I will not torment your Lordship with what is discoursed concerning those great things before your time. I am, &c.

An answer to Cardinal Bonvisi's [1] query if a twelvemonth and a day's possession excludes all pretensions:

Copia rescripti Caesarei nuntio apostolico in causa palatinata extraditi.

Nomine sacrae Caesarae majestatis eminentissimo

---

[1] Francisco Buonvisi (1626–1700), a native of Lucca, went to Vienna in order to induce Leopold not to break with the French (1672), and thereafter became regular envoy at the Emperor's court. His post was not an easy one; the Imperial ministers suspected him of being a friend of France and worked against him. Buonvisi himself was candid to the point of tactlessness and resolutely refused to interfere in Imperial affairs; he exercised, however, a personal influence on the Emperor. He had been made Cardinal in 1681.

domino cardinali nuntio Bonvisi ad eiusdem inter-
rogationem et instantium an juxta imperii leges
praetendens successionem in feudo, nec eiusdem
possessionem intra annum et diem apprehendens
beneficii possessorii excidat? perbenigne respon-
dendum, leges imperii in hoc capite a jure communi
Romano et feudali non discrepare, adeoque, prae-
tendentem successionem in feudis imperii aliisve
bonis, competente via contra eum qui in capescenda
possessione praevenit posse agere, et uti etiam post
lapsum anni et diei omnibus beneficiis in possessorio
et petitorio jure communi statutis, si autem neglecta
via juris et competentis judicii, sibi ipsi jus dicere,
et possessionem ab alio apprehensam propria
authoritate et facto occupare praesumat eum jure
suo cadere et in alias etiam poenas pro circumstantia-
rum qualitate incidere. Quod reliquum est sacra Caesarea majestas eminentissimum dominum cardinalem
gratia et benevolentia sua Caesarea propense com-
plectitur. Signatum Viennae, 10 martii, 1686.[1]

Ratisbon, 15/25 March, 85/6.

My Lord (Middleton):

After having taken a great deal of rest our Diet
rouses and becomes very active. On Saturday last
were dictated two commissions decree[s], which were
brought hither, as I am informed, by a courier of the
Elector Palatine's as he passed by this place in his
return from Vienna to Heidelberg.

The one concerns the Duke of Holstein Gottorp,[2]
and mentions that whereas the Diet, by a conclusion
made by them the 31st of August last, thought it
reasonable that the said Prince should be restored
to the possession of his country, of which he is

---

[1] For a translation of this letter see Appendix.

[2] Christian Albert, Duke of Holstein-Gottorp (1641–94),
succeeded his father Frederick III in 1659. See Introduction,
pp. 37–40.

unjustly ousted by the King of Denmark, and in order to it entreated his Imperial Majesty to employ his good offices and mediation. The Emperor now offers his mediation and invites the Electors of Saxony and Brandenburg and the house of Brunswick to assist him with their mediations; that in case the King of Denmark should refuse this accommodation, they may take other measures to persuade him to be reasonable. The other commission decree is touching the limits. The great difficulty has been about agreeing the place of treaty. The Electoral College has still been for this town, and upon the considerations I have formerly mentioned. The Emperor offers to advance all that is necessary on his part towards perfecting this business, so that the poor people who suffer under the domination of the French may be delivered from that hardship, and desires the Diet to do all they can on their part, and proposes to them three places for the treaty, viz: *Worms*, *Speyer*, and *Frankfort*, and likewise desires the Diet at the same time to deliberate upon and promote the *puncta securitatis publicae*, meaning the alliance of Franconia, which is designed (as I have formerly writ) to be renewed very suddenly.[1] This will oblige the States of the Empire who are in the alliance to maintain their proportion of troops to be ready on occasion, notwithstanding the fifty Roman months they are to pay. This makes some murmur, and it is thought that this decree which the Emperor designs in favour of the Elector Palatine has been purposely delayed till that tax was passed.

If the post comes in time enough from Vienna, your Lordship shall know what comes from thence in a paper enclosed to Dr. Wynne. Pray, my Lord, keep me alive in the memory of those you think convenient, and always reckon me, as I am, &c.

[1] See Introduction, p. 30.

1686

Ratisbon, 25 March/4 April, 86.

To my Lord (Middleton):

About the conclusion, touching the fifty Roman months, which the Electoral College refused to send to the Emperor's commissioners by a general deputation as was wont: pretending they were denied the honour of punctilios due to them; therefore the minister of Mayence carried it alone.

Ratisbon, 29 March/8 April, 86.

My Lord (Middleton):

The Diet is at present in devotion, and will not be at leisure till after the holydays to mind worldly matters.

Besides the business of Hamburg there has happened an hostile action at Vienna which may retard the accommodation[1] which was expected. Monsieur Marenholt, the Duke of Zell's envoy at that court, has made a new invasion on the person of Monsieur Schafftheusen,[2] who was sent with Monsieur Mylden by that town to the Emperor. Monsieur Marenholt attacked him as he was taking the air without Vienna in his coach with his colleague, forced him out of the coach, and cudgelled him. The pretence of the quarrel is this: Marenholt had the copy of a letter, which he pretended was sent by Schafftheusen to his masters at Hamburg, giving a hint, that if they would open their purse, and give fourscore thousand crowns among the courtiers at Vienna, the Emperor might be brought to recall the com-

[1] MS. 'accomedation'.

[2] John Schaffshausen (1643–97), senator of Hamburg, was sent in July 1685 to Vienna with a colleague to inform the Emperor of the true state of the dissensions (both external and internal) in Hamburg. In March 1686, the two envoys were the victims of a violent assault by the Lüneburg-Zell envoy, von Mahrenholtz, in the open streets of Vienna, the result of which was that the Emperor forbad von Mahrenholtz his presence and demanded his recall.

74

mission he has given the Duke of Zell, and oblige him to draw his forces out of their country. This he showed to some of the ministers. The town of Hamburg received such a letter, but as a thing supposed, made it to be burnt by the hands of the hangman, and sent a letter to Schafftheusen to be delivered to the Emperor, in which they say they shall look on Marenholt as the forger of the former letter till he produces the man from whom he received the copy. Upon the knowledge of the contents of this last letter (a copy whereof was sent to Marenholt by a friend of his from Hamburg) the cudgelling ensued. The Emperor has forbid Marenholt the court, and writ a letter of complaint to his master. The Elector of Brandenburg is very angry, having passed his word to the Hamburgers for the security of their ministers, and has it in his power to be revenged of Marenholt he having some fiefs which [he] hold[s] of the Elector. The Prince of Anspach is dead of the smallpox, and we hear the Marquis of Bareit is very sick.

The Elector Palatine's minister was to see me yesterday. Among other things he told me his master relies much upon his Majesty, and hopes he will continue to assist him with his good offices in France, and at the Diet if there be occasion.

'Tis said there will be a reply put in to the French memorial; as soon as it is delivered I will send it to your Lordship.

I send you enclosed the Emperor's answer[1] to the nuncio in the case of the Palatinate.

If the news comes from Vienna before this post goes out it shall be enclosed to Dr. Wynne. I am, &c.

The Duke of Hanover[2] has begun the military execution he threatened in Mecklenburg.

---

[1] See p. 71. The Letterbook has a note : 'vide two pages before for the Emp^{rs} answer.'

[2] Ernest August, Elector of Hanover (1630–98), brother of

1686

To my Lord Middleton, with the conclusion of
the Diet touching Simmern and Lautern, possessed
by the Elector Palatine. Item there was sent there-
with the Elector Palatine's memorial dictated the
19th instant with the *documenta* requisite to make
good his title thereunto, and were as follows:

Vendredi le 19 avril l'Électeur Palatin a fait
dicter ici un mémoire touchant les prétentions de
Madame d'Orléans dans lequel on montre clairement
que son Altesse Électorale n'est pas d'intention de
prendre pour aucun fondement de ses prétentions
sur les duchés de Lautern et Simeren la *possession
prise*, mais qu'elle a pour fondement les constitutions de l'Empire la brille d'or Imperatoris Caroli
quarti, constitutiones Sigismundi declaratorias de-
pactorum familia Palatina, la paix de Westphalie, et
autres actes de l'Empire, dans lesquels il se voit
clairement que les princesses ne succèdent jamais
dans les biens féodaux[1] si non après la mort[s] de
toute la lignée masculine. Et comme son Altesse
Electorale Palatine a fait démontrer clairement tout
ceci à l'envoyé de France, Monsieur l'Abbé de
Morelle,[2] ce dit envoyé a prié de lui montrer les
actes et documents pour en tirer un extrait; ce qu'on
lui a accorder, avec protestation pourtant que ce
serait fait seulement pour montrer le grand respect qu'on a pour le roi, et qu'autrement on n'était

George William, Duke of Zell, concluded a defensive alliance
with the Emperor for ten years in 1674 and in 1683 bound himself by an agreement to furnish the Emperor with 10,000 men
for the Turkish war. In 1692 he obtained his dearest object,
conferment of the electoral dignity on his house.

[1] MS. 'feudeaux'.

[2] Jean Morel, Abbé de St. Arnould (d. 1719), was sent to
Heidelberg by Louis in 1685 on the business of the Duchess
of Orleans' claims. He adopted a high tone, and demanded
from the Elector Palatine the family acts and letters of investiture to verify the origin of all the Elector's possessions.

pas obligé de lui exhiber ce qu'on avait entre les mains pour soutenir ses droits. Ces sont les documents:

1. Constitutio Rupertina Anno 1395 nimirum Ruperti Secundi Electoris Palatini filius, qui a été fait Empereur après, nous montre par les paroles suivantes que les princesses ne peuvent succéder dans les biens feudataires:

Toutes les princesses aussitôt qu'elles sont mariées seront obligée de renoncer à l'héritage et succession de tous les principautés, provinces, sujets, et à tout ce qui en dépend pour jamais, ou jusqu'à ce que tous les héritiers mâles de la maison Palatine et de la maison de Bavière sont morts; et alors il sera permis aux filles ou princesses de la maison Palatine de succéder dans les biens féodaux.

2. La disposition du Prince Palatin nommé *Stephan*, père de tous ceux de la famille qui vivent présentement, consiste en les paroles suivantes l'an 1444: les filles n'auront point de droit sur les seigneuries, châteaux, provinces, ni sujets qui en dépendent, et se contenteront de l'argent comptant qu'on leur donnera pour la dot, et cela pour toujours, jusqu'à ce que la lignée masculine Palatine est entièrement morte.

3. L'an 1511 la Princesse Palatine Helena mariée à Henry Duc de Mecklenbourg renonce par un acte solennel à tous biens féodaux Palatins.

4. La Princesse Palatine Amelia mariée à George Duc de la Pomeranie renonce solennellement à tous droits du Palatinat l'an 1512.

5. La Princesse Dorothéa mariée à Guillaume Duc de Sax renonce par un acte solennel au droit du Palatinat l'an 1560.

6. De même fait la Princesse Palatine Kunigund Jacobe fillia Frederici tertii Electoris Palatini mariée au Comte Jean de Nassau l'an 1580.

7. De même renonce la Princesse Palatine Dorothéa mariée au Jean George Prince d'Anhalt l'an 1595.

On a ici averti Monsieur l'Abbé Morelle de bien
marquer, que les filles et princesses de la maison
Palatine ont été obligeés jusqu'au temps de Frédérique le quatrième de renoncer non seulement aux
biens féodaux,[1] mais aussi aux allodiaux, ce qu'on
a changé après, en permettant aux filles Palatines le
pouvoir aussi de prétendre aux meubles et biens
allodiaux[2] quand leur lignée masculine va manquer.

8. La Princesse Louise fille de Frédérique le 4
Élector Palatin, et mariée au Jean Duc de Deux-
ponts renonce par un acte solennel au droit du
Palatin l'an 1612.

9. Le même fait la Princesse Elisabette fille de Frédérique 4 Electeur Palatin et mariée l'an 1616 au
George Wilhelm Prince Electoral de Brandenburg.

10. La Princesse Palatine Henriette fille de l'Électeur Palatin Frédérique le quint et mariée l'an 1651
à Sigismund Ragotzi Prince de la Transylvanie
renonce à tous droits Palatins.

11. Le même fait la Princesse Sophia fille de
l'Électeur Palatin Frédérique Cinquième et mariée
l'an 1658 au Duc de Brunswick[3] comme Évêque
d'Osnabruch.

Il faut donc savoir que par ces actes les princesses
Palatines sont toujours obligées de se contenter de
leur dot, et résigner après à tous droits Palatins
pour elles et pour leur héritiers, de la sorte qu'elles
renoncent à toutes prétentions tant des biens allodiaux que féodaux et cela pour toujours jusqu'à ce
que la lignée masculine Palatine est tout à fait ex-
tirpée.

12. Dans l'original du traité de mariage qui fut
fait l'an 1671 entre Monsieur et Madame d'Orléans
il se trouve au the article. 'La Princesse sera auto-

[1] MS. 'feudals'.   [2] MS. 'allodials'.
[3] MS. 'Brunsweig'.

risée par ledit Seigneur son futur époux pour renoncer comme elle renonce dès à present à tous droits successifs en tous les bien souverains et féodaux paternels et maternels situés en Allemagne se réservant seulement ses droits aux biens allodiaux de sa maison situés hors d'Allemagne.'

13. Copie de la quittance sur le payement de la dot de Madame d'Orléans signée de la propre main de Monsieur et de Madame d'Orléans. 'En conséquence du susdit payement Madame, autorisée ainsi de Monsieur son époux, en réitérant la renonciation qu'elle a faite par ledit contract de mariage, d'abondant renonce par ces présentes a tous droits successifs en tous les biens souverains et féodaux paternels et maternels situés en Allemagne se réservant seulement ses droits sur les biens de même qualité situés hors d'Allemagne, et les allodiaux de sa maison selon la coutume de ladite maison Électorale Palatine.

14. Tout de même se trouve-il dans la procuration de Monsieur et Madame d'Orléans ledit acte de quittance aussi bien que la renonciation réitérée.

15. On à montré à Monsieur de Morelle hoc passu dans la lettre féodale que l'Empereur d'àprésent a donnée au dernier Électeur Palatin Charles Louis[1] que tout ce que l'Électeur Palatin a acheté ou possède per modum pignoris ou per héritage, soit châteaux, provinces, duchés, principautés, sujets ou biens *nullo excepto* demeure attaché au fief de l'Empire.

Ratisbon, 19/29 April, 86.

To my Lord Middleton with the Duke of Zell's letter to the Emperor, a copy of verses, and about two little places on the other side of the Elbe taken by the said Duke from the Hamburgers and fortified.

[1] MS. 'Lodovig'.

1686

The Verses[1]   Ditto.

Since love and verse, as well as wine,
Are brisker where the sun doth shine,
'Tis something to lose two degrees,
Now age itself begins to freeze:
Yet this I patiently cou'd bear ⎫
If the rough[2] Danube's beauties were ⎬
But only two degrees less fair ⎭
Than the kind[3] Nymphs of gentle Thames
Who warm me hither with their beams:
Such power they have, they can dispense
Five hundred miles their influence.
But hunger forces men to eat,
Tho' no temptation's in the meat.
How wou'd the ogling Sparks despise
The darling damsel of my eyes,
Did they behold her at a play
As she's trick'd up on holiday,
When the whole family combine
For public pride to make her shine!
Her hair[4] which long before lay matted
Are in this day comb'd out and plaited,[5]
A diamond bodkin in each tress
The badges of her nobleness;
For ev'ry stone, as well as she,
Can boast an ancient pedigree.
These form'd the jewel erst[6] did grace
The cap o' th' first Graf o' th' race,
Now preferr'd by Gräfin Marian
T'adorne the handle of her fan.
And, as by old record appears,
Worn since in Kunigunda's[7] ears,

[1] Printed in 1696, 1697, 1704; see *ante*, p. 62, note 1.
[2] 1697 'rich'.   [3] 1697 and 1704, 'bright'.
[4] 1697, 1704 'locks'.
[5] MS. 'pleated'.   [6] 1697, 'crest'.
[7] 1697, 1704, 'Renigunda's'.

80

Now sparkling in the fräulein's hair: ⎫
No serpent[1] breaking in the air ⎬
Can with her starry head compare. ⎭
Such ropes of pearls her hands[2] incumber
She scarce can deal the cards at ombre:
So many rings each finger freight
They tumble with the mighty weight;
The like in England ne'er was seen
Since Holbein drew Hal and his Queen.
But after these fantastick fights
The lustre's meaner than the lights;
She that bears this glitt'ring pomp
Is but a tawdry ill-bred ramp
Whose brawny limbs and martial face
Proclaim her of the Gothic race,
More than the painted[3] pageantry
Of all her[4] father's heraldry.
But there's another sort of creatures,
Whose ruddy look and grotesque features
Are so much out of nature's way,
You'd think them stamp'd on other clay:
No lawful daughters of old Adam.
From[5] these behold a city madam
With arms in mittens, head in muff,
A dapper cloak, and rev'rend ruff:
No farce so pleasant as this malkin, ⎫
The pretty jet[6] she has in walking[7] ⎬
And the soft sound of high Dutch talking ⎭
Here unattended by the Graces,
The Queen of Love in a sad case is.
Nature, her active minister,
Neglects affairs, and will not stir;
Thinks it not worth her while to please,
But when she does it for her ease.

[1] 1697, 1704 'rocket'. [2] 1704 'arms'.
[3] 1704 'mangled'. [4] 1704 'the'.
[5] 1697, 1704 'mongst'. [6] Strut or swagger.
[7] 1697 This line is the third of the triplet; 1704 omitted.

Ev'n I, her most devout adorer,
With wand'ring thoughts appear before her;
And when I'm making an oblation, ⎤
Am fain to spur imagination ⎬
With some old¹ London inclination. ⎦
The bow is bent at German dame,
The arrow flies at English game.
Kindness, that can indifference warm,
And blow that calm into a storm,
Has in the very tend'rest hour
Over my gentleness no² pow'r,
True to my countrywomen's charms
Whilst³ kiss'd and press'd in foreign arms.

Fragments left out:⁴

With thousand diamonds whose prices
You must not guess at by their sizes;
Their antique cut, and want of lustre
Which in a shop will not pass muster,
But by the laws of heraldry
Th'ear's the judge and not the eye.
Let them who live in plenty flout,
I must make shift with sauer kraut;
What matter is't what this stone cost,
Or what t'will yield since it can boast.
These are the charmes of this great nation;
No coquetry nor no belle passion
To force the lock of nature's door
And make her lavish out her store.
Diff'ring in faith, in birth and dress, ⎤
When I ingeniously confess ⎬
They all agree in ugliness, ⎦
The virgins of the Church of Rome, ⎤
The daughters wrought on Luther's loom, ⎬
Have in this world the same, sad doom. ⎦

¹ 1704 'sham'.   ² 1704 'a'.   ³ 1697, 1704 'when'.
⁴ The following lines are deleted in the MS.

Ratisbon, 26 April/6 May, 86.

My Lord (Middleton):

It is talked here as if the alliance of Franconia[1] would come on again; the Emperor and the Spaniard being persuaded they shall have a great advantage by it, and that all the Princes and States who have a mind to enter into it will send their deputies to Au[g]sburg, where there is to be a meeting to that purpose in June next.

The Diet have made a conclusion in favour of the Duke of Mecklenburg-Schwerin,[2] making a proportionable deduction in the matriculate[3] of the Empire for the town of Wismar and its dependencies, which was given to the King of Sweden by the treaty of Westphalia; the Duke paying the tax hitherto, which was paid while the family was in possession of that place.

On Saturday last was dictated a commission decree, by which the Emperor desires that the Prince of Dietrichstein (his Grand Maître d'hôtel) and the Prince of Waldeck[4] may be received and allowed their vote and session in the College of Princes.

[1] An allusion to the Luxemburg Alliance of 1682 between the Emperor and the Franconian and Upper Rhenish Circles, of which the Augsburg Alliance was an extension.

[2] Christian Louis, Duke of Mecklenburg-Schwerin (b. 1623, began his rule in 1658, and died in exile at the Hague in 1692). He became a Roman Catholic and ally of Louis XIV. In 1648, by the Treaty of Westphalia, Wismar and other parts of Mecklenburg were surrendered to Sweden; the duchy was recompensed by the secularized bishoprics of Schwerin and Ratzeburg.

[3] The matricula 'was the list of the contingents in men and money which the several states were bound to furnish to the Empire' (Ranke's *History*).

[4] George Frederick, Prince of Waldeck (1620–92), a Saxon by birth, entered Leopold's service and was promoted to the rank of Field-marshal. The title of Prince was conferred on him in 1682, and the following year he took part in the defence of Vienna.

We know not yet what particulars are certainly
resolved on to be executed the next campaign. I
hope by Thursday to be able to give you some
information of these matters. I am, &c.

Ratisbon, 29 April/9 May, 86.
My Lord (Middleton):
Here is arrived lately Count Lamberg,[1] who has
been long expected in quality of first commissioner
for Austria. This occasions new disputes about
ceremonials. The Electoral College has refused to
visit him, saying the ministers of the College of
Princes (though they are the last comers) ought to
make them the first visit. The Emperor, who would
gain this point, has made it be contested formerly.
The College of Princes will not see him without he
will promise to return their visit, which is contrary
to his instructions, he being to imitate the Count de
Windisgratz in an inferior post. He has given me
notice of his arrival in a long compliment he sent
me by his secretary, and I intend to go and see him
to-morrow.

No expedient is found yet for delivering the two
last resolutions of the Diet to the Imperial commission; the Electors being resolved not to deliver
them as they did that of the fifty Roman months,
with a protestation of their rights, lest it should
grow into a custom and the difference never come
to be decided about the alliance. Count de Crécy
touching the limits; Count de la Tour Taxis[2] about

[1] Leopold Joseph, Count of Lamberg (1654–1706),
succeeded Wassendorf as governor of Upper Austria (1686).
He remained in Ratisbon until 1699. Skelton described him
as 'a man of no parts or education, a good, toping fellow'
(Discourse to Hyde; *Hyde Correspondence*, i. 636). Cf., however,
Etherege's verdict, p. 142.

[2] Inigo Lamoral, Count of Thurn and Taxis, usually called
Count de la Tour, born at Brussels 1653, commanded the
Bavarian cavalry which fought against the Turks in Hungary.

5,000 Turks being come to Esseck; and touching the victory obtained by General Mercy against Tekely near Segedin.[1]

Ratisbon, 10/20 May, 86.

To my Lord Middleton about the meeting of the ministers of the Electors of Brandenburg and Saxony the houses of Brunswick[2] and Hesse and Cassel at the fair of Leipzig[3] with an account of the design of these princes.

Ratisbon, 20/30 May, 86.

My Lord (Middleton):

Yesterday the Prince of Dietrichstein was by a conclusion of the Diet admitted into the College of Princes, and allowed to take place and give his vote as descended to him from his father. The obtaining of this last favour has occasioned some debates and delays, but it being the Emperor's earnest desire it should be so the College of Electors agreed to dispute it no farther in case the College of Princes, whom it immediately concerned, did first consent to it, which they did accordingly. The father of this prince was received into the College conditionally that it should not descend to his posterity

---

[1] Peter Grafen Mercy defeated Tököly, who was marching with a body of Turks to the relief of Munkács on April 24, 1686. He was informed by spies of the presence of 4,000 Turks, 7,000 Tartars, and 300 Hungarians on the other side of the river Theiss near Szegedin. He surprised the enemy and routed them at the first shock, taking 350 prisoners, with baggage and colours. Tököly was forced to swim the river, narrowly escaping with his life. General Mercy died of a sabre wound in the head, at the siege of Buda, 1686: 'regretted by everybody in general and particularly by the Duke of Lorraine, who was well acquainted with his bravery and military talents' (*Memoirs of the Duke of Berwick*, 1779, i. 12). Hughes wrote to Trumbull on May 10/20 confirming and describing the victory (*Hist. MSS. Com.: Marquess of Downshire*, vol. i, p. 166).

[2] MS. 'Brunswig'.   [3] MS. 'Leipzwig'.

unless he purchased a principality in the Empire, which should descend with it, which was not performed; but the Emperor in favour of the son (who is his Grand Maître de la Maison) has raised an estate, which he has given him in Tyrol, into a principality, and taken care he should lose nothing by the neglect. To-morrow the conclusion will be passed for receiving the Prince of Waldeck likewise into the College. &c.

Ratisbon, 7/17 June, 86.

To my Lord Middleton:

About the Brandenburg troops being dissatisfied with the changing of their route; of their slow march, and the great mischief they have done in their passage through Silesia.[1]

About Chancellor Stratman's[2] being sent to the Elector of Bavaria to dispose him to comply and be content with the resolution of the council of war which is: to make one army, and that the Elector should command under the Duke of Lorraine[3] at the siege of Buda, notwithstanding the promise

[1] Their march had been retarded by differences which had arisen with the Duke of Zell.

[2] Theodore Henry Strattmann was promoted to the responsible post of Court Chancellor (1683). He negotiated the marriage between the Emperor's daughter and the Elector of Bavaria, and later adjusted the quarrel between this Elector and the Duke of Lorraine. In 1687 he was active to secure for the House of Hapsburg the succession in Hungary; he remained in power until his death in 1693. He was greatly esteemed for his frankness in speech and action, and as virtual prime minister served the Emperor with devotion and tact.

[3] Charles, Duke of Lorraine, born at Vienna 1643, was deprived of his rights of succession by the Treaty of Montmartre in favour of Louis XIV. After vain intercession he was ordered to leave Paris and became the lifelong enemy of France. In the Imperial service, with the help of Sobieski, he relieved Vienna in 1683, took Neuhäusel by storm in 1685, Buda in 1686, and reduced Transylvania by his victory at Mohács in 1687.

made him by the Emperor of commanding an army apart;[1] with the reasons for attacking Buda and Erlau or Alba Regalis.

About the King's letters received from Sir Gabriel Sylvius,[2] and about the debates in the Diet concerning the French King's contraventions since the concluding of the armistice.

Of a letter to be writ to the French King upon that subject from the Emperor in his own, and the Empire's name.

Ditto.

Sir (Br. Wynne):[3]

I have not this week received any letters from England, which is a thing that touches me here as near as ever a disappointment did in London with the woman I loved most tenderly; but I flatter myself in this case, as I used to do in the other, that it is some misfortune and not your want of kindness has been the occasion. I have writ my Lord all the news we have, which you have constantly the perusal of. That which makes me break off this letter so abruptly is the news I have just now received of Mr. Fitzjames's[4] being arrived in this town, which

[1] The Elector had urged that he was entitled to a separate command as a German Prince and the Emperor's son-in-law.

[2] Sir Gabriel Sylvius, English envoy extraordinary to Denmark, was a native of Orange, who passed to the service of the Duke of York. His embarkation for Denmark in 1685 was witnessed by Evelyn (*Diary*, Everyman ed., ii. 228). He was recalled in 1689.

[3] Perhaps Wynne was brother-in-law or stepbrother to Hughes, though the word brother was used loosely for more distant relationships.

[4] James Fitzjames, Duke of Berwick (1670–1734), the natural son of James II by Arabella Churchill, was educated in France, and served his first campaign at the age of fifteen under Charles of Lorraine at the siege of Buda. He was created Duke of Berwick in 1687, and served in Hungary again in that year. He became a French subject in 1702, and was created Marshal of France in 1706.

I hope you will take for an excuse for my silence till next post. I am, &c.

Ditto.

Sir (Sir Gabriel Sylvius):

I had the favour of yours of the 22nd of May last with two letters enclosed, the copies of which I long since received from England. I shall let them lie by me till I have further instructions, and you may assure the prince,[1] when there is occasion to serve him here, I will be a very faithful and industrious solicitor in his business. The campaign is like to begin very late in Hungary, &c.: The news, as in the foregoing to my Lord Middleton, adding: We have long known here you need not to have apprehended anything from the Swedes, Bremen not being able to furnish the King of Sweden with 20,000 crowns, which he demanded to defray the charge of the twelve hundred men he was to send into Hungary and Pomerania, being more indigent than that province.

When anything happens worth your knowledge in my sphere I shall not fail communicating it to you being

Sir, &c.

To Sir Peter Wyche.[2]   Ditto.

Sir:

I received yours of the 26th of May with the letters enclosed from Sir Gabriel Sylvius. I am extremely beholden to you for the favour, and am sorry I am forced to give you the trouble of conveying another to him.

[1] George of Denmark.

[2] Sir Peter Wyche (1628–1698), born in London, educated at Oxford, Cambridge, and the Middle Temple, was knighted by Charles II at the Hague in 1660, and was one of the original members of the Royal Society. In 1669 he was envoy extraordinary in Russia, and afterwards English Resident in Hamburg until 1689.

The news part as in the foregoing letter, adding: After you have adjusted your preliminaries and come to a close treaty with the Duke of Zell, the main article I hear he will insist upon is to be well reimbursed the charges he has been at in executing the Imperial commission, and your town of Hamburg must help to feed the troops his territories are overstocked with.

When they come to action in Hungary I will constantly acquaint you with what comes to my knowledge, being very sensible how much you have obliged me to be

Sir, &c.

Ratisbon, 10/20 June, 86.

My Lord (Middleton):

I have sent you enclosed the conclusions of the two Colleges upon the debates I mentioned in my last of the 7th instant. That which is remarkable in that of the Electors is their resolution that the business of the limits, and the execution of the armistitia, shall be treated of here, contrary to the intention of the Emperor expressed in the commissions decree he sent them some time since. According to these conclusions the Imperial commission sent to Monsieur de Crécy a writing mentioning the contraventions of his Christian Majesty, which contains only the lands he seized in Brisgau in lieu of the revenue the Emperor detains belonging to the University of Fribourg, and the cutting down of woods in the Black Forest, which they compute to be to the value of 200,000 crowns, a good sum as wood is sold in these plentiful countries. A copy of this with Monsieur de Crécy's answer I intend to send by the next post; all this buzzle is only to incline the States of the Empire to enter more willingly into the alliance which is now a going to be conferred about at Au[g]sburg.

1686

Chancellor Stratman[1] is returned to Vienna, and has happily brought the Elector of Bavaria to comply with the Emperor's desires so that Buda is to be beseiged by the whole army under the command of the Duke of Lorraine. They began their march from Raab to Barkan on the 13th instant new style, whence the Elector and the Duke are to take several routes, and to rejoin at Buda, the Elector commanding a body apart thither; and it is so ordered that in his way, he is to have the honour of taking two little places Hatwan and Pest;[2] it is not certain whether he will succeed in the first, but such care has been taken that there is no doubt but the last will capitulate upon his lying[3] down before it. The Brandenburg troops were not arrived when they began to march, but they were within three days' journey and will overtake them on the way.[4] The twelve hundred men, that have been long expected from Sweden, are now hastening towards Hungary, Bremen having made a shift to make up the 20,000 crowns that was demanded of them.

The 7th instant, about one in the afternoon, Mr. Fitzjames[5] came very well hither, with the gentlemen that attend him; their horses were harassed with the journey, but [a] little rest will set them right again; he stayed here that night to refresh

[1] See *ante*, p. 86, note 2.

[2] The Imperial army was to march direct to Buda, whilst the Elector of Bavaria at the head of 24,000 men on the other side of the Danube was to hinder communication between Buda and Erlau (Eger) by taking Pest and Hatwan. Actually on June 23rd the Turks abandoned Pest on the approach of the Bavarians, but the Count of Stainau failed to attack Hatwan, whose garrison had been reinforced.

[3] MS. 'lyind'.

[4] The Brandenburg troops did not arrive in Pest until July 3rd (Jacob Richard's *A Journal of the Siege and Taking of Buda*, 1687).

[5] See *ante*, p. 87, note 4.

himself and embarked the next morning by 5 o'clock for Vienna, having a great impatience to be at the camp, where he will arrive in very good time. I am, &c.

Ratisbon, 1/11 July, 1686.

My Lord (Middleton):

The day before yesterday, according to the direction I had from Sir Gabriel Sylvius, I delivered his Majesty's letters concerning the Prince of Denmark's business;[1] that for the Emperor to the Imperial commission, and that for the Diet to the Director of Mayence. I had a favourable audience from both, and many assurances that, if there were any occasion, they would be ready conformable to his Majesty's desire to serve the prince in a cause that appeared to them so very just. The Bishop of Passau desired a copy of the letter; he has undertook to send it the Emperor that he might the better recommend the business to his Imperial Majesty, which I gave him accordingly. The Director has promised me (in case the Diet think of writing to his Majesty) to get Defender of the Faith inserted in his titles, which has been omitted in some former reigns.

It is reported that the deputies assembled at Augsburg are come to a conclusion, and that the alliance is made upon the same foot it was before: that is there is a particular alliance between the three circles of Swabia, Franconia, and Bavaria for their mutual defence; and the two circles of Franconia and Bavaria have entered moreover into another alliance into which the kings of Spain and Sweden

[1] Prince George had married Princess Anne, sister of James II, in 1683. In June the Danes took possession of the two villages of Tremsbüttel and Steinhorst in Holstein in the name of Prince George as security for the 150,000 crowns, with interest, which the Duke of Holstein's officers confessed they owed to the Prince.

are admitted. I shall be able by the next post to give
your Lordship a more perfect account of this matter[1]

The deputy of the Elector of Brandenburg has
by his master's orders acquainted the Diet that his
Imperial Majesty and his master have by a treaty
adjusted the differences which were between them.
The Elector has resigned all his pretensions to the
principality of Jägerndorf[2] in Silesia, and likewise
all his pretensions there (upon the death of the late
Prince of Brieg) to Brieg, Liegnitz, and Wohlau.[3]
In consideration of which the Emperor has given
him the baillage or circle of Leubus [sic][4] in Silesia,

[1] The Alliance of Augsburg was concluded on July 6th;
see Introduction, p. 30. The King of Spain was included by
virtue of the provinces he held in the circle of Burgundy; the
King of Sweden as Duke of Pomerania.

[2] Jägerndorf, a fief in Silesia, was acquired at the beginning
of the fifteenth century by the Hohenzollerns, and belonged
to Brandenburg until Prince John George, a zealous Protestant, declaring war in 1620 against the King of Bohemia, was
despoiled of the duchy by the Emperor. The Elector of
Brandenburg declared the confiscation illegal and asserted
that it did not preclude other members of the House of
Brandenburg from their rights.

[3] MS. 'Lignitz and Olau'. In 1537 the Elector of Brandenburg and the Duke of Liegnitz had made a compact according
to which the longer lived family should receive the three fiefs.
The King of Bohemia, ruler of Silesia, compelled the Duke
of Liegnitz to abandon the treaty, but the Elector of Brandenburg considered he had exceeded his powers, and in 1675, on
the extinction of the Liegnitz line of Lower Silesian Dukes by
the death of Duke George William, the Elector of Brandenburg claimed the three duchies. The Emperor refused to
recognize his right, and the relations of Emperor and Elector
were embittered by the complications arising between them
with regard to this inheritance and that of Jägerndorf. In
March 1686 Frederick William concluded an alliance with the
Emperor by which, in compensation for abandoning his
claims to the other Silesian duchies, he received the circle of
Schweibus. See Introduction, p. 36.

[4] The circle of Schweibus formed part of the principality of
Glogau. It was about 1,300 square kilometres and was valued

FRIDERICVS GVILLELMVS   MARCHIO BRANDENBVRGENSIS,
SACRI ROMANI IMPERII   ARCHICAMERARIVS ET ELECTOR,
DVX MAGDEBVRGI PRVSSIÆ IVLIÆ,   CLIVIÆ MONTIVM ET POMERANIÆ
    BVRGGRAVIVS   NVREMBERGENSIS
PRINCEPS HALBERSTADI=   ENSIS ET MINDENSIS,
COMES   MARCHIÆ   ET   RAVENSPVRGI   &c.

La Blondeau Sculp.   Io. Iacobus de Rubeis Formis Romæ ad Templ. S. Mæ de Pace cum Priu. S.P.

FREDERICK WILLIAM, THE GREAT ELECTOR OF BRANDENBURG

on the confines of Poland, and has discharged from all dependence certain lands the Elector held of the crown of Bohemia.

Yesterday the Elector Prince Palatine with the Archduchess his Princess[1] passed by this town in their journey from Vienna to Heidelberg. The Emperor has lent them his barges, and defrays their charges as far as Ulm.[2] They came ashore and were magnificently treated by the Prince of Passau. The same evening they embarked again and continued their way. I am, with much duty, my Lord, &c.

Ratisbon, 5/15 July, 86.

My Lord (Middleton):

The Diet have not as yet made any recess in the matter of the French contraventions, though it has been long expected. They give out it will be done this week.

The design, as I have mentioned formerly, is that a letter shall be writ in the Emperor and Empire's name to his Christian Majesty to redress the grievances that have been so much talked of here lately, and till it be done they say they cannot come to treat of the limits, nor the execution of the truce, much less of a peace. Our deputies which went from hence to the conference at Augsburg are on their

by the Emperor at only 1,200 or 1,300 florins. The country was of no value from the economic point of view, as it was lacking in water and of a sandy soil. The Emperor nevertheless had refused to counsel its abandonment in November 1685, and the conditions offered by Brandenburg were again rejected in January 1686. In March of that year an underhand arrangement was secretly made with the Prince Electoral, by which he consented to annul the gift after the death of his father. Under these circumstances the treaty was finally signed on April 1st.

[1] John William, Elector Prince Palatine (1658–1716), had married Josepha, daughter of Emperor Ferdinand III.

[2] Halfway between Ratisbon and Heidelberg.

way back. At their return I hope to have a copy of their conclusion, which will shew the nature and extent of the alliance made there.

I gave you an account in my last letter of the composure of the differences between the Emperor and the Elector of Brandenburg. The name of the little country in Silesia granted to the Elector is Suibus [*sic*] and not Leibus, as I writ before.

There is an old difference between the houses of Brandenburg and Saxony lately revived about the principality of Quernfurt, the Regence of Magdeburg having cited the Prince of Saxon-Weissenfels[1] to come and do fealty for the four baillages Quernfurt, Dahme, Jüterbock, and Berg, which compose the principality, as holding of Magdeburg. When Magdeburg[2] was, by the Treaty of Münster, given to the Elector of Brandenburg these four baillages, which depended of that bishopric, were given to the Elector of Saxony and made part of the circle of upper Saxony, and have continued so ever since, they being before a part of the lower Saxony, in which the bishopric is situate. In 1660 the Emperor raised these baillages into a principality which bears the name of the biggest. Saxon-Weissenfels received the investiture from the Emperor, and was admitted to sit and vote in the College of Princes by the Diet, though upon some disputes of precedency he has never took his place there. The Emperor at present seems to take great care to reconcile all private differences, and the deputy of Saxony told me he hoped this would be amicably composed. All these

[1] John Adolph I, Duke of Saxe-Weissenfels (1671–1697), inherited the dukedom in 1680.

[2] By the treaty of Münster (1648) Brandenburg was promised the archbishopric of Magdeburg on the death of the then administrator, the Duke of Saxe-Weissenfels; this event took place in 1680, when the Elector secured the lands of the archbishopric and compelled the citizens of Magdeburg to do homage to him.

things make the French jealous that, in case the Emperor has good success this summer in Hungary, the Empire will endeavour to recover what they have parted with by the armistitia.

The Duke of Holstein-Gottorp, who has been some time in Flanders, had a minister at Augsburg but he could not get to be admitted to the conference. The Electors of Mayence[1] and Treves[2] have some time designed a visit to the Elector of Cologne[3] at Bonn,[4] which they intend suddenly to perform. I send your Lordship enclosed a letter from my Lord Mountjoy[5] from before Buda; it came to my hands by this day's post, and therefore I trouble you with no other news from thence. I am, &c.

Ratisbon, 12/22 July, 8[6].

My Lord (Middleton):

The day before yesterday (being Saturday) his Majesty's letter concerning the Prince of Denmark's business was dictated in the Diet. Monsieur de Schnolsky, the King of Sweden's minister here, who likewise is for the affairs of the Duke of Holstein-Gottorp, endeavoured to cavil at the direction, it being *legatis, abligatis et deputatis*, from whence he inferred that it made a distinction between the College of Electors and that of the Princes, which the College of Princes will not allow of. The Count de Windisgratz has still taken their part in this,

---

[1] Anselm Francis, Archbishop and Elector of Mainz.

[2] John Hugo, Archbishop and Elector of Treves (1676–1711). [3] See *ante*, p. 60, note 1.

[4] MS. 'Boon'.

[5] William Stewart, Lord Mountjoy (1653–92), served in Hungary as a volunteer, was dangerously wounded at the capture of Buda, and returned to Ireland in 1687. Hughes in a letter to Trumbull, May 10/20, announced his arrival in Ratisbon with other Irish noblemen and thirty horses (*Hist. MSS. Com. : Marquess of Downshire*, i. 166).

which makes the misunderstanding between him and the Electors; but knowing how nice these gentlemen are I had, before I delivered the letter to the director, examined the form with some precedents and found it *verbatim* with that which his late Majesty writ to the Diet in 1680 which was so well received, and intimating this to the College of Princes they are very well satisfied. This Monsieur de Schnolsky is a terrible critic and fell upon the word *pigebit*, which happens to be in the letter, and, had I not found means to compose things amicably between him and the word here, I should have been obliged, notwithstanding the respect due to his years, to have engaged Mr. John Cook in the quarrel. Schnolsky concluded with an old proverb: that one tale is good till another is heard, and threatened to put in a memorial to acquaint the Diet with the whole state of the matter; but I met him by chance yesterday and found him in better humour. He allowed it a good debt, though the money was not lent but assigned to the prince by the King of Denmark, his brother; that the Duke of Holstein was drawn in and overseen to give a new mortgage for this part of the 300,000 crowns which he agreed to pay[1] to the King of Denmark after the peace made between them; having already secured the whole sum by a former mortgage; that the Duke did this without the knowledge of those who managed his affairs, and that otherwise he would have informed him that the two baillages[2] had been engaged before to the Count of Königsmark, of which he knew nothing; his conclusion was that since things stood as they did there was nothing to be thought of but paying the money, which he said was not yet ready, but they were using all means to raise it suddenly; which done he hoped there would be no difficulty

[1] MS. 'play'.
[2] Tremsbüttel and Steinhorst. See p. 91, note 1.

made of restoring the possession of the baillages. This week the Count de Crécy intends to put in a memorial to press the treating of the limits and the execution of the armistitia, to suppress the great noise of the French contraventions.

I have the conclusion of the three circles and the heads [of] the other alliance,[1] which is kept so secret but I cannot get them translated before the next post.

I expect this day letters from the camp before Buda; as soon as they come I will enclose the contents. I am, &c.

Enclosed a list of the slain and wounded in the assault made the 13th July, new style.[2]

Ratisbon, 15/25 July, 86.

My Lord (Middleton):

I send your Lordship enclosed the substance of the recess[3] made at Augsburg for the three circles. I cannot yet procure that which is agreed for the great alliance into which strangers are admitted. The foundation of it, which I have from good hands, is to bring the French King to satisfy the Empire concerning the contraventions which have been so much complained of lately. It is signed in the name of the Emperor, the house of Austria, the Elector of Bavaria, the circle of Bavaria, the circles of Franconia and Burgundy, the house of Saxony, and the King of Sweden, only as he is one of the States of

[1] With Sweden and Spain.
[2] On July 11th a breach had been found and Lorraine decided to attempt a lodgment therein. The assault was begun at 7 p.m. on July 13th; after an hour's obstinate fighting the breach was gained. After maintaining their position for two hours the allies were compelled to retire. According to Jacob Richards's account the casualties amounted to 1,000 soldiers and fifty volunteers. The *London Gazette* reported (July 22–6) that of the twenty English involved only Fitzjames and five or six others escaped unhurt.
[3] A resolution, decree, or act of the Diet.

H

the Empire,[1] and the house of Hesse and Cassel. There is an article in this alliance which permits the Emperor to take into it whom he shall think fit as well foreign powers as States of the Empire, and the kings of Spain and Sweden will be hereafter received without any limitation. The Elector Palatine, who was not named at the conference for good reasons, will be admitted likewise by the Emperor into the alliance when it is thought convenient. Monsieur de Rachelius, who was at Augsburg on the behalf of the Duke of Holstein-Gottorp, could not get his master accepted but he is referred to the Emperor's pleasure. The army agreed to be raised by the confederates is to consist of 60,000 men;[2] all the particulars are not yet agreed of and there is to be suddenly another meeting at Nuremberg where the business is to be made perfect.

The Prince of Waldeck moved the Elector of Brandenburg at Dyrmont in his way to Cleve to enter into this alliance, but he answered that for several reasons he knew he should be able to do more for the Empire by keeping himself out of it. These matters have made Monsieur de Crécy give in a memorial to the Diet which was dictated the day before yesterday and is to be considered of tomorrow, a copy of which I send your Lordship in French. I am, &c.

My Lord (Middleton): Ratisbon 19/29 Aug., 86.

Yesterday Monsieur Wampel, the Elector of Bavaria's deputy here, having received orders to attend the assembly at Nuremberg departed from

[1] The King of Sweden became a member of the Empire on the cession to him by the Peace of Westphalia of Pomerania, Wismar, Bremen, and Verden. Etherege errs in including Saxony in the alliance.

[2] These were to be led by the Prince of Waldeck, but figured on paper only. The Emperor undertook to contribute 16,000 men, Bavaria 8,000, and Spain 6,000.

hence for that town. Monsieur Schnolsky, the Swedish minister, in a letter from thence, says they are like to do great things towards the perfecting and strengthening of the alliance made at Augsburg, and that many ministers are met there, particularly from the house of Saxony, one from the Elector Palatine, and Monsieur Rook[1] from the Elector of Brandenburg. The French say it is only an artifice to augment the meeting, and Monsieur de Crécy assures me upon his knowledge the Elector of Brandenburg has nobody there on his behalf.

Yesterday likewise the Imperial commission sent a paper to the said Monsieur de Crécy complaining of a new contravention, viz. that a burgomaster[2] of Breisach[3] came to a burgomaster of Kenzingen (a town belonging to the Empire in Brisgau) attended with seven or eight troopers and told him they had received several fugitives, Hugenots or deserters, and if they continued to do so and did not deliver them up, the garrison of Breisach would take satisfaction, threatening them with military execution. This paper, in words which have more force than any they have used before, demands that this should be redressed, and all the other contraventions formerly mentioned, the bridge that is building at Hüningen,[4] etc.

Monsieur de Crécy told the messenger he must return the same answer to the Imperial commission which he had done to the papers they had sent him before; that the truth and justice of these matters was to be examined and would plainly appear when

[1] Melchior de Ruck, a confirmed enemy of France, whom the Elector of Brandenburg had sent to Vienna in September 1685 to offer the Emperor troops.

[2] MS. 'burrowmaster'. [3] MS. 'Brisac'.

[4] Hüningen was within the jurisdiction of the Margrave of Baden-Durlach on the Rhine, a little north of Basel. The French began to build a fort of six bastions to cover the bridge.

the execution of the armistitia was treated of; that, for his part, it is long since he has had full power to determine all things in controversy; that it is evident the Empire is unwilling to have things fairly ended by not empowering any to treat with him; that he would send it the King his master, who had many complaints to make on his part, as should appear when they might be amicably redressed, but that he did not think it fit to make a noise with them now, having no such alliances to carry on as had been not long since made at Augsburg and were now improving at Nuremberg. There is a decree of commission to the same purpose of this paper which will be suddenly dictated to the Diet. It will be time enough after we see what becomes of Buda to trouble your Lordship with the reasonings of several ministers here on these matters; much depends on the success of that siege.

I am with all duty—

Ratisbon, 26 Aug./5 Sept., 86.

To my Lord Middleton ⎱ of the taking of Buda.[1]
and my Lord Sunderland ⎰

Ratisbon, 31 Aug./10 Sept., 86.

Sir (Sir William Trumbull):[2]

.   .   .   .

I am told there is a stop put to your going for Turkey. The merchants petitioned when Sir Wil-

[1] Buda fell on Sept. 2nd, new style.

[2] Sir William Trumbull (1639–1716) was appointed envoy to the French court in 1685 and ambassador to Turkey in 1686. He landed at Constantinople in August 1687. Among his friends can be numbered Pepys, Pierre Bayle, Dryden, and Pope. According to Burnet, 'He was the eminentest of all our Civilians . . . a learned, a diligent and a virtuous man' (*op. cit.* ii. 501).

liam Soames[1] was named, but their petition was rejected, my Lord Chandois, not deserving the favour of the court, I believe serves them at a cheaper rate than ordinary. Get some friend to learn among the merchants for how many years he agreed with them, how near his time is out, and how much yearly they allow him. My Lord Winchelsea[2] had 10,000 reichs thalers[3] per annum, and 2,000 gratuities allowed him. Sir Daniel Harvey[4] had the same allowance, but the company disputed the gratuity. What Sir John Finch[5] had I know not, but I fancy my Lord Chandois,[6] being looked upon as a disaffected person, serves them at an under rate. The King's having no good opinion of him was the reason he was intended to be recalled. The charge, if looked into, is not so great as the company will pretend in setting out Sir William Soames. The same presents will serve, and it is no more than what they gave him for equipage, which I think was but

[1] Sir William Soames, English ambassador in Turkey, died on June 2, 1686, at Malta, on his way to Constantinople. Clarendon writing on July 29, 1686, exclaims: 'What will happen upon the death of Sir William Soames? Will my Lord Chandos be continued in Turkey, or will the King recommend another ambassador to the Company' (*Hyde Correspondence*, i. 513).

[2] Heneage Finch, 2nd Earl of Winchilsea, was sent in 1661 on an important embassy to Sultan Mahomet Chan IV, of which he published an account in the same year. He remained ambassador at Constantinople for eight years and died in 1689.

[3] reichs thalers = rix dollars.

[4] Sir Daniel Harvey (d. 1672) succeeded Lord Winchilsea as ambassador in Turkey. Etherege was for a short time his secretary. See Introduction, p. 8.

[5] Sir John Finch (1626–82), a physician, succeeded Harvey as ambassador at Constantinople in 1672. He returned to England in 1682 and died in London of pleurisy.

[6] James Brydges, Lord Chandos (1642–1714), was Finch's successor as ambassador to Turkey, 1680–6. In August 1686 the Turkey Company petitioned against his removal on the plea that they had lately been at great charge in fitting out Sir William Soames.

£600; I am sure not more than £800. If your friends press hard at court you may get over this rub, and if you do let me know it and I will think of a way to inform you of all that is necessary in that employment. I am, &c.

Ratisbon, 2/12 Sept., 86.

My Lord (Middleton):

. . . There are about 3,000 Lüneburgers admitted into Hamburg with Chovet[1] (the Duke of Zell's general), who have all given their oath to the magistrates. They have made a sally and killed about 150, some say more, of the Danes.[2] About eight or nine of the Council of Thirty which is broke are in hold, and are like to suffer; they made the faction which was to give up the town to the King of Denmark, as it is said, on the 2nd of this month, the same day Buda was taken.[3] I do not hear the Elector of Brandenburg's 6,000 men, who are sent to defend the place, are arrived yet, he promises to make them up [to] 15,000 if need requires.

Monsieur Christhoussen, the King of Denmark's minister in the Zellish court, told the Duke that his master's design was so well laid that all Europe could not disconcert it. Nevertheless it is believed here, he has missed his opportunity. Of the Empire's being dissatisfied with this enterprise, and of their suspecting the French King to be privy to it; of Moldavia's subjecting itself to Poland; about

[1] Jeremias Chauvet, in the service of Brunswick-Lüneburg-Zell.

[2] The citizens of Hamburg had asked the Elector of Brandenburg and the Prince of Lüneburg for assistance against the Danes. On Aug. 31st, 2,000 Lüneburgers and 300 horse entered the town, and were followed a little later by five Brandenburg regiments.

[3] See *ante*, p. 66, note 2. Two of the leaders of the Council of Thirty, Jastram and Schnitger, were executed on October 14th.

the contraventions, and the commissions sending
Monsieur de Crécy's answer back because it was not
in Latin; of his excusing it by saying it was no more
than a discourse by the by, that none ever pretended
in familiar talk to make another speak what language
he pleased; about the assembly at Nuremberg; and
of the Elector Palatine's giving 1,000 foot and 400
dragoons to be admitted into the alliance; and of the
Duke of Holstein's being likewise admitted for
1,000 foot.

Ratisbon, 9/19 Sept., 86.

My Lord (Sunderland):
. . . About the differences between the Count
de Windisgratz and the Electoral College and of
Monsieur de Crécy's improving them. . . . It
followed *in haec verba*. The Count de Windisgratz
is about 56 years of age, tormented often with the
gout and gravel, which adds to his natural ill
humour. He has children by a former wife which
he neglects, being fond of some he has by a lady to
whom he has been married some few years. She
was maid of honour to the Empress Dowager, and
esteemed a great ornament to that court. She is very
like, and full as handsome as, Mrs. Betty Mackerel,[1]
but more affected than Mrs. Middleton.[2] The

[1] Betty Mackerel was an actress at the Drury Lane Theatre
who played Ariel in Duffett's *Mock Tempest* in 1674. Her
reputation was none of the best, and there are many coarse
allusions to her in lampoons of the time.

[2] Jane Middleton (1645-92), a beauty of the court of
Charles II. Daughter of Sir Robert Needham, she married
Charles Middleton, 1660. Her first lover may have been de
Grammont, and among his successors may be numbered
Viscount Ranelagh, Ralph Duke of Montague, Waller the
poet (with whom she terminated a liaison in 1686), St.
Evremond, and Lord Rochester (Wilmot). A three-quarter
length portrait of her by Lely in Hampton Court shows her
to have been of the languorous, voluptuous, blonde type.
Grammont speaks of her as 'one of the handsomest women in

Count is of a temper so jealous, that he tormented
her before her time, when he was her lover; if he
observed her speaking to any man in the drawing-
room he would get her in to a corner, and pinch her
black and blue, and she was resolved not to have
him had not his tears to the Empress softened her to
impose her commands to marry him. He is hot and
imperious, and uses those of the Diet who have
some dependence of him as scurvily as he does his
domestics. He has had experience in affairs and
understands his master's interest, but will sacrifice
anything to his pride and ambition; and indeed all
his passions are so violent that he does him little
service for want of conduct. These qualities, some
of his countrymen say, got him this employment;
the ministers at Vienna for their own quiet favouring
him in this honourable occasion of his absence. He
has been formerly employed in the French court, and
has twenty times told me how he was received there;
with as much heat as an old lady tells some pleasant
passage of her youth which warms her. His conversation is so loud, he is vehement even in trifles,
and he speaks French as well as my Lord Peterborough.[1] If you flatter him the lion becomes a
lamb, and, without examining anything you advance,
will, like the Lord Chamberlain in *Hamlet*, cry, 'Oh!
very like a weasel.'

The Bishop of Passau is a good old man who
loves his quiet, without either genius or experience,
defers generally in all things to the Count, and looks
as meekly as the chief of your commission eccle-
siastic.[2] Of contraventions and alliances.

town', but 'the indolent languishing airs she gave herself did
not please everybody' (*Memoirs*, pub. Sonnenschein, pp.131–2).

[1] Henry Mordaunt, 2nd Earl of Peterborough (1624?–
1697), was in France from the outbreak of the Civil War to
1642, and for a short period in 1646.

[2] James II, in the teeth of great opposition, had set up an
ecclesiastical commission in July 1686.

Ratisbonne, 10/20 Sept., 86.

Monsieur (le Febure):[1]

Bude fut prise lundi le second de ce mois; on commença à donner l'assaut à 4 heures après midi, et l'on entra la ville sur le 7 heures du soir. Le Gouverneur s'était retrenché dans sa maison avec 50 janissaires, ou il fut tué; mais son lieutenant fut pris prisonnier. On fit passer tous par le fil de l'epée hormis la sexe dont nos amis, selon toute apparence, ont fait un beau butin.

Si ce n'était pour la maison de Monsieur le comte de Crécy, Ratisbonne serait un triste séjour.

Je n'ai pas vu la Dindonelle depuis votre départ et je suis plus sensiblement touché de la perte de vous que vous ne le devez être pour tous les beautés d'ici. Je suis

Monsieur,
Votre très affectionné et obéissant serviteur
G.E.

Ratisbon, 13/23 Sept., 86.

My Lord (Middleton):

I have nothing to acquaint you with about the Diet. The ministers here talk as if his most Christian Majesty was gathering some troops together about Strasbourg, and it is not to be wondered at after the taking of Buda considering the great noise has been in the Empire about making alliances.

They continue to treat still at Hamburg,[2] and it is hoped that business will be fairly composed.

Here is a letter printed which I saw last night, but cannot yet get any copies of it, dated the 14th of August last at Nuremberg, said to be writ by the Duke of Holstein-Gottorp to his Majesty,

---

[1] See *post*, pp. 382-4.
[2] The mediation of Brandenburg caused a cessation of hostilities. A treaty was set on foot and about September 20th the Danish forces were withdrawn.

occasioned by his Majesty's writing to the Diet
in the Prince of Denmark's business. It is an
humble remonstrance of his misfortunes. Pray let
Mr. Wynne inform me whether his Majesty has
received any such letter; by the next post I will send
you a copy of it. I believe it was penned at Nuremberg at the last assembly there by Monsieur
Schnolsky, the Swedish deputy here, and Monsieur
Rachelius, that Duke's minister there; the contents
of it being what Monsieur Schnolsky has told me
before in discoursing about that matter.

I received this day a letter from my Lord Mountjoy[1] from Vienna, who designs to go post through
Bohemia homewards. He tells me he thinks the
council of war will order the army to their winter
quarters, sending only a strong detachment into
the upper Hungary, who are to endeavour the taking
of the castle of Segedin,[2] that they may be able to
command the Theiss.

Three hundred prisoners belonging to the Elector of Bavaria, being ordered to be brought from
Buda to Vienna in boats with a guard, perceiving
the soldiers negligent seized on their arms, killed
them, and made their escape. I am, &c.

Ratisbon, 20/30 Sept., 86.

My Lord (Middleton):
Since my last the Imperial commission have sent
a paper to Monsieur de Crécy, which he refused to
receive, the commission having sent back an answer
of his to a former paper because it was not in Latin.
This paper contains a fresh complaint of a fortress
his Christian Majesty has built to cover the bridge
of Hüningen.[3] The business of the limits has been

[1] See *ante*, p. 95, note 5.
[2] Szegedin or Szeged, about 100 miles south east of Buda
on the river Theiss.　　　　　[3] See *ante*, p. 44, note 4.

again proposed in the Diet, but the ministers of Austria staved it off pretending they are not instructed. There is a commission decree dictated against the King of Denmark for his enterprise at Hamburg, in which the Emperor expects that the States of the Empire will so resent it that, without making any reflection on the reason which that King alleges in his excuse, and without losing any time because of the dangerous consequences of the affair, they will forthwith let him know by a conclusion of the several colleges what their intentions and resolutions are in this matter. There is annexed to this decree an *avocation* sent by his Imperial Majesty to the King of Denmark with an *inhibition*. There is likewise an *excitation* which is not annexed and other orders according to the constitutions of the Empire sent to the circles of upper and lower Saxony, the circle of Westphalia and the King of Sweden.

The Duke of Holstein-Gottorp is lying at Hamburg like the cripple at the pool of Bethesda, and now the waters are troubled would be glad of a helping hand to lift him into his country. I find the Empire very inclinable to what he desires, but it is generally believed this difference will be suddenly composed by the inclination of the parties and the mediation of several powers, who think it their interest to have it ended. I am, &c.

Ratisbon, 4/14 October, 86.

My Lord (Middleton):

Mr. Wynne in his letter of the 17th of September complains that you have received none from me since mine of the 26th of August; where the fault lies I know not. I have not been wanting in my duty, having writ twice a week constantly to your Lordship.

It is now a dead time. The campaign is in a manner

ended, and the Diet has not yet entered into matter about the French contraventions. It is said they will begin this week, and we shall see how much stronger their faction is, who are for the alliance of Augsburg, and consequently for the writing in the name of the Emperor and Empire to demand satisfaction of his most Christian Majesty, than theirs who would treat of the execution of the armistice. If they seem violent in this matter it will make people believe they intend to make a peace with the Turk, which I cannot think they design till they are masters of *Erla* and Alba Regalis. I rather find by the discourses of the chief ministers that they conclude the French King, notwithstanding his greatness, not in a condition to enter in to a war against them without running greater hazard than his prudence will consent to. So that all these negotiations will make him only endeavour to secure himself and not provoke him to attack them; and the fresh contraventions may furnish them with pretences, when they shall think it convenient, to tax him with the breaking of the truce.

The Dutch Gazettes (among many others) have a lie in them which I find by some letters I have read is believed by many: that his Christian Majesty should order Monsieur de Crécy to demand the original of the alliance of Augsburg. Of whom should he demand it? it is no act of the Diet to whom he is sent, but a league concluded among confederate princes towards whom he is not impowered. Want of matter of fact is the occasion of this impertinence, which I hope your Lordship will have the goodness to excuse.

We know not here how far the treaty between the King of Denmark and the town of Hamburg is advanced; by what I have heard is insisted on on both sides, it will take up some time to reconcile things.

If I had the honour now and then to receive some assurances of your Lordship's favour in this dull place it would keep up the spirits of, &c.

Mr. Fitzjames was expected at Vienna on the 11th instant, new style.

Ditto.

To Mr. Wynne telling him that he had his visits constantly returned (though nothing can have less truth in it);[1] that one of the Diet having lent money to another was offered to be paid back in French money, which the person refused to accept of calling it the money of corruption; that grave fops abound here; that nature, who is the best poet and in all her works shews the inclination she has for a comedy, could be though[t] degenerated into a farce to give a description of them; that the fowls at the Bishop of Passau's feast for the taking of Buda were brought from the bishopric to save charges; that they stunk; and that he had given some three oams of Birish wine amongst the people, which might have cost him about 40/- English [money];[2] that the Count de Windisgratz at his feast had, as it was computed, thrown out at the windows about 10 crowns to outdo the Bishop in magnificence. &c.

Ratisbon, 7/17 Oct., 86.

My Lord (Middleton):

The Electoral College yesterday made a conclusion, and delivered it in to the College of Princes, about the treaty of the execution of the armistitia and the limits. By the next post you may expect a copy of it, together with the resolution of the other colleges. The substance of the conclusion is that that treaty ought to be begun and effectually under-

---

[1] The secretary's acid comment.

[2] MS. '40s Engl.' 'Oams' presumably is a mistake for 'omers.'

taken in this town, where the grievances will appear and be most conveniently redressed; that in the meantime his Imperial Majesty was to be humbly desired that he would be pleased to write in his own name and in the name of the whole Empire to his Christian Majesty, and at the same time represent to him likewise by his envoy in that court,[1] in an efficacious and feeling manner, the griefs that the States of the Empire suffer, and demand a just remedy of them; and to this end to make a remonstrance be made by word of mouth to the French plenipotentiary[2] here.

The deputy of Burgundy[3] has acquainted the other deputies of the Diet that the French King has made a post with his arms be set up very near the gates of Namur, which puzzles the Spaniards so much that they know not what to do in the case and therefore desire counsel.[4] He says if they go beyond the bounds set, his Christian Majesty will say they waste his countries; if they pull down his arms, they have broke the peace; and in case they protest against it, that is doing a thing which can have no effect so that Spain is the poor victim still; for while the Empire takes Neuhäusel she loses Luxemburg,[5] and now they have taken Buda the French have set up posts with their King's arms even before the gates of Namur. The other ministers, not knowing what to advise him, have taken further time to consider of his proposition.

The Swabian troops are marching what haste they can home, that circle being alarmed with the fort which his Christian Majesty built[6] to secure his bridge at Hüningen. &c.

---

[1] Lobkowitz.   [2] Crécy.
[3] Neuforge.   [4] MS. 'council'.
[5] The Turks surrendered Neuhäusel to the Imperial forces in September 1685. Luxemburg fell to the French in 1684.   [6] MS. 'build'.

Ratisbon, 21/31 Oct., 1686.

My Lord (Middleton):

I send you at length the conclusion perfect. I doubt not but Mr. Poley[1] in his time sent copies of the conclusions made the 13th of January, 1683, and the 10th November, 1684 to which this present relates. That of the 13th of January prescribes the manner of treating, with which the Count de Windisgratz is much dissatisfied. Since he cannot carry the point he pretends against the Count de Crécy in the ceremonial, notwithstanding the addition of his new character of ambassador extraordinary; this was moved to be inserted in the electoral's only with design to make the Austrian ministers, who influence the towns, inclinable to omit the mentioning the contents of the conclusion of the 10th of November, which orders a strict and severe inquiry into the griefs and contraventions; but both parties stood firm and gave and took of [one] another. This has made much work, for the post couriers go and come very often, and it is thought the Count de Windisgratz will do all he can to hinder the Emperor's confirming of this conclusion. Spain and Sweden are very active to embroil this matter, and the French take particular notice of their goodwill.

The Count de Crécy sent an express yesterday to the King his master. I am, &c.

Of Five Ecclesiæ[2] and Segedin being taken.

Ratisbon, 4/14 Nov., 86.

My Lord (Middleton):

Yesterday the conclusion concerning the taking of winter quarters by force and exactions, &c. was

[1] Edmund Poley, Etherege's predecessor in Ratisbon, was then envoy extraordinary to the King of Sweden. He died in 1714, it is said by his own hand.

[2] Quinque Ecclesiæ, the town of Fünfkirchen, or Pécs, in Hungary.

passed by the three colleges with the word *exaction*, the Diet being in an humour to call things by their proper names, notwithstanding all that the ministers of Brandenburg and Brunswick could do to persuade them to the contrary.

The Count de Lamberg[1] told me yesterday that Don Pedro de Ronquillos[2] had penetrated in the English court the design his Majesty has to besiege Philipsburg,[3] and a courier has passed this place lately dispatched from Heidelberg to Vienna, which has given a further alarm of this design. He told me, more over, they have had notice that a chiaus[4] has been privately at Paris to endeavour to make a league between the Grand Seigneur[5] and his Christian Majesty against the Empire. Having heard from some ministers here that the Dutch ambassador, Van Citters,[6] had written a letter to the States his masters, in which he says His Majesty told him with his own mouth that the French had made an alliance with the Turk to attack the Empire on both sides, I asked him, to see whether he would own this report which is spread by some ministers, if he was not fully convinced of the truth of this matter by the letter Van Citters had sent his masters. But the thing was too gross for him to swallow, though there are some who will not stick at a bigger gudgeon. He gave as little credit to Van Citters as the States his masters had done. This with a slip of the

[1] See *ante*, p. 84, note 2.

[2] The Spanish ambassador in London since 1674.

[3] By the Treaty of Nimeguen Philippsburg had been restored by Louis to the Emperor. It was the first fortress to fall to the French on their invasion of Germany in 1688.

[4] A Turkish messenger.

[5] The Sultan Mohammed IV.

[6] Arnold van Citters, Dutch ambassador in England. Cf. Macaulay's assertion that Van Citters conveyed to William of Orange full and accurate intelligence of all that passed in the English Court.

same pen some months since in a business as unlikely make that minister's letters have no better
reputation than his country's gazettes. Notwithstanding all these real or pretended apprehensions,
the Emperor makes no haste to confirm the conclusion made about the treaty. The meeting which
was to be about this time at Nuremberg is adjourned
sine die. Nevertheless the deputies concerned in the
alliance of Augsburg receive daily the ratifications
from their principals; even that from Sweden is
come in a fine silver box, besides other ornaments,
and to-morrow the Imperial commission intend to
celebrate St. Leopold's day with a Dutch[1] feast and
a Dutch comedy.

Mr. Wynne has an Italian gazette in which is all
that is come from Vienna by this post. I am, &c.

Ratisbon, 8/18 November, 86.

My Lord (Middleton):

On Saturday last the Prince of Waldeck was
installed by the under marshal of the Empire, the
Count de Papenheim, in the College of Princes.
This thing has been long put off by reason of a
dispute between the Elector of Mayence and the
Imperial commission; these saying that the assembly
for that ceremony ought to be called together by
a decree of commission and the other maintaining
it ought to be by a bill of convocation which he
commonly sends over night to the several members
of the Diet to meet the next day about such or such
a business. The Director[2] being better versed in the
records proved he was in the right and got the better
in this dispute.

The same day was dictated a decree of commission
touching the baillage or lordship of Jeveren situate

---

[1] Dutch = Deutsch (German) frequently.
[2] See *ante*, p. 60, note 5.

between l'Ost-Friese and Oldenburg[1] now in the
possession of the King of Denmark formerly belonging to a prince of the house of Anhalt, for which the
Emperor declares, pursuant to a conclusion formerly made in the Diet, as you may read in the enclosed. This baillage was in the time of Charles
the Fifth, by the consent of the then owner, made a
fief, and annexed either to the county of Burgundy
or to the Duchy of Brabant, and does not depend
immediately of the Empire but only as to its general
sovereignty. The French pretend it holds of Burgundy, and the Spaniards of Brabant. It is a little
thing but very fertile, and lying conveniently for
the King of Denmark. When the house of Anhalt
refused to do his Christian Majesty homage for it,
he desired his said Majesty to grant him his title,
which was done accordingly, and, it may be, not
without some consideration. Upon this the King
of Denmark took the castle by surprise, and afterwards insensibly made himself master of that small
territory. The French say the King of Denmark is
not obliged by the truce, and Monsieur de Crécy
tells me when he was urged to treat of this matter
at the time of the making it he always eluded it by
saying that he was not instructed in that affair; that
it does not concern the Empire, and therefore is not
to be restored as part of those lands the King his
master possessed himself of since the first of August
1681;[2] but that it concerns the crown of Spain, to
which nothing was to be restored but what was
taken after the yielding of Luxemburg, before which
time the King of Denmark was in possession of
Jeveren. I find the French are not very positive it
depends of Burgundy, but the Spaniards are very

[1] Jever, the capital of the principality, is thirty-three miles
NNW. of Oldenburg.
[2] By the Truce of Ratisbon the French King was to hold only
those lands that had been assigned to him before Aug. 1, 1681.

positive it depends of Brabant. But the French say let it depend of either the proper time to examine this right is when a general peace shall be treated of, and then the histories of Charles the Fifth will make it clear. The consequences which this business may have confirms some, who are jealous before, that the conclusion about the treating of execution of the armistitia, &c. will not be confirmed.

We have no news by this post from Vienna. Mr. Fitzjames is not yet arrived here. I am with all duty, &c.

Ditto.

Sir (Sir William Trumbull):[1]

By this time you know that the secretary of that embassy is allowed six hundred lion dollars[2] a year which is paid by the merchants; that the company esteem him their servant, and pretend a right to choose him;[3] if you think fit to have a private secretary you must pay him yourself, but you may endeavour to get the company to approve one whom you shall recommend. The man who enjoys the place at present is one Mr. Cooke,[4] who has been long in Turkey, and their ancient servant. I know not whether you will like his countenance and his principles; they are both very odd. He has had much

[1] See *ante*, p. 100, note 2.

[2] Lion dollars were Dutch rix dollars, so called because they bore the device of the lion of Nassau. They were adopted by the Turks and were in circulation throughout the Turkish dominions.

[3] The English ambassador in Constantinople drew his salary (£2,500 a year) from the Turkey Company, i.e., 'The Company of the Merchants of England Trading with the Levant Seas'. The principal part of the ambassador's mission was to promote trade and protect those engaged therein (see G. F. Abbot, *Under the Turk in Constantinople*, p. 7). The Company's Elizabethan charter empowered them to choose the consul or vice-consul.

[4] Thomas Cooke was also cancellarius to the English factory at Constantinople.

experience in the country, and is of an humour that agrees with that people; is a man of good acquired and natural parts, but I fear you will not find them turned to your liking. He is reserved and subtle; if he is not disaffected to the Government he is beholding to his being at so great a distance. Sir Dudley North[1] has been secretary to the company at Constantinople. &c.

Ratisbon, 11/21 Nov., 1686.

My Lord (Middleton):

On Tuesday last the ninth instant, in matters of consequence a man cannot be too exact, the three colleges met in the *Neben Stube*,[2] the room where the general conferences are always held, and, after a grave debate which took up some time by reason of unhappy difficulties which I shall acquaint you with anon, a conclusion was unanimously made, that they should go and see a farce that afternoon to which they were invited by a deputy from a company of strollers who are lately come from Nuremberg to divert us here. The minister who was sent on this embassy (either through ignorance of the customs of this nice place, or through an excess of civility, a common error in their politics), when he made his compliment to the several members of the Diet without distinguishing between the colleges, laid them all on promiscuously with *illustrious* and *excellence*; this had spoiled his business had not some good-natured husbands who considered the inclinations of their wives bestirred themselves

---

[1] Sir Dudley North (1641–91) accepted an offer of management of an important business in Constantinople, and rapidly rose to be the leading merchant in the Turkey Company, of which he was elected treasurer. In 1680 he returned to England, leaving his business to the charge of his brother.

[2] The former Nebenstube, or Nebenzimmer, may still be seen in the old Rathaus at Ratisbon.

and becalmed the most tempestuous spirits. Then it was considered whether they should be distinguished by their seats. The theatre being no better than a barn and improper for so great a ceremony they resolved to meet *pellmell*. There was a quota collected, and they taxed themselves at 4*s*. a head, reserving the liberty to bring their families. The deputies of the towns would have modestly declined the being on the same foot with the other colleges, but the *excellence* which had been advanced to them made their excellencies *make them* advance the money. There is a comedian[1] in the troop as handsome at least as the Fair Maid of the West[2] which you have seen at Newmarket and makes as much noise in this little town, and gives as much jealousies to the ladies as ever Mrs. Wright[3] or Mrs. Johnson[4] did in London.

The importance of this letter will let you see his Majesty does not misemploy the money he allows me, and I hope persuade my Lord Treasurer[5] to remember me when the good time comes.

This is all has been done in the Diet since my last, and it is but very reasonable they should breathe a while. I just now received a letter from Mr. Vaudrey,[6] which makes me expect Mr. Fitzjames here to-morrow or next day. I am, &c.

[1] The first mention of Julia.

[2] *The Fair Maid of the West*, by Heywood, was probably acted at Newmarket during one of the summer racing seasons. Etherege may have been alluding to a particular actress or amateur who took the title role.

[3] Mrs. Wright was an actress in Davenant's Company in 1670.

[4] Mrs. Johnson, an actress in Davenant's Company 1670-3.

[5] Lord Rochester.

[6] Mr., afterwards Sir Edward, Vaudrey was Fitzjames's tutor. Several payments to him for the use of Fitzjames are recorded in *The Secret Service Expenses of Charles II and James II*. He was knighted in May 1687, and attended his charge (now the Duke of Berwick) in the campaign as in the previous year.

1686

Monsieur Barrillon:[1]

Ne vous attendez pas à une excuse que je doit faire de n'avoir pas répondu à une lettre que vous m'avez fait l'honneur de m'écrire.[2] Vous savez les obligations que je vous ai des honnêtetés que j'ai reçues de Monsieur de Crécy, mais vous ne savez pas le mal que vous m'avez causé. Je paye bien cher les plaisirs que j'ai en me divertissant quelquefois avec Madame la Comtesse à l'hombre. Les deputés subalternes d'Autriche n'osent pas me donner pratique et moi je ne me puis pas résoudre à faire une quarantaine pour entrer chez eux. Il est vrai que leur maître Lieutenant le Comte de Windisgratz après lui avoir fait une requête en forme me permettait, quand il n'était point incommodé de la pierre, de la goutte, ou de la jalousie, de me venir planter à sa gauche dans sa salle d'audience et après y avoir été bien ennuyé, de lui en faire des compliments. Pour me consoler de ce malheur vous devriez faire en sorte qu'on ne s'oublie pas tout à fait de moi dans les bonnes compagnies où vous allez. Mon correspondant sur les affaires de la bassette, Monsieur Corbet, ne m'en a pas envoyé des nouvelles il y a longtemps; assurément que j'en suis en peine; la bassette a ses charmes en certains endroits, et j'aimerais mieux y perdre mon argent en voyant Madame Mazarine[3] que de gagner les bonnes graces de toutes les dames et même de demoiselles d'ici. Si

---

[1] See *ante*, p. 54, note 1.   [2] See *post*, pp. 345-6.
[3] Hortense, Duchess of Mazarin, the famous favourite of Charles II, found refuge in Whitehall in her flight from an insanely jealous husband, and died in Chelsea in 1699. Lucas (*Lives of the Gamesters*) writes, 'for Gaming her Lodgings were more frequented than the Groom Porters, in which she was as great a Proficient as any at that time' (p. 249); and later, 'She would play as fair as any Person when she found her Gamester play only upon the Square, for she play'd so well that scarce anyone could match her' (p. 256).

j'osais m'étendre sur ce chapitre-là je ne vous dirais pas si tôt que je suis &c.

Ratisbon, 18/28 Nov., 86.

My Lord (Middleton):

It is a very dead time for news here; we have nothing now from Vienna but what comes in the Italian gazette, which is constantly sent to Mr. Wynne.

The Prince of Ettingen has a minister here who has long waited for the instalment of his master, which will suddenly be effected. The Austrian ministers say the Emperor will in a little time send a ratification of the conclusion made for treating of the execution of the truce and setting out the limits, and will only change some things in the manner of treating; this will bring the business of the con-commissary and all those little disputes again on foot which were before the treating of the truce, and, it is not unlikely, break the neck of what may be expected from thence. I am, etc.

Ratisbonne, 16/26 Nov., 86.[1]

J'étais surpris d'apprendre que ce joli gentil-homme travesti en Italien hier au soir était le Baron de Sensheim. Je ne savais pas que les honnêtes gens se mêlaient avec des laquais ramassés pour faire les fanfarons, et les batteurs de pavés. Si vous avez quelque chose à me dire faites le moi savoir comme vous devez, et ne vous amusez plus à venir insulter mes domestiques ni ma maison. Soyez content que vous l'avez échappé belle et ne retournez plus chercher les récompenses de telles folies. Pour vos beaux compagnons j'ai des autres mesures à prendre avec eux.

A Monsieur Sensheim.

[1] For the circumstances which called forth this letter see *post*, pp. 391–3.

1686

Ditto.

Monsieur Sensheim's answer to the Stadtkämmerer Wielden: er war ein Reichs Cavalier und hatte ebenmässig ein Session im Reichstag; er war auch nicht sein Kammerdiener der den englischen Herrn Abgesandten offendiret hatte sondern er selbst. Also dass wenn er wollte satisfaction haben sollte er ihm geben auf was Ort und Weise er sie verlanget.[1]

Ratisbon, 22 Nov./2 Dec., 86.

My Lord (Middleton):

. . . This Prince Ettingen has had the Emperor's letters to be admitted to have session in the Diet these many years, and has had now for some time a minister here to solicit it; but he is opposed by his cousin, the Comte of Ettingen, who is President of the Aulic Court,[2] and in favour at Vienna. There are differences between them about the dividing of an estate, and the President is unwilling the Prince should have it in his power to make advantage of the privileges he will have to his prejudice. This makes the Emperor's ministers here do all they can to delay the receiving of him till those disputes are determined. The Prince has hereupon declared that he will not make use of his privileges to stop any legal proceedings between him and his cousin, and it is believed a decree of commission will be ordered ere long to perfect what the Prince desires.

About the King of Poland's being displeased with his Holiness, for not bestowing a cap on the Bishop of Beauvais, the only person he named, and for

---

[1] He was a member of the Diet and had accordingly a seat in the Diet; also it was not his (Sensheim's) valet, but he himself who had given offence to the English envoy. So that if he (Etherege) wished to have satisfaction, should he notify him (Sensheim) of it by a gentleman he would give it to him in whatever place and manner he desired it.

[2] Wolfgang IV of Öttingen, an active privy councillor.

promoting two of his subjects who stood not well towards him.

Ratisbon, 25 Nov./5 Dec., 1686.

My Lord (Middleton):

The Emperor's ratification of the conclusions made for treating of the execution of the truce and limits was sent hither about a fortnight since and has been kept secret by the Imperial commission till this week. This, and some conferences which the commissioners have had in private with the Austrian ministers, has made many jealous. There was a design to gain some points by an after game which could not be carried when the conclusion was passed. It is said that, by some members appointed for that purpose, the pulse of the colleges was felt; the business was to have had the Diet, as it is conjectured, give the substance of the letter which the Emperor is to write to his Christian Majesty which is to consist of griefs, and by that means have engaged them to allow the griefs which the moderate party look upon as complaints till they are further proved. This being gained they intended at the beginning of the treaty to have the Diet to have ordered the redressing of these griefs to have been first treated of, as things most materia[l] for the execution of armistitia. This would have made a rupture, and the French would have looked upon the armament which is to be treated of at the same time as no other than the whole Empire's entering into the alliance of Augsburg. Finding no likelihood of succeeding in this, yesterday the decree of commission for the ratification of these conclusions was given to the Director of Mayence, who found it so uniform to the intentions of the conclusions, that he stayed not to have the Elector his master's approbation but dictated it that very morning, and it had the applause of all the Colleges. In my next I will send your

Lordship a copy of it in form, and then I shall have little to trouble you with till after the holidays, the Diet not intending until they are over to debate of any business.

By what the Emperor has done it appears he intends to pursue the war against the Turks, though the Grand Vizier[1] in a late letter has given him fair warning: he says God has chastised them because his predecessor unjustly broke the peace with the Empire, and that in case he will not consent it should be renewed and be the occasion of the effusion of more blood, God would in their turn chastise him and his for their obstinacy. In the meantime General Leslie[2] was mistaken in the letter I mentioned in my last. Caposwar[3] is surrendered. The garrison has liberty to march out with what they could carry to Segeth, and there were fourteen pieces of cannon found in the place. There is no credit to be given to what I mentioned concerning the King of Denmark's 5,000 men for the Emperor's service, for the project which some pretended to have of that treaty is false. I am, &c.

Ratisbon, 29 Nov./9 Dec., 86.

My Lord (Middleton):

I send your Lordship a copy of the Imperial decree which I promised in my last. I had not then seen it, and I find it much short of what I expected from the general applause it had at first. The place

[1] Kara Ibrahim.

[2] Count Leslie was a brigadier-general under the Elector of Bavaria.

[3] Kaposvár, thirty miles north-west of Fünfkirchen in Hungary. It was captured by Louis of Baden, after an attack lasting several days and the loss of about 200 men. The *London Gazette* (Nov. 29–Dec. 2) reports that twenty-four pieces of cannon were found and that the garrison with its baggage was conducted to Segeth (= Szegedin). Baden afterwards sent his troops to their winter quarters.

named where the Treaty shall be, is ratified. The Emperor says he will not be wanting to facilitate things on his part, and that he will write the letter mentioned in the conclusion. It is left dubitable to whom the States of the Empire are to address their griefs, and the ministers are of diverse opinions as to that point. The manner of treating, which is inserted in the conclusion, is not so much as taken notice of in this decree. This shuffling and cutting make some think the game that is expected will not be played fairly.

The French King is building another fortress in an island about the height of Hagenau on the Rhine.[1] The adding this link to the chain of strong places he has already there makes more murmuring here.

The conclusion lately made about taking winter quarters by force and exactions, is not yet confirmed by the Emperor, and the Elector of Brandenburg has sent a regiment of horse and four companies of foot into Mecklenburg. Upon the complaint of the Regence[2] to him, he has answered them it is necessary he should do it for securing the quiet of the lower Saxony. I am &c.

By an express from Vienna to one of the ministers of Austria we are informed that the Empress Dowager is dead.[3]

[1] This fort, opposite Rastatt, was further north than that at Hüningen. The following June 8,000 men were being employed on the work. The fort was built to prevent approach to Strasburg through the then extensive Hagenauer forest.

[2] The governing bodies of certain European towns were so called.

[3] Eleanor of Gonzaga, daughter of Charles, Duke of Mantua, married Emperor Ferdinand III in 1651; by him she had two daughters:

Eleanor Mary, married (a) Michael Wisnowitski, King of Poland, (b) Duke Charles of Lorraine.

Mary Anne Joseph, married Philip William, Electoral Prince Palatine.

She died, aged 59, on December 6, 1686.

1686

My Lord (Middleton):

The conclusion I formerly mentioned about taking winter quarters by force and exaction is not likely to be confirmed, the Emperor not being willing to do a thing which would disoblige the houses of Brandenburg and Brunswick, whom he may have need of. The fifty Roman months which have been granted to his Imperial Majesty are instantly required to be paid by the Imperial towns, which they refuse alleging, especially those of the circles of Franconia and Swabia, that they have satisfied their shares, in the entertainment of those troops they have sent three years together into Hungary; and the town of Frankfort, which began the business, have sent back the assignation which the court drew upon them, and have protested against it.[1] I know not how the treaty for the execution of the truce, &c. will go on. It seems to me the Imperial commission have no mind to facilitate that business.

The Count of Windisgratz (the last time the Diet met which was on Monday) causing the Director of Mayence to be solicited to put the memorials touching the fort of Hüningen into deliberation he refused;[2] answering it was contrary to the intention of their conclusion. The Director was likewise desired to give under his hand the complaints which have been sent him of griefs, but he said they were only given in to be dictated and that he was not to sign copies and give them out to any other use; that the Austrian ministers had heard them dictated and might take out copies if they pleased. All this tends to what the alliance of Augsburg pretends : that the contraventions are in the first place to be redressed and therefore to be first treated of.

That alliance, which seems to sleep, is active

[1] MS. 'them'. [2] MS. 'which he refused'.

underhand, and a letter has been lately writ from hence by the secretary of Holland, at the instance of the Swedish minister[1] here, to Monsieur Valkenier to desire him to hasten the States his masters' resolution about entering into it. I am, &c.

[*See also Appendix, page* 436.]

Ratisbon, 30 Dec./9 Jan., 1686/7.

My Lord (Treasurer):[2]

I have often thought of the assurances your Lordship was pleased to give me of your favour before I left England, and you have made them so good to me that, had I durst follow my own inclinations, I had tired you with so many acknowledgements, I should almost have made you repent of your goodness. I have been sparing in giving your Lordship an account of what passes here out of the apprehension of giving you a double trouble. If I have been to blame I desire Mr. Shorve may have order to correct me that I may not commit the same fault hereafter.

I find many doubtful in their judgements here whether the Emperor will make another campaign in Hungary, or think of making an advantageous peace, which doubtless the Turks will offer him. If we may believe what is writ from Vienna there are already many competitors for the embassy of Constantinople;[3] if this be so in all likelihood the treaty for the execution of the truce, notwithstanding [it] has been advanced, will proceed no farther.

It is reported here that his Christian Majesty, after the Fort Louis[4] is in a condition to defend

---

[1] Schnolsky.   [2] Lord Rochester.

[3] Mr. Abbot remarks that though this embassy was a byword for difficulty there were never wanting keen candidates (*Under the Turk in Constantinople*).

[4] The name of the fort being erected at Seltz near Hagenau (see *ante*, p. 123, note 1).

itself, intends to build another between Philippsburg and Mannheim; and though he pretends all is but to secure himself against the alliances which are made, the Emperor does not like he should be so much master of the Rhine.

It is evident the *chicane* about the treaty has been hitherto on the Emperor's ministers' side, and one of them told me yesterday, whom I pressed a little in discoursing of this matter, that their care should be to convince the world of the contrary, in case there happened a breach between them and the French. I had said to him before, when he asked me concerning the sea preparations[1] which his Majesty made against the spring, that I was confident his Majesty intended nothing but the securing himself at home, and the preserving of the peace of Christendom, that the confederates might pursue their victories against the common enemy. They are very jealous of his Majesty, especially if they should begin with the French, and the Dutch use all means to increase their suspicions, suggesting his Majesty has a design against them on purpose to hinder them in assisting the alliance of Augsburg, into which they are to enter and to be a main pillar of that building. A good part of Monsieur Caunitz's[2]

[1] Lord Rochester had procured £400,000 towards the repairing of the fleet. Orders were given to put the whole fleet in a condition to go to sea, though England was at peace with all her neighbours. The priests fostered the idea that these preparations were intended against Holland and that France and England would suddenly make war upon the States. The knowledge that the French desired above all things an embroilment between James II and William of Orange lent plausibility to the supposition (Burnet, *op. cit.* ii. 383–4).

[2] Domenic Andrew, Count of Kaunitz (1642–1705), as the Emperor's envoy in the Bavarian court, obtained troops for the Hungarian campaign. At the end of the year 1686 he was sent on a mission to London. He was ordered to co-operate with the Spanish ambassador, in seeking to secure friendly

business in England is, I believe, to find out the inclinations of our court in this matter. Here, as well as in Holland, are tricks used to make the Protestants believe his Majesty is of intelligence with the French King for their extirpation. Amongst other lies in a gazette not long since it was said that Prince George was turned Roman Catholic, and the discourse was that his Princess was to inherit in prejudice of the Princess of Orange.[1] The last week in the gazette of this town, which was taken out of some Dutch news, it is said that his Majesty on the return of Mr. Fitzjames will legitimate him in order to something farther.[2] I will not trouble

relations with the Imperial court, to make clear to James II the real designs of Louis XIV and to try to obtain an alliance for the protection of the peace against further French aggressions. On his return he was appointed to settle the disputes about ceremonials at Ratisbon, to attempt to stir the Electors to combined action with regard to the limits and to endeavour to recruit soldiers to fill up the depleted ranks of the Imperial infantry.

[1] From dispatches from the French embassy in London we learn that Louis desired his ministers to insinuate to James II that he would help to transfer the succession to Princess Anne on the condition of her becoming a Roman Catholic. The plan had been set forth in a minute by some fanatics, and was handed about among Jesuits and Roman Catholics until it fell into the hands of the Dutch ambassador, who gave the paper to the King. James pronounced it a vile forgery contrived by a Dutch pamphleteer, and protested that no such scheme had ever entered his mind, yet a few days later Barillon reported that James had begun to listen to suggestions with respect to changing the succession, and that though it was now obvious that Anne was too attached to the Church of England there was reason to hope that both Princesses might be excluded in favour of some Roman Catholic (Macaulay, *op. cit.* ii. 118–19).

[2] Fitzjames was legitimized on his return to London. Only a small Jesuitical faction had ever seriously thought of setting him up as a competitor of the Princess of Orange, and there is no reason to suppose that James ever had in mind such a scheme.

your Lordship with the idle reasonings which have been made by cabals upon this story.

The Emperor's ministers, who have been hitherto more careful of themselves than of the husbanding of their master's treasure, are hard put to it to find the money necessary to make recruits, far from being able to disburse what the auxiliaries will require. They depended on the fifty Roman months, which have been granted, but the Imperial towns make a difficulty of paying that tax, and some have protested against the assignations which have been drawn upon them towards the making of recruits: urging they have paid their shares in the disbursements they have made for the troops they have sent three campaigns together into Hungary. There is a clause in the conclusion which gives this tax which says it shall be lawful for them to deduct these charges, but being weak it is not doubted but they will be forced to compound. This may be a reason that the Imperial army may not answer expectation the next year if the war continues against the Turk.

The tediousness and impertinence of this letter will incline your Lordship to forgive me if I have committed a fault in not troubling you oftener. I wish your Lordship all manner of happiness this new year, begging the continuance of your favour to &c.

Ditto.

To my Lord Middleton of the Count de Thun's being sent to Munich to dissuade the Elector of Bavaria from his intended journey in to Italy. . . . The Emperor is jealous it is intended a journey of debauch, that Prince being something that way inclined and many have said he designed it partly in spite: a lady being removed for whom he had some consideration: you might, if her good man had thought of it, have seen her in England.[1] The States

[1] The Elector of Bavaria evinced a passion for the Countess

of this country use likewise their endeavour to divert him from this resolution, it being their interest since he asks of them 100,000 crowns to defray his expenses.

Enclosed this French song following:

> Garde le secret de ton âme,
> Et ne te laisse pas flatter,
> Qu'Iris épargnera ta flamme,
> Si tu lui permets d'éclater :
> Son humeur, à l'amour rebelle,
> Exile tous ses doux desirs,
> Et la tendresse est criminelle
> Qui veut lui parler en soupirs.
> Puisque tu vis sous son empire,
> Il faut lui cacher ton destin :
> Si tu ne veux le rendre pire
> Percé du trait de son dédain :
> D'une rigueur si delicate
> Ton cœur ne peut rien espérer,
> Dérobe donc à cette ingrate
> La vanité d'en triompher.[1]

Ratisbon, 31 Dec., 86.

To my Lord Middleton : of the Elector of Bavaria's journey to Venice, and of the Elector of Brandenburg's forbidding his ministers to vote till the Diet pass a conclusion about the cloister of Lockum and about his dédommagements for the war begun '79.

Sir (Mr. Guy):[2]   Ratisbon, 1 Jan., 86/7 new style.

The date of this letter is enough to make you expect a compliment, but I have given and received

of Kaunitz (Maria Eleanora of Sternberg) and an aversion for his wife Maria Antonia, daughter of Leopold. The Electress complained to her father, and refused to live with her husband if Kaunitz returned to Munich, so he was sent on the mission to England (p. 126, note 2).   [1] MS. 'trionfer'.

[2] Henry Guy (1631–1710), Secretary to the Treasury; pay-

so many in this formal place that I cannot think of one to my mind. Be satisfied that every day I wish you increase of happiness in what is possible, for let me tell you, however we may flatter ourselves, the least addition of days and much more of years to the number we have already cannot do us much good.

I have troubled my Lord Treasurer with a tedious account of the news of this place. I hope his goodness will forgive me, and you must forgive me the not having writ to you oftener since it has been occasioned by a fit of sickness I have had this winter. I am now so well recovered that my heart begins to be sensible again. I dare not boast of what is more to the purpose : here is at present a lady who lives commonly near Nuremberg, she is so very handsome, that it may be said she has robbed the whole country, for the rest of the women look as if nature had spared from them what she has bestowed on this. She is as fière as she is fair which may be allowed to a beauty that has no rival.[1]

I send you [a] French song which she has been the occasion of. Mr. Vice Chamberlain is so able a Frenchman that I fear his criticisms, but pray tell him I am not the only man who have engaged myself in a love business without considering whether I was able to go through with it. I beg the continuance of your favour, and do not doubt but you will help Mr. Robson[2] to succeed in what nearly concerns Sir, &c.

ments from public funds passed through his hands until 1688. A boon companion of Charles II, he appears to have been proficient in understanding court methods, and died leaving an estate said to have been valued at £100,000.

[1] The comedienne Julia.

[2] Thomas Robson, clerk and paymaster of import bills and ambassadorial bills of exchange.

Ratisbon, 10/20 January, 86/7.

My Lord (Middleton):
The Diet have assembled twice or thrice since the holidays, but the time has been only spent in conversation. Nothing is expected to be done towards the execution of the armistice till the griefs are delivered in here in Latin, from whence they are to be sent to the Emperor in order to draw up the letter which he is to write to his Christian Majesty concerning them. The delays which are used will take up so much time that it is not likely the treaty, if it is intended, should have any effect till the Imperialists have had the advantage of seeing what another campaign in Hungary will produce.

I find Monsieur de Crécy much dissatisfied with these proceedings. Yesterday he dispatched an express to his master and told me that if they think to talk first of contraventions the answer he had to make was that there were none, but when I urged the bridge at Hüningen and the cutting of wood in the Black Forest, he replied the one they gave occasion for and that the other was of little value : that all the rest were but complaints of such as were his master's subjects who, if any wrong were done them, should address themselves to him and not to the Empire to be relieved. What will become of this matter you are best able to judge, but by what I understand here I believe the Emperor and the Empire will not treat of a *paix décisive*, which is the business of the execution of the truce, they being firmly persuaded that the French will not conclude it but on condition things may remain as they are now.

The gentlemen of the alliance of Augsburg, as I find by their discourse and practices, esteem his Majesty to be of intelligence with the French to oppose their designs. They talk much of preparations made for sea[1] and would alarm the Empire with them, being so ridiculous as to affirm that Holland is a branch of the great body. I am, &c.

Ratisbon, 13/23 Jan., 86/7.

My Lord (Middleton):

Since my last the Electoral College, by way of discourse among themselves, have declared that it is fit something should be done to shew they intend to treat of the execution of the truce before the griefs can be ready, and proposed the giving of the mutual guarantee. This has been occasioned by a letter, which is yet a great secret, that the Emperor has writ to the several Electors: the substance of which is that he is informed from sure hands that his Christian Majesty designs to undertake something against the Empire next spring, and desires them to assist him with their advice (the French endeavouring to cut off the good intelligence which ought to be between those considerable branches and their body) that they may unanimously take their measure to prevent the mischief intended. In case this guarantee should be resolved by the College of Electors it is believed the College of Princes, in which the Austrian ministers have the great sway, will not concur with them in it. They are more inclined to treat of the armament for the public security and only forbear it to save appearances. They know if the French King begins, though it is their fault the armistice is not executed, the calumny will be generally laid on him, especially by the Protestant party who are animated by other reasons than that of the Emperor's being engaged at present in a war against the Turks.[2]

The offers the Imperialists pretend the Turks have

[1] See *ante*, p. 126, note 1.

[2] By the revocation of the Edict of Nantes in 1685, and the consequent persecution of the Huguenots.

made them, in case they will make a peace with them, are so extravagant that the artifice plainly appears and the design they had in it is no less subtle: which was to frighten the French in making them believe they had it in their hands to make an advantageous peace whenever they pleased. I am, &c.

Ratisbon, 17/27 Jan., 86/7.

My Lord (Middleton):

The Diet have not as yet deliberated of any business. The Count de Crécy has orders not to press them but only to expect what they will do. The Austrian ministers say his Christian Majesty has set them a time (which is till the end of March next) to treat of the execution of the armistice. Monsieur de Crécy has not prescribed them this time by any instruction he has had. It is supposed they have the notice of it from Rome: his Christian Majesty having informed his Holiness with his intention in this matter.

The Emperor's ministers do not seem so much alarmed at this as to mend their pace: they only say it is impossible in so short a time to do what the French expect from them. They would not stick at the giving the mutual guarantee, if the word of the Empire might be taken, but the scruple is about the security. It has been owned to me that the project for the armament for the public security, which according to the late conclusion made here was to be treated of alternatively with the execution of the armistice, is drawn up privately and that there is only wanting to make it perfect the naming of a general and of a town where the *caisse*[1] is to be established. They would fain effect this that they might have a body of men on the Rhine next spring to protect them from what they apprehend from

[1] Presumably a place where the money was to be collected.

the French.[1] That which makes the accomplishment of this delayed is the desire some Princes of the Empire have that their troops may have employment, they having more on foot than they can well maintain with which they watch to make an advantage when there is an occasion. In a word the Empire would willingly treat of the execution of the truce as far as concerns the redressing of the griefs but cannot find in their hearts to conclude a peace with the French upon such hard terms as they made the truce. The French will have the peace treated of, as it ought to be, according to the eleventh article of the armistitia and if it be not they do no[t] think it reasonable to wait till the Empire be at leisure to attack them. I am &c.,

I hope your Lordship will be so kind as to make me a friend in the treasury upon the change which I hear is to be.

Ditto.

My Lord (Sunderland):[2]

(The news as in the foregoing letter till to this place.) . . . The Emperor is a little dissatisfied with the Elector of Bavaria. The Count de Thun stays at Munich till his return from Venice. The ministers of Austria say the Elector is abused by the French, who put unreasonable jealousies in his head to make him suspect the Emperor.[3]

Here is a talk of a splendid embassy to be sent to the Porte. It is to consist of three, and the Count

[1] The apprehension was of a French attack on the Palatinate. 'La question de l'armement ou de la securité publique et la question des limites sont les deux questions qui se présentent par intervalles devant la diète et qu'elle ne résout jamais' (G. Pagès, *Le Grand Électeur et Louis XIV*, p. 576).

[2] See *ante*, p. 59, note 1.

[3] Louis XIV did his best to increase the Elector's dissatisfaction at the treatment accorded to him with regard to the command in Hungary insinuating that the Emperor was afraid of giving him too much power.

de Windisgratz is confidently named to be one. He may meet with his match if he comes to treat about ceremonials with the Grand Vizier. They had got a trick to print in the newsbooks of this town several things which might be prejudicial to his Majesty, pretending they took them out of some Holland gazettes. I complained of this to the Count de Lamberg, who has checked[1] Monsieur Scherer on it. He is one of the underministers of Austria who has the overlooking of these matters. He is extreme violent against the French, and believes England has too good a correspondence with them. Nevertheless the dapperspruce Doctor (whom I should overmeasure if I should call him the Mr. Yard of Ratisbon) upon this reprimand has promised to mend his manners.

I do not doubt but your Lordship will be careful of the work of your own hands, and secure me a friend in the treasury in the change which is like to be. I am.

Ratisbon, 24 Jan./3 Feb., 86/7.

I send your Lordship the copy of a medal made lately in silver at Nuremberg upon the taking of Buda. It is called Joshua. *Pello duos* is the anagram of *Leopoldus*.[2] I will send you the original when I

[1] MS. 'chacked'.

[2] I owe the explanation of this reference to the courtesy of Mr. Allan, of the Department of Coins and Medals at the British Museum. The medal is described by Jules Jergina in the Review *Szazadol*, 1884, pp. 787–8. The face presents the fortress of Buda, together with the surrounding district; above, the bust of Leopold; below, the inscription: INFELIX BUDAM/LVDOVICVS PER/DIDIT OLIM/HÆC ARMIS CÆDIT NVNC/LEOPOLDE TVIS/A. 1686. D.2.SEP. On the obverse is depicted between two armies a man in a helmet with a sceptre in his right hand and a shield in his left hand, in front of him the sun following the moon with the inscription: STAT SOL LUNA FVGIT DUM/IOSVA PVGNAT ET ORAT/SIC EGO PELLO DVOS! SIC LEOPOLDUS ERO!

have an opportunity. I would not venture it in a letter, fearing the weight should make it miscarry. The French look on this as a libel.

Here has been nothing done yet towards the advancing of the treaty for the execution of the truce. The Imperial commission expect instructions from Vienna, and it is believed they have received them and will suddenly give in a commission decree, the contents of which will give some light into what is intended. They are in a great apprehension of his Christian Majesty's proceedings.

The Count de Crécy has told the members of the Diet, they are not to expect anything should be proposed by him upon the return of the courier he has sent to France: that the King his master had acquainted his Holiness with his mind that he might impart it to the Emperor, and that he intended to take his measures according to the answer which the Emperor should give thereunto.

The Bishop of Salzburg is very sick, and this day the Count de Lamberg, who is a chanoine of that place and one whom the Emperor has a design to advance, is by his Imperial order gone from hence for that town to brigue[1] in case of a vacance. I am, &c.

Ratisbon, 27 Jan./6 Feb., 86/7.

My Lord (Middleton):

Here has been nothing yet done in the Diet. They continue consulting at Vienna what they shall do concerning the treaty of the execution of the armistice. The time draws near which the French have fixed to be satisfied in this business: they are resolved not to lose the advantage of being beforehand this

Round the circumference of the medal is another inscription with the initials I.W. The silver medallion, which measured 48mm. in diameter, was struck by Wolrab, an engraver of Nuremberg.

[1] To contend or solicit by intrigue (obsolete).

spring in case the Empire will not secure them by a peace from what they apprehend when the war with the Turk is ended. The French complain the Emperor is very slow in his deliberations, nevertheless they think he will be forced at last to comply with what they desire.

Two days since the courier the French plenipotentiary sent to his master returned hither, and this morning he has dispatched him back again. He tells me the King his master has ordered him, while this matter depends, constantly to inform him whether anything be done in it or no by way of express, and that the substance of this is that the Emperor's council have not yet determined anything in it. I believe his Christian Majesty is impatient to know what the Emperor resolves, and thinks he may guess at it by what he may learn from hence before he can receive the certainty from Rome.

By the many visits Monsieur de Crécy has lately made I imagine he has endeavoured to find out what Electors and Princes of the Empire are well disposed for the treaty, and has informed his master of them: for on my discoursing with him on this subject he told me several ministers were already instructed in the matter.

The Count de Windisgratz has been taxed with the discovery of a secret, which has made the French more earnest in the pressing of this affair. He was pleased, after having examined himself, to do me the honour to say he never spoke of it to anybody but to me, and that he did not tell it me directly, but only by seeming to consent to several things I discoursed of, and that if ever he recovered the use of his hands again, which were then very gouty, he would be revenged (but he was pleased to be so favourable as to explain himself)—by writing. This secret has hardly been one to any shopkeeper in this town this half year, and a child by their proceedings ever since I have been here might have guessed at it. It is *that they never intended to keep the truce any longer than they should think it convenient, it being made so much to the prejudice of the Empire.* This has been owned to me out of vanity by some ministers who were violent for the alliance of Augsburg when they put no confidence in me, esteeming his Majesty to have too strict an alliance with France upon my first acquaintance with them.

The morning Mr. Fitzjames went from hence &c.; the story about the compliment Sir George made to Schnolsky upon his journey to Augsburg (wishing his coach might break on the way because he went with a design of making an alliance against France); of his Honour's not being taken notice of notwithstanding the compliment he made the Imperial commission upon the taking of Buda; of Count Lamberg's civilities; of Sir George's applying himself to him alone, who may perhaps be made first commissioner, which is a dignity the Empire will never suffer the Comte of Windisgratz to rise to; of his denying at last to have trusted his Honour with anything, but that he thought of this so late that all the ministers take his first word and no man will believe me whatever I say to the contrary. I am, &c.

Ratisbon, 31 Jan./10 Feb., 1686/7.

My Lord (Godolphin):[1]

I no sooner received the news of the change which was to be in the Treasury but I straight fixed my

---

[1] Sidney, Earl of Godolphin (*c.* 1645–1712), was appointed first Lord of the Treasury in 1684. Together with Rochester and Sunderland he enjoyed the confidence of James II. Etherege writes to congratulate him on his reappointment to the first Lordship of the Treasury in succession to Rochester. Burnet says ' his incorrupt and sincere way of managing the concerns of the Treasury created in all people a very high esteem for him' (*op. cit.* ii. 113).

thoughts on your Lordship to be my patron. The virtues which you enjoy proper for such a trust, your great experience in those affairs, the confidence which his Majesty has in you, and the particular esteem he has for you made me not doubt but you would be one of the commissioners.[1] Could I show as much judgement in the performance of my duty as I have done in this choice I should not despair of meriting your Lordship's favour, and your justice would allow me what I must wholly expect from your goodness. Instead of congratulating your Lordship I should congratulate his Majesty and the kingdom on this occasion, for you will have the trouble wholly, and they will have the greatest share of the profits of your honourable employment. I have long wish[ed] for a pretext to write to your Lordship, and I hope you will think this so lawful a one that you will forgive my presumption. I shall be modest at first and not importune you with a long letter. If I could by any way learn that your Lordship desires I should acquaint you immediately with what is done here, you would find me very diligent to gain your good opinion.

I am too lazy and too careless to be ambitious, but it is so pleasing an advantage to have the reputation of your favour that the hope of it is enough to change the natural inclination of My Lord, &c.

Ditto.

My Lord (Dover):[2]

I have been long an admirer of your virtues without suspecting your lovingkindness was one of

[1] The others were Lord Bellasye, Lord Dover, Sir John Ernle, and Sir Stephen Fox.

[2] Henry Jermyn, Earl of Dover (*c.* 1636–1708), in his early years surpassed in profligacy his notorious uncle Henry Jermyn, Earl of St. Albans. Etherege writes to congratulate him on his appointment as one of the commissioners of the Treasury. He was a Roman Catholic.

them. Did I not know the perfect resignation you have to his Majesty's pleasure I should wonder at your courage in loading yourself at first setting forth with the most weighty charge in the kingdom. Sir Jo. E[rnle] and Sir S. F[ox],[1] who began with carrying a calf, may bear this ox without staggering, but what a fine thing will it be to you, who have never scarce sullied your fingers with telling of silver, to cast up a monstrous exchequer account whose head is as big as a million while the tail dwindles into a halfpenny farthing. However honourable your title is, you are no other than one of the first cash-keepers in the nation; but what is not a man of honour capable of undertaking when he is called to serve so gracious a master? I doubt not but you will govern the Treasury with as much address and applause as Lucullus did of old the Roman legions, and, were I to be an eyewitness, I should see you lose your case with the same temper I have seen you lose your money.[2] I know not whether I ought to rejoice or condole with you since I think you sacrifice yourself in this matter, but you must give me leave to congratulate my own good fortune now you are placed in a post from whence you may more powerfully continue the dispensing of your favour to My Lord, &c.

Ditto.

To my Lord Middleton: of his Majesty's health being drunk the first at the Count de Crécy's feast; of my Lord Taaffe's opinion touching the proposi-

[1] Sir Stephen Fox (1627–1719) was successively clerk of the green cloth, paymaster general of the forces in England, and, in 1680, one of the Lords commissioners of the Treasury. So that his appointment in 1686 was but a reinstatement in an office held before.

[2] Dover was a lifelong gambler. Ruined by play he sought to retrieve his fortune by means of lucrative posts (Macaulay, *op. cit.* i. 558).

tions made to his Highness by the French King (wherein he calls them *horribles et telles qu'on n'impose qu'aux vaincus*[1]); of several states of the Empire being dissatisfied, if not jealous, that the affair is so long deliberated on at Vienna: it being of so great consequence to the whole Empire, they think it but reasonable it should be communicated to the Diet to debate what answer is fit to be given; of speaking in favour of his Honour to the Commissioners of the Treasury; of the story about his gaming being false.

Ratisbon, 2/12 Feb., 86/7.

My Lord (Taaffe):[2]

I believe the report of my going to Sweden is grounded upon a mistake. I should be sorry to leave the Empire before I have the honour of being personally known to your Lordship and in the happiness of your conversation forget the chagrin which the dullness of this place occasions. I need not trouble you with discoursing of the reasons which have made the French King make the propositions at Rome in this conjuncture. You are so clear-sighted that you do not want any illuminations I can give.

The French urge the treating of a peace is part of the execution of the armistice; your Lordship will best judge of that by reading the 11th article.[3]

Some ministers here are so passionate that it makes them unfit to serve their masters as they

[1] MS. 'vencus'.

[2] Francis, Viscount Taafe and Earl of Carlingford (1639–1704), born in Ireland and educated abroad, served at the siege of Bonn, 1673, and the relief of Vienna, 1683. James II recommended Fitzjames to his care. In 1687 he was given the command of an Irish regiment in the Austrian service. The Duke of Berwick testifies to his culture and sagacity without sharing the opinion of other authorities as to his military ability. [3] See *post*, p. 151.

might do. I am confident the King our master will do all he can that these differences may be happily composed for the benefit of all Christendom, and will never contribute to the unlawful oppressing of the Empire. Judge you how grateful it is to me to hear his Majesty called *bon Français* and to have it said *that the Empire is too poor to purchase so good a friend*! I have a great esteem for the Count de Lamberg; he is a gentleman; besides his other merits he knows how to live, which is a thing most of our Doctors are to learn. I have applied myself wholly to him and endeavoured to cultivate a friendship with him since I had reason to think the Count de Windisgratz slighted our nation. Your Lordship is not ignorant of the zeal his Majesty and all his good subjects shewed for the prosperity of the siege of Buda. I made my compliments to the Imperial commission for the taking of the place, and yet when several cavaliers were invited among the ministers, I was thought unworthy to partake in the public rejoicings. This was blamed by all the ministers, and the reflection I made upon it has been the cause I have not since made my court—for I can give it no less a name, he never making any return of civilities—to the Count de Windisgratz. Upon his being lately taxed with having discovered a secret, upon which some say the proposition of Rome is founded, he was pleased to say if ever he spoke anything of it, it must be to me. I do not doubt but he has discoursed of this business to several, and did not so much think to whom he had trusted the secret as to whom he had given occasion to disclose it; as for me I protest, upon my honour, I know of no secret he trusted me with, and, in case he should have trusted me with any, I am too honest and too reasonable a man upon a private pique to revenge myself on the whole Empire whose prosperity I sincerely wish.

I have received no certain news of what his Majesty intends to do for Mr. Fitzjames. I send your Lordship all the news the last post brought me out of England, and shall be overjoyed to have a good opportunity to shew you how faithful I am.

Ratisbon, 3/13 Feb., 86/7.

Sir (Mr. Skelton):[1]

I had the good fortune, by reason of the distance I am at, not to know of the danger you were in in your passage from England, before I knew you were safely arrived at Paris. I take it very kindly that you ordered Captain Slater to make me the offer of doing me what courtesies you could in your station. I am sorry to find by the other part of his letter that you have had an occasion to apprehend I have been wanting in what is due to your merit. In mine he will shew you the answer I made him as to those matters, and, had I not the testimony of all that are honest here to vindicate me, I doubt not but my own word would be taken against whatsoever malicious reports have been in Holland to the prejudice of

Sir, &c.

Ratisbon, ditto.

Sir (Captain Slater):

I received yesterday a letter from you dated at Paris the 28th of December last.[2] I know not by what fate it was sent to Rotterdam, where it lay in the

---

[1] Bevil Skelton (fl. 1661–92), English envoy at the Hague. He sent warnings of William's intrigues to James, with the result that the former endeavoured to have him recalled. His repeated blunders caused his removal to Versailles in January 1687, where he supported the attempt of Louis XIV to hinder the invasion of England by advancing troops towards the Dutch frontiers. Burnet characterizes him as 'the haughtiest but withal the weakest man that he [James] could have found out. He talked out all secrets, and made himself the scorn of all Holland' (*op. cit.* ii. 302).   [2] See *post*, pp. 351–2.

post-house till an English merchant was so kind as to redeem it, and send it to me. The truth is the business you write to me about might better be cleared in Holland than here. Judge you how much I was surprised with what you tell me the reports in Holland accuse me withal; I, whose conduct ever since I have been in the Empire, has been quite contrary! I have had often occasion to speak of Mr. Skelton, but I have always done it in such a manner that I have not only done justice to his merit but, according to my poor ability, paid some part of the obligation I owe him. How could a man who is so jealous for all that concerns his Majesty as I am censure the negotiations of a gentleman who has so eminently signalized himself in his service?

As for Sir Robert Peyton[1] I am not to be informed of his crimes. I have told the whole history of his behaviour since the beginning of the plot, and satisfied all honest and reasonable men that the States only take it ill that their country cannot be an inviolable sanctuary for all rebels. I know nothing of any letters Peyton had sent to Mr. Skelton, but was told by some ministers here (who hold a correspondence with Valkenier, who has been

[1] Sir Robert Peyton was examined by the council in connexion with the Presbyterian plot, and committed to the Tower for conspiring to levy war against the King, January 1679/80. The chief witness having retracted, Peyton was discharged in May. In 1681 he demanded satisfaction for being expelled the House of Commons, and was again imprisoned in the Tower, but discharged after two months. In 1684 a warrant was out against him for seditious words, and in 1685 the Grand Jury found bills against him. In November 1686 he was reported lately taken in Holland, but rescued by the rabble, and in December the States General complained to James that Skelton had tried to seize him and transport him to England on one of the King's yachts, though he was now a citizen of Amsterdam. Peyton's outlawry was reversed in 1689, but he died of fever the next month (Luttrell's *Relation of State Affairs*, i, *passim*).

some time since recalled from hence by his high and mighty masters), of the breach of faith you mention, to which I answered I did not believe Mr. Skelton ever made him any promise; that Peyton might write to him but that I could not imagine any use was made of his letters but to communicate the contents of them to his Majesty. This is not the first trick has been played me since my being here, and is not the last. Mr. Skelton knows by experience the temper of the Dutch: how little they value a lie to do a man a good turn, especially those his Majesty employs now they esteem him to have a strict alliance with France. Valkenier was long here after my arrival, and used all the means possible to persuade me to visit him; but upon the certain knowledge I had that he, receiving the false news of a victory the late Duke of Monmouth was said to have in the West,[1] had made it be printed here and sent it with great joy to several of his friends, I never would be prevailed with. He is a true burgess of Amsterdam, and since his departure has supplied our gazettes here with lies from his own country, among which there have been some dangerously reflecting on his Majesty; but upon my complaint they have commanded not to do the like for the future. Whether the reports you talk of come from this source or any other they are wholly false, upon my honour. I take your good intentions very kindly, but pray rectify your mistake hereafter, and do not let any idle reports make you have an ill opinion of, &c.

If Mr. Skelton desires to know what passes here

[1] The advanced guard of the Royal army under the Duke of Grafton met with a setback at Philips Norton. They were marching along a lane under fire from both sides when their way was obstructed by a barricade of fire from in front. The troops lost heart and turned back suffering over a hundred casualties. Their retreat was intercepted by rebel cavalry, but they cut their way through.

he may freely command, who have ever had an inclination to serve him.

Ratisbon, 7/17 Feb., 1686/7.
My Lord (Middleton):
Though nothing has been done here lately, yet I think it my duty to acquaint you how matters stand. The Count de Windisgratz says they intend forthwith to treat of the execution of the truce; whether by this he means the peace which is proposed by France or has a design to elude it, I know not. The Director of Mayence on Saturday, which was the last time the Diet met, asked by way of discourse of the ministers of Austria what the Empire was to trust to in the present conjuncture, and Monsieur Scherers answered him that they expected instructions from Vienna upon the proposition made at Rome as on this day or Thursday next.

Monsieur de Barrillon and the Count de Caunitz[1] have no doubt acquainted you in England with what the proposition is. It seems a little hard for the Empire to grant by a peace not only what they have given but for twenty years by the truce, but likewise all the French are now in possession of that is: the bridge and the forts on the Rhine, without which his Christian Majesty cannot secure the keeping of the peace. But the Empire may thank those gentlemen who, when it was their business to take notice of anything, made such a cry about contraventions and such a noise with their alliance of Augsburg, the letters of the burgess of Cologne and of Treves, the defence of the alliance of the Princes of the Empire (in which the libeller has taken a great liberty in talking of his Majesty) and with their threatening medals.[2] These very persons now endeavour to exasperate the Reformed Princes of the Empire upon the propositions being made to his

[1] See *ante*, p. 126, note 2.　　　[2] See *ante*, p. 135.

146

Holiness, and would have it believed the Elector of Brandenburg particularly is very much incensed at it, but I have reason to think not to that degree they give out. I am, &c.

Monsieur de Villars,[1] who is sent by his Christian Majesty to condole the death of the Empress Dowager, arrived here last night on his way for Vienna.

Ratisbon, 10/20 Febr., 86/7.

My Lord (Middleton):

The Diet met yesterday, and the Austrian ministers, by order from the Imperial commission, acquainted them that the Emperor had sent a copy of the proposition made at Rome by the Cardinal d'Estrées[2] on the behalf of the French King, together with his answer thereunto in a circular letter to all the Electors and considerable Princes of the Empire.

This way of proceeding will spin out time, for it will be a good while ere the ministers here can receive instructions from their masters on this matter.

The Emperor's answer to the proposition, as it is said, is in general terms: *That he is, and always has been ready to observe the truce and to treat of the execution of it.* Whether this will satisfy his Christian Majesty,

[1] Claude Louis Hector, Duke of Villars (1653–1734). He was ordered to stop at Munich on his way back from Vienna in order to try to win over the Elector of Bavaria to the French cause. He accompanied the Elector to Hungary, and found the occasion favourable for exciting the jealousy of Maximilian against Charles of Lorraine. He received the title of Duke in 1705.

[2] Cardinal César d'Estrées (1628–1714) was sent to Rome to treat of the delicate affair of the French King's right to receive the revenues of the vacant bishoprics. He forwarded zealously the interests of his country, which, on the death of his brother, the Duke D'Estrées, were exclusively confined to his care. In 1693 he concluded a reconciliation between the Pope and the French clergy.

who expects a peace should be concluded, is a question.

By the last post from Rome we had the news of the death of the Duke d'Estrées.[1]

Ratisbon, 14/24 Feb., 86/7.

Sir (Mr. Wynne):

I received yours of the 28th of January, and thank you very heartily for the pains you have taken in sending me so much of the news of the town.

I have nothing worth troubling my Lord with this post. The Emperor's answer to the F[rench] King's proposition made at Rome was only read to the Diet, and no copies of it given out by the Austrian ministers, so that it is impossible to have it in form as yet. The Emperor protests by all that is holy he has a design to keep the truce very religiously, but I find his Christian Majesty will not be satisfied with this general answer. Copies of this answer are sent to his Holiness, to Monsieur de Lobkowitz,[2] and I doubt not but to Monsieur de Caunitz to be communicated to his Majesty.[3] The Electoral College stay for instructions upon their masters receiving this answer, which is sent them, as I writ my Lord word in my last, in a circular letter. This business is kept off as long as it can from coming to be debated here, and though there are many who think it unreasonable to yield to what the French desire, the necessity which lies upon the Empire at present will frustrate whatever they endeavour to the contrary, and the whole Electoral College seem impatient till his Christian Majesty is satisfied, being more justly apprehensive of the mischief which may

---

[1] The Duke d'Estrées (1625–87), brother of the cardinal, was appointed French ambassador to Rome in 1672. He died on January 30th of apoplexy.

[2] Envoy extraordinary from the Emperor to the French court.   [3] James II.

follow in case he is not than the Spaniards and Swedes, who are moved by different interest. It is not unlikely likewise that the Emperor's ministers may distinguish between what is the interest of the Empire, and that of the house of Austria. While this depends it takes up all the talk here, and we know as little as you what success the officers have had in the recruits they are making for the next campaign.

I must entreat you to let Mr. Robson[1] know I am in great want of his assistance, and I hope before this reaches you he will let me know I may draw a bill upon him. I am.

The Marquis d'Albeville[2] has not yet I suppose had leisure to give me notice of his being in Holland. Pray send me word what delays Mr. Poley.[3]

Ratisbon, 17/27 Feb., 1686/7.

My Lord (Middleton):

The Emperor's answer to the proposition made by his Christian Majesty at Rome is kept so close by his ministers here that no copies of it have been imparted yet to anybody but a favourite or two of theirs, who have been great promoters of the alliance of Augsburg. The reason of this, as it is thought, is: that it may have time to make some impression on the spirits of people before the French

[1] See *ante*, p. 130, note 2.

[2] Ignatius White, Marquis d'Albeville, a native of Ireland, replaced Skelton as English envoy at the Hague 1687, and assured Prince William and the States General that James II was resolved to maintain an alliance with them. Of the Jesuitical cabal, he tactlessly revealed the designs of the court with regard to his co-religionists. Burnet says that 'tho' he had learned the little arts of corrupting Under-Secretaries, and had found out some secrets by that way, which made him pass for a good spy; yet, when he came to negotiate matters in a higher form, he proved a most contemptible and ridiculous man, who had not the common appearances either of decency or truth' (*op. cit.* ii. 415).   [3] See *ante*, p. 111, note 1.

have made any observations on it. Nevertheless I have had the favour to hear it cursorily read over together with a copy of the letter sent to Rome and of the circular letter sent with it to the Electors; as soon as I can procure these things in form I will send them to your Lordship that you may, if you think it necessary, compare them with what is communicated to you by Monsieur de Caunitz.

There are two memorials given in by the Cardinal d'Estrées[1] to his Holiness: the first exposing the reasons which made his Christian Majesty believe that the Emperor, as soon as he had ended the war with the Turks, intended to turn his and the Empire's arms against him, which made him endeavour to secure himself by building the forts, &c.: and press the treaty of the execution of the truce. The contents of the second is that hearing the Emperor was inclined to treat of a peace, his Christian Majesty was willing to have a perfect assurance of a thing he so much desired, acquainting his Holiness upon what terms he would conclude it, provided it was determined by the end of March; expecting by his mediation the Emperor's answer hereunto.

The Emperor in his answer urges there is a contradiction in these two memorials, to clear which it is necessary to know how the second came to be delivered. Cardinal Ranucci,[2] the nuncio at Paris, told Monsieur de Croissy[3] that he had advice that the

---

[1] See *ante*, p. 147, note 2.

[2] Cardinal Angelo Maria Ranuzzi (1626–89) was sent as nuncio to Paris on the birth of the Duke of Burgundy, 1683, and remained there as the Pope's representative until 1689. Ranuzzi personally enjoyed the favour of Louis XIV and was of 'une conduite sage, une humeur douce et aisée', qualities necessary in a post rendered difficult by the political opposition of France and Rome.

[3] Charles Colbert, Marquis de Croissy (1625–96), a brother of the great Colbert, was French Secretary of State for Foreign Affairs.

Emperor was disposed to treat of a *paix décisive* with his Christian Majesty. Monsieur de Croissy asked him if he had it from such good hands as that he might acquaint his master of it. The Cardinal told him he might; upon this Monsieur de Crécy was writ to, to have his opinion of the matter. Monsieur de Crécy writ word back that he believed it only a trick to know what the King his master would insist upon in treating of a peace, and that, in order to bring this about, Monsieur de Lobkowitz [1] was instructed to advance this to the nuncio. I am apt to believe something of this for, after the conclusion was confirmed for treating of the execution of the armistice, asking one of the ministers why they did not fall to work he told me the French expected they should treat of a peace and that it was to be considered what terms they would insist upon since they had cause to apprehend they would have things to remain on the same foot they were, without redressing the griefs. The substance of the rest of the answer is: that the Emperor and Empire have observed the truce; that the alliance of Augsburg and the armament talked of were only defensive and intended for nothing but a guarantee for the observation of it; but that the French had contravened it. This Monsieur de Crécy says is leaving a gap open for a rupture whenever they please, and chicaning still upon the same point they have hitherto done to hinder the execution of the truce; that as to the treating of a peace the time and place may be named according to the eleventh article of the armistice which says: *Pacis tractatus (quibus finitis hoc armistitium cum omnibus suis hic positis conditionibus cessat) confestim inchoentur et tempus atque locus hic determinetur,* but that nothing presses, there remaining yet above seventeen years of the twenty for which the truce is made to conclude it in.

[1] See *ante*, p. 148, note 2.

The letter to his Holiness is more moderate than that which is sent with this answer to the Electors, which strives to exasperate them by all ways against his Christian Majesty's proceedings. Notwithstanding all this I find the Empire generally disposed to satisfy his Christian Majesty; especially the three ecclesiastical electors,[1] who by reason of their neighbourhood have more cause to apprehend the consequence of a rupture. Those who are unwilling to comply I believe necessity will bring them to it at last.

I am sensible I trouble your Lordship with things you are much better informed of than myself, but the desire I have not to be wanting in my duty I hope will make you excuse the impertinence of &c.

Ratisbon, 21 Feb./3 March, 1686/7.
My Lord (Middleton):

I have sent your Lordship enclosed, according to my promise in my last, copies of the two memorials in Italian as they were delivered at Rome by the Cardinal d'Estrées, together with the Emperor's answer to them in a Latin letter to his Holiness. The circular letter to the Electors and Princes is in Dutch.[2] It is the same in substance with the Latin, only the epithets are sharper and the expressions stronger in some places. The Imperial commission had a conference the day before yesterday with the Austrian ministers about this business, which we expect will be suddenly deliberated of in the Diet. I am, &c.

Ratisbon, 24 Feb./6 March, 86/7.
My Lord (Middleton):

I send your Lordship enclosed the three decrees of commission which were given in by the Imperial

[1] Of Mayence, Treves, and Cologne.
[2] Dutch, i.e. Deutsch (German).

commission the night before last night to the Director of Mayence, and dictated the next morning in
the Diet. The first is for hastening the treating of the
limits, and what else concerns the execution of the
truce. After this commission had been dictated the
Emperor's ministers pretended to be concerned it
was done so soon, and that they had a design to have
withdrawn it lest his Christian Majesty might take
it ill that this business was pressed before he had
declared whether he was satisfied with the Emperor's answer to his propositions made at Rome.
The French look upon this as a trick to make his
Holiness believe they have still been forward to
treat of the execution of the truce.

By the contents of this commission, and of the
conclusion lately made to treat of these affairs, the
griefs, which have made so much noise, will come
to be treated of and breed all those delays which his
Christian Majesty would have avoided.

As to the sufficient power which the commission
says is come some time ago it is not known whom it
is granted to. If it be to the Count de Windisgratz
alone it will revive an old dispute which will occasion more delay, for the Empire will never consent
it should be otherwise than in the Imperial commission. As for the time of this power's coming
hither, *the some time since*, it is said to be a week or a
fortnight, but it is generally believed it came but by
the last post.

The Count de Windisgratz and Monsieur Scherer
his creature, who treat all the ministers as spies for
the French who have any conversation with Monsieur de Crécy, have vowed the ruin of Monsieur de
Jena,[1] the chief minister of the Elector of Branden-

[1] Godfrey de Jena (1620–1703) was appointed deputy at
Ratisbon in 1662, a place he kept for a quarter of a century.
The clarity and accuracy of his dispatches are remarkable,
and their contents range from secret intrigues to the latest

burg here, and have accused him in a letter to the
Elector: that he should give his suffrage *de speranti*,
that is, in hopes it would be approved by his master;
when there was not long since a guarantee proposed
in that college for securing the observation of the
truce: that it was but reasonable that some caution-
ary towns should be, by the Empire, put into the
hands of his Christian Majesty. But the whole
Electoral College have vindicated him, and the
Chancellor of Mayence has given it under the great
seal of the Empire that it is false, and de Jena has
publicly in the Diet given the lie to those who gave
the information.

The second decree of commission against the
King of Denmark touching the bishopric of Lübeck
is looked upon to be very briskly given by the
Emperor against the King at this time. In the last
war between the French and the Empire the King
of Denmark, being then an ally of the Emperor's
His Imperial Majesty, in part of satisfaction for the
troops he furnished, assigned him winter quarters
in several places among the rest in the lands belonging to the town and bishopric of Lübeck; which
contributions the King of Denmark has yet left
uncollected, having a design to work in time the
family of the Duke of Holstein-Gottorp out of the
possession of that bishopric. That King some time
since demanded a sum of money from the chapter
as due to him upon this account, but at the same time
made them understand underhand that in case they
would choose one of his younger sons coadjutor
in reversion after the Duke of Holstein's two sons

lampoons. His recall in February 1687 was suspended and
he was still officiating at Ratisbon on the death of Frederick
William. In the minister's defence it may be said that he was
probably ignorant of the secret treaty between Brandenburg
and Austria, and that he may have received orders from the
pro-French Meinders at home which did not correspond with
the Elector's wishes. See Introduction, pp. 36–7.

and himself (who are all three already coadjutors, the father having the surveyance of his two sons) they might that way pay the debt; otherwise they must expect the King would make a military execution. The chapter were inclinable, but the Emperor made them know it was against the canon. The substance of the Bishop's letter, which is said to be annexed to this commission, is no other than that the chapter fearing the military execution, which the King of Denmark does not openly threaten, are disposed to grant the King his demands.

The third decree of commission is the approving of the conclusion concerning winter quarters which was joined with the conclusion by which the Roman months were granted. Here are several conjectures what should be meant by the public and laudable example mentioned in this commission; the thing is something obscure, but the true meaning is the Emperor, finding the towns stand upon the dédommagements in the collection of this tax, and that it is necessary he should approve of this conclusion hopes all the towns will follow the good example, which some have shewed which have been wrought upon, and paid without scruple. I am, &c.

Ratisbon, 28 Feb./10 March, 1686/7.

My Lord (Middleton):

I received yesterday your Lordship's circular letter about regulating of extraordinaries.[1] I have been so modest in that point that I cannot think I have contributed anything towards the making of that order.

My being in your Lordship's province recommends me to your care, but I have a better title to it: the many precedents I have of your favour. It is natural to think we are a little hardly dealt with

[1] See *post*, p. 349.

when we are retrenched a bounty we have been used to, though we are conscious of our own want of merit, and I do not doubt but you will represent my condition to the Lords of the Treasury. You know it is very much for me to be three-quarters of a year in arrear in a town where there is no credit.

Nothing has been done in the Diet since my last. The Emperor's ministers have had a private conference, but it is not yet known what is resolved among them.

The Count de Lamberg is not yet returned from Salzburg; the Bishop still continues ill, and though the Emperor's physician, who attends him, says he will re-establish him in his health it is not believed he will recover. I am, with all duty, &c.

Ditto.

Sir (Mr. Wynne):

. . . I have not yet been acquainted with Monsieur d'Albeville's[1] arrival in Holland, though he has writ to Abbot Fleming[2] about regulating his chapel. I suspect his secretary, consul Petit, may have done me some ill office, for he has broke off long since the intelligence he held with us in Mr. Skelton's time, upon my refusing to allow 80 dollars per annum to a friend of his, as he pretended, who was to furnish me with a written gazette from those parts. I did not think I was to be so ill a husband of His Majesty's money.

[1] See *ante*, p. 149, note 2.
[2] Placidius Fleming was the abbot of St. James's, or the Scotch monastery in Ratisbon. His career (1672–1720) was distinguished by able administration, strict discipline, and the organization of a seminary connected with the monastery for the education of young Scotsmen of good family (see *Edinburgh Review* for January 1864). During Hughes's envoyship he engaged in Jacobean intrigues, and the envoy describes him as 'of a most violent, daring humour and as dangerous and desperate as any Jesuit in the world'.

The Marquis d'Albeville's harangue to the States is printed here in French.

Some ministers here who are of the Reformed religion report that my Lord Castelmain,[1] at the magnificent treat he gave to the prelates at Rome, drew a curtain behind which was his Majesty's picture with John Calvin under his feet, drawn so like that he was to be known.[2] I am, &c.

Ratisbon, 3/13 March, 86/7.

My Lord (Middleton):

On Monday, the last of February, a decree of commission, a copy of which I send your Lordship enclosed, was dictated in the Diet, by which the Emperor requires one hundred Roman months of the States of the Empire to enable him to carry on the war against the Turks.

The reason the Imperial commission had to be dissatisfied that the three decrees of commission, which I sent you the last week, were so soon dictated

[1] Roger Palmer, Earl of Castelmaine (1634–1705), husband of the notorious Duchess of Cleveland, mistress of Charles II. An ardent Roman Catholic, he was sent in 1686 as ambassador to the Pope. Macaulay has pointed out the impropriety of entrusting to a man of such unpleasant notoriety a spiritual mission to an austere pontiff. The Pope received him coldly and delayed granting him a public interview. The preparations for the great occasion commenced in Easter 1686, and were only completed the following November. Macaulay describes the procession, the banquet, and the allegorical paintings (one of which represented St. George with his foot on the neck of Titus Oates) which adorned the façade of his palace. The Pope refused the ambassador's request of preferment for the Jesuit Petre; Castelmaine retaliated by circulating a memorial reflecting on the Pope, and was promptly dismissed (Macaulay, *op. cit.* ii. 82–6).

[2] Luttrell reported that letters from Rome spoke of Castelmaine's 'having sett up the armes of the pope and his majestie over his palace at Rome, with several devices of the Catholick religion triumphing over heresy' (*op. cit.* i. 393).

was: that they intended this should have been dictated with them.

The ratification of the conclusion made against taking winter quarters by force gave an insight to what has followed. The ministers here expect instructions from their masters about granting this money, and it is thought they will receive them suddenly; the Emperor doubtless having felt the great ones beforehand.

We have no news yet how his Christian Majesty likes the Emperor's reply to his propositions. Several members of the Diet seem impatient to know it. I find by the Count de Crécy it will not satisfy, it appearing, as he says, by several clauses in it, that the Emperor desires to have his hands at liberty, and his master expecting to be very well secured that nothing shall be undertaken against him when a peace shall happen to be made with the Turk.

The demanding at this time the hundred Roman months makes the French more jealous; they being persuaded his Imperial Majesty does not intend to make above this campaign against the Turk. This money, they say, will come too late to do him any service this summer, and that it seems rather to be a fond provided for some other design.

The Count de Crécy has been sometime collecting into method all that has passed between France and the Empire since the peace of Münster till now. I believe the latter part of it will be made use of to show who has delayed the treating of the execution of the truce. I have found by discoursing with him of the hardness of the propositions, that he was of opinion his master would abate if the Emperor would come fairly to a treaty; for in all manner of dealings more is asked than is thought will be given in order to make a good bargain. There are very few precedents, I think, in history of countries and towns which have been quietly restored by princes to whom they have been granted for a considerable number of years, especially when the situation makes them convenient for them. There was a proposition for a truce made at Rome in the beginning of Henry the Fourth's reign between him and Spain for ten years. But the Cardinal d'Ossat,[1] as appears by a letter of his to his master, would let him by no means consent to it, but stood upon having the towns, which the Spaniards had taken in that war, delivered back and a peace concluded; urging that in the ten years the Spaniards would fortify them so well that they should not be able to retake them. The Empire has fallen into this inconveniency, and what they have yielded for twenty years is already so well fortified that they will have much ado to recover it, let them begin when they please. After this oversight, or this necessity, the difference is not so very great between the securing of the observation of the truce and the making of a peace.

The Emperor intends to have no other auxiliaries this campaign than eight thousand men of the Elector of Bavaria, fifteen hundred of the circle of Swabia,[2] and fifteen hundred of that of Franconia, and the upper Rhine, together in all eleven thousand, but it is thought the Elector's troops will not be complete.

The Empress lay in of a daughter on the 6th instant, new style, and yesterday a decree of commission was dictated to acquaint the Diet with it.

The Elector of Bavaria returned on Saturday last to Munich, and is gone already for Vienna. I am, &c.

Ditto.

Sir (Mr. Wynne):

I must desire the favour of you to acquaint my Lord that Monsieur Valkenier, who was not long

[1] Cardinal Arnaud d'Ossat, French diplomat (1536–1604).
[2] MS. 'Swabe'.

since here from the States of Holland, is coming back with the character of envoy. I formerly acquainted his Lordship with the reasons why I did not visit him; which was chiefly because he had shown great demonstrations of joy upon the report of a victory which the late Duke of Monmouth had got against his Majesty in the West,[1] causing the lie to be printed here, and dispersing it among such as he thought it would be welcome to. It goes against my stomach to have any commerce with such as I know to be no well-wishers to his Majesty's prosperity, wherefore I desire to have orders in this case that I may know better how to behave myself when he arrives. I let my Lord know by a letter I sent him not long since that there was a misunderstanding between the Count de Windisgratz and me and how it happened. The malice which has been used to ruin some ministers of the Diet who live civilly with the Count de Crécy by forging of many lies against them makes me think I ought to be so cautious as to desire nothing may be believed at court to my prejudice till my answer be heard. Though there is a truce between the Empire and France some of the ministers of the Emperor cannot forgive a man who does not live in open hostility with the French; such is the good breeding of this place. My conduct has been to live well with all who have a due regard to his Majesty's *dignity*. My conversation has been impartial, and I have given, according as I have been able, an account of matters without any inclination or favour to either party. I am, &c.

Ditto to Mr. Maule.

The substance of the letter was: that no pleasure but the seeing of him in England could be greater than the receiving of a letter from him; that it is no

---

[1] See *ante*, p. 145, note 1.

new thing to be his debtor, seeing he had neglected one post since he had received his letter;[1] but that it was no less troublesome to write upon duty and neglect writing to him than it is to a wife with whom her husband impertinently employs the kind hour in which she had a rendezvous with her lover. That his letter made him (Sir George) of good humour, and the like favour now and then would render him less sensible of the loss of country and friends; that every line of his letter was full of entertainment but that which charms the most is the assurance of his kindness. That Sir George is fond of being a man of business; that there is a greater reformation in him than he can imagine, and that he is no more guilty of those errors which he has known him commit when necessity had got the better of his judgement; that upon receiving a letter from his Lady and being called rogue at 800 miles distance it makes him cry in consideration of my Lord Mulgrave,[2] *solamen miseris*, &c.

Ditto.

To my Lady thus:

I beg your pardon for undertaking to advise you. I am so well satisfied by your last letter of your prudence and judgement that I shall never more commit the same error. I wish there were copies of it in London, it might serve for a pattern for modest wives to write to their husbands. You shall find me so careful hereafter how I offend you that I will no

[1] For Maule's letter see *post*, p. 352.
[2] John Sheffield, Earl of Mulgrave (1648–1721), was made Lord Chamberlain on the accession of James II. On March 11, 1685/6, he married Lady Conway, whom Luttrell designates as 'a great fortune'. According to Burnet 'he was . . . a man distinguished by fine parts. . . . His moral character was entitled to no respect. He was a libertine without that openness of heart and hand which sometimes makes a libertine so amiable' (*op. cit.* ii. 95).

more subscribe myself your loving, since you take it ill, but Madame
Your most dutiful husband G.E.

Ditto.

Sir (Mr. Corbet):

I am much obliged to you for the favour you did me in delivering a letter I enclosed to you for Mr. Maule. He has sent me one in return, and I leave you to imagine how welcome it was from one whom I so very much esteem, being both extreme pleasant and kind. I have answered his by the last post, but had not time then to satisfy my inclinations in writing to you and cherishing your friendship, which I reckon among those things, which are most dear to me. Besides your other merits the opinion I have of your sincerity makes all that comes from you have more charms than I know in Ratisbon or Nuremberg; and I should have known few solid pleasures since I left England had not your kindness been bountiful to me.

I find a convenience now and then in this country, but can boast as little success in the pursuit of what I have loved as Captain Pack[1] himself; but I have more passive love, and endure the torment without making so much noise; in a word *les badinages* is all the freedom has been allowed me by these sort of mistresses.

I have good greyhounds, and coursing is one of my greatest recreations. We have such plenty of game that now and then I start six brace of hares in

---

[1] Possibly the Captain Pack mentioned in the *Memoirs of the Verney Family*, ii. 448: 'Capt. Bellinger and Capt. Pack fought in Leicester Fields, the former was wounded but parted by Harry Wharton and Mr. Smith.' Thomas Cartwright records in his *Diary* under the date April 20, 1687, that he spoke with Captain Pack at the King's levee, whilst Luttrell notes that he was deprived of his commission on Sept. 8, 1688 (*op. cit*. i. 460).

a day. When I was in Holland I won near two hundred pounds and lost near the same sum at my first coming hither, which has given an occasion for an idle report, as I am informed from London. I have not played at anything but sixpenny ombre these thirteen months, and am rather a winner than a loser since I saw you. I am in a post where I have more business than people believe; and the desire I have to discharge myself as well as I can of my duty, makes me apply my head to it, and has in a manner quite allayed the passion I had for play.

I was very sorry though I did not wonder to hear of Dr. Conquest's[1] indiscretion in the coffee-house. I should be glad if Charles Boyle[2] would play the brave and come this campaign into Hungary that I might show him, though he has forgot me, I am still the same man on his score. If Whitaker would bear him company he should stay and pass the time at chess with me till the warriors returned again, but nothing can be more grateful to me as an occasion to shew you how faithfully I am, &c.

Ratisbon, 7/17 March, 86/7.

My Lord (Sunderland):

I have given my Lord Middleton constantly the best account I have been able of what has been done or discoursed of here, and am confident when there has been anything worth your knowing it has been imparted to you; wherefore I shall not trouble your Lordship with any idle repetitions.

How his Christian Majesty will approve the answer the Emperor has sent to his propositions, and whether the Empire will grant his Imperial

[1] 'Dr. Conquest a popish physitian, having lately spoke words of the prince and princess of Orange, hath occasioned much talk' (Luttrell, *op. cit.* i. 393, Jan. 1686/7.)

[2] Probably Charles Boyle, 2nd son of the Earl of Burlington, afterwards Earl of Clifford.

Majesty the supply of one hundred Roman months which he in a very humble manner desires, are the two businesses which employ everybody's expectations at this time. Monsieur de Crécy by his last letters from Paris, which are not very fresh, finds, as he tells me, his master will insist upon what he has proposed; that it was the Emperor's ministers' own seeking that the treating of a peace was inserted into the armistitia; that the Cardinal Ranucci [1] was put upon making an overture for treating of a peace only to discover what his Christian Majesty's demands would be; which considerations make him more firm in his resolution, joined with the want of sincerity which he pretends to discover daily in all the proceedings of the Emperor's ministers. That if they had not endeavoured to have eluded the treating of the execution of the truce he had not been forced for his own security to have made these propositions, which, however hard they seem, his Christian Majesty says they grant him nothing but what he is in possession of, and has an undoubted right to till the twenty years are expired; in consideration of which he gives up many considerable pretensions he has in the Empire (though it be hard to guess what these pretensions are—now, in case there be a rupture, they will be made out no question). Besides, his Christian Majesty urges that he has sat still and looked on while the Emperor has conquered a whole kingdom, and perfectly secured himself against his ancient enemy the Turk, and that it is but reasonable he should be secured in his turn against those arms whose victories he has favoured.

We are told here, how true it is your Lordship best knows, that Monsieur de Caunitz's chief business in England [2] is to entreat his Majesty to use his good offices to persuade his Christian Majesty to

[1] See *ante*, p. 150, note 2.   [2] See *ante*, p. 126, note 2.

accept of the Emperor's word as a sufficient guarantee for the observation of the truce; his Christian Majesty giving his reciprocally.

By this time you know the full contents of Monsieur Dykvelt's[1] errand. It has been long reported here that one part of it was to know the reason of his Majesty's arming,[2] which to me seems as saucy and impertinent as if a yeoman should send to a gentleman, his neighbour, to ask him why he wears a good sword.

I have writ to my Lord Godolphin and my Lord Dover[3] to beg their favour in the Treasury, but I have but little confidence in my letters and therefore must once more beg your Lordship to speak to them in my behalf. I know the consideration they have for your word, and when they look upon me as your creature it will supply my want of merit. I am, &c.

Ditto.

To Mr. Wynne, desiring to know Count Caunitz's business in England. N.B. a Fr[ench] [?] quest.

[1] Everhard van Veede, Herr van Dykvelt, was dispatched to England in 1687 with orders to expostulate with James II on his policy at home and abroad, and to attempt to bring him to a better understanding with William. He had besides a private mission to the opposition, in which his conduct was guided by instructions drawn up by Burnet. He arranged secret interviews with Devonshire, Halifax, Danby, Shrewsbury and other malcontents, in an endeavour to ascertain their views as to the policy of James. It was as a result of Dykvelt's embassy that William concluded that he must abandon all hope of bringing England into the Continental alliance whilst James II remained on the throne.

[2] Cf. Russell, *Letters*, 1810: ''Tis said the King is not pleased with the Envoy Extraordinary the States are sending over; he is one it seems entirely in the interest of the Prince' (p. 116); and 'he is allowed to be a man of parts and integrity; what his business is, everyone is left to his own guess as yet' (p. 222).

[3] See *ante*, pp. 139–40.

1686/7

My Lord (Middleton):

On Tuesday the 8th instant, new style, the Count de Crécy received the King his master's reply to the memorial given by Monsieur de Lobkowitz about the propositions made at Rome. Everybody here seems to be well satisfied with it, and I am very glad to hear it said the peace of Christendom is secured by his Majesty's mediation. Copies of this have been sent to all Christian courts, and you have had it before it came hither. The Imperial commission have not yet communicated this in form to the Diet, who have done nothing since my last to your Lordship, so that I have nothing more to acquaint you with by this post than that the Count de Lamberg arrived here likewise on Tuesday and that I have an hour this afternoon to visit him.

The most violent spirits here begin already to gain a good temper, and I hope, now there is no danger of the public peace's being broke, the ministers will no longer live in a state of war, and that I may play quietly at cards with the Countess of Crécy without giving the Austrian[1] jealousy.

The design of betraying Buda to the Bassa of Alba Regalis[2] is at large in the gazettes I send to Mr. Wynne. I am, &c.

[1] MS. 'Austrician'.

[2] One Lieutenant Fincke, of Finckenstein, agreed with the Bassa of Alba Regalis to open to the enemy one of the sally-ports of Buda on the night of March 8th for 10,000 ducats. The plot was discovered by a Christian slave who was in the room when the Bassa was discussing the design. This slave being ransomed a few days afterwards, hastened to give an account of what he had heard to Major-General Becke, the governor of Buda, and the traitorous lieutenant was seized. He confessed, but urged that he never intended to perform what he had promised; nevertheless he was executed after torture on April 9th.

Sir (Mr. Dryden):[1]

You know I am no flatterer, and therefore will
excuse me when I tell you I cannot endure you
should arrogate a thing to yourself you have not
the least pretence to. Is it not enough that you excel
in so many eminent virtues but you must be a
putting in for a vice which all the world knows is
properly my province? If you persist in your claim
to laziness you will be thought as affected in it as
Montaigne is, when he complains of the want of
memory. What soul has ever been more active
than your own? what country, nay what corner of
the earth has it not travelled into? whose bosom has
it not dived into and informed itself there so perfectly of all the secrets of man's heart that only the
Great Being, whose image it bears, knows them
better? I, whose every action of *my* life is a witness
of my idleness, little thought that you, who have
raised so many immortal monuments of your industry, durst have set up to be my rival. But to
punish you I will distinguish: you have no share in
that noble laziness of mind which all I write make[s]
out my just title to, but as for that of the body I can
let you come in for a snack without any jealousy.
I am apt to think you have bated something of your
mettle since you and I were rivals in other matters,
though I hope you have not yet obtained the perfection I have heard Sir Charles Sidley[2] brag of:
which is, that when a short youth runs quick through
every vein and puts him in mind of his ancient
prowess, he thinks it not worth while to bestow
motion on his *et caetera muscle*.

[1] MS. 'Dreyden', i.e., John Dryden, the poet. This is in
answer to the letter of Dryden's on p. 265.

[2] Sir Charles Sedley (*c.* 1639–1701), poet, playwright, and
man of wit, notorious for the indecent frolics described by
Pepys (*Diary*, July 1, 1663, and Oct. 23, 1668).

Though I have not been able formerly to forbear playing the fool in verse and prose I have now judgement enough to know how much I ventured, and am rather amazed at my good fortune than vain upon a little success; and did I not see my own error the commendation you give me would be enough to persuade me of it. A woman, who has luckily been thought agreeable, has not reason to be proud when she hears herself extravagantly praised by an undoubted beauty. It would be a pretty thing for a man who has learned of his own head to scrape on the fiddle to enter the list with the greatest master in the science of music.

It is not to contend with you in writing but to vie with you in kindness that makes me fond of your correspondence, and I hope my want of art in friendship will make you forget the faults it makes me commit in writing.

I have not time now to acquaint you how I like my employment. Nature no more intended me for a politician than she did you for a courtier, but since I am embarked I will endeavour not to be wanting in my duty. It concerns me nearly, for, should I be shipwrecked, the season is too far gone to expect another adventure. The conversation I have with the ministers here improves me daily more in philosophy than in policy, and shows me that the most necessary part of it is better to be learned in the wide world than in the gardens of Epicurus.

I am glad to hear your son is in the office; hoping now and then by your favour to have the benefit of a letter from him. Pray tell Sir Henry Shere, his honesty and good understanding have made me love him ever since I knew him. If we meet in England again he may find the gravity of this place has fitted me for his Spanish humour.

I was so pleased with reading your letter that I was vexed at the last proof you gave me of your laziness, the not finding it in your heart to turn over the paper. In that you have had the better of me; but I will always renounce that darling sin, rather than omit anything which may give you an assurance of my being faithfully yours, &c.

Ratisbon, 14/24 March, 86/7.
My Lord (Middleton):
On Friday last the Duke of Lorraine caused a memorial to be delivered to the Diet, a copy of which I send your Lordship with this, which was dictated, and the same day the Diet adjourned till after Easter.

When they meet again I believe the first thing that will be done will be the communicating to them his Christian Majesty's reply to the Emperor's letter sent to him upon his propositions.

The Austrian ministers think it a hard case to be obliged to renounce to their griefs; that which makes them have more repugnance to it is the desire they have to manage the Protestants, whom they think it their interest to court now, as the French kings have thought[1] it theirs formerly. The Swede is very active to keep these griefs awake, having no hopes of getting anything while things are quiet, but doubtless will think it fit to let them sleep at present. So that after all their noise and buzzles[2] about these matters they have, without getting anything, given an occasion for the building of the bridge at Hüningen and the Fort Louis; and repent too late they did not, as they were advised, pursue the war in Hungary without taking notice of what the French did till the[y] found the time more proper. But though they have not mended their affairs they have given his Majesty an occasion to convince the world of the pious and great design he has of preserving the peace of Christendom. I am, &c.

[1] MS. 'thôt'.
[2] Perhaps = bustle. N.E.D. has no record of such a use.

1686/7

Sir (Mr. Skelton):

I received the favour of yours of the 7th instant yesterday, and am very glad to find you open your heart so freely to me. I protest to you upon my *honour*[1] I am so sure of the *innocence of mine*, as to those matters which have been *maliciously* reported of me, that there is not *one thought* which ever passed in it concerning you which *I can wish you should be ignorant of.* I have been so far from being *guilty* of what you have heard of me either in Holland or at Paris that *all honest people* here *can witness* that when you or any of your actions have been talked of I have spoken in *your behalf* with no *less heat* than I could have done had my own *life* or *reputation* been in question. In this I did not only an act of *justice*, but *gratified my own inclination*, which has been, ever since I had the good fortune to be more particularly acquainted with you at the Hague, *to endeavour to deserve your friendship.*

I have always lived without *art* and *dissimulation*, and should not have the *confidence* were I the least *in the wrong* to say so much in my vindication. I have said more to *satisfy* you than I should have done to satisfy one who is indifferent to me. The *esteem and kindness* I have for you make me impatient you should have any jealousy of me, and the greatest favour you can do me will be to *examine this thing to the bottom*. With the news as in the foregoing letter, &c.

Sir (Mr. Vaudry):[2]

Though I naturally love writing as little as you do, yet you had not been so long without being importuned by me, did I not know a letter from hence would be much about as acceptable as

---

[1] This and following italicized words ironically underlined by the secretary.   [2] See *ante*, p. 117, note 6.

of the prius & great Defeui he has of preserving the peace of Christendome. Iam &c.

Dito

Sr (mr Skelton)

I received the favour of yours of ye y Instant
yesterday, and am very glad to find you open
your heart soe freely to me. I protest to you
upon my honor I am so sure of the Innocence of mine as to those matters, wch have
been maliciously reported of me, that there
is not one thought which ever passt in it
concerning you wich I can wish you shou'd
be ignorant of. I have been so farr from
being guilty of what you have heard of me
either in Holland or at Paris, that all honest
people here can witness that when you —

SPECIMEN HANDWRITING OF HUGH HUGHES, ETHEREGE'S SECRETARY
(*From the Letterbook*)

Mademoiselle Regal[1] in London. The fugitive Protestants of Austria, and the pillage you saw at Buda, are very fine booty indeed compared with what you get by rifling[2] in the richest city in the world, setting other matters aside, for beauty!

I am told from the secretary's office that you come this year again into Hungary. I recommend, if it be so, to your care the only happy hour I expect in this country; the seeing you in your journey that way.

In obedience to Mr. Fitzjames I writ to my Lord Taaffe. I wish I could often give him proof of the pleasure I have in obeying him *himself*, and the favours he did me here have so charmed me that I have vowed myself wholly to his service.

The Elector of Bavaria is come back from Vienna to Munich. He assisted, while he was there, several times at the Council of War, in which it has been resolved that the army next campaign shall be divided into two bodies, and that he shall command apart; but this resolution is made with so many restrictions as, in case the Turk with his greatest force makes head in Hungary, or that the Grand Signor comes to command in person &c., that the judicious believe the army will be kept entire, and the Elector disappointed as he was the last year.

We hear not yet of any more than of eleven thousand auxiliaries, viz., three thousand of the troops of the circles, &c. My Lord Taaffe will give you the best account of these matters (of news, viz.), and, if he please, inform you of what projects have been proposed to begin the campaign with. It is impossible they should come so early to my knowledge.

Pray be so kind as to believe no man is more sincerely than myself. . . .

[1] See Vaudrey's letter, p. 358. Hugh Hughes, in a letter dated 2/12 Feb.1692, calls her the Baroness de Royal, and states that she had married the Baron de Metternich, Brandenburg minister for Magdeburg, the previous year.   [2] MS. 'riffling'.

1687

My Lord (Rochester):[1]

Though it has pleased his Majesty, after having given yourself and the world all the honourable marks possible of his being highly satisfied with your prudence and good services, to ease you of many cares, the most painful charge in the kingdom made you hourly labour under, and give you more time to enjoy yourself in the management of which Treasury you will find a more real satisfaction, yet your Lordship can never recover a perfect liberty; you must expect ever to be followed and persecuted by the impertinent acknowledgement of those poor grateful men who have been obliged by your bounty. The share I have had of your favour, and the generous assurance you gave me of it when I left England, have made such an impression in me that I cannot forbear troubling you, without thinking I

[1] On December 17, 1687, Rochester was dismissed from the office of Lord Treasurer with a pension of £4,000 per annum for two lives on the Post Office, and some Irish lands. For some time Rochester's influence had gradually been passing to Sunderland and the Jesuitical cabal. The ecclesiastical commission was instituted against his wishes (though he yielded so far as to consent to serve on it); the Parliament was prorogued indefinitely, in spite of his opposition; envoys were ordered to reserve their important secrets for private communication to the King or Sunderland. Meanwhile Rochester's enemies were persuading James II that the Lord Treasurer was behind the nation's obstinate resistance to his designs, and were filling letters with calumnious assertions. Sunderland finally suggested to the hesitant King that the proof of Rochester's obedience should rest on his willingness to become a Roman Catholic. Rochester, aware of what was at stake, did not scruple to prevaricate and assume the attitude of a man open to conversion. Finally, he promised to do all that the Roman Catholics desired except renounce his religion. James at his dismissal owned that no fault could be found with the way in which Rochester had managed the Treasury, but asserted that it was necessary for the Lord Treasurer to share his own opinions.

neglect my duty. I hope your Lordship will let me see you forgive me this presumption by continuing on all occasions your goodness to me.

Since the arrival of Monsieur de Caunitz your Lordship knows better than I do what has passed concerning the execution of the truce, which has been the only business of moment here. The French expect when the Diet meets again, they being now adjourned till after the holidays, the Imperial commission should communicate in form the reply his Christian Majesty has made to the Emperor's letter sent in answer to the propositions made at Rome. I cannot yet make any judgement what will be done in this matter, but I am apt to think, by the measures I have observed the Emperor's ministers take, they will put off the imparting of it in form as long as they can; they being unwilling the contraventions should die without being examined. They may think fit to let them sleep till they see the success of the next campaign, and accordingly wake them when they please by pretending the Emperor can only answer for himself and not for the States of the Empire who pretend to be grieved. If the French perceive this they will press the communicating of this matter, and his Christian Majesty will desire the word of the States of the Empire as well as the Emperor's to secure the observation of the truce, as he did lately, in the difference between the Elector Palatine and Madame d'Orleans about the possession. When the next campaign is begun and anything happens worth your Lordship's knowledge you shall not fail to have an account of it from, &c.

Ditto.

Sir (Mr. Guy):[1]

I have enclosed a letter for my Lord Rochester, knowing I could not put it into better hands to be

[1] See *ante*, p. 129, note 2.

delivered for my advantage. The experience I have of your favour to me gives me more confidence to trouble you, and gives me at the same time an assurance that you will forgive me.

While all the great and happy seek your friendship, you are generously industrious to find out occasions to oblige the unfortunate. All the return you are like to have from me is only poor acknowledgements while I live, and, when I die, such another legacy as was left you by our friend Thomas Nailer.[1] Mr. Robson has let me know what you have done for me in the Treasury; considering the little leisure you have, and that ceremony is as unsufferable to me as noise was to Morose[2] . . . you have answered me the best way with your money.

Pray make my compliments to my Lord Godolphin and my Lord Dover. I intend to do it suddenly myself, for it is as great a pleasure to me to discharge my duty to the men whom I am obliged to honour as it is to a lover to discharge the impatience he has in his veins on his mistress. Pardon the lasciviousness of my thoughts; my body is become almost as modest as your own, and I know not a woman whose favours I so passionately desire, as I do the opportunity to shew you how faithfully I am, &c.

Ratisbon, 24 March/3 April, 87.

My Lord (Middleton):

On Sunday last, the 27th Martii new style, the Elector of Bavaria arrived at Munich from Vienna. He is returned, as it is said, very well satisfied with the caresses he received there, and the assurance

---

[1] Guy was the residuary legatee to Thomas Naylor, a man of great wealth, who was buried in Westminster Abbey on Nov. 12, 1686.

[2] In Ben Jonson's '*Epicoene, or the Silent Woman*'. The play was revived at the Restoration, Pepys witnessing a performance on Sept. 19, 1668.

which is given him that he shall command the body of an army apart the next campaign. The French laugh at this and say he will be deceived as he was the last year; that you may better judge of this I enclose you a paper of news.

Though it has been given out that the Emperor intends to have no more auxiliaries than the eleven thousand I mentioned formerly, his ministers have solicited the Electors of Saxony and Brandenburg for other troops; but I do not hear yet they have been successful.

The Emperor writ the 8th of March to the circles of Swabia and Franconia to recruit what troops they have, and to raise each of them one or more regiments of foot, which he may make use of in case of need. The Emperor has sent other letters to some Imperial towns to forward them in the instructing of their deputies here for the granting of the hundred Roman months he has desired.

I shall not be able to tell your Lordship till after the holidays how his Christian Majesty's answer is liked, by which he accepts of the Emperor's word for the observation of the truce. I am, &c.

Ditto.

Sir (Mr. Fitzjames):

It is a little confident for a poor man at this distance to put in to make his court to you with the throng of great ones who encompass you at London. Could I have found out a way to have contributed from hence anything towards the advancing of your pleasures I should sooner have congratulated with you all you have enjoyed since your return to England. You have yet but tasted the weak beginnings of that happiness which will daily grow stronger and attend you all your life long. I wonder in an age, and in a place where you have so much business for your love to hear, your ambition is so active to

bring you back to Hungary. Sure some cruel nymph
will not let you snatch a sprig of myrtle till she can
in revenge take her arms full of laurel. If this resolution hold I hope you will not skip Ratisbon in your
journey, nor make any difficulty of coming to an
éclaircissement with me about the secret of it. There
are bright English eyes more fateful than the glittering scimitars of the Turks.

If I have leave now and then to come into your
memory it will be a favour much above the merit of
Sir, &c.

Easter Monday, Ratisbon, 28 March/7 April, 87.
My Lord (Middleton):

My last to your Lordship was of the 24th instant,
and I had no sooner sent it to the post but I learned
the same day the Imperial commission had given
the enclosed decree, which was dictated in the
dictature, a thing which is usual though the Diet be
adjourned.

It is only a bare communication of what has
lately passed between his Christian Majesty and the
Empire. The French seem satisfied with this, the
Emperor tacitly approving what they desire. I had
reason to think they would not have made such
haste to communicate in form his Christian Majesty's
final declaration, they seeming unwilling to give
any distaste to the Protestants, who are most concerned in the complaints which have been made
here of contraventions. But though I was mistaken,
the way the Emperor's ministers have taken may
come to the same end; for by virtue of another
decree of commission, when time shall serve, the
Emperor may desire the States of the Empire to
deliberate on this matter and give their approbation
of it, the present decree of commission being only
to lodge these papers in the Diet. They endeavour
to flatter the Protestants with the hope of this, but

they are ill satisfied, and are suspicious there has passed more between his Holiness the Emperor and the French King than they are acquainted with. The Swedish minister[1] is much out of countenance (to find himself deceived by those, whose secrets he thought nobody knew so well as himself) to find all the pains he has taken about the alliance of Augsburg come to nothing, and that there is no likelihood of any work yet awhile in Christendom for these idle fellows his master has to spare. Some say the States of the Empire are generally dissatisfied that a business of this moment should be only imparted to them after it was determined, and that without asking their approbation. All I can say to this is that I know the French do all they can to maintain a quarrel between them and the council at Vienna. The season is very backward here, which makes me believe the campaign will begin late, though the recruits are ordered to be in Hungary by the middle of May. The Elector of Saxony has excused himself from sending the Emperor any troops this year. The Emperor has a minister at Berlin who is treating for troops as offers a great sum of money, as the Count de Lamberg tells me, but how much this sum is or what men are[2] desired is not yet known, and very few think the negotiation will succeed. I am, &c.

Ratisbon, 9 April, 87.

My Lord (Taaffe):

The favour I have received of your Lordship of the 3rd instant is no less welcome to me here, than an advantage got against the Turks is to you at Vienna. I know there are idle people all the world over, who take too much liberty in talking, which made me never take any notice in my letters into England of what I mentioned to your Lordship,

---

[1] Schnolsky.   [2] MS. 'is'.

especially since it came out of the mouths of Protestants, some of which in this country are as true blue as many of ours. As for the *fierté* of the Count Windisgratz, not to trouble myself to give it a more proper name, the civilities I receive from the Count de Lamberg make over and above up what I lose by it.

Mr. Fitzjames is to be speedily made Duke of Cumberland, some say of Berwick; the Earl of Powis[1] is to be made a marquis; Arthur Herbert[2] is fallen into his Majesty's displeasure upon what account I am not informed. He is a man of a violent temper, open and obstinate to the last degree, and has still been a declared enemy of my Lord Dartmouth's.[3] His place of Master of the Robes is said to be given to my Lord Thomas Howard,[4] his regi-

[1] William Herbert, Earl of Powis (*c.* 1617–96), the head of the Roman Catholic aristocracy in England, was created Viscount Montgomery and Marquess of Powis in 1687. He was moderate and tolerant, and accepted with reluctance the privy councillorship offered him in 1686.

[2] Arthur Herbert, Earl of Torrington (1647–1716). James II appointed him rear-admiral of England and Master of the Robes 1685, counting on his support as M.P. for Dover for the repeal of the Test Act. Herbert refused to comply and was dismissed from all his employments. 'He was indeed a man abandoned to luxury and vice. But, tho' he was poor, and had much to lose, having places to the value of £4,000 a year, he chose to lose them all rather than to comply' (Burnet, *op. cit.* ii. 365). Burnet's estimate of Herbert's character confirms Etherege: 'he was upon every occasion so sullen and peevish, that it was plain he set a high value on himself, and expected the same of all others'. His private quarrel with Dartmouth, 'who, he thought, had more of the King's confidence than himself, was believed the root of all the sullenness he fell into towards the King' (*op. cit.* ii. 491–2).

[3] George Legge, Baron Dartmouth (1647–91), under James II became master of the horse and governor of the Tower, and in 1688 was given chief command of the fleet.

[4] Lord Thomas Howard, Lieutenant of the West Riding, and a rigid Roman Catholic, was sent ambassador to Rome 1688.

ment of foot to my Lord Hunsdon,[1] that of rear-admiral the King keeps in his own hands.[2]

Since the Diet has been adjourned by reason of the holidays the Imperial commission have given a decree which was dictated in the dictature, by which his Imperial Majesty has communicated to them all that has passed in the business of the truce between him and the French King. I believe it is in order to prepare them for the granting the hundred Roman months, which are desired.

I wish it were in my power to give you daily proofs how faithfully I am, &c.

Ratisbon, 31 Mar./10 Apr., 87.

My Lord (Middleton):

Having at present no business of the Diet to trouble you with I have made choice of this time to acquit myself of a promise I made some time since to the Abbot of the Scots Benedictines[3] here. Your Lordship knows by experience how impossible it is for any of our country to be in this place without being very much obliged to him, his greatest care, next to that which he has for his cloister and matters of religion, being to do good offices to strangers. I am confident to tell your Lordship no news when I acquaint you that his piety, his courtesy, his industry, and his good husbandry are the wonder of all who know him and the poor condition of his monastery; and I do not doubt but your Lordship will be very glad to have an occasion to give him a

[1] Robert Carey, Baron Hunsdon, son of Sir Horatio Carey, succeeded to the peerage in 1677. He became the colonel of an infantry regiment in Ireland.

[2] Luttrell reports (February 1686/7) that Sir Roger Strickland had succeeded Herbert as vice-admiral. His official appointment dates from Oct. 30, 1687.

[3] Abbot Fleming; see *ante*, p. 156, note 2. He had been granted a bounty of the value of fifty guineas on Dec. 26, 1685 (*Secret Service Expenses of Charles II and James II*).

proof of your favour. The monastery, you know,
bears his Majesty's name, and was founded by
Prince William, brother to Achaius, King of Scots,
in the time of Charlemagne.[1] It has been richly
endowed, but was so ruined in the long war, in
which the Swedes made such havoc in the Empire,[2]
that it has not now above one hundred pounds a
year left to maintain the Abbot and the religious
men, which nevertheless are kept up to the number
of twelve. A little after my arrival here the bishop
of this place and Freisingen,[3] died, and Prince
Clement, brother to the Elector of Bavaria,[4] who
is now about fifteen years of age, was made bishop
of the two bishoprics. The temporals, which are
three score and ten thousand crowns a year (that
of Ratisbon being twenty, and that of Freisingen
fifty), are put into the hands of commissioners,
and will remain so for ten years, to be disposed
of by his Holiness to pious uses. The most considerable part of this revenue is given to the Elector
towards the maintenance of his troops during
the war against the Turks, but there is yet so much

[1] The Church of St. James, or the Scotch Church in Ratisbon, derived its name from the monastery of Irish Benedictines
(i.e. Scots) to which it was attached. The usual legend of its
foundation is that one Marianus left Ireland on a pilgrimage
to Rome and stopped on his way at Ratisbon. Here he was
directed by the Hermit Muriherdach to pray for direction as
to whether he should continue his journey or remain where
he was. In a dream he was desired to spend the remainder of
his days in Ratisbon, and on coming out of St. Peter's church
rays of the sun struck his eyes, finally determining him to give
up his pilgrimage. The Abbess Wila consigned the church
to the Scots monks, who added thereto a monastery.

[2] In 1633 the Swedes under Bernhard von Weimar forced
Ratisbon to surrender, after a short siege, and ravaged the
town.

[3] MS. 'Frizing'.

[4] Prince Joseph Clement of Bavaria (1671–1723), son of the
Elector Ferdinand, was chosen Elector and Archbishop of
Cologne in 1688.

indisposed of as will over and above answer the
modest desires of the Abbot, which are only to
have a small pension ordered him by his Holiness
during those ten years towards the repairing of his
monastery, which is much ruined, and the putting
him and his religious out of that *miserable wanting
condition they are now always in.* The Cardinal of Norfolk[1] is his friend, and will favour him in all he can,
and does not doubt, if his Majesty would by a gracious letter appoint him to make use of his name
to his Holiness, but the thing would be granted.
The Abbot as well as myself refer this wholly to
your Lordship to judge whether it be convenient
to move his Majesty in it, and beg the favour that
you will order Mr. Wynne to acquaint us with your
Lordship's opinion. I am, &c.

Sir (Mr. Wynne):   Ditto.

The enclosed to my Lord is about a business
which concerns my Lord Abbot Fleming. Neither
myself nor he do question but if there be occasion
you will contribute all the good offices you can.
I have desired my Lord to appoint you to make us
know what is his opinion in the matter. If his Lordship thinks fit to acquaint his Majesty with it, and
that his Majesty will be graciously pleased to order
a letter to be sent to the Cardinal of Norfolk about
it, pray let it be enclosed to me that I may give it to
the Abbot to be sent accordingly. I question not
but my letter will be communicated to you, which
makes me say no more but that it would be pity
so ancient a monument of the piety of the princes
of our island should go to decay for want of a little
charitable assistance.

[1] Philip Howard, called Cardinal of Norfolk (1629–94),
third son of Henry Howard, Earl of Arundel, became Cardinal
Protector of England and Scotland in Rome and chief adviser
to the Holy See in matters relating to Great Britain.

1687

The Diet assembled yesterday, but all that was done was the putting off of the business of the hundred Roman months for eight days longer.

A letter I had from my Lord Taaffe of the 3rd of April, new style, tells me the Duke of Lorraine was expected at Vienna in four or five days to confer about the operations of the next campaign.

We have frost, snow, and hail here, and our Easter this year is as cold as your Christmas is usually. I am, &c.

Ratisbon, 31 March, 87.

My Lord (Chamberlain):[1]

Never lover was more agreeably surprised with the favour of his mistress than I have been with the letter you have done me the favour to send me.[2] I am yet too[3] overjoyed, though it is three days since I received it, that my mind has not regained the temper which is necessary to make you a reasonable answer. You must excuse therefore the impertinences of what I write, as women do the imperfect speeches of those who love too well to express themselves handsomely. The pleasure you have given me makes me forgive the malice you have shewed in putting me in mind of my being old. I have always by my way of living taken care to banish age from my thoughts, and what have I done to provoke your envy, who are young and vigorous, to remember me that I bear a burthen on my [back][4] humour makes me insensible of? It is but seldom I have had occasion in this grave place to draw my bow, and when I have I did not perceive my nerves were slackened. You should quietly have let me alone till age had surprised me and not have wounded my imagination with your raillery. You are

[1] Lord Mulgrave; p. 161, note 2.
[2] See *post*, pp. 357–8.
[3] MS. 'to', perhaps, for 'so'.   [4] MS. 'back' deleted.

more cruel than the murderers of Caesar; they gave him the death he wished, but you have attempted to make me old against my will. Nevertheless since my time cannot be long I will prepare myself for taking my leave of the pleasures of this world by being in charity with you, and wishing the happiness you enjoy may be daily increased, though none besides yourself can think it uncomplete. When the ladies know me to be good for nothing it will be a comfort to me if I can find opportunities to assure you that I am, &c.

Ratisbon, 4/14 April, 87.

My Lord (Middleton):

My last to your Lordship of the 31st of March was about a business which concerns Abbot Fleming. He tells me when he was in England you would have advised him to ask his Majesty's letter to the Pope, rather than to the Elector of Bavaria, which cost him the trouble and charge of a long journey to no purpose. He hopes your Lordship will think fit to move his Majesty in what he humbly desires now, it being only his Majesty's letter to the Cardinal of Norfolk to give him authority to use his Majesty's name to his Holiness in his behalf.

There has happened a difference between two Protestant princes of the Empire lately; the Elector of Brandenburg and the Duke of Zell, touching a commandery called Gartau,[1] which lies on the Elbe. This commandery, as it is said, has always been held of the house of Brunswick, and when it was alienated by the Knights of Malta they were acknowledged as lords, and all into whose hands it has come since have ever owned them as such. The present possessor, a gentleman whose name is Beulau, is a subject of the Elector of Brandenburg, and was summoned by him to come and do him fealty for

[1] Gartow in Hanover, not far from Wittenberg.

183

this commandery, the Elector pretending that all the commanderies in the Empire which are in the hands of Protestants depend of him as their great prior or master. Beulau, though strictly charged to the contrary by the Duke of Zell, has acknowledged the Elector his lord, and the Elector in a solemn hunting, according to the custom here, to set out his limits included these lands. The Duke of Zell, at the same time, put a company of foot into the house to keep the possession, and lodged three or four more companies thereabout to support them in case they should be attacked. The Duke of Zell has since writ a letter to the Elector in such high terms that they have both given order to their troops to march towards the said commandery.

The Duchess of Hanover [1] is now at Berlin, and it is thought she may facilitate the making up of this business. The occasion of her journey thither is to compose another difference, which is between the Prince Electoral and his wife, her daughter, which I am trusted with as a secret.

The French have been some time ill satisfied with the Elector of Brandenburg's conduct as to their affairs, and have broke off the secret alliance they had with him, and disappointed him of a sum of money which would have been welcome at this time. I am, &c.

Ratisbon, 7/17 April, 87.

My Lord (Middleton):

The Diet have not done anything since the holidays. The day before yesterday we received the news of the death of Louis Marquis of Brandenburg; he died of a violent fever at Potsdam on

[1] Sophie, Duchess of Hanover (1630–1714), the twelfth child of the Elector Palatine Frederick V; her daughter, Sophie Charlotte, married Prince Frederick of Brandenburg in 1686.

Easter Monday. He wanted about six weeks of twenty-one years old. The Electoral Prince is still indisposed, and it is thought he may languish some time, but will never perfectly recover; these two are the only princes which remained of the first bed.[1] Louis was married to the heiress of the house of Radsville[2] in Lithuania, and has left without children the richest and the handsomest widow in the Empire.

The affliction the court of Brandenburg is in upon this misfortune has made them neglect instructing the Elector's ministers here in the difference about Gartau which I mentioned in my last, and hindered me from sending you a copy of the letter writ by the Duke of Zell to the Elector, which would have given you a perfect insight into all the disputes which are between them. It is reported here they are as good as composed, but one of the Elector's ministers told me yesterday there were great endeavours used, but it was not yet effected.

The Elector of Bavaria and all that court are gone to Lemsberg,[3] where he will stay and heron-hawk till the end of this month, and then return to Munich. His minister at Vienna has obtained of the Emperor three hundred thousand florins, which is to be paid

[1] The Margrave Louis was the second son of the Elector's first marriage with Louise Henriette of Orange. The second Electress, Dorothea of Brunswick, tried to force her husband to give her son the advantage over her stepsons. Hence when Louis died suddenly in the midst of an attack of scarlet fever his elder brother, the Prince Electoral Frederick, attributed his death to poison administered by his stepmother or her confidante, the Duchess of Holstein-Weisenberg. Apprehensive that another dose was being prepared for him he hastily left Potsdam, together with his wife, and retired to Cassel. An inquest was held, but no crime was discoverable. The event gave rise to a conflict between the Elector and his son, which was not settled until November 1687.

[2] The daughter and heiress of Prince Radziwill of Poland.

[3] Probably Lemberg, a village in the Palatinate, three miles east of Pirmasens.

to the Elector when he comes thither towards the defraying the charges of the campaign.

I do not hear the Emperor has yet agreed for any other auxiliaries than those I have already spoke of. I am, &c.

Ratisbon, 11/21 April, 87.

My Lord (Middleton):

The instructions the ministers have received, concerning the hundred Roman months which have been demanded, are so various, some of their principals limiting them to twenty, others to thirty, none exceeding fifty, that the Imperial commission do not think it fit this matter should be yet deliberated on in the Diet.

Some spirits here have been disturbed upon the news of his most Christian Majesty's intending to visit Luxemburg this spring, but, upon receiving copies of the letter which he commanded Monsieur de Croissy to write to Cardinal Ranucci about that journey, they were quieted again.

It is said here Mr. de Lobkowitz will have order to deliver another memorial to the French King, desiring an explanation of part of the last paragraph of his Majesty's answer to his last memorial; by which it is implied the contraventions should not be examined, and it is likely it is done already. This will be known to your Lordship before it can come to us. The Emperor's ministers are very unwilling[1] the griefs which have made so much noise should be wholly abandoned, or at least seem so to satisfy their confederates of the alliance of Augsburg and to remove the apprehensions of the Protestants whom they may have need of; for I have reason to doubt, by what I know of men and matters here, that it is possible[2] the truce should be kept, though it linger out some time longer.

MS. 'unwillingly'.   [2] MS. 'impossible'.

The Emperor, by a letter to the circle of Swabia, desires 4,000 men of them this campaign (which is the same number they furnished the last), and that they may be in Hungary by the 15th of May. The Diet of the circle of Franconia is to meet on the fourteenth of this instant. I am, &c.

Ditto.

My Lord (Duke of Berwick):[1]

I have received with much joy the news of his Majesty's creating you Duke of Berwick. You had no need of a title to make you great; the care nature has taken in forming of your mind and body has made you eminently so, and you alone can make yourself greater by the way you take to improve your virtues. Nevertheless the glittering favours of fortune are necessary to entertain those who, without examining any deeper, worship appearances. Besides, she is a mistress you are resolved to court, and it is a pleasure to have her kind. May she always lead you by the hand and never let you make a false step to disoblige her.

The same letters confirm to me your coming into Hungary again. Though you are cruel to the ladies in England in depriving them of the only delight of their eyes I hope you will be good-natured to a poor man who reckons on the happiness of seeing you. Let the convenience of the Danube move you in my behalf; it will be as sensible [an] affliction as can touch me to lose the least opportunity of giving you a proof how faithfully I am, My Lord,

Your Grace's, &c.

Ratisbon, 14/24 April, 87.

My Lord (Middleton):

The circle of Swabia in their general assembly have shewed themselves unwilling to give the

---

[1] James Fitzjames had been created Duke of Berwick, Earl of Teignmouth, and Baron Bosworth.

hundred Roman Months, and there is such an indisposition in the other States of the Empire as to this matter that I believe it will not be proposed again yet awhile.

The design of delivering another memorial to his Christian Majesty to desire him to explain himself about the contraventions which I mentioned in my last of the 11th instant, is come to nothing; it being either a project of the Count de Windisgratz, which is not approved at Vienna, or not thought convenient now that King intends to visit Luxemburg.

The Elector of Bavaria comes to-morrow to Straubing,[1] seven miles from hence, where he meant to have taken a review[2] of his troops, but being informed that in this season it would do much harm to the country he has ordered them to be drawn thither by degrees, and to be embarked both horse and foot on the Danube, and their general rendezvous to be at Pressburg. After two or three days' diversion in coursing, for which that country is proper, the Elector returns to Munich. There has been a great noise in the court at Berlin about the death of Prince Louis, it being the general opinion there he was poisoned.[3] That which gave the ground for this suspicion was the virulence of the matter which came from him after his death, which not only stained but ate[4] into silver; but upon opening of him it is said the physicians found it was an impostume which broke within him. It was affirmed here the Duchess of Hanover[5] had made a journey to this court, which I took notice of formerly to your Lordship, but I cannot believe, no letters having spoke of it since, that she has been there.

[1] A town on the right bank of the Danube, twenty-five miles south-east of Ratisbon. Etherege was probably reckoning German miles. [2] MS. 'reveue'.
[3] See *ante*, p. 185, note 1. [4] MS. 'eat'.
[5] See *ante*, p. 184, note 1.

The Duke of Hanover, with a very magnificent train, goes this spring to Aix-la-Chapelle to drink the waters.

There has been a new conspiracy in both the Hungaries in which Caraffa[1] has run great dangers of his life, but we know not yet the particulars. I am, &c.

Ratisbon, 18/28 April, 87.

Sir (Mr. Corbet):

Yesterday your letter of the 30th of March came to my hands, and gave me a pleasure which nothing but the like proof of your kindness can give me here. If my ghost be as restless when I am in the other world as my mind is now I am in another country, my friends must expect to be much haunted; it will cost them some frights, and, it may be, some money to lay me.

There is not a day but my thoughts dog you from the coffee-house to the play, from thence to Marylebone,[2] always concerned for your good luck, and in pain I cannot make one with you in the sports you follow. Some of the ancients have imagined that the greatest torment of the dead was an impatient longing after what they delighted most in while they were living, and I can swear by my damnation in Germany, this hell is no jesting matter. Now Mr. B— is promoted I hope Mr. Swan will be mounted. I am sorry on so good an occasion I have not a quibble in my head which would pass muster. I pity Mrs. Debora's loss in Mr. Whitaker's being gone to board in another quarter; if he happens into

[1] Antony, Count of Caraffa, commanded in Upper Hungary. He captured Munkács and received the Order of the Golden Fleece for his part in the storming of Belgrade. Etherege alludes to his discovery of a new rebellion about to break out in Hungary; the conspirators were apprehended and the four leaders executed.

[2] MS. 'Marribone', where there was a famous bowling green.

a house with Mr. Crown[1] John's songs and Joseph's voice will charm the whole family.

I find the colonel is resolved to blaze to the last as well as myself. Methinks I see in a triumph of our present loves a Cupid, for fear of burning his fingers, with a little piece of a torch on a saveall. He has beauty, the strongest cordial to keep up his spirits; I have only a plain Bavarian with her sandy coloured locks, brawny limbs, and a brick complexion, and yet I find myself often very hearty.

Pray remember me kindly to all my friends, and particularly to Tom Maule. I am very sensible of the trouble the correspondence you have with me gives you. I shall not tire you with any tedious acknowledgements, but only assure you you oblige one who cannot be ungrateful and is extremely

Sir, &c.

Ditto.

My Lord (Middleton):

The Diet meet daily though nothing is done. The business of the Austrian ministers when they are assembled is to dispose them to grant the hundred Roman months, in which they meet with more difficulties than they imagined. The Electors, though they give nothing themselves but are only to seem well inclined to draw in the other States of the Empire, nevertheless some of them, as the Elector of Saxony, and it is thought the Elector of Brandenburg too, will not shew their good inclinations but upon conditions which are very hard to the Emperor. I believe all the reformed princes will endeavour what they can to necessitate him to make peace with the Turk in a short time, that the Empire may be in a condition to turn their arms that way

---

[1] John Crowne, the dramatist. The most popular of his plays was the comedy *Sir Courtly Nice*, 1685. He contributed some songs to Motteux's *Gentleman's Journal*, 1691–2, which were set to music by Henry Purcell.

which they judge most for their interest. Several of the princes and the whole College of the Towns, who find they are the dupes in this matter, vigorously oppose it.

The business which they talk of deliberating of next is the abuses about the money, which are indeed very scandalous; some princes, especially Anhalt[1] and Saxon-Gotha, having coined new florins whose intrinsic values are not the third part of what they should be. This has made the town of Nuremberg put forth a prohibition against those florins, and the Prince of Saxon-Gotha has writ a very sharp and threatening letter to the town on this occasion.

The Emperor, who desired at first but fifteen hundred men of the circles of Franconia and the upper Rhine, and as many of the circle of Swabia, for this campaign, has since desired the same number they furnished the last. As I have writ to you formerly, I know not of any success yet his ministers who solicit troops in several courts within the Empire have had. The general rendezvous is appointed to be the 15th of May, and it is said there will be a body of an army detached to secure the new conquests on the Drave; we know nothing more of what is intended this summer. I have sent an extract of a letter and other letters of news to Mr. Wynne to be communicated to you. I am, &c.

Ratisbon, 25 Apr. / 5 May, 87.

My Lord (Middleton):

The Austrian ministers here continue endeavouring to dispose the Diet to grant the Roman months which have been desired. The last week they proposed to Mr. Sawer, the Bishop of Bamberg's deputy, who is their agent in most matters, to have it deliberated on in the College of Princes, but he

[1] Prince John George of Anhalt, the brother-in-law of the Elector of Brandenburg.

told them he was yet so doubtful of any success that it would do better to defer it longer. The Swedish minister, Monsieur Schnolsky, has at length received instructions in this matter, and bawls out he is ready to give the whole hundred, or one hundred and fifty if they had been demanded. In the meantime the Imperial commission, who think it would look ill if they should get nothing, would be glad if they could compass half.

The Count de Lamberg tells me the Emperor's troops are complete, not only the horse but the foot, and that by the prudence and industry of the officers the recruits consist all of good men fit for service. The Elector of Bavaria has made a review of his recruits at Straubing, and his men begin to embark there the 2nd of May, new style, and will be all embarked by the 16th for the general rendezvous in Hungary. We hear not that the Emperor's minister in the court of Brandenburg[1] has obtained any troops for this campaign. That Elector has recalled the commission which he gave to inquire into the manner of the death of his son, the Prince Louis. The humour which was taken out of his stomach and put on a silver plate ate[2] quite through it. It is believed all over Germany he was poisoned, and the dose is said to have been given him in a dish of coffee.

I asked the Count de Lamberg what had been done in the treaty with the Muscovite ambassadors at Vienna, but he told me he knew not, it being kept secret; the Emperor to that purpose naming those who have negotiated with them. He told me the envoy which was sent from Poland, as he believes, was chiefly to find out and give an account of what should be concluded with these ambassadors,

---

[1] Baron Francis Henry, of Fridag, one of the cleverest Austrian diplomats of the day, had been sent to the Brandenburg court in the spring of 1685.   [2] MS. 'eat'.

though it is said here that envoy came to desire the Emperor to supply the King his master[1] with money towards the carrying on the war against the Turks and to join with him in the conquest of Transylvania, which that King would have in recompense for saving Vienna and the hereditary provinces;[2] and that he asks this by the instigation of the Protestants in Hungary who border on that country and hope to find him less severe to them than the Emperor. I am, &c.

Ratisbon, 28 April / 8 May, 87.

My Lord (Middleton):

It was concluded in the assembly of the circle of Swabia, the 30th of April, new style, that the sum of what it has cost this circle in contributing these four years last past to the war against the Turks should be cast up and sent to their deputy at Ratisbon to be shewn to the Diet, and that, on this consideration, they would not give anything towards the hundred Roman months which are desired. This is an ill precedent and is like to do much prejudice to this matter. This tax by the number of months and the noise it makes one would think, should it be granted, would bring in millions, but I am assured by a person who is to be believed that the letters he has received from the chief officers of the Treasury own no more came into the Emperor's coffers of the fifty Roman months last granted, than[3]

---

[1] MS. 'Mr'.

[2] John Sobieski, King of Poland, had marched to the relief of Vienna, at the urgent call of the Duke of Lorraine, with 26,000 men, and was in supreme command at the battle which saved the city on Sept. 12, 1683. After this achievement he was able to do little to assist in driving the Turks back, hampered as he was by domestic troubles, pro-French intrigues among his nobles, and the pro-French sympathies of his wife.   [3] MS. 'and'.

one hundred thousand crowns; this is not strange considering that the great ones only give in form to draw in others, and that the towns insisted on dédommagements.

The Elector of Bavaria, in consideration that the Emperor has refused to let him march his cavalry through his country, has refused to give the circle of Swabia leave to march their cavalry through Bavaria, though the circle made use of the letter which the Emperor writ in their behalf to desire the favour of the Elector. The circle have acquainted the Emperor with this, and we shall know suddenly how the matter will be adjusted. The charge, if they are obliged to embark them on the Danube, will come to three score thousand florins. The Emperor's ministers say the Elector has no reason to refuse the passage on that account since the charge he has been at in embarking his horse was considered in the three score thousand florins which his minister has obtained at Vienna.

The next week the two regiments of foot of Swabia are to pass through this town, and 450 men of the circle of Franconia, being the recruits they send to their troops who have quartered this winter in Hungary.

The Elector of Brandenburg and the house of Brunswick have made their complaints and given in their pretences about Gartau to the Diet, but they intend not to meddle with it, saying it is more properly a law suit and ought to be brought before the Chamber of Spire;[1] though these Princes were very hot and gave order to their troops to march, there is no fear of bloodshed; the Protestant interest will amicably decide this quarrel. I am, &c.

I just now received the news of the Bishop of Salzburg's death, which may occasion some changes

[1] The German supreme court was located at Spire in Bavaria.

here, the poor Prince of Passau having quite lost his memory.

Ditto.

Sir (Mr. Wynne):

On Tuesday last the Count de Lamberg came to see me, and shewed me a letter which he had received that day from the Count de Caunitz, his cousin, three days fresher than yours of the 8th of this instant, which came to my hands on Sunday. He tells us the Duke of Berwick comes into Hungary; if he does pray let me know when he leaves you that I may the better judge at what time he may pass by here in case he comes this way. The Count de Lamberg would fain have a good English gelding[1] of about £50 or £60 price, and has desired me to write to somebody who has an interest to let one be bought and brought with the Duke's equipage. He, as well as myself, believes this letter will come too late, if it does not pray beg the favour of Mr. Vaudrey, and tell him besides the obliging the Count and me the gelding will be a good letter of exchange at Ratisbon, and that, as it is but reasonable, we will stand to all accidents.

Another part of Mr. de Caunitz's letter say[s] some of the spiteful people of this place have written something to do me ill offices. I know it is not unlikely, being well acquainted with the Count de Windisgratz's nature. Pray endeavour to find out what this is. His Majesty did not send me hither to make my court to the proud and fantastic humour of any man, but to live well with all, and to give an impartial account of affairs, and I have carried myself with that civility and moderation that nothing but a malicious lie can do me any harm. I am.

[1] English horses were in great esteem in the seventeenth century. Chamberlayne (*State of England*, 1684) boasted that 'for war, for coach, for highway, for hunting, there are nowhere such plenty of horses'.

1687

My Lord (Middleton):

We know not here anything of what has passed in the Council of War at Vienna touching the designs at the opening of this campaign; it is kept so secret that what has been talked of is but by conjecture. I cannot believe the Emperor's army will be so considerable this year as it expected, for the Count de Lamberg two days since told me the letters he has lately received are so differing concerning the recruits of the infantry that he does not know what to think of the business, whether they are well restablished[1] or no. The Elector of Brandenburg has promised to furnish the Emperor with some troops in case they could agree on the conditions, and the Emperor's minister in that court was treating when the Elector excused himself on the difference which happened about Gartau, and, though it is not like to have any evil consequence now, I do not hear that that treaty goes forward.

The news here is that Mr. de Schomberg[2] coming to Berlin, the Elector has made him feldmarschal or lieutenant-general of all his troops and governor of Prussia, which he has accepted, and that he intends to make this campaign in Hungary as a volunteer. The Duke of Lorraine is very glad of this, but others who fear his criticisms are very much alarmed.

The business of the Roman months advances but

[1] An old alternative form of 're-established'.

[2] Frederick, Duke of Schomberg (c. 1615–90), born at Heidelberg, became a French subject. He was made Marshal of France, but quitted his adopted country on the Revocation of the Edict of Nantes 1685. He was invited to Berlin by the Elector of Brandenburg, and, with the consent of Louis XIV, accepted the position of general of all the Brandenburg forces and the governorship of Prussia. Schomberg joined William of Orange on his expedition to England, and was killed at the battle of the Boyne.

slowly, and the Austrian ministers have hitherto
endeavour[ed] in vain to get a casting voice, though
that will not do their business according to an
article in the treaty of Münster, by which it is provided that no State of the Empire shall be taxed but
by its own particular consent; this was then promoted by the French and Swedes to lessen the power
of the Emperor.

The Elector of Bavaria has desired of his bailiffs,
and all other his civil officers, a loan of one hundred
thousand crowns, to supply his occasions this campaign, which they have with heavy hearts consented
to.

The Count de Lamberg expects daily orders from
the Emperor to go to the Election at Salzburg,
where there is already in the chapter great briguing.
I am, &c.

Ratisbon, 5/15 May, 87.

My Lord (Middleton):

Since my last of the 2nd instant, I have seen a
letter which Mr. de Rébenac,[1] the envoy of France
at Berlin, has writ to the Count de Crécy, in which
he says that the Elector has made Mr. de Schomberg
general of all his troops and given him an absolute
power; that he has a regiment of dragoons, with
a pension of twelve thousand crowns a year, is made
governor of Prussia, and is admitted to the secret
council. This the maréchal has accepted of, provided it may be with his most Christian Majesty's
good liking. The Elector has spoke to the envoy
to move the King in this, urging he cannot give a
better proof of his intention to maintain a good
correspondence with him, and of his having no
design to employ his forces against his interest, than

---

[1] François de Pas, Comte de Rébenac, envoy extraordinary
from France to Brandenburg. He was ambitious and arrogant and by his contemptuous and haughty attitude did much
to quicken the animosity of the Elector against the French.

by putting them so absolutely into the power of a
maréchal of France so renowned for his fidelity.

As to the design Mr. de Schomberg is said to have
of going into Hungary, it is news the Count de
Windisgratz has received from Vienna which I
cannot yet confirm.

The circle of Swabia have sent their last resolution to the Emperor and the Elector of Bavaria,
which is that they will forthwith disband their
cavalry in case the Elector persist to refuse them
passage; they expect an answer to this.

Though there is yet a talk of dividing the army,
the Emperor having no more auxiliaries than those
I have formerly mentioned, I believe it a thing
unpracticable. It is not known what is resolved in
the Council of War, but it is most likely some small
detachment will be sent towards the Drave to secure
the places which were taken at the latter end of the
last campaign, and that this will open with the siege
of Alba Regalis. &c.

Ditto.

Sir (Mr. Wynne):

I was last night with the Abbot Fleming, with
whom I drank your health. We hope you will not
neglect soliciting my Lord about obtaining his
Majesty's letter to the Cardinal of Norfolk, and will
take care to let us know what is resolved in the
business.

The Count de Lamberg, who went from hence
yesterday for Salzburg to the election, which is now
briguing there, shewed me a letter from Mr. de
Caunitz to him, in which he owns the Count de
Windisgratz had writ to him concerning me. Nobody can imagine the pride and malice of that man,
who esteems himself the emperor of this place, and
cannot suffer any one who will not neglect all
besides to cringe to him. This I do not think becoming

a person whom his Majesty employs. The only pique he has to me is because I would not play the fool to please him; he has endeavoured to play me many mean tricks as: to hinder me from the liberty of coursing, to make my footmen be enrolled by officers who have made levies here, but I have had the good luck to get the better of him in all, and now we live on the foot of a cold civility. I only mention this to you that you may give me notice in case anything should be spoken to do me a prejudice, not that I have reason to fear any ill office from Mr. de Caunitz, who seems to believe the character his kinsman the Count de Lamberg gives of me rather than that he had from the Count de Windisgratz.

I have not yet had an account of my pension from those I employ to receive it. Pray present my service to the Privy Purse and tell him I am very sensible of his favour. I am sorry I am in a post where I can only return him a compliment for it. I am, &c.

Ratisbon, 9/19 May, 1687.

My Lord (Sunderland:)

Though the Diet and I cannot agree in all things in one thing we are very well met; they are as idle and, it may be, as negligent as I can wish to be, they seldom have much business, and have the best art of spinning out a little to all the advantage of loss of time. No schoolboy is more fond of a holiday, and they have the pleasure of keeping them double by reason of the two religions professed. This was a fine place for your Lordship to choose to send me to correct the laziness of my nature, but yet you have not quite lost your aim; the sense I have of your benefits has so spurred me up that I have twice a week given the best account I have been able to do of what has passed in the Empire, which begins to beget in me such a relish of business that I should be more vain of making a good dispatch than of writing a witty letter. I shall endeavour by fitting myself for this to show my gratitude to your Lordship. I know it will be more acceptable than any dull acknowledgements I can make.

I find in the news I received yesterday from England that his Majesty, upon the death of the Duke of Bucks,[1] intends to give your Lordship the garter.[2] I have never known you ambitious of anything but of serving him well, which assures me this is a voluntary act of his favour; honours of this kind cannot make any great impressions of joy in you, but since they are not the unhappiest, nor it may be the unwisest, who can please themselves with toys, I wish you may be as fond of it as some I have known, and that you may wear it with as much pleasure as I have done in my younger days the favours of a mistress. Your goodness makes me so much belong to you that I share in all the good fortune that befalls you, and there is always self-interest in the case when your prosperity is wished by, &c.

Ditto.

My Lord (Middleton):

The Elector of Bavaria has not yet sent an answer to the last message which was sent to him about the passage of the troops of Swabia, but it is believed he will permit them to pass through his country after all these difficulties, having granted the like favour to

[1] George Villiers, Duke of Buckingham, one of the most celebrated of the Restoration wits and a personal friend of Etherege's, had retired on James's accession to his manor at Helmsley in Yorkshire. He died, aged 61, on April 15, 1687, in the house of a tenant at Kirkby Moorside, of a chill caught whilst hunting, and was buried on June 7th in Henry VII's Chapel, Westminster Abbey.

[2] Sunderland was granted the order of the garter on April 26th and was installed a knight on June 23rd.

GEORGE VILLERS DUKE OF BUCKINGHAM.

the troops of Franconia and they going[1] to be joined to that part of the army in which he is to command.

The circle of Franconia have concluded in their Diet, which was held the 8th of May, new style, that they will send into Hungary, besides the 1,500 men which have wintered there, 500 more to serve there, or the whole rest of the troops of the circle, which make in all 4,000 men, in case the Emperor desires them, but desire to be excused from contributing to the tax of one hundred Roman months, as the circle of Swabia has done before them; and it is said here the Emperor has required them to send their whole troops, which looks like the giving over the hopes of getting the hundred Roman months. The Emperor has no other auxiliaries this campaign than the Elector of Bavaria's troops and those of these two circles, and nobody here yet knows certainly what is the design this year, though all guess it is to besiege Alba Regalis.

The Prince of Passau, who is become altogether uncapable and was never fit to be employed in affairs, has desired the Emperor's leave to retire to his bishopric; it is said the Emperor has granted it him for a month only, but it is certain he will come hither no more, and this is only an artifice of the Count de Windisgratz to gain time to endeavour to be received as principal commissioner; but besides the general aversion the Diet has for him they will never receive any one in that quality, who is not a prince of the Empire.[2] This will make a long vacation here, for I am confident nothing will be done till there be a new principal commissioner, so that all the news I am like to furnish you with this good while must come from the camp.

[1] MS. 'being'.
[2] It was customary for the principal or first commissioner to publish the resolutions of the Diet. The Prince of Passau left the charge to Windischgrätz the second commissioner.

1687

The regiment of Mr. Bielk,[1] general of the Elector of Bavaria's cavalry, went from hence this day, and reckon to be at Pressburg the latter end of this month; their colonel is not yet returned from Sweden, whither he had the Elector's leave to go; their lieutenant-colonel, which is the youngest of the Königsmarks who were in England, is at Vienna. I am, &c.

Ditto.

Sir (Marquis d'Albeville):

I long since by the gazettes learned of your safe arrival at the Hague, and have waited till something which might be for his Majesty's service should give me an occasion of writing to you and congratulating you thereupon; but nothing falling out yet to that purpose I have taken the liberty to write to you, and to assure you that when there does I shall not fail to inform you of it. If there be anything else in which I may serve you in your own particular in the station I am in, you may freely command, etc.

Ditto.

Sir (Mr. Wynne):

If anything had offered itself which had been necessary for his Majesty's service to have been communicated to the Marquis d'Albeville I should not have omitted the doing it. I consider that above all things, and can never neglect it for a foolish punctilio. I have writ to him to offer him my service, and to let him know I am ready to receive his commands in what may be for his Majesty's. I wonder at the article you send me word is in his extraordinaries, having never heard from him or his secretary; if he has sent those prints to anybody else at the Diet I humbly conceive they had been better sent to me, who am employed by his Majesty. I could have

[1] Bielk, a Swedish colonel and governor of Pomerania.

made use of them to return the obligations I have
to some ministers who impart their prints and papers
to me; but, to be plain with you, I believe his secretary Petit the cause of this misunderstanding, who,
upon my refusing to allow him fourscore crowns
a year for a manuscript which I did not think fit to
fling away his Majesty's money upon, broke off an
intelligence he held with your brother, as I have
mentioned in a letter I writ formerly to you. We had
in Mr. Skelton's time some gazettes from him, but
Mr. Petit sent them generally the day after the fair,
that is the next week after he had made use of them,
but since Mr. d'Albeville arrived we have had none,
so that I believe Mr. Petit has put in that article for
prints in the Marquis's extraordinaries for some
former pretensions of his own. I am, &c.

Ratisbon, 12/22 May, 87.
My Lord (Middleton):
The Prince of Passau left this place yesterday
morning at four o'clock, and, a day or two before he
went, he sent to the Director of Mayence to desire
him to acquaint the Diet with his going and to dispose them to send him a deputation to make him a
compliment thereupon. The Director answered
that he was ready to serve the Prince, but that the
Diet could not send a deputation without he would
acquaint them in form by a decree of commission
with his departure, and that he might remember
upon his last leaving this place for a while, and not
doing of it the members of the Diet only sent their
secretaries or some other domestic to wish him a
good journey.
The Prince, the day before he went away, sent a
decree of commission accordingly, though he stayed
not to receive the benefit of it, which makes it
plainly appear it was a contrivance of the Count de
Windisgratz, and more especially a clause which is

inserted in the commission, which says that the Prince hopes his absence will not prejudice the public, but if there be any urgent affairs the Diet may communicate their acts to his excellence the Count de Windisgratz, who represents the Imperial commission in his absence. This has occasioned some consultations here privately among the ministers, and particularly the College of Electors, who are not yet resolved whether they shall let this decree of commission sleep without being dictated, the Prince being gone, or whether they shall dictate it with a strong protestation against the Count's pretensions. It is generally thought that the Count, if he has reason to apprehend the last, to avoid the disgrace will secretly cause the decree of commission to be withdrawn.

Yesterday arrived here an express to acquaint the[1] Count of Lamberg that the election at Salzburg will be on the 15th of June next, though other letters say on the 30th. The Count de Lamberg was gone before to Passau, being a canon of that place as well as of Salzburg, where he intended to stay till he had notice from his friends that things were disposed according to his desire. The competitors for this great archbishopric are the Count de Kimburg, nephew of the last bishop, but the chapter are not well inclined for him, his uncle being so liberal to him in his lifetime that they think not only the church but every one of them have suffered by it; another is the Count de Wolckestein, an Austrian, and a Count de Thun, I think a brother of him who was in England; both these have advantageous characters and are exceeding well spoken of, but it is thought by many the Count de Lamberg will carry it.

The Count de Crécy has received a letter of the 8th instant from the King his master, which acquaints him that the King is perfectly satisfied that

[1] MS. 'to'.

the Emperor intends to observe the truce by what has passed between Mr. de Lobkowitz and Monsieur de Croissy. Lobkowitz has told de Croissy that the Emperor is contented that the griefs, which have hitherto been complained of, shall be no more mentioned, but desires there may be no new occasion of complaint; that the règlement of the limits may be treated of, and the Emperor engages that he will faithfully observe the truce during the whole term. Monsieur de Croissy has acquainted Mr. de Lobkowitz on the behalf of his King that he will give no occasion of complaint, and that, in case there happen any, things shall be amicably accommodated; that as to the treaty for regulating the limits it would take up more time than the treating of a peace, which ought to be done forthwith, which being perfected the other treaty will be useless; and that he will faithfully observe the truce during the whole term. All this was by word of mouth, but the Count de Crécy believes Monsieur de Lobkowitz will give in a memorial to the same purpose. I believe you have had an account of this before from such as know the particulars better than I do. Nevertheless I think it my duty to acquaint you with what I know of this matter. I am, &c.

Ditto.

My Lord (Middleton):

The troops of Franconia are expected to pass by here on Saturday next; many will have it that they send no more than 500 men to join with their troops which quartered this winter in Hungary, and not all the forces of the circle.

The circle of Swabia, foreseeing the Elector of Bavaria would persist in refusing them leave to pass with their cavalry and baggage through his country, dispatched the secretary of the circle to Vienna to solicit the Emperor, in case the Elector should refuse them, that they might have liberty to march through Bohemia. The secretary returned on Monday last at night, not being able to obtain this, but the Emperor has promised them that in case the circle will bring them by water to Vilshofen[1] at their own charge he will defray them the rest of the way into Hungary. The Diet of the circle is to meet after to-morrow to determine of this affair. The great preparations which have been made for carrying both ammunition and provisions down the river this campaign make many think it will open, not with the siege of Alba Regalis, but with the siege of Esseck, to cut off all manner of relief which may be expected from Belgrade by the places the Turks hold in the lower Hungary.

Ditto.

Sir (Mr. Boyle):[2]

Did I not know you to be one of the most careless men in the world I should imagine you were the most ungrateful, so wholly to forget me who loved you so entirely. It is long since I writ to you, and, having received no answer, I am grown spiteful enough to wish you had so just an excuse for yourself as having been a year in Ireland. I need not tell you I am good-natured; I who have forgiven so many mistresses who have been false to me can well forgive a friend who has only been negligent. My heart was never touched for any for whom there remains not still some impression of kindness. Pray, if you can spare one quarter of an hour from the pleasures of London to please an absent friend, send me some news of all my friends, particularly of my Lord Dunbar[3] and of Ned Lee whose prosperity I have always wished. Let me know how Mrs.

---

[1] On the Danube, thirteen miles WNW. of Passau.
[2] Probably the Charles Boyle mentioned on p. 163.
[3] Robert Constable, Viscount Dunbar (c. 1651–1714).

Hughes[1] has disposed of herself; Mrs. Davies has
given a proof of the great passion she always had
for music, and Monsieur Peasible[2] has another
(guess) bass to thrum than that he played so well
upon. Make the kindest compliment you can for me
to Mrs. Willis,[3] and let me know how she and her
little family does. That you may know I am not
altogether idle here, and to oblige you to do the like
for me, I must tell you I have stolen this little time
to write to you, while no less than twenty chanoi-
nesses are expecting me in a wood by a fountain
with music and a collation. Notwithstanding the
resentment I ought to have against you I am very
faithfully, &c:

Ratisbon, 16/26 May, 87.
My Lord (Middleton):
The Duke of Mecklenburg-Schwerin[4] has caused
a memorial to be given in to the Diet signifying that
the King of Sweden, since the fort which he had
built on the river Warnemont[5] near Rostock was
demobilised by an Imperial execution, he still exacts

[1] Possibly Mrs. Margaret Hughes, the actress, see *post*,
p. 290.
[2] James Paisible (1656?–1721), flautist and composer, born
in France, came to England 1680. On December 4, 1686,
Paisible procured a licence for his marriage with Mary Davis.
It is just possible that this was the actress, famed for her
singing and dancing, who became the mistress of Charles II.
According to a note in Goodwin's edition of Cunningham's
The Story of Nell Gwyn (pp. 51–2), she left her house in St.
James's Square in 1687, after which date nothing is known of
her. Paisible was later connected with the theatres, supplying
overtures and musical interludes for performances.
[3] Possibly the lady mentioned in the Savile Correspondence:
'Lord Culpepper returned from Paris with Mrs. Willis, whom
he carried thither to buy whatsoever pleased her there and
this nation could not afford' (1667).
[4] See *ante*, p. 83, note 2.
[5] The name of the river is Warnow; Warnemünde is a
port on the Baltic, eight miles from Rostock.

imposts of all the vessels which come into Rostock, keeping a man of war or two before the port to compel them, so that the said town receives no advantage by the ruin of the fort. The Swedish deputy here pretends that by an agreement made in 1679 between the King and the Duke of Mecklenburg-Güstrow,[1] who divide these imposts, his master has right to exact them, having the consent of Mecklenburg-Güstrow, upon whose land the fort of Warnemont stood. Mecklenburg-Schwerin protests against this agreement, saying that the town of Rostock and the dependences remain in common between the two Dukes by the pacts of their family, and desires the agreement may be annulled and the town relieved from the douane.

On Saturday last 300 men of the troops of Franconia arrived here and embark this day for Hungary. The Emperor has writ a letter, which the Comte de Hohenloe[2] has delivered to the directors of this circle, by which he presses them to send with all speed the rest of the troops the circle maintains into Hungary, and the directors have summoned the whole circle to meet and consult whether it be convenient to leave themselves without any forces in case of accidents.

Ditto.

Sir (Betterton, the player):[3]

A poor man who has lost the enjoyment of his friends and the pleasures of London ought to use all the means he can to divert his chagrin and pass

[1] Gustave Adolphus, Duke of Mecklenburg-Güstrow.

[2] Louis Gustave, Count of Hohenlohe, Imperial envoy to the Franconian and Upper Rhenish circles.

[3] Thomas Betterton (c. 1635–1710), the famous actor, first appeared on the stage in 1660. He was much esteemed by Charles II; Pepys, Pope, Steele, and Cibber all laud his acting. He appears to have led a conspicuously blameless life, marrying in 1662 an actress, Mary Saunderson.

away the time as easy as is possible. In order to this I am often forced to trouble my acquaintance in England, and I do not doubt but you will forgive me my making bold with you among the rest. I have three in my little family who now and then give me a little music; they play very well and at sight. We have all the operas, and I have a correspondent at Paris who sends me what is new there. If you would do me the favour to procure me some of the best composition with the several parts, and let them be given to Dr. Wynne at my Lord Middleton's office, he will take care to send them to me. I shall esteem myself much obliged to you for this courtesy, and your kindness will be greater if now and then you give me an account of the stage and of other matters which, you shall judge, I will be glad to hear of. You will not mistake if you have the same opinion of me you had formerly, for I assure you I am not changed in my inclinations and can never be otherwise than—

My humble service to Mrs. Betterton.[1]

Ratisbon, 19/29 May, 87.

Sir (Mr. Wynne):

I have nothing this post worth informing my Lord of. We are like to have a long vacation here since it has pleased his Imperial Majesty to give the Prince of Passau, the head of his commission, leave to retire for some time to his bishopric to endeavour to recover his understanding, which has always been infirm and is now in a deep consumption.

When the news comes in from Vienna I will enclose it for my Lord. The letter I send you for Mr. Guy may help Mr. Robson in his soliciting my

---

[1] Mrs. Betterton is said to have been an admirable actress who was famous in the roles of Queen Katherine and Juliet, and whose Ophelia was a worthy counterpart to her husband's Hamlet.

business in the Treasury. It is not good to be much in arrear, and the 30th of this month I have a year's entertainment due, besides all my extraordinaries ever since I have been abroad. I am, &c:

Sir (Mr. Guy): Ditto.

The assurance you are pleased to give me of your kindness comforts me almost for all I have lost in England. You are so generous you do not only assist me in what is necessary, but you contribute towards my pleasure; you do not only take care to make me be supplied with money, but you give yourself the trouble to write to me, and were I in a better condition, I know so well how to value things I should prefer this favour to the other. I know you have but little time to spare from public affairs, and that little, in charity, which begins at home, you should employ in pleasing of yourself, but you are so prodigal you throw away part of it in delighting so poor a man as I am, who can make you no return but in kind wishes. May the women love you for what you have done, and may the men you oblige be all as sensible and as grateful as I am.

As soon as the campaign is begun I intend to write to my Lord Godolphin. The business of the Diet for the most part is only fit to entertain those insects in politics which crawl under the trees in St. James's Park, and I am not so vain as to think my dull imaginations capable of making his good nature receive them well. Make my court for me to him and to my Lord Dover, and tell them I think it is more for their ease to take your word for my receipt of their benefits than to exact a tedious acquittance under my own hand. If it be possible for them to think I merit their favour it must be by your means, and I shall ascribe to you what Horace does to the Muses, *Quod spiro et placeo si placeo tuum est*. I am, &c.

Ratisbon, 23 May / 2 June, 87.

My Lord (Middleton):

The circle of Swabia have accepted of what the Emperor offered, and concluded in their assembly, held the 27th of May, new style, to embark their cavalry and send them to Vilshofen at their own charge, where the Emperor has commissioners who are to take care to convey them from thence into Hungary at his charge. Nevertheless they have sent an express to the Elector of Bavaria to desire that their baggage may have leave to pass by land. The foot of this circle are embarked at Ulm, and we expect them here daily; the horse will come some ten days after them, it taking up time to fit floats and boats for them.

Mr. Cutts[1] arrived at this town last night and took a boat and went down the Danube for Vienna this morning at 4 o'clock. Two days before passed by here one Ashley, who has been a lieutenant in Sir Edward Hales's[2] regiment. I enclose in this the gazettes and a paper of news from Vienna. I am, &c.

Ditto.

Sir (Mr. Will Richards):

... Pray remember my humble service to my Lord Lumley.[3] I am very sensible of the obligations I have

[1] John Cutts, afterwards Baron Cutts of Gowran, Ireland (1661–1707), was among the English volunteers in Hungary in 1686, and distinguished himself at the siege and capture of Buda. As a result of his heroism he received the appointment of adjutant-general to the Duke of Lorraine.

[2] Sir Edward Hales was admitted to the rank of colonel of a foot regiment in 1673. He became a Roman Catholic on the accession of James II, a fact which led to the celebrated test case decided in Hales's favour.

[3] Richard Lumley, 1st Earl of Scarborough, a Roman Catholic and a favourite of Charles II. He collected troops in Hants against Monmouth, and became colonel of the carabineers, of which these formed the nucleus 1685. In 1687 he

to him, and tell him I had taken care to have paid a little debt of ten guineas before now if those I employ in my affairs in England had not been negligent. I have heard of the success of *The Eunuch*,[1] and am very glad the town has so good a taste to give the same just applause to Sir Charles Sedley's writing, which his friends have always done to his conversation. Few of our plays can boast of more wit than I have heard him speak at a supper ;[2] some barren sparks have found fault with what he has formerly done on this occasion only because the fitness of the soil has produced too big a crop. I daily drink his health, my Lord Dorset's,[3] Mr. Jepson's,[4] Charles Godfrey's, your own, and all our friends'; but this is not much you will say for one who lives in this drinking country; that you may

was converted to Protestantism, laid down his commission, and signed the invitation to William, for whom he undertook the North.

[1] Sedley adapted Terence's *Eunuchus* as *Bellamira, or The Mistress*, a satirical, witty, licentious comedy after the manner of Etherege. It was acted at Drury Lane in May 1687, and during the first performance the roof of the theatre fell in. On May 12, 1687, it was acted at Whitehall.

[2] Sedley was noted for his witty conversation. Cf. Pepys: 'I happened to sit near to Sir Charles Sedley; who I find a very witty man, and he did at every line take notice of the dullness of the poet and the badness of the action, and that most pertinently; which I was mightily taken with.' Oct. 4th, 1664; see also Feb. 18, 1667.

[3] Charles Sackville, Earl of Dorset (1638–1706), wit, courtier, and patron of letters, was the companion of Sedley and Rochester in their notorious excesses. He retired from court on the accession of James II, and concurred in the invitation to William. His gaiety and wit secured his popularity, but he was also a generous patron. Etherege dedicated to Dorset (then Lord Buckhurst) his first play, *Love in a Tub*.

[4] Probably William Jephson, of the Secretary of State's office, who was appointed Secretary of the Treasury in 1689. Henry Savile, writing to the Earl of Halifax, speaks of 'my Lord Dorset's friend Jephson' (Savile Correspondence). See Introduction, p. 12.

then take it more kindly I wish it as heartily as I do my own, and though I have no very good memory for other things I never forget the least favour which has been done me, and therefore you may be confident I am (D. Will).[1]

Ratisbon, 30 May / 9 June, 87.

My Lord (Middleton):

This morning the troops of Swabia arrived here in their way to Hungary; they disembarked in a meadow about a mile from hence and marched into the town, the Marquis of Baden-Durlach, who commands them in chief, being at the head of the infantry, which consists of three regiments and, by what I could judge by the sight I had of them, make three thousand men complete, all lusty fellows and not very ill clothed; the regiment of horse which ought to be a thousand to make up what this circle is to furnish, is a little behind the foot on the Danube, and is [2] expected to arrive and land and march likewise through this place this afternoon to be embarked on the other side of the bridge.

The Count de Crécy, who has long solicited to be recalled, or at least to have leave to go for some time to Paris to look after his private affairs, has with much ado obtained of the King his master permission to go thither, but with a strict charge not to be absent from hence above two months, to be counted from the day of his departure; the time limited him being so short he has been in doubt whether he should accept the party, but is now resolved to begin his journey one day this week, taking his Lady and a few domestics with him only, leaving his children and most part of his family behind. Monsieur Krischman,[3] who is a German-born but naturalized a

---

[1] Possibly standing for 'Dear Will'. [2] MS. 'are'.
[3] Hereafter written as Frischman.

Frenchman, one of the ablest men here, and has been long employed by the French King, is charged with the care of informing that court of what passes in the plenipotentiary's absence; but that which moved his Christian Majesty to grant this favour to his minister is the confidence he has nothing will be done in the Diet till the campaign is ended.

I send your Lordship enclosed all I have from Vienna by this post. I am, with all duty, &c.

Ratisbon, 2/12 June.

My Lord (Middleton):

The circle of Franconia send the rest of their troops into Hungary, and this morning two thousand foot marched into this town, where they are to be embarked on the Danube. Though it was expected the cavalry of Swabia, as I writ you word by my last of the 30th of May, should have arrived here the same day the foot did, they are by some accident retarded and are not yet come hither. The artillery and baggage belonging to the troops of this circle are stopped at Heumau,[1] a village belonging to the Elector Palatine about four or five leagues short of this place. They were to go by land into Hungary, but the Elector of Bavaria will not permit them to pass through his country. The Swabians pretend this is hard, they paying to the last penny for every thing they have, but others say they make bold to take free quarters. However this is, the Margrave of Baden declared when he went from hence he would stay at Linz with his regiments and not stir one foot farther till the artillery and baggage had joined him. The little disputes which have unluckily happened concerning the forces belonging to these circles have and will retard the operations of the campaign, it being more than time they were at the general rendezvous already.

[1] Hemau, about fifteen miles west of Ratisbon.

I send your Lordship the extract of part of a letter from Munich, which confirms the news we had before of the extraordinary accident which happened in Citta Nova near the Cape of Istria.

We have here the copy of a memorial given to his Majesty by the Count de Caunitz, dated the 19th of May last, by which he desires his Majesty to become guarantee of the observation of the truce, as he is of the peace of Nimiguen upon which it is founded. Here is a party among the deputies of the Diet, which I need not name, who are not well pleased the Emperor has done this without asking first the approbation of the Empire.

The Count de Crécy sets forward for France, on the terms I mentioned in my last, the day after to-morrow.

If I receive any news from Vienna this day I will enclose it for your Lordship, being with all duty, &c.

Ratisbon, 6/16 June, 87.

Sir (Mr. Wynne):

Yesterday I received yours of the 20th of May, for which I thank you. I will endeavour to accommodate myself with saddles here since the opportunity is lost of sending them.

I have nothing of moment to write to my Lord, and therefore I have rather chosen to send you a paper of what news we have to be given to him.

I wonder I cannot get the least word from you concerning Abbot Fleming's business.[1] I believe it was not seasonable at that time to desire his Majesty's letter to the Cardinal of Norfolk to make use of his name in it to his Holiness, in regard of his obstinacy in refusing those reasonable things his Majesty desired of him; but since his Holiness has since complied, and granted that by a bull which he

---

[1] See *ante*, pp. 179–80.

refused to do at the ambassador's instance, it may be a more proper time now for my Lord to move his Majesty in it. I am &c.

Ratisbon, 9/19 June, 87.

My Lord (Middleton):

Yesterday being Wednesday, the 8th instant, the Duke of Berwick came in good health to this town between 5 and 6 in the afternoon and embarked for Vienna before 5 o'clock this morning; his equipage followed about 8, which, with the little rest it had here is much recovered. The Duke intends to make what haste he can to join the Duke of Lorraine, who, with the main body of the army, is already passed the Sarowitz,[1] as you will find by the paper of news I send you. His equipage is to follow him with what convenient speed they can. The regiment of horse belonging to the circle of Swabia, who according to my last arrived here on Sunday, and disembarked according to the custom to let the boats and *radeaux* the better pass the bridges, made bold to march three German miles to a place called Vader before they embarked again, and did much mischief to the country; but it is thought the Elector of Bavaria will account with them for it when they return.

The Count Charles de Schomberg, third son to the maréschal, is made governor of Magdeberg.

The Elector of Brandenburg has recalled his old minister Monsieur de Jena,[2] who has served him twenty years in the Diet, to gratify a faction here, which has much dissatisfied the French. I am, &c.

Ditto.

My Lord (Sunderland):

. . . (News about his Grace the Duke of Berwick's arrival as in the foregoing letter); it followed:

[1] The Sárviz canal.
[2] See Introduction and *ante*, p. 153, note 1.

I am charged to make your Lordship many compliment[s] from him, which are full of kindness and
esteem, but I should wrong him in endeavouring to
express them since they must needs lose much of
that grace and obligingness with which he spoke
them. Imagine therefore what will best please you
on this subject. My Lord Charles[1] tells me you are
pleased to continue me in your favour, which is the
welcomest news I could hear from England. I wish
I could do something to deserve it, in the meantime
I will be careful not to do anything which may make
me forfeit so great a blessing. I am, &c.

Ratisbon, 13/23 June, 87.
Sir (Marquis d'Albeville):
    I am ashamed I have been so long without
acknowledging the favour of yours of the 2nd
instant, but I doubt not but you will forgive me
considering the hurry I have been in in providing
boats and other necessaries for the transporting the
equipages belonging to our volunteers, who are
gone into Hungary, and the making of our countrymen welcome in this place. The Duke of Berwick
arrived here on Wednesday last, and the next morning embarked on the Danube with my Lord
Charles Hamilton, my Lord Dongan,[2] and Sir
Edward Vaudrey, to make what diligence he could,
according to his Majesty's order, to join the Duke of
Lorraine, who with a good body of the army, all
the troops being not yet arrived at Barkan, particularly those of the circle of Swabia and what are this
year sent by the circle of Franconia, is already

[1] Lord Charles Hamilton, son of Charles Hamilton, 5th
Earl of Abercorn, took part in the battle of Mohács and gave
the King an account of the fighting on his return to London
in November 1687.

[2] Walter Dungan, styled Lord Dungan, was born abroad,
but being naturalized was M.P. for Naas in the Parliament of
James II.

passed the Sarwitz and marches towards the Drave
to hinder the Turks from repairing the bridge at
Esseck; but I fear he will come too late, we having
a report that that work is already perfected and that
the enemy have a body of men on this side the
river. The Elector of Bavaria, who has been a little
indisposed, had not yet left Vienna. When our post
comes in I will enclose what news it brings to-day.

Monsieur Valkenier, who came hither some time
since from the States of Holland, has given me notice
of his arrival; when he was here before I made him
no visit, being credibly informed that he, receiving
the false report that the late Duke of Monmouth
had routed his Majesty's forces at Philips Norton,
sent the news to many ministers to whom he thought
it would be welcome, and was the occasion of the
printing of the lie here, it being sent him by
some brother citizen of Amsterdam; but meeting of
him lately by accident and protesting upon his
honour he did not with any malicious design to
disserve his Majesty, but only dispersed it as he used
to do the other news which comes from his country,
the Secretary of State[1] has left it to my choice
whether I will see him or no, and I intend to give
him a visit this week. I write this to you because I
know the Prince of Orange has been told I neglected
him, that you may tell his Highness, if you find it
convenient, the reason of it.

There has happened a thing which has made me
omit the visiting the Count de Windisgratz, who is
joined in commission with the Prince of Passau, but
by reason of the Prince's infirmity he in a manner
does all and the other is but a cipher. It would be
too tedious to give a character of the man and to let
you know how he is embroiled with most of the
Diet, particularly with the Electoral College. We
lived some time very well together and I made him

[1] Lord Middleton.

a hundred visits, all which time he never so much as sent a man to make me a compliment. Upon the taking of Buda I sent to congratulate the Imperial commission, but they, when they made their public rejoicing and invited the ministers and many cavaliers of this town, to the wonder of everybody never took any notice of me. I, considering the zeal his Majesty had showed for the success of that siege and how many English gentlemen had perished at it, thought I could not but resent for the honour of our nation. This has made the Count tax me for being of the French faction, but all the account I have given of affairs into England, before the business of the truce was settled, show that I have behave[d] myself according to my instructions with all the impartiality imaginable. If I have visited the Count de Crécy more than the Emperor's ministers it is because I was admitted without ceremony, which is the plague of this place, there being scarce another house here where I could enjoy my freedom and find any diversion, and his Majesty did not send me hither to live in solitude. The Count is so revengeful he will not stick at anything to do a man a mischief he has a pique to. Valkenier, whom I suspected, to justify himself to me told me the Count had owned to him that he has writ against me into Holland, and I believe has been the occasion, by the falsehoods he suggested, of a difference between Mr. Skelton and me. He has writ likewise into France, to Vienna and into England, but I have not had much difficulty to get the better of him, truth being on my side. I let you know this lest any indirect means should be used to do me any ill offices with you. Those whom his Majesty employs, in my opinion, should omit nothing to have a good understanding, and I shall be very careful to do you all the service in my power, especially in letting you know what is done here and in Hungary to help you a little to pay such as communicate things to you in kind. You will very much oblige me, when you have leisure, if you do the like for me. This day the hundred months which the Emperor has desired, and have laid dormant for some time, are waken and put into deliberation, with what success you will know hereafter. I am, with much esteem and sincerity, Sir, &c.

Ditto.

Sir (Mr. Petit):

As a farther answer to your letter of the 6th instant I may add this. Sir George received a letter from Captain Slater upon Mr. Skelton's arrival at Paris in December[1] last, wherein he was pleased to acquaint him of several reports which were in Holland, that in his discourses here he frequently made reflection on the conduct of Mr. Skelton in his negotiations abroad, without giving him any account from whence these reports might come, which were nothing but lies and inventions of somebody who intended to do him ill offices with Mr. Skelton and breed a difference between those whom his Majesty employs in his service. This bred a jealousy in Sir George, and particularly of those who grew cold in their correspondence, and I must freely tell you that I received but two letters from you in more than two months after Mr. Skelton left Holland, and now and then one, but very seldom after the refusal of the newspaper. The letters which were enclosed to you were enclosed by order from the Secretary of State, and the two or three packets which were enclosed after Mr. Skelton's leaving Holland were not sent with a design to put you to any expense, for, in case it be not paid you elsewhere, you need but send me a note of what it comes to and you shall receive it; but Sir George has since discovered from whence these falsehoods

---

[1] See post, pp. 251–2

arise, which is from the mean malice of a great minister here,[1] who, 'tis not unlikely, either has or will endeavour to play him the like trick with the Marquis d'Albeville. He is very sorry any accident should make him suspect you are not of the number of his friends, and he will endeavour to make amends for the mentioning of your breaking off the correspondence[2] by clearing the mistake and by doing you all the kindness which is in his power. I know not whether I may hope for your correspondence hereafter seeing[3] you tell me you have omitted writing to me since the Marquis's arrival by order to save needless postage, and I shall not dare, till you are pleased to give me leave, put you to the unnecessary charge of hearing from Sir

Your most humble servant
H[ugh] H[ughes].

Ratisbon, 13/23 June, 1686.

Sir (Mr. Wynne):

Yesterday I received yours of the 27th of May, together with the part of the *Hind and Panther*[4] enclosed in another packet; pray let me know how this poem is approved by the court.

Mr. Petit has writ to your brother to excuse his breaking off his correspondence. This is one part of his letter: 'I know I have omitted writing to you since the Marquis's arrival, which I did by order to save needless postage', but I have writ to the Marquis[5] this day, and I believe their minds will change, wherefore I would desire you to keep it to yourself. I had some reason to be jealous of Mr. Petit, but I am of opinion it was groundless, for meeting Mr.

[1] Windischgrätz.
[2] Petit had evidently been rebuked as a consequence of Etherege's complaint, see *ante*, p. 156.   [3] MS. 'being'.
[4] Dryden's poem *The Hind and the Panther*, in which he defended Roman Catholicism, had just been published.
[5] The Marquis d'Albeville; see *ante*, p. 217.

Valkenier by accident, and taxing him with the divulging and occasioning to be printed the false report about the skirmish at Philips Norton, he protested he only did as he used to do with news sent him out of his country, and that upon his honour he had no intention to do his Majesty any ill service; he likewise protested he had done me no ill offices in Holland, but that the Count de Windisgratz has owned to him privately since his return hither he had writ into Holland, to Paris, Vienna, and into England against me, and I am persuaded from this source had sprung those lies which made a misunderstanding between Mr. Skelton and me and that Petit is innocent. Upon this éclaircissement, this confidence, and the liberty which is left me to do what I think fit, I intend to see Monsieur Valkenier.

I wish you all happiness and am

Dear Sir . . .

Pray press Mr. Robson to solicit for six months' entertainment, and not to let my extraordinaries run on farther. I wonder at their not being paid, they being so very reasonable.

Ditto.

My Lord (Middleton):

On Friday last the Count de Windisgratz delivered a decree of commission to the Diet, which was dictated the same day. It is the Emperor's approbation of a moderation of matricule[1] made in favour of the Count de Lovestein. The decree was only signed by the Count, but it was in the usual form, in the name of the whole commission, though the Prince of Passau is absent. This day the hundred Roman month[s] which have slept so long are intended to be put into deliberation again.

The Count de Jörger,[2] an Austrian, is declared

[1] See *ante*, p. 83, note 3.
[2] John Quintin Jörger (1624–1705), a Protestant by birth,

governor or major of Vienna in the place of the old Count de Staremberg,[1] who died sometime since.

The Count de Fürstenberg,[2] Dean of Salzburg, who formerly refused the bishopric of Münster, has a mind to this, as it is reported, and the chapter are inclined to choose him; their only exception to him is that he is too old, as their only exception to the Count de Lamberg[3] is that he is too young. In a few days now we shall see who will be the lucky man.

The ministers here are full of the praises of his Majesty's justice and piety upon the memorial given at Paris by Mr. Skelton, occasion upon one given to his Majesty by the Count de Caunitz desiring he would be guarantee of the observation of the truce as he is of the peace of Nimeguen, upon which it is founded. I am, &c.

Ratisbon, 16/26 June, 1687.

My Lord (Middleton):

The hundred Roman months were marked in the paper of things intended to be deliberated on by the Diet on Monday last, but the Austrian ministers, the Count de Windisgratz's creatures, not being able to prevail that the decree of commission, which was left by the Prince of Passau upon his leaving this

---

was converted to Catholicism and appointed governor of Lower Austria 1687. His activities greatly benefited Vienna, and he was especially solicitous of public security; reorganized the fire brigade, police, and detective force, revised the market regulations, and repaired the pavements.

[1] Conrad Balthasar, Count of Staremberg (1612–87), president of Lower Austria, died on April 10, 1687, in the 75th year of his age.

[2] William Egon of Fürstenberg (1629–1704) received the cardinal's cap 1686. In 1688 he was elected coadjutor to his old friend the Archbishop of Cologne, but the Pope refused to ratify the election, and Louis XIV compensated him with the Abbey of St. Germain-des-Prés.

[3] Lamberg was only thirty-three years of age.

place, should be first dictated, in which there is a clause that gives the Count the title of excellence and hopes he will be permitted to act as principal commissioner in the Prince's absence, neither that nor any other business has been deliberated of, and it is likely will not till the Count has carried his point. The College of Electors, for several reasons which you have been troubled with formerly, have protested against his pretensions several times, but the Count hoped at this time, the Count de Crécy being absent and Monsieur de Jena the Brandenburg minister being disgraced, who most violently opposed, he might obtain his desires, and indeed many of the electoral began to lose heart, but some who wish not the Count's success in this matter have taken the pains to set before them the dangerous consequences of their compliances, upon which they have taken fresh courage and are resolved not to yield. This trifle will put a stop to the deliberating of affairs which are necessary for the good of the Empire. I have a copy of his Christian Majesty's answer to this memorial given by Mr. Skelton touching his Majesty's becoming guarantee for the observation of the truce. I do not find it is yet communicated to the ministers here, and therefore cannot say anything concerning their opinions of it. It is quite opposite to the alliance of Augsburg, and destroys the redressing of what they call contraventions.

As soon as the post comes in I will enclose the news from Hungary. I am, &c.

Sir (Mr. Robson):   Ditto.

I pray do me the favour to pay to William Bridgeman,[1] esquire, the sum of twelve guineas, being a debt I have long owed him, and you oblige, &c.

[1] William Bridgeman, secretary to Lord Sunderland and the Admiralty.

Sir (Mr. Bridgeman):

Though I have been negligent in writing to you I have not forgot how much I have been obliged to you, and particularly the debt I owe you; and to convince you of it I have enclosed a note and a letter to Mr. Robson for the payment of it. My Lord Dongan,[1] when he passed by here, told me you would do him the favour to send his letters to him, and I have promised him to forward them in case they are directed to me. I pray give the paper of news to my Lord,[2] and give me some proof of your kindness by doing me what friendly offices you can with him. You may be confident wherever I am I shall always be, &c.

Ditto.

Sir (Mr. Robson):

I must desire you to move my friends in the Treasury for me; there was six months' entertainment due to me in May last. I pray press my extraordinaries very earnestly, for they are very reasonable and will begin to grow stale. It is a very troublesome thing to be in debt, and particularly here I have known so much the inconvenience of it that I hope you will endeavour to prevent it. I have sent Mr. Bridgeman, who will deliver you this, a note for twelve guineas on you; pray let him receive it.

I hope you will suddenly send me some good news that I may be in a condition to make a compliment to Mrs. Robson, without making of you jealous of, &c.

Ratisbon, 20/30 Junii, 87.

Sir (Mr. Wynne):

I received yesterday your favour with the second and third part of the *Hind and Panther*, which I have not yet read quite over.

[1] See *ante*, p. 217, note 2.   [2] Lord Sunderland.

Nothing is done here, the Count de Windisgratz being gone to Etting[1] to pay a vow he made to the Holy Virgin in the last fit of the stone he was tormented with. Wherefore I have not writ to my Lord, only enclosing for him what news is come to us from Vienna this day.

On Friday last my Lord Kenoul[2] with Captain Brown went from this place towards Hungary. I have not yet heard from any of our volunteers in those part[s], but I learn in a letter from Vienna, of the 26th instant, new style, that the Duke of Berwick is arrived in that town in good health. You will see by the paper I send you for my Lord in what condition thing[s] are in Hungary, and that we cannot be long without hearing of some considerable action. I am.

Ratisbon, 23 June/3 July, 87.

My Lord (Middleton):

Having no business to acquaint Mr. Secretary with at present I hope you will excuse me to him, and by your interest prevail with him to forgive the liberty I take of writing only to my Lord Middleton. I have had the honour to know your Lordship long, and when you were not so great I loved you no less than I do now. The favours which fortune bestows move the weak to admire and the false to flatter; I look upon them as fine clothes which are ornaments to such as nature has been kind to, and never fail to make them more loathsome who have no merit. Such as are immediately distinguished from other men by heaven, will ever be preferred by me to such who only wear the marks [of] a Prince's kindness. You see what a fine courtier I am like to make, if ever I come back to England. I do not doubt but you have done me many benefits in my absence,

---

[1] Ötting, about sixty miles from Ratisbon.
[2] George Hay, 5th Earl of Kinnoul. See *post*, p. 262.

and I must thank you for choosing the most generous way of doing them, which is without letting me know anything of it. I dare not mention anything of London to you; the air of the town may be so altered that I shall be thought to talk like an Indian. Some of my countrymen who have passed this way have given me faint descriptions, by which I guess a little at the countenance of things.

Mr. Wynne has sent me the *Hind and Panther*, by which I find John Dryden has a noble ambition to restore poetry to its ancient dignity in wrapping up the mysteries of religion in verse. What a shame it is to me to see him a saint and remain still the same devil. I must blame the goodness of my constitution which cannot be much altered since my mind is not much changed from what it was at the gravel pits.[1] I saw a play about ten years ago called the *Eunuch*, so heavy a lump the players durst not charge themselves with the dead weight, but it seems Sir Charles Sedley has animated the mighty mass and now it treads the stage lightly.[2] He had always more wit than was enough for one man, and therefore does well to continue his charity to one who wants it. Dryden finds his *Macflecknoe* does no good;[3] I wish better success with his *Hind and Panther*.

I am apt to think your good nature makes you steal

[1] Probably an allusion to the gravel pits at Kensington.

[2] See *ante*, p. 212, note 1.

[3] Etherege presumably means that it did not have the desired effect on the object of its satire, Shadwell. He must have been particularly interested in the poem on account of its references to himself:

Let gentle George in triumph head the stage;
Make Dorimant betray and Loveit rage;
Let Cully, Cockwood, Fopling, charm the pit,
And in their folly show the writer's wit. . . .
When did his [Jonson's] Muse from Fletcher scenes purloin,
As thou [Shadwell] whole Eth'ridg dost transfuse to thine?

some nights from your business to enjoy your friends. I will not desire you now to speak about anything which may concern me at court, but in return I hope you will put some of my old acquaintance in mind of me. I can never forget those who have obliged me, and have drunk many a grateful cup to their memory; how much Rhenish wine have you made me swallow for your share! You who have given me so much cause to be ever, &c.

Ratisbon 27 June / 7 July, 87.

Sir (Mr. Wynne):

You may be pleased to let my Lord know that on the 30th of June, new style, Johannes Ernestus de Thun, brother to the Count of that name who was envoy in England, was elected archbishop of Salzburg; he and the Count de Fürstenberg had equal voices, but the good old Dean generously gave his own voice to the Count de Thun to help him to carry it.

I send you the copies of Mr. Skelton's memorial and his most Christian Majesty's answer to it concerning the guarantee as they have been printed here. In the French King's answer these words with the line under them are left out in the printed copy which is dispersed over the Empire: soit sous le prétexte des griefs des ministres Protestants ni sous quelque autre que ce puis être, &c. Some think it done with a design, others think it an error, but it is traced to come from Monsieur de Staremberg, the Holland minister at Paris, and given by Valkenier to the man who occasioned it to be printed here.

Here is great intriguing to get the decree of commission read which was left by the Prince of Passau when he went from hence, which does insinuate the giving the title of excellence to the Count de Windisgratz by the Diet, and their admitting him to execute the function of principal commissioner. The Prince's College is managed by the Count's creatures, but the College of Electors stand firm, though fair word and threats have been used to move them. I shall not trouble you with particulars without something happen in this business worth my Lord's knowledge. I enclose the news we have from Vienna, and am, &c.

The Princess Palatine, who is to be Queen of Portugal,[1] was about a fortnight ago in these parts incognito to pay some vows she had made before she begins her journey, and particularly at the Holy Virgin of Etting, eighteen miles[2] from hence, who bestows her blessing on the marriage bed.

Ratisbon, 30 June/10 July, 87.

My Lord (Middleton):

The Diet has been once assembled since my last: the College of Princes urged the dictating the decree of commission left by the Bishop of Passau; the College of Electors consented to the dictature, but with a protestation in writing against the pretensions of the Count de Windisgratz, provided also that the deputation of Austria would charge themselves with the protestation, which the ministers of Austria refused, and threatened the Electorals that, in case they did not dictate it, the Emperor would send a decree of commission, in which he would name all those who opposed it as his enemies. Upon this the Electorals refused absolutely to dictate it till they had acquainted their principals how nearly this matter concerned their privileges, and the threats that were made them, and should receive instructions thereupon; so that this affair, which has

[1] The Princess Maria Sophia Elisabeth, aged twenty-one, married Peter II of Portugal.
[2] German miles; see *ante*, p. 226, note 1.

been long managing underhand, is come to be an open war between the two factions.

On Monday last arrived here George Pitt's two sons, and embarked yesterday morning for the army.

I send your Lordship the news I have by this day's post from Vienna, and am with all duty, &c.

Ratisbon, 5/15 July, 87.

My Lord (Middleton):

I received this day a letter from Mr. Wynne of the 17th of the last month, in which he tells me you had had none from me in fifteen days. I am sorry my letters come not more regularly to you; it is none of my fault, for I write to you constantly twice a week. I gave order some time since they should be sent by the way of Holland, though not under Mr. Petit's cover, believing that way they might sooner reach you, and do not know how the mistake has happened but I will examine the thing and take care the order you sent me shall be executed.

The news we receive from Vienna comes hither on Mondays and Thursdays in the afternoon, which are our post days for Holland, so that we are forced to visit our friends here, who communicate what they have to us, to get what we have from Vienna translated and writ fair; nevertheless I have not failed to send what comes to my knowledge to you by the same post, but it was impossible for me yesterday to send you the enclosed relation, as I have mentioned to Mr. Wynne in the letter I writ to him, promising you should have it by the Flanders post, which sets out this day. I am fain to make use of that way now, there being no possibility of sending by Holland these two days.

I have not yet had a word from any of the Duke of Berwick's company. I ascribe it to the great diligence they have made to be with the Duke of

Lorraine. I wish them safe there, for the Turks of Alba Regalis are a little troublesome to those that go down the Danube without a good convoy. I am, &c.

This day we have the news of the death of the Princess Electoral Palatine. Fr[ench] N[e]ws.

Ratisbon, 7/17 July, 87.

My Lord (Middleton):

To-morrow the Electoral College is to give in their resolution concerning the dictating the commission decree left by the Bishop of Passau.

I sent your Lordship on Tuesday, the 5th instant, by the way of Brussels, the particulars of what had been done by the Duke of Lorraine since his coming to the Drave.

I send your Lordship now by the way of Holland, under Mr. Petit's cover, the news we have this day from Vienna, with a letter from Pettau of the 9th instant, new style, from Mr. Leslie, the Count's kinsman.

We expect the Count de Lamberg's return hither every day ; his arrival will be a great help to me in furnishing you with an account of what passes this campaign by reason of the good intelligence which he has from many of his relations and acquaintance in the army. I am &c.

It is said here the Emperor intends after the campaign to send my Lord Taaffe to relieve the Count de Caunitz.

Ditto.

Monsieur (de Gennes):

Vous m'avez tant roué d'excellence que j'ai envie de vous bien donner du marquis, si je ne faisais pas conscience d'ôter les armes de la main de notre ami le Norman à cette heure qu'il se batte contre l'ennemi commun de la Chrétienté. Je n'ai pas le temps de barbouiller beaucoup de papier à présent,

231

c'est pourquoi je vous dirai seulement que
Mr. L'Évêque continue à être bien exact dans toutes
ses fonctions. Il donna hier un grand fête à Madame
la Comtesse[1] de Stubenberg et à toutes les plus jolies
Fräuleins d'ici. Mr. de Stocken et moi fûmes ses
coadjuteurs, tout se passa de sa part avec beaucoup
de cérémonie et de magnificence, et de la nôtre
avec beaucoup de réjouissance. La petit Stubenberg
devient tous les jours plus jolie et plus mûre et je
crois que les doux zéphyres qui soufflent les amants
feront bientôt épanouir ce petit bouton de rose.

Monsieur le Comte et Madame la Comtesse de
Windisgratz surprirent Monsieur Stocken et moi
l'autre jour dans le bois auprès de la fontaine où
nous faisions[2] bonne chère avec Mademoiselle de
Vernerin. La Comtesse se jeta presque hors de son
carosse pour voir ce qui s'y passait et allongea le
cou jusqu'à ce que nous fûmes à perte de vue. Pour
me venger un peu après j'étais dans une assemblée
où Mr. le Comte vint lui-même pour rappeler sa
femme à la maison, le crasseux écuyer ayant
negligé son devoir ce jour-là, je la pris par la main
et elle fit beaucoup d'effort pour me l'arracher;
j'ai tenu ferme et lui dis en français: je ne pouvais
pas me dispenser de conduire une personne de sa
qualité et de son mérite dans son carosse. Elle
me dit beaucoup de chose[s] en allemand que je
ne pouvais, ou que je ne voulais pas entendre; la
plus grand part de la compagnie se mit à rire et
elle fut obligée d'appeler à l'aide pour me faire dire
que cela ne se pouvait faire. Nous n'avons pas
encore fait le voyage de Nuremberg quoique je sais
que les belles Zinzendorfs[3] y sont de retour, mais
nous espérons de les voir bientôt. Mademoiselle
de Windisgratz est bien plus amoureuse de Monsieur
de Stocken que je n'étais jamais d'elle. Toutes les

[1] MS. 'Countesse'.　　[2] MS. 'fesions'.
[3] See Appendix, p. 410.

belles lui en veulent et il est chassé par une meute de Fräuleins. Cela qui fait que je le plains est qu'il y a si peu de gibiers dans cette ville qu'elles ne peuvent pas prendre le change. Il court risque d'être mis en pièces et Dieu sait que le tout n'est qu'un petit morceau et à peine peut rassasier une.

Adieu, mon cher, vous m'avez tant rebuté de la cérémonie que je ne veux pas vous faire d'autre compliment que l'ordinaire. Je suis &c.

Ratisbon, 14/24 July, 87.

My Lord (President): [1]

Our post days for England happening to be the same the post comes in here from Vienna, I have so little time to get the news which comes from the army translated and transcribed that I cannot send it so regularly as I would to your Lordship's office; but I will never be wanting when anything of moment falls out to give your Lordship notice of it. The enclosed papers will acquaint your Lordship with all we know of what has passed on the banks of the Drave, but I find in a private letter, which comes from a gentleman I am well acquainted with who is a volunteer in the Elector of Bavaria's troops, that the Elector was not the 10th instant, new style, passed the bridge at Mohatz, and they did not reckon to pass it till the 12th. The Elector, when the Duke of Lorraine sent to him to come and join him, intended to have besieged Great Waradein, and had taken his measures so well that it was believed he would have succeeded. The ambition he has of doing something considerable alone made him not well satisfied with the message he received to march towards Esseck. He once had a design to have sent an express to communicate the plan he had drawn of this siege to the Council of War, and to have stayed in the upper Hungary till he received

[1] Lord Sunderland.

their answer, but, believing the Council would carry it against him and that it would occasion the loss of much time, he let himself be persuaded to comply with the Duke of Lorraine's desires.

It was believed here at first the guarantee which was desired by the Count de Caunitz would have no effect, since the French would never consent to it but on such terms as are expressed in the answer to Mr. Skelton's memorial, and the Empire would have nothing mentioned but the truce that they may come again, when they think fit, with their griefs. The French have quitted the design of making the fort at Trarbach,[1] and some say upon his Majesty's causing to be represented to the most Christian King the farther jealousies it will give the Empire, but the French agent here says it is because the earth is not proper for the work.

I wish I knew how to deserve the favour I hear your Lordship shows me on all occasions; though I have no other merit I will never want that of being, &c.

Ditto.

My Lord (Middleton):

Yesterday the Electoral College deliberated about the dictating the decree of commission which concerns the Count de Windisgratz's pretensions, and had declared their resolution therein, but that the College of Princes was up so that it is put off again till to-morrow.

The Count de Lamberg, who arrived here on Friday last, is to go the next week for Passau, where the chapter, by reason of the infirmity of the Bishop, intend to name administrators to manage the

[1] In May orders had been given for the building of a new fort at Trarbach between Treves and Coblenz. In June the French had formed a camp there of 8,000 foot and 4,000 horse and started work on the fort, which was to be called Mont Royal and to have seven bastions.

revenues of the bishopric, and likewise a coadjutor which it is thought will be the Count, to comfort him for the loss of his expectations at Salzburg.

I send your Lordship with the news we have to-day, a paper which did not come to my hands till the last post was gone. It does not contain much more than what was in the extract I sent you then. I am, &c.

Ratisbon, 18/28 July, 87.
My Lord (Middleton):
The Electoral College on Saturday last made a conclusion about dictating the decree of commission left by the Prince of Passau, a copy of which I send you. The same day the Princes College made a conclusion upon this conclusion, which was not communicated, the Electoral College being risen before they had done, so that the decree is not yet dictated. It is true this decree can have no effect as to the main business, the naming a deputation to compliment the prince upon his departure, nevertheless the Director I think made a fault, which has given the Count de Windisgratz's faction the advantage of engaging the whole College of Princes in their interest. He ought not to have suppressed the decree but with the consent of all the Diet, whom first he ought to have acquainted with his reasons for doing it; though this be not of much moment, they pretend to be jealous the Director may assume a right of suppressing on his own head at some time or other a commission decree which may be of consequence to the Empire.

This great affair has taken up the whole care of the Diet these two months, by which your Lordship may see how hardly the deputies are put to't to find out work to make their principals believe they earn their pensions.

Here has been a report the French had given over

the design of making the fort at Trarbach, but the agent here in the Count de Crécy's absence tells me the work still goes on, though the ground is not proper.

Since my last to your Lordship of the 14th I have seen a letter written by the Count de Staremberg (nephew to him who was governor of Vienna [1] and an officer in his regiment) to some relations he has in this place of the 11th instant, in which he says the Duke of Lorraine and all his army were on the other side the Drave near Walpo; that the Elector of Bavaria came over the river that evening to speak with the Duke, and that the Elector's army was to pass and join them the next day; that 20,000 Turks were entrenched about Esseck, the Grand Vizier being towards the Save with a body of reserve; that they expected suddenly to engage; nevertheless that there was a whisper that the Vizier would propose a peace on such terms as might be accepted. I am, &c.

Ditto.

Sir (Mr. Corbet):

I begin to think I wear out of the memory of my acquaintance in England since I have not had a letter from any particular friend these three months. To comfort me for this I make the best of this place and do not omit any company, or indeed anything which can give me any sort of pleasure. In a former letter to you I desired you to let me know what my Lady Soames [2] does since her return, but I hear honest Sir Henry Shere [3] can give me a better account

[1] See p. 223, note 1.

[2] Sir William Soames married Lady Beata Pope, the sister of Lord Keeper Guildford's wife.

[3] Sir Henry Shere, or Sheres, military engineer and author, served against Monmouth as an officer of artillery, was knighted in 1685, and made surveyor of the ordnance in succession to Sir William Trumbull. He was a member of the Royal Society and a friend of Pepys.

of that than you can. It may be this will come to your hands at Tunbridge;[1] if it does, let my friends know I would willingly lose a hundred or two hundred pounds to enjoy them there this season, but since I cannot immediately have that happiness be so kind to let me have it at second hand. You are able to make the relation of what has passed there almost as pleasant to me as if I had been a partaker.

When you are with Tom Maul make him drink my health; it is the least he can do for a man who loves him so well. I am &c.

Ratisbon, 21/31 July, 87.

My Lord (Middleton):

The College of Princes have made a conclusion concerning the dictature of the commission's decree, which has been long the only business of the Diet. It ends reflecting on the Electoral College, in the same terms theirs, which I have sent you, reflects on them; so that the quarrel is grown higher, and the Electorals are so scandalized at it that they deliberate among themselves whether they shall reply or absolutely refuse the dictating the decree.

The Duke of Mantua[2] has left Vienna and is gone for Hungary; he has had some private conferences with the Emperor during his stay there, and, it is reported, about matters of consequence. Many things are talked of here, but without any grounds, wherefore I think them not worth the mentioning to

[1] Tunbridge Wells: 'at the season the general rendezvous of all the gay and handsome of both sexes . . . Everything there breathes birth and pleasure, constraint is banished, familiarity is established upon the first acquaintance, and joy and pleasure are the sole sovereigns of the place' (Grammont, *op. cit.*, p. 303).

[2] Ferdinand Charles Gonzaga, Duke of Mantua, was an extravagant and dissolute prince who involved his country in useless wars.

your Lordship, who knows that Duke makes many journeys without any design. If I can learn anything from good hands I will acquaint you with it.

Some letters the last post talked of some volunteers being taken by the Turks of Alba Regalis, who had put themselves into a small body and were marching towards the army without a convoy. This put me in pain for George Pitt's sons, who were the last who passed and might likely have been of the number; but it not being confirmed this day makes me hope the advice was false. I have not yet heard one word from the Duke of Berwick's company, though I have writ often to them. It may be they think it not worth while to give notice of anything less than the routing of the Turkish army and the taking of Esseck. Our news this day is little more than the confirmation of what I sent you in my last as you will find by the enclosed. I am &c.

Ditto, new style.

Monsieur (de Crécy):

Le Comte de Windisgratz est devenu beaucoup plus considérable depuis votre départ d'ici, et à cette heure, non pas un petit nombre, mais tout le Collège de Princes courent risque d'être convier à un beau festin après la prise d'Esseck.

Les dernières nouvelles de Vienne disent que l'Empereur n'est pas satisfait de la réponse de sa Majesté Chrétienne au mémoire qui lui a été présenté par Monsieur Skelton et qu'il espère d'obtenir des meilleurs conditions par la médiation de sa Majesté Britannique. Pour moi je n'ai point changé de sentiment depuis que j'ai su que Monsieur de Caunitz a desiré la garantie; et cela qui m'a plus confirmé dans mes pensées est que Monsieur de Caunitz a refusé de donner en écrit ce qu'il a dit en Angleterre sur cette réponse. Toute la conduite de ces affaires a une telle liaison qu'il n'est pas difficile de diviner de ce dont il s'agit à cette heure par cela qui s'est passé.

J'étais bien surpris d'apprendre que vous vous êtes [1] souvenu d'une bagatelle qui me touche dans un temps que mille affaires vous occupent qui vous sont de grande conséquence. C'est une obligation dont je serais toujours reconnaissant. Vous m'avez accablé avec beaucoup d'autres et je serais l'homme le plus ingrate du monde si je ne vous donnais pas en toutes occasions des bonnes raisons de croire que je suis, Monsieur,

Votre très humble et très obéissant serviteur
Geo. Etherege.

Faites, je vous prie Monsieur, mes très humbles baissements à Madame la Comtesse et dites lui que j'espère en peu de temps de baisser les cartes en les lui donnant à l'hombre.

Ratisbon, 25 July, 87.

My Lord (Dorset): [2]

When you consider I have been two years from England without letting you know I am sensible you are the person in the world I am most obliged to, you will have reason to think me very ungrateful, but I know your humour so well you had rather forgive a debt than be troubled with acknowledgement. I hope therefore you will look upon the neglect as the mere effect of laziness, and will easily excuse that vice in me, who am in a country from whence I can send you nothing to contribute to your pleasure. All my business in this dull place is to give a bare account of what is done, which requires only a little plain sense. I have lost for want of exercise the use of fancy and imagination, and am grown so very stupid that when I read a new poem methinks the author should be invited to one of those reverend cells the hermit Lee has

---

[1] MS. 'est'.   [2] See *ante*, p. 212, note 3.

quitted.[1] Lovers have been metamorphosed by the
ancient poets, though churches have not yet;[2] you
and I were ne'er so bold to turn the fair Castle
when she fled us into a tree, not dreaming she would
grow as big as one of Evelyn's oaks,[3] nor ourselves
into bulls when we carried the two draggle-tailed
nymphs one bitter, frosty night over the Thames to
Lambeth. Sertorius aimed to make a milk-white
hind an immortal dame, but his hint's improved by
the lady of the spotted muff's ingracious son. I
cannot guess on whom the Duke of Bucks' mantle
is fallen, but it is MacFlecknoe[4] with doubled
portion of that prophet's art. [There are many
lucky hits, and Bishop Martin is a master stroke.][5]

I am so glad of an occasion of laughing here; it
is no wonder the ridicule gets the better of the
heroic; a letter from Sheppard[6] might get the better

[1] Nathaniel Lee (1653?–92), dramatist, author of the
famous Restoration tragedy *The Rival Queens*, had been
removed to Bethlehem Hospital, insane, on Nov. 11, 1684.
His debauches probably aggravated an original tendency to
insanity. The *D.N.B.* states that Lee was detained for five
years (1689), but Etherege's allusion points to an earlier
though probably temporary release.

[2] An allusion to Dryden's *The Hind and the Panther*, in
which the former animal represents the Catholic, the latter
the Anglican church.

[3] Perhaps in allusion to John Evelyn's attempts in his
Sylva and in a discourse before the Royal Society 1662 to encourage the planting of oak forests in England.

[4] MS. 'MacFl': presumably an allusion to Dryden's satire
as a worthy successor to Buckingham's *Rehearsal*.

[5] The words enclosed in brackets are deleted in the MS.
The Martin in Dryden's *Hind and Panther* represents Father
Petre, the King's Jesuit Confessor.

[6] Sir Fleetwood Sheppard (1634–98), poet and courtier,
the boon companion of Dorset, Henry Savile, and other
rakes. In 1674 Dorset invited him to live at Copt Hall.
Sheppard was appointed steward to Nell Gwyn, and afterwards tutor to her son by the King, Charles, Earl of Burford.
On the accession of James II Sheppard lived in retirement at

of both if he had as great an alacrity in writing as he has in talking; there would be many congratulations if he had liberty granted him in this point; I wish it him heartily, since I never knew he had any further malice in it than making the company split themselves with laughter.

I would gladly be a witness of the content you enjoy at Copt Hall[1] now, and I hope to surprise you there one day, your gravity laid aside teaching my Lord Buckhurst[2] how to manage his hobby horse. I am, &c.

Ditto.

Sir (Dr. Wynne):

The Duke of Holstein-Gottorp has consented to the excluding of the house of Brunswick in the determining of the differences between the King of Denmark and him, and Altona is appointed for the place of treaty. I have not mentioned this sooner because Sir Peter Wyche is better posted to give you an account of it. I make no question but Sir Gabriel Sylvius has informed you that the marriage is concluded between the Prince Electoral of Saxony[3] and the Princess of Denmark, and that you have likewise heard that and the Prince Electoral of Brandenburg will not return to Potsdam, apprehending to live in that court since what has befallen the Margrave his brother.[4]

By this you see we have no news worth send[ing] you from hence except what comes from Esseck,

Copt Hall. He wrote several satires in verse, and was a patron of the poets, being the first to remark Prior's promise.

[1] Dorset's principal seat was at Knole, but he had also a country place at Copt Hall in Essex.

[2] Dorset's son Lionel was born the following January.

[3] Prince John George, afterwards Elector John George IV (1668–94). The marriage did not take place.

[4] See *ante*, p. 185, note 1. The Elector threatened to leave Prussia to Philip, son of his second wife.

which I have enclosed, and desire you to give it to my Lord. I am, &c.

Rattisbon, 28 July / 7 Aug., 87.

My Lord (Sunderland):

By the last post I gave your secretary an account how the Imperialists had missed of their design against Esseck [1] and were repassed the Drave. I send you now the best account we have here of what passed between the two armies when the Duke of Lorraine intended to have attacked the Turks in their retrenchments; it is in Dutch French, and the sense in all places not so clear as I could wish it, but you must allow for the great alloy in the coin of this country.

It is very likely that the Imperialists after this will besiege Sigeth,[2] or Alba Regalis or some other place, to oblige the Turks, if they can, in their turn to pass the Drave; but the year is far spent, and the army has suffered so much in this tedious march that I am afraid now the Turks have got a little heart again no great matter is to be hoped from this campaign. Many excuse the Duke of Lorraine and will not believe the secret was kept as it should have been. It is certain the Grand Vizier this year has behaved himself like a great captain, and all his motions have been regulated on the Duke's; the time which was lost by the water's being so very high, the not being informed of the strength of the enemy, the despising them a little too much, and the being obliged after better information to stay

[1] The repulse of the attack on Esseck was partly due to the imperfect co-operation between the Duke of Lorraine and the Elector of Bavaria. Esseck was an important fortress where the bridge over the Drave was the main link between South Hungary and Belgrade. Lorraine, against his better judgement, attacked the town for twenty-four hours, but was unable to draw the Turks from their retrenchments, and repassed the river on July 23rd.

[2] Szegedin, or Szeged.

till the Elector was joined with his army,[1] all contributed to the misfortune.

I intended to have writ to my Lord Godolphin, but having nothing to acquaint him with but what he will know of your Lordship I thought it would give him unnecessary trouble. I shall never be wanting in anything which may witness how much I esteem him, but I know no better way of gaining his favour than by your Lordship's speaking on my behalf to him which I do not doubt but you will add to the rest of the benefits you have conferred on
My Lord, &c.

Ditto.

My Lord (Middleton):

The Count de Lamberg in the little stay he made here, after his return from Salzburg before he went to Passau, used all the means he could, at the instance of the Count de Windisgratz, to get the Electoral College to receive him as principal commissioner *ad interim*, but it had no other success than the discovering of the Count de Windisgratz's practices, who has protested solemnly that it was so far from his seeking that he knew nothing of the decree of commission left by the Prince of Passau upon his retirement. I send you a copy of the declaration made yesterday by the Electoral College occasioned by a conclusion made in the College of Princes, which I have formerly mentioned. This declaration was delivered to the Director of the Princes' College, who reports that the College could not then deliberate upon it by reason of the absence of Monsieur Sauer, a minister who has fifteen masters, but the truth is they intend first to communicate it to the Count de Windisgratz, and to-morrow we shall see of what metal his cabal is made. I am, &c.

[1] The Elector of Bavaria's march to join Lorraine had been over rough country between Szegedin and Mohács.

Ratisbon, 4/14 Aug., 87.

Sir (Mr. Guy):

. . . The Germans call it a very fine and difficult retreat; it is a good thing when a man is fallen into a bog to have address and strength enough to get out again, but it is better to take such wise measures as not to make the false step . . . news. . .

I wish our friend Mr. Savile[1] as good success in what he is gone into France about as the Christian King has had, and the Marquis d'Angeau.[2]

You have a war in England between the Hind and the Panther. General Dryden is an expert captain, but I always thought him fitter for execution than for council; who commands the Panther's forces[3] I know not. The author of *The Revolter*, while he endeavours to expose the morals of his enemy, exposes more his own dullness by his poetry. The gentleman who has transversed the poem shews that the genius of the *Rehearsal* is not dead with the Duke of Bucks; there are several strokes which show that hand is skilful in the turn of satire, and one line which makes me think he has been acquainted

[1] Henry Savile (1642–87), brother of the Marquis of Halifax, the companion of Killigrew, Dorset, and Sheppard. In July he went to Paris for a surgical operation, from the effect of which he died on Oct. 6, 1687.

[2] Philippe de Courcillon, Marquis de Dangeau (1638–1720), soldier and diplomat.

[3] The Panther represented the Church of England. Among the many replies to Dryden's poem were *The Revolter; a Tragi-Comedy acted between the Hind and the Panther and Religio Laici, &c.*, 1687, and *The Hind and the Panther Transversed to the Story of the City and Country Mouse*, by Montague and Prior. This latter is the only other work of the controversy known to posterity. Mr. Saintsbury has summed it up as containing 'Some tolerable parody of Dryden's own work, and a good deal of heavy joking closely modelled on *The Rehearsal*' (*Dryden*, Men of Letters, pp. 97–8). There is a legend that Dryden wept at receiving such treatment from two young men to whom he had been kind.

with Sir Benjamin, the hero in an Essay of Comedy you have hear[d] of. Let them go on and turn the churches into what beasts they please, I shall never turn my religion, which teaches me to be always obedient and faithful to the King my master.

You are always so forward in doing me favours, that it is superfluous to beg them of you, and I do not doubt but you will help Mr. Robson in getting my extraordinaries now they begin to grow stale, without saying more than that they will come very seasonably to, &c.

Ditto.

My Lord (Middleton):

I send your Lordship the answer the Princes' College have made to the last declaration of the College of Electors touching the dictating of the commission's decree so much contested. Your Lordship may take notice that the conclusion made by the Electorals in 1684, mentioned in their first declaration about this matter, was only a particular conclusion of that College in which the Princes had not concurred. The Princes have, since this declaration, demanded the dictature of the commission's decree of the Director of Mayence, and the Count de Windisgratz yesterday demanded it of him in the Emperor's name, so that on Saturday next we shall see what end this business will have.

We have no other news from Vienna by this post, saving that on the 11th of this instant an express arrived there from the Prince Louis de Baden,[1] which says the Turks have passed the Drave with their whole army, and are so strongly entrenched

[1] Louis William, Margrave of Baden (1655–1707), born in Paris but educated in Germany. He served at Buda, took the town of Fünfkirchen, and burnt the bridge at Esseck. In the campaign of 1687 he had a share in the victory of Mohács, and in 1689 was given command in the Imperial army.

near Darda [1] that it is impossible to attack them. The courier says nevertheless that half an hour after his departure he heard such a terrible noise of cannon and other shot that he believes there might have been some engagement. This makes them expect another express with impatience. Though there was a design to besiege Sigeth I am apt to believe the Turks being entrenched with their whole army within so few leagues off the place it will go nigh to break those measures.

The Prince of Neuberg is sick of a fever, as some letters mention; but I have not in any private letters, though I have seen many of much fresher dates than my Lord Dongan's was, found anything concerning the Duke of Berwick, which makes me think he is not desperately ill, and hope by this time he is recovered. I am, &c.

Ratisbon, 8/18 Aug., 87.

Sir (Mr. Bridgeman): [2]

I had yesterday the few lines you were pleased to favour me with and to show you how grateful I am to those who are willing to remember me I could not omit the thanking of you for them this day. Considering the little time you have to spare from your many painful employments, the obligation is more to me than if I should receive a long letter from an idle fellow; but neither the idle nor the busy are much given to think of a friend so far off as I am. If I have an answer to one letter in three I esteem myself well paid, and if I have none it is not so vexatious, I fancy, as it would be to have two or three answers to a poem had I the skill and genius to write one. I send you what news I have from Hungary, which I desire you to show my Lord.

[1] Fort Darda, on the opposite side of the Drave to Esseck.
[2] See *ante*, p. 224, note 1.

The kindest thing you can do for me in my absence is to preserve me in his memory. I am &c.

Ditto.

My Lord (Middleton):

This day the commission's decree which has been so long chicaned here was dictated, the Electoral College reserving their rights and renewing their protestations against the Count de Windisgratz's pretensions.

All the news I have seen in private letters this day from Vienna is that the Duke of Lorraine and the Elector of Bavaria are encamped with their army near Mohatz and the Turks at Darda, there having not yet been any engagement, and if we may make any judgement from the Grand Vizier's conduct the Christians are not likely to do any great matters this campaign.

I have not these two posts had any letter from our volunteers. I am, &c.

Ratisbon, 11/21 Aug., 87.

My Lord (Sunderland):

I received yesterday your letter of the 26 of July concerning mourning for the Duchess of Modena,[1] and forthwith took care to perform what you commanded me.

On Monday last the 8th instant, in the evening here arrived a staffetta[2] from Vienna, dispatched by a friend to the Count de Windisgratz to let him know the Emperor had received the news of a victory obtained against the Turks the 10th instant,

[1] The Duchess of Modena was the Queen of England's mother. She died in Rome on July 19th, aged 53, after an eleven days' sickness. Luttrell reports that the English court went into mourning on July 31st, and that Whitehall and St. James' were hung with black.

[2] A mounted courier.

new style; the Prince of Savoy [1] brought this welcome message, who was dispatched as soon as the Christians were masters of the Turkish camp. The same night I writ a letter in haste to my Lord Middleton to acquaint him with this action, which I sent by Holland, and, an express parting hence for Paris, I writ at the same time to Mr. Skelton, thinking by the diligence of the express the news might be in England sooner that way.

All the particulars I have yet learned are these: the Imperialists drew up in battle and the Turks drew a very considerable body out of their trenches, intending only to skirmish. The Elector of Bavaria commanded the left wing, in which were many of the young nobility, who were impatient of signalizing themselves, and, it is said, the Turks were engaged by their forwardness to attack them. The Elector himself has a contusion by a blow on the left hand, and the Prince de Comercy, who is reported to have done things beyond belief, is shot through both the shoulders and has lost the greatest part of his regiment; nevertheless the Germans reckon but 500 men of theirs killed, and we hear of no other person of quality wounded, which makes me hope well of our countrymen; it is affirmed the Turks have lost eight or nine thousand who remained dead upon the place, the like number is reckoned to be drowned in the Drave. The Christians entered their camp with them, where their great body of reserve took the fright and dispersed themselves, leaving their artillery and baggage. The artillery is said to be 100 pieces of cannon, great and small, and the riches which were found in their tents incredible. Many here reason

---

[1] The famous Prince Eugène of Savoy (1663–1736) entered the service of Leopold I in 1683. He was sent by the Emperor to the Duke of Savoy, whom he brought into the coalition against the French.

on the consequences of this great victory,[1] but I shall not trouble your Lordship with imaginations; it is likely this ordinary will only confirm what we have heard already; if it bring any other particulars I will enclose them for your Lordship.

Yesterday was dictated a decree of commission delivered by the Count de Windisgratz to acquaint the Diet in form with this victory, which will occasion a conclusion to congratulate the Emperor upon it, who no doubt is infinitely well pleased with his unexpected good fortune; but he cannot be more pleased than I was with what your Lordship so kindly added to your circular letter. I am, &c.

Ditto.

My Lord (Dover):
It is so long since I presumed to trouble you with one letter, that I imagine you begin to think yourself secure from the like persecution, but men in your post lie so open, they must expect to be shot at, and I cannot forbear aiming at you, bearing you an inclination of an older date than I will mention, both for your own sake and my own. You are not only a courtier but a soldier, not only a fine gentleman but a good Christian, and these things help to embolden me to give you a short account of the victory the Christians have gained against the Turks . . . (The news as in the foregoing letter.) It ended: I know so generous a man as you are will help an old acquaintance with a good word, when

[1] This battle is variously called Harkány (Harsan), Siclos, or Mohács. The Grand Vizier, on the track of the Imperial army retreating from Esseck, risked a pitched battle at Harkány and suffered a crushing defeat on August 12th. The *London Gazette* reported 8,000 Turks slain and 100 pieces of cannon captured. This important victory did more than any other single event to overthrow the ascendancy of the Turks in Hungary (*Cambridge Modern History*, v. 367).

you think it convenient in the Treasury, and excuse me the time I make you lose in showing you how faithfully I am, &c.

Ratisbon, 18/28 Aug., 87.

My Lord (Middleton):

I did not think I should have occasion yet awhile to trouble you again with anything concerning the observation of the truce, but spirits here [are] beginning to warm since they know his Majesty has not accepted of the guarantee, on reasons better know[n] to your Lordship than to me; I imagine it may not be altogether unnecessary to acquaint you with the temper I am in, it being a thing which may hereafter disturb the peace of Christendom.

The gentlemen who projected the alliance of Augsburg deny that the Count de Lobkowitz ever told Monsieur de Croissy, upon his Christian Majesty's last declaration before the guarantee was proposed, that the Emperor was willing the truce should be kept without mentioning any more the griefs, which had been complained of.

The French accuse them to be men of evil faith, and say it is that which makes them find often evasions for giving memorials in writing, that they may have recourse to their usual policy, which is to deny what they have said. The Emperor's ministers, together with the Swedish, the Spanish,[1] and Holland ministers here, say that the answer his Christian Majesty has made to Mr. Skelton's memorial, touching the guarantee offered by his Majesty, is contrary to the truce, and that the said King has no right to enlarge any fortifications, much less build any new forts, in any of those places the sovereignty of which is only accorded him provisionally for twenty years. I never heard them give any other reasons for this than that it is against the

[1] Probably de Neuforge. See *post*, p. 379.

very nature of an armistice, which implies a cessation of all manner of hostility, and against all laws, but still in general terms without any particular quotations or precedent. Upon this the French agent here has order to endeavour to remove the impressions this may make on people, and does therefore insinuate that the Emperor's ministers, who have signed the said truce, and all the ministers of the several States of the Empire here at Ratisbon, can, and ought for the truth's sake, to remember that by the truce they have not only by the twelfth article formally renounced to all rights of sovereignty, and yielded the same in the fifth article to his Christian Majesty without any exception or restriction, and promising nobody should disturb him in the enjoyment of his rights, whereof that of building some forts for the security of others he affaires[?] is one; but that they even abandoned the article, which they had prepared in the project upon which the treaty was founded, to restrain his Christian Majesty from fortifying, &c. (a copy of which taken from the original papers I send your Lordship) the 13th of August 1684, being that day rejected by the French plenipotentiary. From whence he insinuates that they cannot, without violating the truce themselves, maintain now that to be contrary to the intention of the truce which they durst not then maintain by the treaty. He insinuates an example from the 29th article of the truce concluded between the Archduke Albert and the States General the 9th of April 1609, by which it is stipulated that there should be no new forts built in the Low Countries during that truce on either side, and from thence concludes that there being no stipulation to the contrary his Christian Majesty may raise what forts he pleases within his dominion for the preservation of what he is to possess for twenty years, according to the tenor of the truce.

The Elector of Bavaria, having heard that the Count de Caunitz had desired his Majesty in the Emperor's name to be guarant[ee] of the truce, has writ to his minister[1] here to inform him what is done in it, seeming to take it very ill that the Emperor did not first acquaint his allies with it, and all the States of the Empire who are generally concerned.

The Diet have made a conclusion to congratulate the Emperor on the victory; the Count de Windisgratz pretends it should be delivered to him as principal commissioner *ad interim*; the Electoral College oppose it, so that this will beget a new war, that being ended which was occasioned by the dictating the decree of commission left by the Prince of Passau. I am, &c.

Ratisbon, 22 Aug./1 Sept., 87.

My Lord (Sunderland):

I sent by Lord Middleton by the last post the best account I then had of the battle given near Siklos. I now enclose for your Lordship a copy of a letter on the same purpose, ordered by the gentleman who writ it to be communicated to me; I made an acquaintance with him on my first coming hither; this is the third campaign he has made in Hungary as a volunteer in the Elector of Bavaria's troops; he is very curious in his observations, and his quality and reputation give him occasion to satisfy himself and his friends. The latter part of this letter is wanting, the time being too short to transcribe it; it was sent with what was copied to Monsieur de Croissy; it gives a description of the Turkish camp and how it was fortified, with a few other particulars, and ends with another article touching the Duke of Mantua, much more pleasant than what is in the part I send you. He had saved himself

[1] Wampel; see *ante*, p. 98.

behind the baggage during the engagement, and could not without much difficulty after the victory be persuaded to enter the enemy's camp to join the Duke of Lorraine. Nothing would prevail till they had assured him *che tutti li Turchi stavano amazzati*;[1] then he let himself be conducted, but with much precaution, finding fault that no more troops were left to guard the baggage during the combat.[2] He has no equipage, the Duke of Lorraine furnishing him by the Emperor's order with all things necessary for himself and his retinue, Monsieur de Gambo not excepted, the most Christian King's minister who is always at his elbow. I am, &c.

Ditto.

My Lord (Middleton):

I send your Lordship a copy of an extract of the propositions made by the Emperor to the nobility of Hungary at Vienna for the better regulating the affairs of that kingdom, which now in all likelihood will be delivered from the tyranny of the Turks. Your Lordship had by the last an account of the battle and victory as it is written to us here from Vienna. I have sent to my Lord Sunderland part of a letter by this post, written on the same subject by a French gentleman who is a volunteer in the Elector of Bavaria's troops. If you have a curiosity to see it, you will find what a resolute enemy the Turk is, and how redoubtable the great Gonzagas continue to be in the person of the present Duke of Mantua.

I send you the little news I have received this day, and am with all duty, &c.

[1] 'that all the Turks were massacred'.
[2] The Duke of Mantua's cowardice was notorious. *Cf. Memoirs of Berwick*, i. 15: 'The Duke of Mantua, who was a volunteer, was not much exposed to danger; for as soon as he saw the Turks advancing to attack us, he retired to the mountain of Harsan'.

Ratisbon, 25 Aug./4 September, 87.

My Lord (Middleton):

The Electoral College have appointed to-morrow to agree on the form in which, according as they have unanimously concluded, they shall severally write to their masters to know their pleasure concerning the Count de Windisgratz's pretensions to be the Emperor's principal commissioner here. The substance of what is intended to be writ is: whether the Electors think it of the dignity of a Diet of the Empire to admit of a principal commissioner who is not a Prince of the Empire contrary to all precedents, and if so whether they think it convenient to receive the Count de Windisgratz as such, who ever since he has been here has violently opposed them in their rights and privileges, endeavouring to put them on the same level with the Princes.

How this matter would go was a question till a few days since a cordelier,[1] in a sermon he preached at St. Ulric's[2] in this town, put all godly people out of doubt, confidently affirming that all Christendom was beholden to a vow the Count de Windisgratz had made who was before, was now, and still should be what he was, in spite of all his enemies, the Emperor's principal commissioner, &c.

There have been disputes whether the glory of the last victory belongs most to the Duke of Lorraine or to the Elector of Bavaria, but this sermon has made some write to their friends in the army who were hotly engaged that they might give over their idle contests, and that both the Duke and the Elector were but the executors of the Count's vow, to whom the cordelier had justly given the laurel.

I sent to your Lordship in my last of the 22

---

[1] A Franciscan friar, so called from his girdle of knotted cord.   [2] A church adjoining the cathedral.

instant, for want of other news, the public written news which comes on post days from Vienna hither. There was something in it concerning my Lord Taaffe in which I imagine there is a mistake which you know how to rectify better than I do. In a visit I made yesterday to the Baron of Frise, the Elector of Saxony's minister, he told me he had received a letter which tells him my Lord Taaffe is made great marshal to the Queen of Poland, the Duke of Lorraine's wife,[1] and that he was a going to Innsbruck[2] to take possession of his office, and that the Duke of Berwick commands his regiment the rest of this campaign. Monsieur Scherer, the second minister for Austria, has read an Italian paper to the Diet which makes much noise here; the business of it is to persuade them, there is a good understanding between the French and the Turks. I asked the Baron if he heard it read; he told me he came late that day to the council, nevertheless he heard part of it; that for want of practising lately the Italian tongue he could not understand it distinctly; that he had a design to have a copy of it, but the several ministers told him Scherer absolutely refused to give any. I told him it seemed strange to me he should read a thing in full Diet and afterwards refuse to trust the ministers with copies of it, it being only matter of news and that it merited their resentment, it looking like imposing on the illustrious assembly; that Diets were not things to be jested with; that either he should not have communicated it to them, or have given them leave to examine it. This, as I am told, is writ by way of letter from a Turk out of their own camp to a Turk who was taken prisoner by the Bavarians. There are several impertinences in it, as that the French in the Turkish

[1] The Duke of Lorraine married the Archduchess Eleanora Maria, widow of King Michael of Poland, in 1678.
[2] MS. 'Insprugg'.

camp advised the taking the Elector of Bavaria as the only means to make an advantageous peace with the Emperor; that there was no hope of coming to treat in earnest of a peace, while the French had so strong a faction in the Vizier's council. If I can possibly get a copy of it from Vienna I will send it your Lordship hereafter. These foolish proceedings daily sawer[?] affairs, as you will see in the billet I send you which was writ to me on this occasion by Mr. Frischman, the French agent here in the Count de Crécy's absence, who is now on his way back.

I send your Lordship to divert you an extract of part of a letter writ by an acquaintance of mine who was present at an interview of two hundred Turks and as many Christians between both armies a few days before the battle on the releasing of a Bassa taken prisoner at Buda,[1] and am, &c.

Ratisbon, 29 Aug./8 Sept., 1687.

My Lord (Middleton):

I gave your Lordship an account on the 18th instant, old style, how matters stood here concerning the execution of the truce; since which time I have seen a copy of a circular letter writ by the Emperor to the Electors on that subject, and more particularly on the building of the fort at Trarbach;[2] a copy of that which was sent to the Elector of Mayence coming to my hands I have enclosed it in

[1] Ishmael Bassa, who had been made prisoner at Buda, was released a few days before the battle of Harkány on the payment of 14,000 crowns ransom. Two hundred picked men from each side advanced, keeping a fixed distance from one another. Dünewald sent two officers as pledges for the two Turks who were to bring the money. The Turks soon became friendly, one going so far as to display his dexterity on horseback. The Bassa on his return to the Turkish ranks alighted, threw himself on his knees and face, lay thus prostrate for some time, and then rose with tears in his eyes (*London Gazette*, Sept. 8–12th).   [2] See *ante*, p. 234, note 1.

this that your Lordship may make a judgement thereof; if the Count de Crécy (who is not expected before the latter end of September) were here I believe I should likewise send you a commentary on it. *I have only made*[1] two or three observations in the margent, where the sense to me seems to be equivocal. It is a maxim among the Emperor's ministers to be always complaining and making of noise on every innovation which is made in the lands yielded by the truce, lest the world should forget they are part of the Empire, and how they came to be divided for a while from the body. The Swede who joins with them is more violent than they, concerned he is out of play, and hoping great advantages from a revolution in the affairs of Christendom; the Spaniard's chagrin and the thoughts he has he cannot be in a worse condition make him blow the coals, and others for other interests add more fuel to the fire.

I send your Lordship likewise a copy of a note written by the French minister, who is without a character here, to a friend and dispersed about the town on the occasion of the Italian paper read in the Diet by Monsieur Scherer, the Count de Windisgratz's humble slave, which reflects on the person of his Christian Majesty. Your Lordship may remember at the time of the siege of Vienna the idle reports which were raised on the taking of the Grand Vizier's cassette.[2] These are much of the same nature. The Elector of Bavaria, concerned that a faction in the Empire would rob him of the glory of the late victory, has sent a particular relation thereof to Munich, which his minister here has given to be printed; it will come out this afternoon in Dutch,[3] but I shall not be able to get it translated before the next post. I am, &c.

[1] Written in margin: 'made by Mr. Frischman.'
[2] MS. 'casset' = casket.   [3] i.e., German.

The hundred Roman months formerly demanded are put in Ensag [?] and the ministers having anew received instructions from their principals will be this week deliberated on.

Ratisbon, 1/11 Sept., 87.

Sir (Sir Edward Vaudrey):

Notwithstanding the lucky success of the Christians against the Turks I have received no news from your army which was so welcome to me as your letter of the 6th of this month, new style. It has almost restored me to that quiet of mind which I lost on the first account I had of the Duke of Berwick's distemper.[1] I hope you have taken care to put all who have the happiness to know him in England as much at ease [as] you have done me; especially his Majesty, who, I am confident, has been in very great pain for him. I cannot but tremble yet when I reflect on the malignity of the disease, and the little relief he could have in those barbarous parts to help him to overcome it. Nothing can give me an entire satisfaction but the seeing him in his return perfectly recovered. Your haste made you forget to let me know where you are, but the freshness of the date of what you write me makes me think you are at Vienna, where you may find all things necessary to assist nature to accomplish speedily what she herself has been long labouring to effect. The Duke must be careful of himself too, not only for his own sake but for the welfare of all those whom his charms have equally engaged with him in whatsoever shall concern him. If our sex be not worth his thoughts let him think on the other, and how severely he has been revenged on them for all the sighs they have cost him. However *fière* some

---

[1] During the attack on Esseck, the Duke fell ill of a violent fever. His indisposition continuing he was compelled to retire to Buda for the recovery of his health.

of them may have appeared, their hearts have been tender on this occasion, and will scarce leave aching till they see him in London again with that vigour and beauty which has never failed secretly to warm them.

I have nothing of consequence from our own country. His Majesty is now in his progress and will join the Queen at the Bath on the 6th instant in order to bring her back. I am, very faithfully, &c.

Ditto.

Sir (Mr. de Paz):[1]

I am very much beholden to you for the trouble you have given yourself in my business in the absence of Mr. Wynne. I shall always have it in my memory, and be willing to serve you in my turn, when I have an occasion. Pray give Mr. Wynne the enclosed bill of extraordinaries[2] that he may get it allowed; it completes the two years I have been out of England. I hope Mr. Robson will solicit this and those he has already, and get them paid altogether. The heat of this campaign is over, so that our news is not worth your knowing. I am, &c.

Ditto.

My Lord (Middleton):

Yesterday the Diet deliberated on the hundred Roman months. The Electoral College is ready to grant the Emperor his desires, the other Colleges are divided on the business; the cabal which join with the house of Austria are for giving all; the house of Brunswick alleges a letter written to the Emperor in which they urge their reasons to be excused; the circle[s] of Swabia, Franconia, and the upper Rhine desire the Emperor's exemption, saying

[1] Samuel de Paz, secretary to Lord Dartmouth, was deputising for Dr. Wynne in his absence.
[2] See *post*, p. 367.

they are not able to pay. In a few days more we shall see what a conclusion this will produce.

I have sent you translated out of Dutch the relation of the battle of Harsan, printed by the Elector of Bavaria's order, which I promised by the last post. The heroic Maximilian, it is said, has changed his resolution of leaving the army so soon, and will stay and endeavour to take Esseck to make his glory complete. I am.

I forgot to acquaint your Lordship with a thing which may be of consequence. Monsieur Scherer, the deputy of Austria, concluded the note he gave for the hundred Roman months with words to this purpose: that the States would, by granting this subsidy, do the Empire an eminent service which the Emperor would acknowledge by endeavouring to make a tolerable peace, or at least a truce, with the Turks. Some say he only meant by this to insinuate it should be the last time he would trouble them in this nature, but the French are not satisfied with this interpretation.

It is now six o'clock at night and the post is not come in from Vienna yet, so that I doubt it will not come time enough to send you the news. What I have said concerning the attacking Esseck I have in a letter from Monsieur Lantery, the minister of Savoy at Munich, of the 9th instant, new style.

Ratisbon, 5/15 Sept., 87.

My Lord (Middleton):

On Friday last the College of Electors and that of the Princes exchanged the conclusions they had severally made in granting the hundred Roman months, being assembled together in the chamber *de re et correlatione*,[1] and this week the general conclusion will be agreed on. The College of Electors

---

[1] The great council-room of the Diet now called the Reichssaal.

were unanimous in the giving of this aid, but some of the Princes,[1] as I have mentioned before, would not tax themselves, and no State of the Empire can be legally taxed without its own consent. Many expedients were proposed to make this conclusion of the Princes more plausible: the dissenters not allowing the word unanimous to be inserted, one proposed the greatest part had granted, another that the College had almost unanimously granted, but these propositions being laughed at, it was subtly proposed that the word unanimous should be left out, which they all agreed to, and those which would not tax themselves are duped with *on a accordé*.

Our last post from Vienna came in a day later than it should have done, and brought us no news save only that a hussar was arrived there who said Esseck did capitulate; but no credit was given to him, not bringing anything from the general, and no courier arriving since to confirm it.

There is no doubt of its being false. If our post be here to-day in time your Lordship shall have the news enclosed. I am, &c.

Ratisbon, 8/18 Sept., 87.

Sir (Mr. Wynne):

I just now received yours of the 26th of August, and hope you have diverted yourself well in the country. The Diet not having yet agreed on the general conclusion concerning the Roman months, I have nothing to send my Lord to-day but the news we receive from Vienna, which I have enclosed for him in this. The Duke of Berwick is pretty well

[1] The Princes were divided: some consented to the tax, others considered themselves too exhausted, a third party were of opinion deductions should be made in favour of those Princes who had sent troops to assist the Emperor; the majority were, however, agreed to the imposition.

recovered of his sickness and is come to Vienna. Most of our country['s] volunteers are at Pressburg, where I hear they intend to stay to see the ceremony of the Archduke Joseph's coronation,[1] which I am told will be about three weeks hence. We have only lost my poor Lord Kenoul, who died at Mohatz a few days before the battle.

I this day was paid £500, which Mr. Robson has taken care to return me; pray thank him for me, and let him know I will do it myself the next post. Mr. de Paz[2] has been so kind as to write to me constantly during your absence, of which I am very sensible, and likewise of the trouble which you on all occasions give yourself in what concerns

Sir, &c.

Ratisbon, 12/22 Sept.

My Lord (Middleton):

The difficulties which the Imperial towns have made about granting the Roman months have for some time retarded the passing of the general conclusion, but it is said it will be infallibly agreed on this day, so that I shall be able to send you a copy of it by the next post.

The greatness of the rivers, swelled by continual rains which have fallen in these parts, have been the reason so great a victory has not had the consequence which might reasonably be expected. The campaign, I find, is ended, and I am afraid the Imperial army will be much ruined with what they have suffered already, and with what they must undergo before they get to their winter quarters. The Duke of

[1] This much-postponed event did not take place until December 9th. The Archduke Joseph (1678–1711), afterwards Emperor Joseph, was the nine-year-old son of Leopold. His coronation marked the recognition of the Hungarian crown as hereditary in the male Habsburg line.

[2] See *ante*, p. 259, note 1.

Lorraine is expected at Vienna so soon as the Elector is gone for Munich.

I cannot give any account of the Duke of Berwick, not having lately had the favour to hear from our volunteers.

The Elector of Brandenburg is sending one Monsieur Schmettau[1] to be his minister here in the stead of Monsieur de Jena, who is recalled and disgraced. This animates the French more against that Elector, he having punished de Jena for having favoured, as his enemies alleged, their interest, and sent one to succeed him who is engaged in a faction at that court against them.

I send your Lordship what news we have from the army. You must not expect any great matters since the operations which were designed are given over. I am, with much duty, &c.

Ratisbonne, ditto, new style.

Je ne suis pas mort, Monsieur, et le mal que j'ai n'est pas à la main comme vous voyez; c'est à l'invincible et héroïque Maximilien que le ciel réserve des blessures si honorables. Vous n'aurez guère de peine à deviner ma maladie quand je vous dirai maudit soit mon jardin, le louage m'en coûte trop cher. C'est s'expliquer aussi nettement que si je m'aurais servi du proverbe si connu aux ouvriers en soie: le chat échaudé &c.[2] Après cette confidence pouvez vous imaginer que c'est une indifférence qui a causé un si long silence. Non, mon ami, c'est

---

[1] Wolfgang von Schmettau was ordered to avoid conflict with the French, not to treat of the peace as this might provoke a rupture, but only to protest prudently against the contraventions. Schmettau, though looked on with suspicion by the French party, behaved with civility and tact to Crécy. His orders were evidence of the Elector of Brandenburg's desire to prolong the peace between France and the Empire.

[2] Chat échaudé craint l'eau froide.

le chagrin et la honte d'avoir goûté de ce fruit malsain que vous m'aviez défendu, qui m'ont empeché de paraître devant vous. Pardonnez une faiblesse qui ne dément point notre origine; tout ce que je sais[1] de nos Fraüleins ne vaut pas la peine de vous le mander. Elles sont insensibles à tout hormis le tonnerre qui depuis peu se fait craindre. Vous savez que j'étais toujours philosophe, mais vous ne savez pas que je change de secte. J'étais peripatetique et j'aimais la promenade, mais tout d'un coup je suis devenu disciple d'Épicure, je me tien, dans ma petite retraite, et je me suis établi pour maxime que la plus grand volupté consiste dans une parfaite santé. Le transport d'une débauche ne paye pas le mal au cœur qu'on sent le lendemain au matin. Ces morales sont admirables, mais je n'ai pas le loisir de m'étendre sur un si digne sujet; pour ces atomes ils ne me rompent guère la tête. Par la grâce de Dieu je sais où mon esprit est borné et je ne me mets guère en peine de savoir de quelle manière ce monde ici a été fait ou comment on se divert dans l'autre; cette grande humilité vous peut persuader que je suis bien préparé pour reçevoir ces lumières et ces rayons dont vous faites mention que la belle comtesse me vient éclairer. J'admire ses beaux yeux, mais j'ai[2] peur que son âme ne soit aussi aveugle que celles des autres mortelles; afin que vous ne vous imaginiez pas une étrange affaire de ce qui est arrivé, sachez que j'en suis déjà si bien sorti que je fus avant hier à la chasse et que mes laquais reportèrent trois lièvres en croupe à la maison dont 'Silk'[3] en attrapa le plus gros. Cette manière d'écrire sans réserve vous doit assurer que je suis, Monsieur, votre très humble et très obéissant serviteur G.E.

[1] MS. 'say'.
[2] MS. 'je'.
[3] Presumably the name of a hound.

Sir (Mr. Poley):

Though I am a great lover of the sun and never cared for trading northward yet the encouragement of a return from you of the 24th of August makes me prefer that traffic to the commerce I have in all other parts. I made the compliment which you desired me to the Countess of Stubenberg, to whom I found it was very agreeable; if I have any advantage in her good opinion I owe it all to my being your countryman.

The Count de Windisgratz, since the retreat of the Prince of Passau, has had a better game to play for what he pretends to than ever he had before; at first his cabal endeavoured to make him be received as principal commissioner *ad interim*, but lately, upon a new negotiation about the delivering the conclusion for congratulating the Emperor upon the late victory, his creatures have changed the question, crying that the Electorals had already acknowledged him as principal commissioner in delivering a conclusion or two to him formerly, which the Electorals did to make him a compliment on his first coming hither after he was received as Con-representant.[1] The Electorals have writ to their principals, and this matter depends till they have received their instructions. The Count, to weaken the Electorals and to strike some terror into them, has taken the advantage, now the Elector of Brandenburg is ill with France, to accuse Monsieur de Jena of being in the French interest, and though the whole College of Electors justified the contrary of what was alleged against him, and that the Director gave him this justification under the great seal of the Empire, the Elector his master has recalled him and

---

[1] The Diet replied that they did not oppose this move because it would have obstructed important business, but that such an innovation must not be repeated lest it should be interpreted as a cession of rights.

he is now at Halle, where he is Chancellor but in disgrace. Monsieur Metternich is in Monsieur Schenbeck's place, as much the Count's humble creature as Mr. de Scherer, and Monsieur Schmettau, who has married Monsieur Fuchs'[1] daughter, is coming hither in de Jena's place.

Instead of troubling you with these impertinences I should sooner have reflected how much they have tired you formerly.

The Electoral and the Princes' College have granted the Emperor the hundred Roman months which have long lain dormant. The Towns make some difficulty in giving their consent, but this day the general conclusion will be passed.

I desired Sir Peter Wyche to give you advice of the victory obtained near Darda, which I hope he did accordingly; the Elector of Bavaria, jealous that the victory was not enough ascribed to his courage and conduct.

Ratisbon, 15/25 Sept., 87.

My Lord (Middleton):

According to my promise in my last of the 12th instant I send your Lordship a copy of the general conclusion about the hundred Roman months which passed in the Diet that same day. The only business which employs the ministers here at present are the intrigues and practices of the Count de Windisgratz's cabal to get the conclusions lately made delivered to him. This being only a matter which concerns the two factions here I shall not presume to trouble your Lordship with the particu-

---

[1] Paul von Fuchs (1640–1704), the clever and influential Brandenburg statesman, negotiator in the Schwiebus question 1686, and in the quarrels between Denmark and Holstein-Gottorp. He was named one of the mediating ministers at Altona, and succeeded, after a journey to Copenhagen, in bringing the conference to a close by a treaty in 1689.

lars of what is done in it. It will be enough if the dispute comes to be ended to let you know what party carries the point. I am, &c.

Ratisbon, 19/29 Sept., 87.

Sir (Mr. Wynne):

I received yesterday yours of the 2nd instant. You may imagine I have been much concerned I have had no better correspondence with our volunteers this campaign that I might oftener give my Lord an account of the Duke of Berwick's health. I did all I could to engage them to it, both by making them very welcome here and writing kindly to them when they were in the army, but I could never draw no more than two letters from them, one from my Lord Dongan after the retreat from the other side of the Drave, and one from Sir Edward Vaudrey upon his return to Vienna, the substance of which I sent into England. I am sorry to hear you were alarmed with the false news of the Duke of Berwick's death, occasioned by that of my Lord Kenoul's at Mohatz. A secretary at Vienna belonging to the Prince of Mecklenburg made that impertinent mistake, which I knew not time enough to prevent the surprise it might occasion, but I hope little credit was given to it, and the apprehension it put the court into made the news of his recovery be received more joyfully. The army drawing towards their winter quarters, and the disputes the Count de Windisgratz has with the Electorals about his pretensions to be principal commissioner here, are the reasons I have nothing worth troubling my Lord with at present.

To answer you touching the proposition the gentleman desired you to make me in his behalf I must tell you I find by your letter you do not well understand the coin of this country. It is very low, and our best *guilders* are not above half good silver, but this is not to the purpose. I will tell you what I receive here for £500 sterling: by a return by way of Amsterdam I had 2,464 dollars, each dollar being a guilder or a florin (which is all one) and one half; the true value of a dollar here, current money, being just four shillings English, so that I had in that return 36 dollars of this country less than the true value of my money, that being the gain of the merchants. If the gentleman will deal as ingeniously as I do, and will be willing the merchants shall not have the advantage of our money sticking to their fingers, I shall accept of the proposition. I am very much.

I suppose you mean ducats by what you name guildiners; each ducat if in gold and [full] weight comes to three florins and one half, the upgelt [?] being counted, which (according to four shillings a dollar) 150 guildiners amount to £70 sterling, but this does not reach the sum of 86 or 87 which you mention, so that I must expect till the gentleman explain himself better, and whether it is current money or what other sort of money I am to receive.

Ratisbon, 22 Sept./2 Oct., 87.

My Lord (Middleton):

I have sent you the copy of two letters: one is the Elector of Saxony's answer to the Emperor's of the 16 of July, which you had some time since, about the building of the fort on the Moselle;[1] the other is the Elector of Cologne's. I had sent them to your Lordship before now but that I found some difficulty to get them translated. In the Elector of Saxony's you will find he is not well satisfied the Emperor proposed the guarantee without his knowledge; many other States of the Empire resent it, as I have intimated to your Lordship formerly. In the Elector of Cologne's there is an article which

[1] Trarbach.

concerns his Majesty, as if he should have declared that the answer which the French King gave to the memorial given him by Mr. Skelton touching the guarantee is conformable to the truce. The ministers are very curious to know what they ought to think of this, and the Director of Mayence desired me in a visit I made him on Tuesday last to clear this matter to him if I could. I told him I knew nothing of it, and that I could not imagine how his Majesty could have any occasion to make any such declaration; the Count de Caunitz, having in a private audience which he had of his Majesty after his Christian Majesty had explained himself, excused himself from giving a memorial of his exceptions to it; what then passed in discourse between his Majesty and the Count I was not informed of, nor could I say anything of his Majesty's opinion on the matter in dispute: whether his Christian Majesty according to the truce might build what forts he thought fit on the lands yielded to him in sovereignty during the term he is to enjoy them.

Yesterday Captain Brown, who came to make the campaign with the late Lord Kenoul, passed through the town, and told me he left the Duke of Berwick perfectly recovered at Vienna; that he resolved to come forthwith for England, and that I might expect him here every moment. My Lord Dongan and Sir Edward Vaudrey are something indisposed, yet they come along with him.

My Lord Charles Hamilton,[1] with his tough constitution is the only man who has weathered out the campaign in constant health. I am, &c.

Mr. Nugent,[2] my Lord Dongan's kinsman, is left very ill at Buda, and 'tis feared will not recover.

[1] See *ante*, p. 217, note 1.
[2] Christopher Nugent, eldest son of Francis Nugent of Dardistown, Meath, and Bridget, the sister of William Dungan, was a soldier of some repute.

1687

My Lord (Middleton):

The cabals and intrigues for and against the Count de Windisgratz's pretensions have been the only business of the Diet this long while. I should persecute you with a long letter, I think to no purpose, should I give you an account of all the particulars of this affair, wherefore I hope you will not think me negligent if I only tell you the Elector of Bavaria, the Elector of Cologne, and the Elector of Brandenburg have sent their ministers instructions in it, which are not to consent that the conclusions of the Diet should be given to the Count de Windisgratz either by a deputation or by the Director, and not to acknowledge any one as the Emperor's chief minister here who is not a Prince of the Empire. This, I suppose, will make the Count despair of succeeding in what he has been long labouring to bring about.

We expect the Count de Crécy here very speedily. I saw a letter written by Monsieur de Croissy to the French agent, in which he tells him the Count de Crécy has received instructions at that court about all which has passed here in his absence, and particularly about the Italian pamphlet which was read in the Diet reflecting on his most Christian Majesty.

In a letter which came hither this week from the Cardinal d'Estrées from Rome I find in justification of his Christian Majesty's building of forts, he alleges, what the Elector of Cologne mentions in his letter to the Emperor, that his Majesty thinks he may do it with[out] contravening the truce. I think it my duty to give your Lordship notice of this, not being instructed what his Majesty's opinion is of the matter, and not having heard he has declared it.

Sir Edward Vaudrey fell very sick at Vienna and

continues still very weak, which has made the Duke of Berwick defer his journey for England.

We have very considerable news this day, which is that Valpo and Esseck[1] have capitulated and surrendered on conditions. I will endeavour to learn what particulars I can, and enclose them in this for your Lordship. I am, with all duty . . .

I find there are no other particulars come by this post than that Esseck was surrendered the 30th of September, and that the Count Dietrichstein[2] brought the news of it to the Emperor.

Ratisbon, 3/13 Oct., 87.

My Lord (Middleton):

The gentleman who is employed for the French affairs here in the absence of Monsieur de Crécy[3] has shown me, since my last to your Lordship of the 29th past, the transcript of part of a letter written by the Prince Herman of Baden[4] to the Cardinal of Fürstenberg,[5] in which he tells him the Emperor is very angry that there have been false reports raised in the Empire reflecting on the French, assuring him there were no papers found in the Grand Vizier's chancellery which may give occasion for

[1] Walpo, with a garrison of 450 men, was the first to yield. On Dünewald's approach to Esseck the Bassa quitted the town, having removed as much as he could. The Turks intended to blow up the fortress, but Dünewald suspected their design and advanced too quickly for them to be able to carry it out.

[2] Son of the Prince of Dietrichstein; see *ante*, p. 85.

[3] Frischman.

[4] Herman Margrave of Baden-Baden (1628–91) was appointed President of the Imperial Council of War and Imperial field marshal 1682. He was present at the relief of Vienna, and baffled the Turks' attempts to make peace 1685. In 1688 he was made principal commissioner at Ratisbon, where he died of a stroke three years later.

[5] See *ante*, p. 223, note 2.

this, and that all the French prisoners taken with the Turks this campaign were renegados who had been eighteen or fifteen years out of their country. The agent has not thought fit to communicate this transcript, nor to let the Dutch[1] know to whom Prince Herman writ the contents of it, being unwilling to make the cardinal more hated by them than he is already, but only by word of mouth has acquainted the ministers that the Prince of Baden, by the Emperor's order, as he believed, to do the French justice and to satisfy their court in this matter, had written to this purpose. The design of this is to undeceive many, and to intimidate such as may be so indiscreet to make a noise yet with these stories. Much care is taken to have a sufficient proof against him who read the Italian pamphlet in the Diet and those who promoted it, and the Count de Crécy is coming with instructions in this business, it reflecting immediate[ly] on his Christian Majesty. Monsieur Scherer, who is naturally very fearful, says the principal commissioner (that would be) gave him the pamphlet to that purpose, and his excellence gives him the lie upon it, though all the Diet knows he had it from him and that he himself turned it the night before into Dutch[2] at his house to entertain an assembly of ladies.

I send your Lordship the particulars concerning the taking of Esseck and Valpo.[3] They seem incredible, but they were given me by the Count of Lamberg, from whom I receive all the civilities imaginable and are the same which are communicated to the Diet. This perfectly convinces me of the great consternation it has been long said the Turks are in, and the great Leopoldus now may take the motto of the first Caesar.[4] I am, &c.

<hr>

[1] Germans.   [2] i.e. German.
[3] See *ante*, p. 271, note 1.
[4] Written in margin: veni, vidi, vici.

My Lord (Chamberlain):[1]

It cannot be unpleasing to the great to have the most inconsiderable men enter into their interest, though all they can do is to make secret vows for their happiness. This gives me the boldness to tell you I have been very much concerned ever since I heard you had left the Bath on a message sent you by my Lord Dover. Till yesterday I learnt you were returned thither to execute your charge. I am ignorant of the occasion of this message, and imagine it might happen on a mistake, knowing you too gallant to be capable of giving an offence there where the news mentions. The love and honour I have for you, and it may be the thoughts of having a person out of court whose favour I confidently rely on, gave me some apprehension, though the consequence has been what I always expected from your prudence. I know not what your Lordship thinks of me, or whether you ever think of me or no, but I assure you I have always a grateful memory of the obligations I have to you, and could not omit this opportunity of congratulating with you at least my own good fortune, knowing you will be still ready to forward what may be proposed for my advantage. I can pretend but little merit, but it may be you may think it enough to be faithfully. . . .

Ratisbon, 10/20 Oct., 87.

My Lord (Middleton):

On Wednesday, the fifth instant, I was taken ill of a fever, which I suppose was occasioned by a very odd surfeit of Danube water. The day before, it being very fine weather here, the Electoral College let me know that they would come and pass away the afternoon in my garden, where I forced

[1] Lord Mulgrave.

myself to give them the best proofs I could of a hearty welcome: beginning myself all the health[s] which are usual on the like occasion, and having wisely, as I thought, given order that my glass should be always three parts water, I behaved myself boldly and to the satisfaction of all my guests, who withdrew one after another according as they felt they had their *rausch*.[1] They went to bed drunk and waked well the next morning; I went to bed with my head undisturbed but my stomach overcharged, and waked about five in the morning with a little shivering which soon turned into a hot fit. I perceived this way the effect of an indigestion, and though I have taken all the care imaginable to relieve my stomach, all I can say is, that this morning I awaked without a fever. I yet keep my bed and eat nothing but broth, which I hope (I knowing nothing extraordinary to communicate to you) will make you excuse my not writing to you with my own hand this post.

Generally once a week or a fortnight here uses to blow a trade wind which makes us see the Diet under sail, though she suddenly casts anchor again, but now we have had a dead calm ever since the instructions of the Electors are come to their deputies against the Count de Windisgratz's pretensions; and the two conclusions which were made a good while since, the first for congratulating the Emperor on the victory and the other for the hundred Roman months, remain in the Director's hands, and there is no talk how or to whom they will be delivered.

By a letter from Savern[2] the Count de Crécy lets us know that he would be at Strasbourg the 13

[1] Were intoxicated. German *Rausch* = carouse; *einen Rausch haben* = to be drunk.

[2] Saverne, or Zabern, a town twenty miles north-west of Strassburg.

instant and set forwards from thence for this place the 15th, so that we expect him here the latter end of this week.

On Friday last my Lord Charles Hamilton passed through this town in company with the Marquis de Créqui and a son of the Count de Roy. I could not see him by reason of my illness, but I sent to know if I could be serviceable to him in anything and to inform myself of the Duke of Berwick. He sent me word that the Duke had had a little relapse but would suddenly be setting forward for England, that my Lord Dongan intended to follow him the Thursday after, so that I expect him here daily.

I send your Lordship the extract of a letter written the 10th instant, new style, from Venice by Monsieur de la Haye, the French Ambassador there, which acquaints you with the manner of taking[1] Castel-Nuovo;[2] though you may have the relation sooner from other parts, yet this coming from so good a hand I thought it not amiss to send it you.

Here has been some time since a rumour as if the Grand Vizier and the Aga of the janizaries had been strangled in a mutiny of the spahis and janizaries at Petewardin, but so little credit was to be given to it that I made no manner of mention of it to your Lordship; but since it is certain there was a mutiny in the Turkish army after their saving themselves on the other side the Drave, which without question was the reason Dünewald had so good a bargain of Esseck and Walpo; the best account of what happened on that mutiny[3] is believed to be in

[1] MS. 'taken'.

[2] On September 28th the Venetians had stormed a breach in the walls of Castelnuovo, whereupon the garrison retired from the lower town to the castle and offered to capitulate on condition they could march out with their arms. The exodus took place on October 1st after a month's siege.

[3] The Turkish soldiers mutinied as a result of the defeat at Harkány. They demanded the head of the Grand Vizier.

the printed gazette which I received this day from Vienna, wherefore I have enclosed it with the other news.

I hear you have our good Abbot[1] with you in England. I need not desire you to make much of him while he stays with you, but I earnestly beg you to do all you can to send him back in good humour, that St. Benedict may speak with reverence of St. Ignatius, and that both their disciples may live in amity. I am, &c.

Ditto.

Sir (Mr. Corbet):

Yours of the 22nd of the last month found me in a violent fever, which is now over, though it has left me so weak I dare not yet venture abroad. I hope this will serve to excuse my not making you any return these two last ordinaries. Your letters are always so welcome to me that, should I take any neglect of writing unkindly of you, I could not but forget it upon the receiving of two lines from you. I wish you had not had so just an excuse for not letting me hear from you before as that which you are pleased to make. I am yet so sensible how much it puts a man out of humour to be ill treated by fortune at play (though I have been long out of her power in that nature) that I cannot blame your omitting a point of friendship on such an occasion; the like has often not only made[2] me forget my best friends for a time, but even a mistress in the height of all my passion. I must tell you nevertheless I am not wholly satisfied with you, because you have left me in pain by not acquainting me that that unconstant lady has been since more favourable to you; I am hearty glad of the account you give me of her smiling on Mr. Maule. I should be in the wrong if I took it ill I have not heard from him who has so many ways of employing every minute of his time better.

[1] Abbot Fleming.　　　　　[2] MS. 'make'.

The Emperor's good luck this campaign, all things well considered, is no less wonderful than that of the gentlemen you name who were concerned in diving for the treasure of the galleon.[1] The easy victory the Turks gave him; their abandoning, the Lord knows wherefore, Esseck, the chief place aimed at, and their letting Dünewald, with a small detachment of the army and an inconsiderable body of Cravats,[2] make himself master, to pin up the basket,[3] of almost all that part of Slavonia which lies between the Save and the Drave. The Venetians have pushed with no less success in the Morea[4] and we see the vast Ottoman Empire, in one ill run which began from the siege of Vienna, moulder away like Skelton's guineas,[5] and its Grand Seigneurs in danger to be reduced to lead the lives of their ancestors the Succomami, and wander up and

---

[1] *Cf.* Evelyn's *Diary*, June 6, 1687: 'There was about this time brought into the Downs a vast treasure, which was sunk in a Spanish galleon about forty-five years ago, somewhere near Hispaniola, or the Bahama islands, and was now weighed up by some gentlemen, who were at the charge of divers, &c. to the enriching them beyond all expectation. The Duke of Albemarle's share came to, I believe, £50,000. Some private gentlemen who adventured £100 gained from £8,000 to £10,000. His Majesty's tenth was £10,000.'

[2] i.e. Croats.   [3] i.e. to close the matter.

[4] Whilst the main Turkish forces were occupied in Hungary the Venetian Republic organized attacks on Greece and the Dalmatian coast. In 1685, with the assistance of German mercenaries, they commenced their conquest of the Morea under the leadership of Morosini. The capture of Koron and Kalamata made them masters of the peninsula of Maina. In 1685 the Turks were defeated by the Germans in an attempt to relieve Nauplia, the surrender of which gave the Venetians an almost complete command of southern Morea. The campaign of 1687 was the most famous of the war. During July the Turkish entrenchments at Patras were carried by storm and the Gulf of Corinth occupied in August. After fortifying the Isthmus the Venetians laid siege to Athens, which surrendered on Sept. 28th (*Camb. Mod. Hist. V, passim*).

[5] MS. 'guneas'.

down with an army of sheep again. But these
reflections savour too much of the place I live in,
and, if I should go on farther, you may think the
politics infectious and believe I may return into
England well enough accomplished to be admitted
to walk with Mr. Spicer and Mr. Vandebendy, and
the rest of that wise company, who never talk of
any affairs but such as do not concern them. London
is dull by accident but Ratisbon by nature. We have
a theatre too, but not only our plays but our actors
would be hissed in a country fair; St. Bartholomew's[1]
is too honourable. We have often lampoons on
the intrigues of state as scurrilous and as witless as
yours can be on the ladies.

Ratisbon, 13/23 Oct., 87.

Sir (Mr. Wynne):

I write this to let you see I am in a fair way of
living again, though I was dangerously ill the last
week; a good constitution, which is the best physician everywhere and almost the only one here, has
soon set me on my legs again. Yesterday was the
first I intended to take a little fresh air, and just as I
was stepping into my coach, word was brought
me the Duke of Berwick was arrived. I went
immediately to see him and saw him look so fresh
and so well after his sickness that the joy of it, I
think, has forwarded much the recovering of my
health. We stayed together till ten at night, and I
took my leave of him at five this morning, not being
able to prevail with him to stay a day and unweary
himself. You will have him before this comes to

[1] St. Bartholomew's Fair was the home of the puppet-
shows and drolls so despised by the regular dramatists and
theatres. Cf. the prologue to Mrs. Pix's *Spanish Wives*:
　　'Drolls shortly will amuse you at the Fair'.
Pepys records on Aug 30, 1667, 'I to Bartholomew fayre, to
walk up and down, and there among other things find my
Lady Castlemaine at a puppet-play'.

your hands for he told me he intended to be in England in ten days, which made me send by him to my Lord what I intended to have writ to his Lordship concerning the Count Caunitz's[1] being made one of the Emperor's secret council, and that there is a treaty in hand about the furnishing the Emperor with some troops the next campaign, but it is not yet perfected, though some give out as it were; as soon as it is I will send you the conditions agreed on.

All the talk now here is of Dünewald's advancing as far as Belgrade,[2] and nobody knows how far he may push the Turks in the consternation they are in; especially if he can, as is endeavoured, engage the army, which in the mutiny have revolted from the Grand Vizier, to accept of conditions offered them.

I have answered your letter long since in which was a proposition for returning my money. I could not guess what you meant by guildiners, but let me know what the gentleman does expect in England for 100 crowns current money here and I will suddenly tell you whether it will be for both our advantages or no.

If you cannot send the black-laced hood and scarlet worsted stockings, which I mentioned in a former letter to you, in any time by our Abbot, pray venture to enclose them in two packets and let me have them by post. I am, &c.

I am just now going to meet on the road the Count de Crécy and his Lady, whom we expect this day.

Ratisbon, 17/27 Oct., 87.

My Lord (Middleton):

I thought I had recovered my health when I writ my last of the 13th instant to Mr. Wynne, but I have

[1] As a reward for his services Kaunitz was made a Privy Councillor and a Knight of the Golden Fleece.

[2] The capture of Belgrade was reserved for the next campaign. It fell on Sept. 8, 1688.

since found I was deceived and I have got a double tertian ague which, though it torments me sufficiently does not make me apprehend the losing of anything but the miserable diversions of this place for a time.

On the 14th my Lord Dongan arrived here and the next day went easily on in a coach for Frankfort, not being yet well enough recovered of his sickness to endure the fatigue of going post. The same day the Count de Crécy and his Lady arrived from Paris.

He was yesterday to see me and I find he has instructions strongly to defend his master's right of building forts in what part he pleases of the land yielded him in sovereignty. Nothing has passed as yet between him and the ministers but visits of ceremony. He gave the Concommissary and not the Count de Windisgratz, who looks upon himself as chief of the Imperial Commission, notice of his arrival. This Count gives out that he has desired the Emperor to recall him from this place, but few believe he would seek of himself to quit an employment which yields him eighteen thousand florins a year. The truth is the Emperor cannot persuade any Prince of the Empire to accept of being principal commissioner while he continues the Count de Windisgratz here with the power he has given him; but upon his being recalled he will find enough who will accept of it, and the Emperor may save his pension of 18,000 florins, which will be a weighty point against the Count, as money matters stand, without he has better friends than he is reported to have among the chief ministers at Vienna. They talk at Vienna and here of two Princes, Saxe-Lauenburg[1] and Herman of Baden,[2] one of which is

[1] Julius, Duke of Saxe-Lauenburg, born at Prague 1641, was brought up a Roman Catholic. He served in the Imperial army and rose to the rank of field marshal. He died suddenly at Reichstadt, Bohemia, 1689.

[2] See *ante*, p. 271, note 4.

to come hither. All the Duke of Lorraine's friends hope it will be Prince Herman of Baden, and it may be the Emperor is persuaded that the President of his Council of War and his general should have a better understanding. I am, &c.

Ditto.

Sir (Mr. Wynne):

I received yours of the 30th of September yesterday, which found me in a fit of a double tertian ague, and, though I hope I may be rid of it before I can have an answer of this letter, yet I must desire you to employ your interest with some friend to inform me of the best way of preparing and taking the quinquina. I know not whom to direct you to since Dr. Short[1] is dead, who was the physician I loved best and chiefly made use of. He has given it me formerly according to Tabor's manner.[2] Pray likewise send me the receipt of what we commonly call the bitter potion, both of that which purges and of that which does not; I am pretty confident I shall have no need of them by that time I have your answer, but it will not be amiss to have them lie by one in this country.

We have lately lost the fine weather we had, and now we have nothing but great fogs, high winds, and almost continual rain, besides the variety of an earthquake which rocked the town so favourably

[1] Dr. Thomas Short (1635–85), physician, became a Roman Catholic and was much praised for his learning. He obtained a considerable practice, but died on Sept. 28th, 1685. Burnet believed he was poisoned by his co-religionists on account of his suspicions of foul play in connexion with the death of Charles II (*op. cit.* ii. 285).

[2] Sir John Tabor went to Versailles to try the effect of his preparations of bark called quinquina on the Dauphin, who was ill of 'intermitting fever'. He was able to cure him when none else could with his 'heavenly drug', which was long after known at the French court as the English remedy (Seward's *Anecdotes*).

the other day that none but such who by experience knew the thing had any apprehension of the danger. I am, &c.

Ratisbon, 20/30 Oct., 87.

My Lord (Middleton):

I have missed three fits of my fever, which was very violent for the time; I am yet very weak, but hope in a few days to enjoy a perfect health again.

All the news this place affords at present is that the Prince Herman of Baden is certainly to come hither as the Emperor's principal commissioner. You will have an account of what the Duke of Lorraine does in Transylvania, how the Turks have abandoned Possega,[1] in Slavonia, on the approach of Dünewald, and how Palotta, near Alba Regalis in the Lower Hungary, is yielded to Esterhasi[2] on conditions in the enclosed news from Vienna. I am, &c.

Ratisbon, 23 Oct./3 Nov., 1687.

Sir (Mr. Guy):

I have spared you so long that I begin to fear you may think I grow negligent in paying you the acknowledgement I owe you. It would be a fine thing if I, who am here at school to learn the affairs and interest of princes, should be such a blockhead

[1] The Turks burnt and abandoned the places left to their charge, vowing they would follow the Grand Vizier to Constantinople for the pay which they had not received. Dünewald, having garrisoned the deserted Possega with 1,000 men, marched on Gradiska. Possega was the capital of Slavonia.

[2] Paul IV Esterhazy de Galantha (1635–1713), born at Eisenstadt, contributed in 1686 to the capture of Buda with the result that in 1687 he was raised to the dignity of a Prince of the Empire. Esterhazy arrived before Palota with 2,000 Hungarians on October 19th and the town soon surrendered. There were but 250 men in the city, of which only one-third were soldiers.

as to forget my own. I wish I were near the sea or some river which runs your way that, instead of this dull tribute, I might send you some of our good wine to put you in mind of me in your cheerful hours.

As for our women they are a commodity which will turn to no account in England, especially to you who, as well as myself, have by a long experience of the frailties of the sex, almost acquired a perfect chastity; but while we approach this virtue let us take care our years do not sour us with any of the common vices of age; let us still preserve our good humour and our good nature, to make us welcome near those young people who possess that plentiful estate we have pretty well run out of, that we may help them rail at the morose and cry out with Falstaff : *down with them they hate us* $\frac{\text{(youth)}}{\text{(young men)}}$.[1] I have lost the conversation of my friends, but the benefit which I enjoy by your favour of not being so uneasy abroad as I might be in another main matter keeps me from being altogether unhappy. This can never be enough owned by my being all my life, &c.

Sir,

Ditto.

My Lord (Middleton):

We are here wishing for the new principal commissioner, though we know not yet when we are to expect him. The Emperor, it is thought to oblige the Duke of Lorraine, and it may be himself chiefly, has removed him from being president of the Council of War, so that he will come hither not well satisfied. Wherefore 'tis believed the Count de Windisgratz is still to continue in the post he is in, to have an eye over his actions, or, it may be, the court lets him remain here awhile not knowing

---

[1] Thus bracketed in the MS.

how to dispose of him. The Count de Jörger,[1] who was some time since said to be made Governor of Vienna, having now that charge certainly conferred on him, a thing the Count de Windisgratz was in nomination for, the Prince Herman of Baden, whose temper is said to be as haughty and as violent as the Count's, will doubtless hereafter occasion some pleasant scenes which may help to divert us. I have been told by two or three ministers, to show the good opinion he has of himself, that passing once through this town he affirmed that in discharging the place he held he had done more than ever Caesar or Alexander did; but I know the injury report does generally to mankind and therefore will not give you his character by hearsay, but stay till I have seen him and know[2] him a little myself.

The Diet has not so much as met lately, and here is a decree of commission not yet dictated, which chides them for their negligence, and gives them three or four points to debate on which are not yet known. The French plenipotentiary has told some of the deputies that in case they touch on the new forts he has instructions to put in a short memorial, which will make the chief sticklers ashamed, if not silent.

I know not yet what new conquest we shall hear of when the post comes in. We are all amazed at the Emperor's good fortune here; I know not what you are in England. I am, &c.

Ratisbon, 27 Oct./6 Nov., 87.

My Lord (Middleton):

His Catholic Majesty has given lately the Golden Fleece to fourteen; among which number are the Count de Caunitz and the Count de Windisgratz; the last has particularly deserved it of him in refusing to sign the truce in the behalf of the Spaniards at

---

[1] See *ante*, p. 222, note 2.   [2] MS. 'how'.

the time when it was signed between the Empire and France, which cost them three millions, besides Luxemburg. He has leave to go to Vienna to receive the order, so that before his return and the coming of our new principal commissary it is not expected much will be done here.

The States of Hungary will struggle at the meeting at Pressburg to preserve their right of election, but as the case stands they will be fain to submit to the Emperor's will.[1]

The Director of the Diet yesterday treated his brethren of the Electoral College, and the French plenipotentiary sat president of the feast. I was likewise invited, and notwithstanding my late sickness I ventured to go, but had liberty to drink what I pleased.

In the evening the Duke of Berwick's equipage arrived here; they rest to-day, and to-morrow continue their journey. I am, &c.

Ratisbon, 3/13 Nov., 87.
My Lord (Middleton):

Now the campaign is ended in Hungary it is beginning at the Diet. Yesterday was dictated a decree of commission which attacks the fortress at Trarbach; it is the consequence of the Emperor's letter to the Electors writ on that subject, a copy of which I sent you some time since. It endeavours also by arguments to confute some remarks which were made on the same letter by word of mouth by Monsieur Frischman, who was agent for the French affairs in the plenipotentiary's absence.

I will endeavour by the next ordinary to get it translated and send it to your Lordship.

[1] On October 31st the Diet at Pressburg recognized the Hungarian crown as hereditary in the male Habsburg line, the Emperor having consented to allow the Hungarians their ancient privileges and to grant a general amnesty.

The Count de Crécy is drawing up a memorial to defend the fortress, which you shall likewise have as soon as it is given in, that you may put the reasons on both sides into the balance and see which bear down the scale.

Though the Emperor's ministers proceed still on their maxim that it is necessary always to be complaining of France, I find many here who think they have no good ground to proceed on unless it can be proved that Trarbach was not of the reunions made before the first of August, 1681. The French can give good proofs that it was, which makes me believe this decree of commission will not have the effect the Emperor's ministers expect, and that the Empire will not declare this is a contravention, and that fresh noise, instead of putting a stop to this, may be the occasion of building more forts.[1]

Last night about 12 o'clock a courier arrived here from the French court; I have not yet learned from the Count de Crécy what his business is. Our last post from Vienna came in so late by reason of the floods which continual rains have occasioned that I could not send your Lordship what news it brought; you lost not much, it was such stuff as is scarce fit for a gazette, nevertheless if anything comes in due time to-day it shall be enclosed. I am, &c.

Ratisbon, 7/17 Nov., 1687.

My Lord (Middleton):

I have sent you, according to my promise in my last, a copy of the commission decree concerning the building of the fortress on the Moselle. The French plenipotentiary is hard at work and we shall suddenly see his memorial in answer to it. I will not trouble you with the discourses and judgements of any of the ministers here till both sides have pleaded.

The day after to-morrow the coronation is to be

[1] See Introduction, p. 31.

at Pressburg, and the States of Hungary have consented to receive the Archduke as hereditary king. I am, &c.

Ratisbon 10/20 Nov., 87.
Sir (Mr. Wynne):

I have nothing of consequence to impart to my Lord this post, and I intend not to trouble him with a letter before the Count de Crécy has given in his memorial to the Diet touching the fort at Trarbach. It is already penned, and he has promised to show me the brouillon to-day.

Yesterday, being St. Elizabeth's day, a Queen of Hungary, the Archduke Joseph was crowned[1] hereditary king of that country, a thing the States consented to in consideration of the great obligation they have to the house of Austria for delivering them [from] the tyranny of the Turks.

I have ordered your brother to send you a copy of the propositions which the Emperor made to those States, as we have them here.

We have our news very irregularly now the court is at Pressburg, and I cannot give you an exact account what progress is made in quartering the army in Transylvania.

Ratisbon, 14/24 Nov., 87.
Sir (Sir Edward Vaudrey):

Since I have had the honour to know the Duke of Berwick I have been so engaged by his charming qualities that I cannot but continually wish for his prosperity, and, though I am too inconsiderable to be able to do him any service myself, I cannot forbear stirring up those who I believe may have it in their power, among which number, the opinion I have of your prudence and experience, makes me

[1] The coronation which should have taken place on November 19th was postponed until December 9th. Saint Elizabeth was the daughter of Andrew II, King of Hungary.

reckon you. Ambition never wants a room in the souls of young men who are born with those advantages his Grace has; yet there is a certain modesty in youth which makes them stand in need of a good friend to push them on, or else they run the hazard of losing the favours of fortune as they often do those of a mistress—for want of being undertaking enough. This is a business most proper for you to mind, and never to let that crowd of pleasures which will be always courting of him make him forget what is more essential to make him great and happy. It is natural to mankind to love them best whom they have most obliged, partly out of fondness for the works which they have brought nearer to perfection, and partly because they think they may have more confidence in them. This makes princes the more they do for their favourites still love them better, and imagine they can hardly give them sufficient proofs of their kindness. Though my Lord Duke has the greatest share in his Majesty's favour it is not impossible this way to improve it, and the fresh marks which he receives of that will increase the esteem and reputation which he has already in the world. The thing I mentioned to you when last l saw you I think almost absolutely necessary for him to get; it is what the favourite has still enjoyed, as you will find if you will reflect in what hands it has usually been. I have been so long absent from court that I cannot judge as well as you of the measures that are to be taken for the obtaining it; nevertheless give me leave to say in general that, as princes make alliances in order to bring about their designs, so courtiers ought to make friendships which may facilitate what they aim at. It is not amiss to be well with some Lord of the Treasury who is most active and has most opportunity of being near his Majesty. He, in case any recompense be required in lieu, may find out a way to make the satisfying of it more easy. The ministers who are most in reputation and can with more freedom speak to his Majesty ought to be sought. They will be always seasonably putting the King in mind of my Lord Duke and of his merit. The approbation of other men, especially of the judicious, makes us grow fonder of what we love, and a prince's inclination by often hearing the object praised seldom fails of growing into a violent passion. Thus women in courts have been talked into their arms, and when their beauty has been decayed have kept their posts by the tongues of their faction. The Garter is a feather he must want in his cap, and he must leave the choice of his wife wholly to the King. It is a presumption in me to write on this subject to you, wherefore I will not tire you with any more impertinences. I hope my Lord Duke and yourself will look on what I have said already as the extravagance of my zeal, and on that score forgive, Sir, &c.

Ratisbon, 21 Nov./1 Dec., 1687.

My Lord (Middleton):

I thought I should have sent you to-day a copy of the Count de Crécy's memorial, which I have so often promised in my letters lately, but the Count, who is not only an able minister but a *bel esprit* and of the Academy,[1] is so hard to please that he is fain to take a great deal of pains, and after all can hardly please himself. I know not whether this is a defect or a virtue in man, but I begin to be sensible it is a sign of growing old,[2] which is no good thing. The order has been changed, the expressions often polished and filed. He has read it to me, and, impartially speaking, I think the French arms had[3]

[1] Crécy had been made a member of the French Academy in July 1679.
[2] Crécy was fifty-eight years old.
[3] MS. 'has'.

not more advantage of the Germans when the truce was signed than his arguments have of the Count de Windisgratz's, who drew up the decree of commission. Nevertheless were he not pressed in time I believe he would be taking of it in pieces again; few have so working and so indefatigable a brain. To-morrow it will be dictated, and on Thursday I hope to be able to keep my word with your Lordship.

The court is still at Pressburg and we have no news of the coronation. That which makes the Hungarians so stubbornly oppose the abolishing the law, which I mentioned in a paper enclosed in a letter to Mr. Wynne, is the severity which was used in the persecution of those who were in the conspiracy with Tekely the last year; many being put to death without the usual forms of justice, and, it is said, they are so much incensed at this that they demand justice of the Emperor against the author of those illegal proceedings.[1]

The last week arrived here Mr. Schmettau, who comes as principal minister for the Elector of Brandenburg. He married Mr. Fuchs'[2] daughter, one of the ablest ministers the Elector has, and who is now employed at the treaty at Altona. Schmettau is well bred, and has the reputation of being a man of parts. He lived formerly in the Court of Heidelberg, and was sent into England by the late Elector Palatine about the jewels which Prince Rupert left to Mistress Hughes.[3] I am, &c.

---

[1] Antony Caraffa presided over a special court at Eperies to inquire into the guilt of Tököly's associates in 1687 with terrible severity and cruelty. He is said to have employed a prostitute as informer, and to have shed much noble blood on mere suspicion. The court was called the shambles of Eperies, and to this day the name of Caraffa is cursed by Hungarians. The inquiry lasted several months, until at the request of the Hungarians the Emperor put a stop to it.

[2] See *ante*, p. 266, note 1.

[3] Margaret Hughes, the actress, was Rupert's mistress, by

My Lord (Middleton):

Since my last of the 21st instant the Count de
Crécy has fancied his memorial is too long and
yesterday was employed in making of it shorter; he
tells me it is now to his mind and that he will
deliver it as it is; but he has deceived me so often
that I shall not mention it any more to your Lordship till I have a copy of it in my own hands.

Monsieur Schmettau whom I acquainted you in
my last was arrived here from the Elector of
Brandenburg, has begun his negotiation very briskly,
giving in to the Diet to-day a memorial which he
brought with him ready penned at Berlin, in which
the Elector asks of the Emperor and the Empire for
dédommagements of what he suffered in the war
before the peace of Nimeguen:[1] three Imperial
towns—Dortmund, Mühlhausen and Nordhausen;
a million of crowns to be raised in the nature of
Roman months; and the first principality which shall
happen to be in their power to dispose of.

These demands are very high, and I suppose the
Elector does not expect they should be granted. I
believe he has chosen his party already, which
cannot be long a secret. This memorial will be forthwith dictated and your Lordship shall have it at
large. The French memorial coming on the neck of
this will make a great noise in the world, and may
cause the Brandenburger's to be more surprising.

whom he had a daughter Ruperta. She ruined her lover, who
left at his death little but a collection of jewels worth £200,000,
most of which was disposed of by lottery to pay his debts.
Mrs. Hughes squandered what was left her by gambling and
was compelled to sell a necklace formerly belonging to
Rupert to Nell Gwyn for £4,520.

[1] In his war against Sweden the Elector of Brandenburg
had captured Stettin and Stralsund, but the Emperor compelled him to restore his gains in west Pomerania at the Treaty
in 1679.

1687

My secretary in the margent of my last letter writ that the Count de Windisgratz had acquainted the Diet with the taking of Erlau; it is true the Count told some of the ministers that it was surrendered on conditions which are yet unknown, and, in case we have no confirmation of it by this day's post, the truth of the advice the Count had is to be suspected. I am, &c.

Ratisbonne, 27e Nov., 87.

Monseigneur (Le Duc de Lorraine):

Je vous envoie une lettre du Roi mon maître laquelle j'ai ordre de vous faire tenir avec beaucoup de soin et je ne peux m'empêcher de me prévaloir d'une si favourable occasion de vous écrire moi-même, et de témoigner à votre Altesse le zèle que j'ai pour son service. Il y a présentement deux ans que je suis ici et un peu après mon arrivée le Comte de Windisgratz me donna de la part de votre Altesse un écrit contenant l'état de ses affaires lequel je conserve toujours auprès de moi pour m'instruire si jamais j'ai l'honneur d'être employé en ses interêts. Il me semble Monseigneur, que toutes les honnêtes gens et tous les bons Chrétiens doivent travailler pour vous à leur tour, c'est un homage qui vous est justement dû puisqu'ils tiennent l'assurance de leur liberté et de leur religion des glorieuses victoires que vous avez acquis avec tant de danger et tant de peines.

J'espère que vous pardonnerez la liberté que je prend pour vous montrer la passion que j'ai d'être estimé

Monseigneur, De Votre Altesse Serenissime le très humble et très obéissant serviteur

Geo Etherege.[1]

A son Altesse Sereine[2] Monseigneur le Duc de Lorraine.

[1] MS. 'Ethrege'. [2] MS. 'ser^{ine}'.

Ratisbon, 28 Nov., 87.

Sir (Mr. Cooke):

I should envy the good fortune of the poor clerk, as you are pleased to call him, who has so long sat at the helm in a Secretary of State's warm office, had I not a particular friendship for him, and did I not know his great parts and industry deserve that profitable and eminent post. Let him live long in perfect health that he may the better taste the happiness he enjoys. In return you can do no less than pity me, who have been forced from the shore of delightful Thames to be confined to live on the banks of the unwholesome Danube, where we have been this month choked with fogs and cannot now set a foot out of doors without being up to the knee in snow. The Muses when they were banished Greece travelled westward and have established themselves in other countries, but could never find in their hearts to dwell here. The mountains are the abode of wolves and bears, and the inhabitants of the towns have something as fierce and rugged in their natures. My weak fancy may well suffer here when the noble genius of Ovid was dejected at Pontus; and you cannot but forgive the fondness I have for London should I cry out when I shut this letter: Hei mihi quod Domino non licet ire tuo. In the meantime I comfort myself as well as I can, forget Julia and suit my inclinations to the divertisements the climate affords, the best of which is hunting.

Manet sub iove frigido
venator tenerae coniugis immemor.

Pray be not so malicious to let the meaning of this come to my wife's ear.

It is not much out of season to wish you a merry Christmas, and so good a stomach to the plum broth as an old servant of my grandfather's had whose only grace all the good time was: God love me as I

love plum pottage. I will find out a way ere long
to engage you and Dr. Wynne to remember me. I
hope when I return into England to find your body
as vigorous as I find your mind in your favour of the
14th of October last to, &c.

Ditto.

My Lord (Middleton):
The Director of the Diet has sent a copy of the
Brandenburg memorial to the Elector his master,
desiring instructions for the dictating of it. I
believe the Empire will delay it as long as they can,
and the holidays now drawing near it will not be
till after Xmas. Upon the adjusting the differences
between the Emperor and the Elector of Brandenburg in Silesia, which was about a twelvemonth
since, the Elector had assignments for money made
over to him on some places in Ostfriese in consideration of his resigning his pretensions to Jägerndorf,[1]
which not being paid, an accommodation is now
treating at Vienna; and I believe the design of this
strong memorial is to facilitate the granting of his
demands in that treaty, or, in case he cannot obtain
them, to excuse himself in some manner to the
Empire should he employ force to compass what
he desires. This seems more credible since in his
memorial the expectation he requires is of that
principality or of an[2] equivalent. The French
plenipotentiary has at length given in his memorial,
and to-morrow it is to be dictated, but it is so long
that I fear I shall not be able to send it your Lordship before this day sennight.
The day before yesterday the Count de Caunitz
began his journey for Munich, for Mayence, and
Treve.
The Marquis of Bareit, finding the coronation
put off from time to time, has taken his leave of the

---

[1] See *ante*, p. 92, note 2.   [2] MS. 'one'.

court at Pressburg and is gone home, having, as it is said, first made an agreement to furnish the Emperor the next campaign with 2,500 men.

We have no news of the surrendering of Erlau, and, it is reported, the Bassa has answered that the place being only blocked up and not regularly besieged it cannot be expected he should capitulate. I leave Sir Gabriel Sylvius and Sir Peter Wyche, it properly belonging to their post, to give your Lordship an account of what passes at Altona.[1]

I am, &c.

My Lord (President):

It seems to me to be very natural for the Imperialists to be daily more sensible of the loss of what they have yielded to the French after their late great and unexpected success in the war against the Turk. The hope of enjoyment after many difficulties strangely increases the flame of a lover, and the hope of being in a condition ere long to be able to dispute with his Christian Majesty that branch of the Empire which is lopped off makes them with more impatience see him endeavour to secure himself the possession of it. In my mind there is nothing shows better than the treaties which have been between princes who was the most powerful at the time of signing them; and the articles which are made to the disadvantage of the weaker are seldom, not to say never, observed after, by some revolution, he is grown strong enough to do himself justice. This has made me think the Emperor's intention to let the French peaceably possess what they have by the truce during the time prescribed is conformable to theirs of restoring it after that time is elapsed; but because things cannot yet come to an extremity I have reason to fear his Majesty may have the same

[1] Where the conference was being held to settle the dispute between Denmark and Holstein-Gottorp.

trouble this spring which he had the last, and that application will be made to him to use his mediation to calm the blustering which the fortress near Trarbach makes this winter. This supposition is the cause of my sending your Lordship the enclosed papers, which will perfectly inform you, if you have occasion to read them, how this matter stands here. There is a decree of commission drawn up by the Count de Windisgratz, in which he uses the best arguments he can to show his Christian Majesty has no right to fortify, and particularly in that place. I am sorry the Count had no better a foundation to build on; he a little exposes his parts, but it is pardonable, being out of the great zeal he has to serve his master. There is another decree of commission which was dictated in the Diet the 14th of August, 1684, the day before the signing of the truce, which not only the Count but all the Emperor's ministers here had unhappily forgot. With these you have the Count de Crécy's memorial[1] which answers the Count de Windisgratz's arguments. I have sent my Lord Middleton a copy of that in Latin which was given into the Diet; this is in French, copied from the original, the Latin being but a translation. A project of this memorial was penned by the Count de Crécy when he was in

---

[1] Crécy pointed out that the Truce of Ratisbon had enabled the Emperor to conquer Hungary, and that the French King was justified in building the forts by possession before the treaty as well as by the Emperor's consent. As precedents he cited the Treaty of 1537, in which it was expressly stated that Francis I was not to erect forts in the county of St. Paul, and the Treaty of Antwerp, 1609, in which it was stipulated that no forts were to be built on either side. Louis had only promised by the 8th and 9th articles of the truce to restore to the proprietors, on their taking an oath of fidelity, the lands lying within his jurisdiction and to leave the inhabitants free to exercise their own religion. Crécy further suggested that the Emperor would not scruple to break the truce at his earliest convenience.

France, and has been printed in Holland under the name of a letter written by his Christian Majesty to the Electors, and was afterwards printed at Paris by that King's order. Precedents out of history, methinks, have much more force in this case than a rule of law or a Latin sentence which may serve to fill[1] up a manifest that has a good army to back it; and ever since I have been here my opinion has been that the Empire had done better to have been quiet till they could have exposed their griefs in that nature. I could offer many examples on the subject in dispute, out of the little knowledge I have in history, no less convincing than those the Count de Crécy has quoted. But I think I have revenged myself enough already on your Lordship for making me a Sir Politic; to be even with me keep me still in business and in that show no favour to

&c.

Ratisbon, 1/11 December, 1687.

My Lord (Middleton): Ditto.

This day the Diet made an end of dictating the Count de Crécy's memorial, and, to save the trouble of transcribing it by reason of its length, they ordered it to be printed yesterday; a copy whereof as it came from the press I send your Lordship, having first carefully examined it. I have sent my Lord Sunderland another copy in French; you have likewise a copy of the decree of commission of the 14th of August, 1684, mentioned in the memorial, which is necessary to be seen, it making out the contrary of some things pretended by the Count de Windisgratz in the last decree of commission against fortifying in the lands yielded by the truce. This was communicated to very few and it may be not sent by Mr. Poley.

You have a paper of the news we have from

[1] MS. 'full'.

1687

Vienna. Some letters seem to doubt whether the coronation would be, as it is marked, the 9th instant. Orders are sent to bombard Erlau to see if the Bassa on that will capitulate.

We know not when we shall have our new principal commissioner, the Prince Herman of Baden, here being a report that he has an ill affair to clear at court with Caraffa,[1] by whom he is accused of having had an intelligence with the rebels in the upper Hungary: the Prince accuses Caraffa of doing many things without commission and secretly animates the Hungarians against him, and that things are pushed so far that they can hardly end without the ruin of one of them. I am, with all duty.

Ratisbon, 5/15 Dec., 87.

Sir (Mr. Wynne):

The memorial given in here by the Elector of Brandenburg's minister is dictated and I shall send my Lord a copy of it translated on Thursday next, till when I have nothing to trouble him with. The Prince Herman of Baden's man of business, Monsieur Batzendorf, arrived here with part of his equipage on Saturday last, but we know not when he will come himself, there being a scurvy business to be cleared first between him and Caraffa, to whom the Duke of Lorraine has given the government of Transylvania. That Duke made but a little stay at Pressburg and is now at Innsbruck. We have yet no certain news of the coronation, but it is generally believed it was the 9th instant. This day's post will let us know the truth of it; if it comes in time you shall have what it brings enclosed for my Lord.

[1] Caraffa accused Herman of Baden of a secret understanding with Tököly. He terrified witnesses into confessing that they had carried letters from the Prince to the rebel. Herman of Baden charged Caraffa with exceeding his commission and acting arbitrarily in the matter of the court at Eperies.

I suppose you may have heard that Draskowitz,[1] who has been more than once a rebel and had his pardon of the Emperor, died suddenly at Pressburg. He was the most violent of all the Hungarians in opposing what the Emperor proposed. Some say he died of an apoplexy, some say of grief to see himself forsaken by his faction, and others of poison; every one may think what he please, he died in very good time to facilitate the ending the disputes there. I am, &c.

Ratisbon, 8/18 Dec., 1687.

My Lord (Middleton):

I send you, according to my promise in my last of the 5th instant, a copy of the memorial delivered by Monsieur Schmettau since his coming hither. You will easily imagine the Empire will never consent to what he demands, and that this memorial only precedes the dédommagement which the Elector his master intends to make himself, as a manifest does a war. He has long had a design of seizing the canonicates and prebendaries,[2] as well Roman Catholic as Lutheran, within his dominions which are reserved by the peace of Westphalia, and to convert them to his own use to make him amends in part for what he has suffered in the war which is mentioned. 'Tis thought this may be put in execution now, together with some farther designs which he may have on some Imperial towns, which by being taken into his protection will be secure from those outrages which they are liable to receive from other princes. This way of doing oneself right by

[1] Count Nicholas Drascowitz was inveighing in the Diet at Pressburg against the innovations to be established by law with regard to the disposal of the Hungarian crown when he was seized with an apoplectic fit, of which he died.

[2] These lay within the three bishoprics of Minden, Halberstadt, and Magdeburg yielded to Brandenburg by the Treaty of Osnabrück.

force is the worst thing which can happen in a government, yet it is usual in the Empire, and indeed where there are so many powerful princes it can hardly be prevented.

On Tuesday, the 6th instant, I sent by Flanders the news I received late on Monday night from Pressburg of the coronation's being on the 9th, and the particulars of the capitulation of Erlau. The court was to return for Vienna on the 13th, but here is a letter in town which says the journey would go nigh to be put off till after the holidays, the States of Hungary having a design to deliver a memorial to the Emperor, to which they desire his answer before he leaves them. It is believed they desire in it the redressing of several grievances, and particularly the abolishing of the tribunal at Eperies.[1]

The business between Prince Herman of Baden and Caraffa, where the Prince is accused of holding intelligence with the rebels, is not yet ended. Bethnehadi, who is one of the three who have sworn to the letter,[2] now says that he did it to avoid the torture and that the letter was forged by the judge who gave him the oath. The house of Baden have protested, that if the Prince do not clear himself of this before he goes for Ratisbon, they will not own him. It is said the court is for Prince Herman, though he has been looked upon as in disgrace ever since he has been named to come hither, and that the nuncio[3] and Spanish ambassador are for Caraffa. I am, &c.

[1] See *ante*, p. 290, note 1.
[2] Bethnehadi, examined before Jörger and the council of lower Austria, charged Geczii and Commendans with having coerced him by threats and promises into owning he had carried the incriminating letter. Terrified by the prospect of the rack he had drawn up a confession and confirmed it with an oath as directed.
[3] Cardinal Buonvisi.

Ratisbon, 12/22 Dec., 87.

My Lord (Middleton):

The Emperor going lately a hunting was, by a sudden flood, hindered from returning to Pressburg. He came to Vienna and lay there one night, and the next day went back, where the settling the affairs of Hungary will keep him yet a month or six weeks.

Prince Herman of Baden is still at court, and his family will not consent he shall come hither till he has justified himself against Caraffa, which cannot be before the Emperor has dispatched the public business with the States.

Here is a report that the Turks have left Gradiska, and that General Dünewald has not men enough to spare to garrison it. In the meantime we have yet no confirmation of their leaving Erlau on the capitulation which I have sent you.

The Diet has shut up shop and you are to expect no merchandise from hence till after the holidays, so that I have nothing to do now but to wish your Lordship a merry Xmas and many happy New Years. Since I am a wishing I hope you will give me leave to wish a little for myself too: that I may live to enjoy your favour long, and be in a condition to show you that I am with all duty, and with a perfect inclination, my Lord, &c.

Ratisbon, 18 Dec., 87.

My Lord (Dover):

The advantage I have had by being sent hither was not enough to make me forget what I left in London; but the honour you have been pleased to do me makes me now forget the loss of all I enjoyed there. Your letter has made me more vain than I ever was on a lucky run at play or on receiving a kind note from a mistress; but this vanity is not the effect of the unjust praise you give me in it, but of the assurance I have by it of your favour. The life I have led has afforded me little time to turn over books, but I have had leisure sufficient while I idly rolled about the town to look into myself and know when I am too highly valued. This makes me sensible I can never be out of your debt by writing: one obliging expression of yours is worth more than a thousand of my airy imaginations; all men must be of my mind who prefer le solide aux badinages. You are naturally gallant, and it has not been the custom of your family[1] to lose that inclination early: this makes me think there may be a beauty who with a few strokes of her pen is able to convince you that one tender word outweighs all the wit which was ever writ. The passion which has most power over me is faithfully to serve his Majesty, and to endeavour to be well with them who by their merit are particularly preferred to his favour. In making my court to you in this nature I am sure I cannot commit the fault which may make me forfeit your good opinion; the price I set on that makes every line you have sent me so dear to me that you may reckon you have already contributed more than I shall be ever able to deserve to the happiness and good fortune of, &c.

Ditto.

Sir (Mr. Guy):

You have made me the most agreeable return I ever had since I traded in letters. I never read anything which has so much of the sublime in it as your short favour of the 9th of November last. The transports of pleasure which it gave me are better arguments for that nobleness of expression, to me at least, than any I find in Longinus; but sublime apart, the plain way you take to assure me of your friendship has much more force than all the froth

[1] Etherege was probably thinking of Dover's profligate uncle, Henry Jermyn, Earl of St. Albans.

of rhetoric. The style you are master of is the best
to persuade the men and the properest to engage
the women. When you would play off your rest
you need but choose your gamester; 'tis your own
fault if the party be refused. While I remember you
of your happiness I cannot but reflect on my misfortune. I want the only charm which so late in the
year is capable to warm them; this confirms me the
cardinal was wise who said: *le belle lettere sono le
lettere di cambio.*[1] You see I know how to value the
proofs I receive of your kindness. I wish I knew as
well how to give you as solid proofs of my gratitude
and of that faithfulness with which I am—

Ratisbon, 19 Dec., 87.
I was very much surprised, Sir, with your letter:
such a proof of being remembered by one I love at
this distance is what I have been little used to. In
gratitude I should say much on this subject, but
I know you will take it as kindly if I only think it.
You may without jealousy let me keep my compliments for those whom I know not how to entertain
without them. The women need not rail at our
changing; few of us have the gift to be constant to
ourselves. Sir Charles Sedley sets up for good hours
and sobriety[2]; my Lord Dorset[3] has given over

[1] The best letters are the letters of exchange.
[2] Sedley is said to have been embittered by the fact that
James II seduced his daughter Catherine. He had sat as a
member for New Romney in the last Parliament of Charles II,
and after that king's death he took an increasing interest and
active share in politics. Macaulay cites his speech on the civil
list after the Revolution as a proof that he was a man of ability.
[3] Lord Dorset married his second wife, Mary Compton, in
1685. She was the daughter of the Earl of Northampton,
and celebrated for her beauty and understanding. This
passage provoked the remark from Macaulay: 'The affection
of Dorset for his wife and his strict fidelity to her are mentioned
with great contempt by that profligate coxcomb, Sir George
Etherege, in his letters from Ratisbon' (*op. cit.*, ii, p. 130).

variety and shuts himself up within my Lady's
arms, as you inform me; and, late as it is, Will.
Richards begins to pretend to secrecy, for the devil
a word he has ever writ me about my Lady Morland.[1]
Notwithstanding the ebbing and flowing in the
flesh, my mind is a kind of lake and has the same
standing pleasures it had in London: wine and
women; but our good fellows are far from being
wits and our whores are yet farther from being
beauties. The town is too little to hide us, and
the liberty of talking is too great, so that poor
lovers, like hares in relieving time, are fain to clicket
up and down in the gardens at midnight. I have a
very convenient one belonging to my house; I wish
the rent of it may not cost me too dear. Some time
or other I have good horses and often go a hunting;
were I to write to Tom Crud or Roger Wood this
would afford me wherewithal to fill one side of
paper. I bungle away now and then a morning at
tennis; here is a pretty carré court and players so
exactly sized for Sir Charles[2] that, were he here, he
would live in it. Here are two very handsome young
ladies, but their unconscionable price is marriage;
nevertheless were I as capable of a belle passion as
some at my age are, they would have cost me many
a billet and much time in tying my cravat at 'em,
but I cannot think of laying a siege, wanting a
stock of things necessary to carry it on and strength
sufficient to maintain the place in case I should take it.

Methinks it is below Bob Woosley's[3] gravity to

[1] The fourth wife of Sir Samuel Morland, the mathe-
matician and inventor. Her name was Mary Aylif, and she
was a woman of low origin and infamous character. The
marriage took place on Feb. 1, 1686/7, a divorce decree being
obtained on July 16th following.

[2] Sir Charles Sedley. See Introduction, p. 15. A carré
court is smaller than a full-sized tennis court.

[3] Robert Wolseley (1649–97), a minor poet best known for
his Preface to Rochester's *Valentinian*, 1685.

engage in a war with the minor poets. I should pity him did I not believe the exercise will do him more good than taking the air at Banstead did. I wear flannel, Sir, wherefore pray talk to me no more of poetry. If you know any friend of ours in whalebone bodice[1] who has an itch that way give him good advice; 'tis time to lay down the cudgels before the women lay us on too heavily.

I have ever enjoyed a liberty of opinion in matters of religion; 'tis indifferent to me whether there be any other in the world who thinks as I do; this makes me have no temptation to talk of the business, but quietly following the light within me I leave that to them who were born with the ambition of becoming prophets or legislators. 'Tis not amiss to see an humble clergy, they are more like the holy men in the primitive time; but it would be very hard to be excommunicated for fornication, it being a point all the differing churches agree in.

You have done very well to excuse me from giving you an account of foreign affairs, and now I reflect on't it would be as impertinent in me as if a solicitor or an attorney should entertain a man who hates a lawsuit with all the causes depending in his county. Besides the diversions I have mentioned, there is one thing which makes me more patiently bear with the loss of my friends in London which no other county can repair, that is the kindness I find from those who manage the Treasury. Were it possible for you to write anything which could be as welcome to you as your letter is to me you should have twenty for one; our imaginations are but the effects of ideas we talk in, and, having but little to work on in this barren place, I hope you will excuse the dullness of, Sir, &c.

[1] MS. 'bodys'. Cf. Ben Jonson, *Elegie* 60:
'The whale-bone man
That quilts those bodies I have leave to span.'

Ratisbon, 22 Dec./1 Jan., 1687/8.

My Lord (Middleton):

At length we have received the news of Erlau's being effectually surrendered; the day the Turks marched out is not expressed; they were about 4,000 men, women and children, of which there were not more than 700 soldiers; the place was well stored with ammunition, but had long wanted other provisions and was much afflicted with sickness.

The Emperor has been troubled with a defluxion, which made him keep in some days at Pressburg, and was the cause of the putting off the carousal designed.

The Jesuits are admitted members of the States of Hungary, contrary to the former constitution.

The Count de Windisgratz went from hence the day before yesterday for Vienna to take the order of the Golden Fleece, the Emperor being expected there after the holidays.

I send your Lordship a paper which is given out by Prince Herman of Baden's partisans to inform people of the state of affair[s] between him and Caraffa. In the meantime Bethnehadi is sent prisoner to Vienna, where the business is to be examined when the Emperor comes thither. 'Tis believed endeavours will be used to moderate the heat of the parties, that the thing may die quietly, and many are of opinion Prince Louis will cut Caraffa's throat before it be ended.

The perambulatory treaty at the court of Brandenburg between the King of Denmark and the States of Holland is concluded; the States having yielded to take off the prohibition which they had imposed on their merchants not to trade into Norway, and that some of their ships shall make that voyage before the following treaty begins. We expected this post the news of its being signed, but it is retarded, the Danish ministers having thought fit first to send [it] to the King their master to peruse.

LEOPOLDUS D. G. ROMAN: IMPERATOR
SEMPER AUGUSTUS, GERMANIÆ, HUNGARIÆ, BOHEM:
ETC. REX. ARCHIDUX AUSTRIÆ. DUX BURGUNDIÆ.

THE EMPEROR LEOPOLD I

The propositions of the Holstein ministers[1] at Altona are something high, methinks, considering the condition their master is in; but they are rather, I believe, to let the world see how much he has suffered than out of any hope they have they should be granted. The conference there is likely to take up much time, and it will be a hard matter to agree things; though I find all who are concerned, by the account we have here, are willing to take pains to bring it to a good issue and secure the peace of the north. The Swede is only suspected to have other intentions, for a very good reason: it being against his interest; nevertheless I find the memorial which was given at Copenhagen by the Swedish envoy, having seen a copy of it, is nothing near so strong as has been reported.

The date of this letter makes me once more wish your Lordship a happy New Year; I look on your prosperity as a kind of good fortune to myself, your favour being the greatest fond which maintains, &c.

Ditto.

(Mr. Maul):

You are so ingenious, Sir, that I know you need but little time to make you perfect in whatever you apply yourself to. This makes me not wonder you are already so arrant a courtier: a poor friend who is unable to do you any service is forgot and the only thing you mind is your interest. This is the third letter I send you without having the favour of one line from you. I should complain did I not think it would be to as little purpose as for an unfortunate lover to reproach a faithless mistress. I know your several employments take up so much of your time that so good a husband of it as you are cannot without regret throw away one minute; but at the

[1] They demanded the restitution of Schleswig, seized by the Danes in 1684. See Introduction, p. 39.

same time I know that they who love well, though never so nearly watched, will find an opportunity to satisfy their inclination. If you think it worth while to appease me, for I could not forbear letting you see I am a little angry, make me an excuse true or false it is all one, it cannot miss of a good effect on a heart which you are master of.

I live in a place of ceremony, and according to the rule I should not congratulate you on your being made Gentleman of the Prince's Bedchamber before you have given me notice of it, but I think you have not much studied those trifles which employ most of the serious hours of the ministers here. But, to be serious myself, I assure you the joy I have when I hear of your good fortune is not at all inferior to that which the greatest men at Whitehall give me when I receive infallible testimonies of their favour, and will never be otherwise, I am so unalterably, Sir, &c.

Ratisbon, 2/12 Jan., 1687/8.

Sir (Mr. Poley):

You had heard from me sooner but that I was in hope of sending you something from the Countess of Stubenberg which might have made my letter more welcome. I was deceived and could get nothing but a compliment in return of your favour. I shall not repeat it, it being the usual one women make when an old acquaintance makes them sensible he has not forgot them. Comfort yourself, poor Aurelia's growing old and cannot send you anything acceptable unless she sends you her eldest daughter.

> No grape was ere so kindly ripe,
> So plump, so smooth, so full of juice.

Wonder not this should be so soon; there is a sort of this fruit which is very early. I know not what Stockholm produces, but all the rest of our fräuleins are but wildings in comparison. Our Souths and our Swans[1] in England might find fault with her courtesy, but all our men would like her face, to pin the basket, my Lady Grafton[2] never had a better; yet I must confess I am a fop in my heart; ill customs influence my very senses, and I have been so used to affectation that without the help of the air of the court what is natural cannot touch me. You see what we get by being polished, as we call it.

Monsieur Schmettau tells me he had the good fortune to see you at Hamburg, and has often mentioned you with much esteem. If the Diet were composed of a few more ministers like him I should spend my time much more to my liking here. Your old friend Monsieur Schnolsky laughs and talks on; is still the same man, nobody can distinguish between his jest and earnest. I had like to have lost him wholly by my being in disgrace with the Count de Windisgratz, but his natural bias inclines him now and then to see me, though he ventures a chiding for it. I have sent you a paper of what has been lately done here, with a little news from other parts. I have only to add that last night we had advice from Cologne that the Cardinal de Fürstenberg[3] is chosen coadjutor there.

[1] Court ladies.   'There's others that say
                          Mrs. South goes astray
                          But that too's a damnable lye'
                          (*Vindication*, 1686, B.M. Harl. MS. 7317).

                          'Widdow Swan
                          For such she is since Ossery is gone'
                                    (*Satire* by Dryden, *ibid.*).

[2] Isabella, daughter of Henry Bennet, Earl of Arlington, married the Duke of Grafton, the second son of Charles II by Lady Castelmain. Her sweetness and beauty were universally commended. Evelyn speaks of her in 1672 as 'a swete child if ever there was one'.

[3] He had been opposed in the election by Prince Clement, nephew of the Elector of Bavaria, but had obtained seventeen votes out of twenty-four. The Grand Chapter had consented

1687/8

The Count de Caunitz[1] has not had very good
success in his two last negotiations, though he has
the Golden Fleece and is made one of the Emperor's
secret council, but the Elector of Bavaria has done
enough the last campaign to merit his friend should
be considered. Tell the Count de Dona[2] I am overjoyed to hear he comes to Vienna and do not despair
of an occasion to see him. I have given you good
measure, and can scarce forbear beginning another
sheet to you, I am so much, Sir, &c.

PS. You are often obligingly remembered by
the Count de Crécy and his Lady; her only quarrel to
you and to me is that we are heretics. I think she
believes you the most obstinate.

Monsieur (Le Comte de Thun):

Depuis que nous nous sommes separé à
Amsterdam je me suis toujours consolé de la perte
que je fis alors en me flattant que je pourrais trouver
une occasion de vous revoir un peu de temps après
que je serais établi ici. Il y a longtemps que je sais
que vous êtes à Munich et, piqué d'impatience de
vous voir, j'ai taché d'obtenir permission de
m'absenter de mon poste pour quelques jours pour
faire ce petit voyage, mais sans y pouvoir réussir.
J'ai appris avec beaucoup de plaisir que la fortune
s'est repentie de vous avoir un peu maltraité en

in November 1687 to the choice of a coadjutor in consideration of the inconvenience that would be caused if the Archbishop died. The Cardinals had prevailed upon the Elector
Palatine to persuade the Emperor to agree by holding out
hopes of carrying the election for a member of his family
(Burnet, ii. 487).

[1] On his return from his unsuccessful mission in England
Kaunitz had been sent as envoy from the Emperor to dissuade the Grand Chapter of Cologne from proceeding to the
election of the pro-French Cardinal of Fürstenberg as coadjutor.

[2] Probably Alexander Count de Dohna (1661–1728),
tutor to the young Prince Frederick William of Brandenburg.

Angleterre, et qu'à la fin elle s'est rangée du côté du mérite et dans des affaires plus solide que le jeu, elle s'est déclarée pour vous et pour votre illustre famille. Si je pouvais savoir que son Altesse Électorale n'irait point ailleurs chercher des divertissements dans ce carnaval peutêtre que je viendrais vous rendre visite et demeurer un jour ou deux pour voir les galanteries de la cour où il y a maintenant un gentilhomme qui est fort de mes amis, Monsieur le Marquis de Duheron, je ne sais si vous le connaissez; ce n'est pas assez de le voir il le faut bien observer car il est adroit à se cacher. Il est homme d'esprit et de cœur et a toutes les belles qualités requises pour le faire bien aimer tant dans les cours que dans les camps. Il n'est pas mal fait et les femmes courraient risque s'il ne négligeait pas trop la barbe. Il a fait plusieurs campagnes en Hongrie et il y a quelques trois années passées qu'il fit une action si belle et si généreuse sur une dispute touchant le Roi mon maître et le feu Duc de Monmouth que tout ce qu'il y a des honnêtes gens de mon pays lui sont redevables. Ne vous laissez pas tromper à son air froid; il est Norman et ne va pas si vite en besogne que les autres français. Si vous lui pouvez rendre quelque bon service où vous avez du pouvoir je vous assure qu'il n'est pas d'humeur d'être ingrat, et si vous en voulez[1] être si fortement caution que je le tiendrai comme fait a moimême. J'ai beaucoup à vous dire de mon pays que vous ne seriez pas fâché d'entendre et quelques choses à vous communiquer qui me touchent dans votre pays; ce sont des affaires plus propre pour une conversation que pour une lettre. J'espère d'avoir l'occasion que je me promet de vous mettre mon cœur en main afin que vous en puisiez toutes les verités, vous qui êtes le plus honnête et le plus généreux de tous les hommes que j'ai jamais connu

[1] MS. 'veux'.

311

ne pouvez pas, sans faire tort à votre grande mérite et à mon peu de jugement, vous méfier que je sois sans aucune réserve &c.

Ratisbon, 9/19 Jan., 87/8.

My Lord (Middleton):

This day we expect to hear that the Emperor is come to Vienna. The settling the affairs of Hungary is put off to another Diet;[1] the season of the year and the absence of the Count de Windisgratz makes the ministers here think of nothing but sliding and feasting. The Count left a paper to be made public when he went for Pressburg, which is a satire on some of the Electorals, who are preparing an answer to welcome him at his return.

This quarrel among our major ministers will not prove so fatal as that which has been between your minor poets.

I am glad to hear our Abbot has got something. I want him here extremely, and would not have my Lord Melford[2] debauch him. I hope he is so continent that nothing can tempt him to leave his old wife and go a whoring into Scotland.

All is in blood and confusion at Constantinople, the rebels wanting money to satisfy the army after the deposing of the Sultan.[3]

[1] The deputies at Pressburg desired that the remaining points should be referred to the next meeting of the Diet rather than, as had been proposed, to commissioners.

[2] John Drummond, 1st Earl of Melfort (1649–1714), Secretary of State for Scotland, declared his conversion to Catholicism and was raised to an earldom in 1686. He is said to have been one of the handsomest men of his time, but of an arrogant disposition and unstable character.

[3] After having obtained the head of the Grand Vizier the mutineers demanded the deposition of Mohammed IV. He was succeeded by his brother Solyman II, who was unable to control the disorderly troops. For some months Constantinople was given over to anarchy and pillage, until the citizens rose and put the ringleaders to death.

This and the height the difference is grown to between his Christian Majesty and his Holiness[1] fills all the politic mouths of this town.

Ditto.

(Mr. Bradbury):[2]

It is so long, Sir, since I have hoped to hear from you that I begin to despair of the favour. I should have considered better how I might be able to deserve your friendship before I relied so firmly on it; more good nature than is usual is required to be mindful of the concerns of a poor man who is at so great a distance.

You gave me long since an imperfect account of what Mr. Smithsby had received of my pension; I remember I excepted against the interest which you reckoned to be due on the bond, to which you have not yet made me any answer; pray adjust the accounts with Mr. Richards and let him send it to me. I referred wholly to you the determining of the suit depending with West and Barbone;[3] it is now five or six months since, and you have not yet acquainted me with so much as your opinion of it. I desired you to employ somebody to search the records about Maynard's business. My cousin Middleton's will would have given some light as to the time; but I know the world too well to be surprised that nothing is done on my behalf. Though you are unmindful of me now, the trouble I have given you formerly will always make me remember the obligation I have to be, Sir, your, &c.

Ditto.

Sir (Mr. Wynne):

I received yours of the 23rd of the last month yesterday, which bring[s] me many kind wishes, for

---

[1] See *post*, p. 315, note 3.

[2] George Bradbury was called to the bar in 1667 and gained for himself a considerable position in the profession.

[3] See Introduction, p. 17.

which I heartily thank you. You must not expect any news of consequence from hence till towards the spring, nor complain that what we send you is not fresh. I have acquaintance which are communicative enough, but our posts come very irregularly, and that which goes to Brussels always advances ours by two days; so that you must have patience till the winter be over. I confess I sent you the news of Drascowitz[1] a month after I knew it, but you have been often even with me, for I have more than once seen the news you have sent me above a week before in written gazettes from Holland. I send you often extracts of letters when the matter is of importance; but I am not so exact when we receive nothing but stuff designed only to patch up newsbooks. The treaty of Altona, the revolutions at Constantinople, and the dispute between France and Rome, must entertain you as well as us yet awhile. I am, &c.

My Lord (President):[2]

I am told from England that all things are now agreed on and that my Lady Anne Spencer is suddenly to be married to my Lord Arran.[3] I cannot but congratulate with your Lordship the choice you have made of so good a son-in-law. Not to mention his other eminent virtues, you know he is an industrious courtier, and, if I may take any measures from the confidences he has often made me, I can assure you he is an able lover. I wish all manner of happiness to the deserving couple, and to your Lordship and my Lady Sunderland all the

[1] See *ante*, p. 299, note 1.
[2] Lord Sunderland.
[3] James Douglas, Earl of Arran, Duke of Hamilton (1658–1712), eldest son of William Douglas, Duke of Hamilton, courtier, diplomat and soldier. He was killed in a famous duel with Lord Mohun in Hyde Park. He married Anne Spencer (1666–90), daughter of the Earl of Sunderland, by whom he had two daughters, both of whom died young.

joy which your indulgence will make you capable of in seeing the young lady well disposed of.

We are very quiet here and do not expect anything should be done in the Diet till the coming of the Marquis of Baden or the return of his adjunct, the Count de Windisgratz. The revolutions which have happened at Constantinople, and the news we have of the great confusion and disorder which continue there, make everybody believe the Emperor will, with much ease, the next campaign push his conquests as far as Belgrade, and oblige the Turks to surrender the rest of the places they have in Hungary. The Emperor, by the last letters from Pressburg, was to be at Vienna the 17th instant, so that we expect to hear he is arrived there by the post which comes in this night. 'Tis commonly said that the affairs of that kingdom, which are not yet settled, will be adjusted by commissioners, but the Count de Lamberg tells me they will remain as they are till another Diet be assembled.[1]

By letters which some ministers here have from Altona I find no good issue is expected from that treaty: the one side being positive to yield to nothing but a compensation,[2] and the other resolving to be satisfied with nothing but a restitution; so that most people think it will be a hard matter to prevent a breach between the two northern crowns.

That which makes most noise now is the dispute between France and the court of Rome, the interdict, and the Marquis de Lavardin's[3] protestation,

[1] See *ante*, p. 312, note 1.
[2] Denmark offered Oldenburg and Delmenhorst to Holstein as an equivalent for Schleswig. See Introduction, p. 39.
[3] Henry Charles, Marquis de Lavardin (1643–1701), was appointed French ambassador at Rome, March 1687. The dispute between France and Rome was over the matter of the 'franchises'. Foreigners had put themselves under the protection of their respective ambassadors at the Papal court, and, lodging in the neighbourhood of their representatives,

'tis thought, will go nigh to cost his Holiness the county of Avignon[1] if not the duchy of Castro too, besides the lessening the terror of his thunder. It is reported here Monseigneur Dadda[2] has spoken to his Majesty to use his mediation in this business and that he had no very favourable answer.

Nobody knows the truth of this better than your Lordship, the continuance of whose favour I continually beg to, &c.

Ratisbon, 16/26 Jan., 87/8.

My Lord (Middleton):

The day has been so often changed on which the Emperor was to leave Pressburg that it is not impossible but he may stay there longer than the 29th instant, though it is positively said he returns then to Vienna.

exempted themselves from the jurisdiction of Rome by pretending they were part of their ambassador's *cortège*. Romans had abused these franchises by using them as sanctuaries from justice. The Pope determined to restrict the privileges of the franchise to the ambassadors' houses and families, and the Imperial and Spanish representatives agreed to quit their pretensions if the French would also consent. Louis XIV rejected the Pope's request, whereupon Innocent refused to receive Lavardin. The French ambassador entered Rome with some troops of horse in a hostile manner, kept guards about his house, and affronted the Pope on all occasions. Innocent would neither admit him to an audience nor receive any message or intercession from the French court (Burnet, ii. 487).

[1] Avignon had been in the possession of the Popes since 1348, when it was sold to Clement VI by Joanna Countess of Provence. In spite of many attempts by the French kings to reunite it with their dominions it remained in Papal possession until 1791.

[2] MS. 'Monsr(g) Dada'. Ferdinand Dadda, domestic prelate to the Pope, had been constantly with the King since his accession, and was a great favourite with the Queen. In July 1687 he made his public entry at Windsor as Papal nuncio to the English Court.

Part of the Marquis of Baden's equipage arrived here the last week, but it is yet uncertain when he is to follow. The Count de Windisgratz is expected to be back about Candlemas; in the meantime nothing is done here but caballing to make the factions stronger.

How to entertain you in this vacation I know not; there are changes in men as in other matters: the passion which was chief minister and disposed of all things may now be in disgrace and another taken into favour. I know you are Mr. Secretary still, but I know not whether you are still the same Lord Middleton I left you. You may be grown as temperate as Sir Ch[arles] Sedley and as uxorious as my Lord Dorset;[1] 'twould be a fine way then to make my court to you to talk of wine and women. No, till you are pleased to instruct me better I shall keep myself upon my guard and be as foppish as any one you have in your province. To show you I am in earnest I will begin from this moment protesting I am with all respect and duty, &c.

Ratisbon, 23 Jan., 87/8.

My Lord (Middleton):

I send you a copy of the articles agreed on upon the surrendering of Mongacz to Caraffa;[2] they are

---

[1] See *ante*, p. 303, notes 2 & 3. This remark is likewise referred to by Macaulay.

[2] Caraffa tendered articles to the garrison which they were compelled to accept: I. Free pardon to all in the town. II. Princess Ragotski and her children to go to Vienna. III. Her real estate to be under the direction of the Treasury, her personal estate to go to her children. IV. Princess to receive equivalent of her dowry. V. Princess to deliver up ducal cap and tokens of authority with which Tököly invested as Prince of Hungary. VI. Arms and ammunition of absent rebels to be given up. VII. Estates in Munkács to be restored to owners. VIII. All to take oath of fidelity and not to leave the province without permission. IX. Deeds and evidence brought to Munkács during the disturbances to be restored

in Hungarian Latin, but you must take them as we have them.

The Emperor invited the Elector of Bavaria to pass the carnival at Vienna, and the Count de Serini[1] went to incline him to it; but he is resolved to go again to Venice, and has appointed the day after to-morrow to set forwards. All endeavours are used to turn him from his design: the Count de Thun, who had leave to go to Salzburg to see his brother, has been called back to his post in haste, and the letters which came from Munich yesterday say the Count de Caunitz is arrived there to use his interest to dissuade the Elector from that journey; but part of his equipage is already gone before, and it will be a hard thing to change his mind.

It is said the Princess of Ostfriese[2] intends to send a minister hither upon the Elector of Brandenburg's having named that duchy in his memorial. It is talked likewise that the King of Denmark intends to send Puffendorf[3] to be his minister here, who is now at his court, having left Sweden on a distaste. He was Chancellor of Bremen, and had a dispute with Welling, who is now at Altona about [a] place in the council, which was determined by the King of Sweden in his prejudice. After having faithfully served the Swedes near thirty years he drew by

to owners. X. Princess's children to be under Emperor's tutelage. XI. Princess to be prohibited from sending to Tököly for consent to yield fortress. XII. Freedom to be given for all to return to homes with food and provisions. The fortress had been able to hold out so long owing to the difficulty of the approaches which afforded no natural shelter. It consisted of three castles on a hill surrounded with a moat hewn out of rock, and was perhaps the strongest place in Hungary.

[1] The Count de Serini had commanded the Bavarian troops in Hungary in 1686.

[2] See *ante*, p. 294.

[3] Esaias Puffendorf, an able diplomat, experienced in the affairs of Sweden and Germany.

degrees what he had in that country out of it, putting it into the hands of a friend of his at Leipzig,[1] and when he was at Hamburg he sent a compliment to the King, his old master, and took his leave of him. That King sent to him and offered to make him his envoy to Holland, but he refused it; he had a pique[2] against the French, and has often made them work in traversing their designs. Nevertheless his Christian Majesty would have received him by reason of his great learning and experience, and have employed him in the Empire, if his religion could have permitted to give him a public character. It is looked on as a very lucky thing at this time for the King of Denmark to have engaged one of the ablest ministers the Swedes had in his service, and the French, since they could not have him themselves, are very glad he belongs to an ally.

Yesterday we had a copy of the arrêt of the Parliament[3] of Paris against the bull touching the quarters.

Ditto.

Sir (Mr. Wynne):

I had yesterday the favour of yours of the 6 January wherein you tell me I shall find by your gazettes you have had long before what I promised you in mine of the 19/29 December.[4] I do not find in your gazettes an account of anything but the ceremonies of the coronation; that, the tournaments and other shows are fit matter for a newsbook. It may be I did not express myself well which may occasion your mistake. What I intended we have yet no good account of here which is: what part of the griefs the Hungarians presented has been redressed, and what part is put off till another Diet;

---

[1] MS. 'Leipswick'.
[2] MS. 'pick'.
[3] MS. 'Parlam–t'.
[4] This letter is not included in the Letterbook.

what institutions have been made for settling the affairs and securing the peace of that kingdom. You cannot have the state of the Prince of Baden and Caraffa's cases since Caraffa has never exposed his case to the public, and the aulic Latin paper which you have is only the Prince of Baden's case, which is divulged by his partisans upon the attestation of Bethnehadi.

Mr. Muddiman has informed me Lord Carlingford[1] is named his Majesty's envoy extraordinary for Vienna, which confirms what I had learned from some ministers here a month ago. I have sent my Lord the little news we have. I am, &c.

Ditto.

My Lord (Carlingford):

I have learnt by my last letters from England that his Majesty has been pleased to name you his envoy extraordinary for Vienna, and cannot but congratulate with your Lordship your coming to a court where you will have so many advantages, both in your affairs and in your pleasures. The memory it yet retains of your father[2] and the great merit and interest of your brother[3] will unlock the hearts of the ministers and engage the civility and respect of the courtiers to you. I wish your Lordship could find out some way to make me serviceable to you in the post I am in, at least for old acquaintance' sake. I must beg you not to rob me of the happiness of seeing you. Make this your road that I may have the pleasure of talking with you and of knowing how our friends pass their time in England, and whether

[1] Nicholas, 2nd Earl of Carlingford, was the elder brother of Lord Taaffe.

[2] Theobald Taaffe, 1st Earl of Carlingford, had been sent on a mission to the Emperor in 1665 to solicit his co-operation against Holland.

[3] Lord Taaffe.

the poor Dog and Partridge[1] is not altogether neglected. A day or two with you will help me to forget what I have suffered since I left them. I have not had any correspondence with my Lord Taaffe since [he] has been in Tyrol. News, &c. I am, &c.

Ratisbon, 26 Jan./5 Feb., 1687/8.

Sir (Marquis d'Albeville):

I am sorry to find by what is communicated to me by some ministers, my friends, that the ungrateful people you have to deal with comply no better with his Majesty's amicable intentions. The many lies which fly about the Empire to blacken the just and reasonable designs which his Majesty has at home come for the most part from that nest where Ferguson[2] by connivance, and Burnet[3] by allowance, sit brooding. I am industrious to undeceive as many as I can, and have exposed the calumny and knavery of

[1] A tavern where the wits met in Fleet Street. Cf.:
  'So what he writes is but translation
  From Dog and Partridge conversation.'
                    Alexander Radcliffe's *The Ramble*, 1682.

[2] Robert Ferguson, 'the Plotter', conspirator and pamphleteer, became involved in the Argyll insurrection and was compelled to take refuge in Holland. He was chaplain to Monmouth's army on his invasion, 1685, and was excepted from the amnesty of 1686. He accompanied William's expedition.

[3] Gilbert Burnet (1643–1715) historian and bishop, on the accession of James II was taken into the confidence of the Prince of Orange and urged William to have a fleet in readiness but not to move until his cause was of sufficient importance to justify him in all eyes. James remonstrated with William about the favour he showed to Burnet, and the latter was dismissed as a preliminary to Albeville's arrival in Holland. Nevertheless William continued to consult him and he was naturalized as a Dutch subject. He was outlawed by James and a prosecution for high treason was set on foot against him.

many reports and printed papers; had I the advantage of being better informed it may be I might do better services.

Monsieur Schmettau, the Elector of Brandenburg's minister here, had advice by the last post that the preliminary treaty between Denmark and Holland at that court, which has been looked on as concluded this good while, is now broke off.

The Emperor has used all means to dissuade the Elector of Bavaria from going to Venice this carnival, but to no purpose, for he began his journey the day before yesterday, and has taken the Electrice with him, but intends to ease himself of her by the way and leave her at Innsbruck with her aunt[1] till he returns. Most think he goes only to divert himself, though it is given out he lays hold on this opportunity to talk personally with the Prince of Tuscany[2] about a marriage with Mademoiselle de Bavière.

Knowing it necessary that those whom his Majesty employs abroad should hold a correspondence with one another to enable them better to do their duty, I could not forbear any longer writing to you, though I have had no notice of your arrival in Holland. I will not omit any occasion to inform you of all matters of consequence which come to my knowledge here, and shall always look on it as a happiness when I may give you a proof of my being very faithfully, Sir.

Ditto.

To Mr. Wynne of the apprehension of finding an answer to Lavardin's protestation in the gazette and of inviting Monsieur d'Albeville to write.

[1] Eleanora Maria, Queen of Poland, wife of the Duke of Lorraine.

[2] The son of Cosmo III de' Medici was reported to be betrothed to Princess Yolanda, daughter of the Elector of Bavaria, already in May 1687.

Ratisbon, 30 Jan./9 Feb., 1687/8.

My Lord (Middleton):

You will find by the paper which is enclosed, if you think it worth your while to read it, that the States of the Empire are not very well disposed to satisfy the Elector of Brandenburg in what he demands of them by his memorial which I sent you about a month ago. We shall see more when the principal commissioner is come and the Diet begins to deliberate on affairs. Monsieur Aveman, the minister which was expected for Ostfriese, arrived here on Friday last.

The Elector of Bavaria left Munich on Wednesday last about 4 o'clock in the morning, after having spent that night with the divertisements of the apartments,[1] a French comedy, and a ball. He intended in his way to Venice to have taken the Electrice with him and to have left her at Innsbruck till his return, but she makes that journey herself, attended only by fifteen persons, that she may not put the Duke of Lorraine to too much charge. Monsieur de Coloverat, who is gone to give formal notice of the King of Hungary's coronation to their Catholic Majesties, was then at Munich to receive their Highnesses' commands for the Spanish court.

The Holland minister has received a printed libel

---

[1] A 'jour d'appartement' at Versailles is described by the Duchess of Orleans in a letter to the Electress Palatine (*Letters of Madame*, I. 60–1). Various rooms were devoted to special amusements. Thus guests would be ushered into the first drawing-room, where violins were playing for dancing; the King's throne was in the adjoining room, where concertos and choral singing were in progress. Next there would be a bedroom, with tables for card-playing and another for games. Thence one entered an antechamber, in which a billiard table stood, and finally there were one or two refreshment rooms. Some guests would settle down to their favourite amusement, others would wander from room to room listening to the music or watching the gaming.

from his country which is dispersed among those of the reformed religion here. It is a pretended answer of the pensioner Fagel[1] to a letter which he affirms to be writ to him by J. Steward, an advocate, by his Majesty's command to know the Prince and Princess of Orange's sentiments on the taking away the Test and abolishing the penal laws. I have taken care to undeceive many who by means of this pamphlet had a prejudice to your proceedings in England, and have used the best arguments I could to satisfy them of the reasonableness and justice of his Majesty's design in that matter. I am, &c.

To Mr. Wynne with a touch about postscripts.
Expressions in a letter to Mr. Richards of the 2/12 Feb., 87/8.

It is well known when play or women are in the case I am no sleeper. I am ashamed to have given you so much trouble, but, over shoes over boots,[2]

[1] Casper Fagel, Grand Pensionary of Holland. James Steward, a Scotch lawyer, undertook to represent the King's intentions to the Hague in such a manner as to incline the Prince to a better opinion of them. He wrote several letters to the Pensionary and pressed him to persuade the Prince to concur with James in the repealing of the penal laws. He urged the inconsiderable number of Papists and the severities to which the laws subjected the Dissenters. William desired Fagel to reply by a declaration of his intentions. Fagel in his answer announced that though William desired toleration he could not approve the removal of the tests, which he considered a necessary safeguard against the Roman Catholics. Whilst he disclaimed the right of interference he condemned the methods of James, and protested his duty and affection to the King, though insinuating that his Declaration was illegal. Steward carried the letter to the King, and Burnet having translated it into English, it was published with the title, 'A Letter to Mr. Steward, giving an account of the Prince and Princess of Orange's thoughts concerning the Repeal of the Test and Penal Laws', 1688.

[2] Expressing reckless continuance in a course already begun (N.E.D.).

pray continue your care. Remember me to all my friends at the Rose[1] and do not forget the lily at the bar. I am sorry for the bright nymph who you write me word is under a cloud; I made hay with her, I confess, while the sun shined, and have run the risk with many more, who were nothing near so handsome, of having a sad occasion to mark a black day in my almanac. You may venture to send me the scandal you mention; now I am growing grave I would not lose anything which may make me laugh.

Ratisbon, 6/16 Feb., 87/8.

Sir (Mr. Wynne):

While we have no principal commissioner here we have so little news stirring that I wonder how I am able to hold any correspondence with you.

The news you send me about the decree obtained against Prince George in the Chamber of Speyer I knew before, but had no instructions farther than delivering his Majesty's letters to the Emperor and Diet in that business.

What success Sir Peter Wyche may have in composing of it with the Duke of Holstein I know not, but we hope here for little good success from the conference at Altona, especially since the death of Monsieur Ulkins,[2] the most prudent and the most moderate minister that Duke had.

The Elector of Bavaria's voyage, which has made so much noise, was broke that day he should have set forwards. The Austrian ministers ascribe the reasons of it to several affairs of State; but some letters which I have seen from that court ascribe it

[1] The Rose Tavern in Covent Garden, a favourite resort of the players: Haines speaks in his *Reformation* Prologue of 'my dear, dear paradise the Rose'. Cf. 'Near to the Rose where Punks in numbers flock' (*Satire* by T. G., *State Poems*, vol. i).

[2] Andrew Ulcken, an able diplomat, thoroughly versed in the whole state of the controversy, died on January 23rd.

to what men at his years are very subject to, a new passion for Mademoiselle Vehlin, one of the Electrice's maids of honour, who, 'tis believed, has sacrificed herself for her mistress's interest, for she may go a considerable snack while he stays at Munich, whereas, had he gone to Venice, the poor Princess had never been called to twelve.

Long before I received your newspaper of the 20th of the last month I knew the answer the Dutch had made to Monsieur d'Albeville's memorial concerning Burnet;[1] and though I had no advice from England that the letter printed under Fagel's name was a libel, my own reason told it me and I have been industrious to hinder the reprinting of it here; which Valkenier had not failed to do in case I had not spoken to him roundly about it.

The Elector of Cologne furnishes the Emperor for the next campaign, which will begin early, as it is said, with 1,200 men at seventeen crowns a head and 400 gratis, and his coadjutor, the Cardinal of Fürstenberg, has offered some on his own score, but how many or upon what conditions I know not; the Elector of Mayence 300, and the Elector of Saxony one regiment.

We expect the Count de Windisgratz's return in March next, but we know not when we may have the Margrave of Baden, the court at Vienna having done nothing towards the giving him that satisfaction which he and his family expect before he comes hither. I enclose the news which comes by this post, and am, &c.

[1] Albeville demanded that Burnet be banished from Holland in pursuance of an article of the treaty between England and the United Provinces relating to rebels or fugitives. Burnet defended himself before the deputies of the States of Holland, with the result that a memorial was drawn up in answer to Albeville insisting on the rights of a naturalized subject, by which the King's complaints could only be dealt with in the Dutch court.

Ratisbon, 13/23 Feb., 87/8.

To brother W., of an envoy from Tuscany expected at Munich to treat of the marriage of Mademoiselle de Bavière.[1]

My Lord (Arran):[2]   Ditto.

It is one of the boldest actions of a man's life to marry. Whoever passes that Rubicon has need of the fortune of Caesar to make him happy; but you have made so prudent a choice that you have secured to yourself all the joy I can wish you. The charms my Lady Anne has in her own person are sufficient for this work were they not joined with that of being so nearly related to my Lord President.[3] In this alliance you seem to have had an equal regard to your love and your ambition. The daughter is the most beautiful object that you can sigh for, and the father is the best appui this can desire. But to be less serious with your Lordship, I have had the honour of your confidence and you have told me of mighty deeds you have performed. I should be glad to be satisfied whether you are as great a hero now you fight in a good cause as when you drew your sword in a querelle d'allemande;[4] the truth is that sort of courage is a little too violent for the present purpose. The business you have now on your hands is to be spun out in length and not to be ended at once. Now the crowd of compliments is over I hope your Lordship will pardon my presuming to write to you and to felicitate you on this occasion, since the most devoted of your clan is not with more passion than I am, &c.

Ratisbon, 16/26 Feb., 87/8.

My Lord (Middleton):

Should I stay till the Diet gives me occasion of writing to you I know not how long I should wait.

[1] See *ante*, p. 322, note 2.   [2] See *ante*, p. 314, note 3.
[3] Lord Sunderland, her father.
[4] Underlined in malice by Hughes.

Those who are unacquainted with the proceedings of this assembly would wonder that, where so many ministers are met and maintained at so great a charge by their masters, so little business is done, and the little that is so slowly. All the news we have now is from other parts and you have it as soon as we if not before us. I send you what comes from Vienna, but that at this season is very inconsiderable.

All my acquaintance in London are either so busy or so lazy that I have very seldom the favour of hearing from any of them. This makes me a perfect stranger to the town, and I know not whether there be any such thing as love or good fellowship stirring. I was thinking of inviting Mr. Julian[1] to a correspondence that I might at least know how scandal goes, but Monsieur Valkenier saves me that labour. You have never a libel fixed up in Whitehall or dispersed elsewhere that he has not an account of in his circular letter from Holland. I should enlarge this if I durst make bold, but I think it better to forbear till I know whether your Lordship is grown too grave for raillery. Be what you please you can never be more happy than you were in Mr. Fox's days. Alas! against my will in this hard-hearted place there is not a maid of honour about court, no not my Lady Etherege, who leads a more virtuous life than I do. Not to affect to be le chevalier à bonne fortune the best adventure I have had here has been with a comedian no less handsome and no less kind in Dutchland[2] than Mrs. Johnson[3] was in England. Our ladies are ill-natured for want of good examples; those of Vienna, as fame says, and you ought to

---

[1] A notorious professional writer of lampoons and libels:
'Julian's so furnished by those scribbling Sparks
That he pays off old Scores and keeps no Clarks'.
　　　　　　　Prologue to Ravenscroft's *London Cuckolds*.
[2] i.e., Germany.
[3] An actress in Davenant's company.

know whether she be a liar, have souls as great and sensible as either of the Cooths ever had, or the more heroic Clambrasil. You see, my Lord, what idleness produces; had I any business your modesty would not have been offended with these loose lines by &c.

Ratisbon, 20 Feb./1 Mar., 1687/8.

My Lord (Middleton):

I met yesterday the Swedish minister here, Mr. Schnolsky, by accident, who told me Mr. Poley, according to the instructions he had received, had had audience of the King his master and had acquainted him with his Majesty's mind touching the affair between the King of Denmark and the Duke of Holstein; and that his master had ordered Monsieur Lionberg,[1] his envoy in England, to return his answer there. He told me likewise he had received a packet from court, with the substance of what Mr. Poley said, together with what Monsieur Lionberg was instructed to answer to it, and that his orders were to communicate them both to me that I might send them into England, to the end that his Majesty and his ministers might see whether Monsieur Lionberg had not mistaken himself in anything; and that he was ready to do it when I would give him an hour, which we agreed to be on Wednesday next. It is not amiss to see but I shall carefully examine the business before I charge myself with these papers, the proceeding being odd and irregular. I saw yesterday a letter from the Abbé Bidal, his Christian Majesty's envoy at Hamburg, who says the Duke of Holstein has given his reply to the Danish plenipotentiaries, by which he seems resolved not to be satisfied with anything

[1] Baron Hans Barikman Leijonberg, envoy in England since 1672.

but his being restored to a part of Sleswick,[1] and that he finds the King his master will be obliged to have the Duke more plainly spoke to so that he may see it is not his interest to harken to what the Swedish ministers[2] suggest and hope to be restored by a war, but to comply and accept of a compensation. The Count de Crécy tells me the Swedes abate a little of their heat on his master's declaring that whosoever shall attack the King of Denmark, either on this score or any other, he will assist him with all his power. I am, with all duty—

Sir (Marquis d'Albeville):

On Friday last I received the favour of yours of the 19th instant, in which you have very much obliged me by the assurances you give me of your kindness. It is a pleasing thing to believe we are well in the opinion of good men, but to be able to flatter ourselves that those whom we esteem and honour have on their side some consideration for us is the greatest happiness in the world. By this you may guess how welcome your letter was to me; the great qualities you possess long ago engaged my inclination, but the zeal you have for his Majesty's service has completed the work, and no person has a greater share in my affection. Upon spreading the libel, which goes under Monsieur's Fagel's name, by the Holland minister among those of the Reformed religion here, I was so lucky to make a true judgement of it, and had an opportunity to convince many of the justice and reasonableness of his Majesty's design in abolishing the Test and penal laws. It has ever been the practice of factious knaves to amuse the world with sham letters, and I could

[1] The Duke refused to abate his demands or accept of Oldenburg and Delmenhorst as an equivalent.

[2] Sweden had requested Denmark to restore Schleswig to the Duke.

not but be very much surprised to see the name of
so eminent a person as is the Pensioner of the high
and mighty States prostituted in this nature . . .
News as in the foregoing letter till to this place.
. . . The Count de Crécy shewed me yesterday a
letter which he had just received from the Marquis
de Lavardin in which he tells him the arrest[1] of the
Parliament of Paris with the harangue made by
Monsieur Talon[2] were affiched against the basilic
of St. Peter's and in three score several places in
Rome to the great astonishment of the people. By
his Holiness's command they were pulled down by
the public officers. Many deliberations have been
what is to be done in this case, but there is nothing
yet determined. In another letter from the Cardinal
d'Estrées it is said some spirits too violent were for
excommunicating the whole Parliament, but his
opinion is it will end in the excommunication of
Monsieur de Harlay[3] and Monsieur Talon, the

[1] Fr. *arrêt*, i.e., decree.
[2] At the assembling of the Parliament Talon, the King's
advocate, representing the King's council, set forth the obligations of the Church to the French kings, and asserted that the
privileges and franchises were immunities the Crown had
long possessed; that the rights of the Crown could admit
of no regulation or bounds but such as were proposed by the
King; that the censure of the Church and the power of the
keys were abused when they served temporal ends, and that
ambassadors were exempt from ecclesiastical censure. He
complained that the Pope refused the bull to nominations for
vacant bishoprics and archbishoprics which was the right of
the King of France. The Parliament pronounced that Talon
be admitted an appellant as of abuse against the Papal bull
and ordnance with regard to the franchises, declared them to
be void, forbade their dispersal, and ordered the suppression
of copies; suggested that Louis should prohibit commerce with
Rome and that the sentence should be affixed in public places.
[3] Achille de Harlai, Count de Beaumont (1639–1712),
attorney-general, provoked the appeal against the Pope on
Lavardin's excommunication (Jan. 1688) and was made first
President of the Parliament of Paris, 1689.

procureur and advocate general. In another part of Monsieur Lavardin's letter he said the Spanish minister, in an audience he had of his Holiness, obtained the confirmation of the Tenth of Parma and told him he could not undertake anything against France, but that he would do all he could to maintain the peace in Italy. The Emperor's minister told his Holiness that his master could not turn his arms westward without doing a manifest injury to all Christendom.

I know you are in a very busy post, wherefore it is not reasonable you should trouble yourself to write, but on extraordinary occasions; but pray let your secretary constantly let me know what passes, since it may contribute to his Majesty's service. I am, &c.

Ratisbon, 23 Feb./1 Mar., 87/8.

Sir (Mr. Wynne):

You may be pleased to tell my Lord that the Swedish minister has not yet been with me to communicate what I mentioned in my last of the 20th instant.[1] I hope he has advanced more than was necessary in this matter; I wish it with all my heart, for he has a good character that way, and it would spoil one of the best comedies we have here if he should go out on't.

The Marquis d'Albeville has given me an account of the answer the States have made to his Majesty's demand of his regiments in Holland,[2] and I must

[1] See *ante*, p. 329.

[2] There were three English and three Scotch regiments in the service of the States. James II suddenly wrote and desired that they should be sent over to him; the States replied that they had paid levy money for them, and that they served without any reservation to the effect that the King could call for them at his pleasure. Orders, however, were given that the officers (many of whom were Catholics and had been causing dissensions) might have leave to go on application (Burnet, ii. 453–4).

confess I am not so much offended at the injustice of
their proceedings as I am ashamed of the behaviour
of the officers, who at once seem to forget the loyalty
they owe to their King and the love they ought to
have for their country. I cannot but say this since I
have the displeasure daily of hearing our politicians
here reason on a thing so very extraordinary. I
knew many of them when I was at the Hague, and
find them so changed that I doubt not but great
industry has been used to debauch them. Many
excuse them on the score of religion,[1] but I know
not what religion, for I am sure the Christian
religion teaches us to be obedient to our lawful
sovereign. It has been the endeavour of factious
spirits to make his Majesty's subjects jealous of him
in matter of religion, but all the impartial world
see that too many of his ungrateful subjects give
just cause to be jealous of them in matter of moral
honesty. I am, &c.

Ditto.

Sir (Marquis d'Albeville):

Though I have nothing worth acquainting you
with by this post I could not omit the acknowledging
the obligations I have to you for your favour of the
24th of the last month. The answer the States have
made to his Majesty's demand of the regiments in
their service makes the greater part of the entertainment of the ministers here. For my part I
wonder not so much that those high and mighty
lords should want the justice to comply with his
Majesty's desire as I do that our countrymen should
want that loyalty for their King, and that love for
their country, which every true English heart uses
to be touched with. This makes me ashamed and
angry. I knew many of the officers when I was at

[1] There were both Protestants and Catholics in the regiments; Etherege, of course, alludes only to the former.

the Hague, and found them then so well inclined
that I could not have imagined in so little a time
to see that noble ardour extinguished which they
had for his Majesty's service.[1] I doubt not but much
pains and address has been employed to debauch
them; there are who pretend to excuse them on the
score of a tender conscience, which sucks in the
jealous bait which cunning knaves fish with. I
know not what religion they can pretend to be of,
the Christian religion carefully teaches obedience
to their sovereign. All who are not blind see that
his Majesty's word is sacred and unviolable, never
prince was so firm to his promise. What pity 'tis
so many brave, well-meaning men should be misled
by factious spirits, who make them suspicious of the
designs of so good and so righteous a King. All
their arguments are grounded merely on presumption. I wish his ungrateful subjects did not give
him evident cause to be jealous of them; does not
his Majesty equally employ according to his
promise his subjects of different religions? and no
man wants his favour who is not wanting in his duty;
besides, what prince is more merciful, more bountiful, and take[s] more particular care to advance
all those who have any merit? I beg your pardon
for saying so much on a matter which you are
better able to discourse of than I am, but the
inclination I have had for many of these officers
has made me give way to the transports of my present
passion. I hope in a little time they will be sensible
of their error, for I cannot but believe that most of
them are without malice mistaken, honest men. You
cannot send any news which will be more welcome
to, Sir, your most humble and most obedient
servant.

[1] Etherege was at the Hague at the beginning of the reign
of James II; he forgot the effect that the Declaration of
Indulgence would be likely to have on Protestants.

Sir (Sir Peter Wyche):

I am in possession of your favour of the 4th of February, and though according to the Altona treaty, I ought to offer you nothing less than an equivalent, yet you must be content at least for the present, to construe this as an act of the sincerity, justice, and inclination I owe you; though you receive nothing proportionable to what your kind letters justly claim. Our cat, the Count de Windisgratz, being absent here is nothing but playing. We morris-dance it all the night till the day peeps in upon us and sends us home to season us for another meeting. Though you see we do nothing, yet I should be glad to hear you at Altona do something, especially since you have nothing to excuse you as to want of matter to work upon. To speak plainer, I do not mean yourself, who as I am informed, are[1] to appear at the conference by his Majesty's instructions. I wish you all the success which the zeal for his Majesty's service and your own satisfaction can propose to you. I am, &c.

G. E.

Ratisbon, 27 Feb./8 Mar., 88.

My Lord (Middleton):

I have not yet seen the Swedish minister since he told me he had order to communicate to me the answer Monsieur de Lionberg was to make to the instances Mr. Poley has made at that court; but I have seen it since in a letter from Copenhagen, which likewise informs me Monsieur Puffendorf[2] is on his way hither where he is to be the King of Denmark's minister. He has orders to call at the courts of Lüneburg, but it is thought what he is to negotiate there will not take him up much time, it being well advanced already. Though I question

---

[1] MS. 'is'.   [2] See *ante*, p. 318, note 3.

not but Sir Peter Wyche gives you a perfect account
of what passes at Altona, I hope your Lordship will
not think it impertinent in me to let you know that
yesterday I saw a letter of the 28th of February, new
style, from the Abbé Bidal[1] in which he says he has
had an audience of the Duke of Holstein-Gottorp,
in which he pressed him very much to accept of the
counties of Oldenburg and Delmenhorst as an
equivalent; representing to him that in case they
were of a less value than the Duchy of Sleswick the
King his master offered to employ powerful offices
by the King of Denmark that he may obtain a
supplement; that he ought not to put his hopes in a
war which he could not be certain would be sincerely
undertaken for him; and that, in case it should, the
success would always be doubtful; and that he was
farther to tell him from the King his master that
having procured the peace of Europe with so much
pains, he would employ all the means he had in his
hands to hinder the disturbance of the public quiet,
and therefore it would do better he should consent
to an accommodation, which could not be made but
by accepting those counties as an equivalent. I am,
&c.

Ditto.

(Mr. Jepson):[2]

Yesterday, Sir, I received your favour of the 25th
of January. I doubt whether you have ever been so
unhappy to be so long absent from what you love
as to be perfectly sensible of the joy it gave me.[3]
Nature, you know, intended me for an idle fellow,
and gave me passions and qualities fit for that
blessed calling, but fortune has made a changeling
of me, and necessity now forces me to set up for a
fop of business. Ned Russell has been more the

[1] See *ante*, p. 329. [2] See *ante*, p. 212, note 4.
[3] MS. 'you'.

object of my envy than the ablest minister I know
is. How pleasanter it is to jolt about in poor hackney
coaches to find out the harmless lust of the town
than to spend the time in a room of state in whispers
to discover the ambitious designs of princes. A
letter from you so fires me with the thought of the
life I have led that I can hardly forbear to rail at that
I am condemned to. There is but one I like worse,
which is that of a clergyman.[1] The mischief they
daily do in the world makes me have no better an
opinion of them than Lucian had of the ancient
philosophers; their pride, their passion, and their
covetousness makes them endeavour to destroy the
government they were instituted to support, and, instead of taking care of the quietness of our souls, they
are industrious to make us cut one another's throats.

I am beholden to you for leading me behind the
scenes. You put me in mind of the time I have well
employed there. Sarah Cooke[2] was always fitter
for a player than for a Mrs., and it is properer her
lungs should be wasted on the stage than that she
should die of a disease too gallant for her. Mrs.
Percivall[3] had only her youth and a maidenhead to
recommend her, which makes me think you do not
take it to heart that Mrs. Mumford is so discreet.

[1] One has only to glance at a few Restoration comedies to
realize in what contempt the average clergyman was held.
On the other hand, great preachers like Tillotson and Stilling-
fleet were much esteemed.

[2] Sarah Cooke was an actress in the King's Company
(1677–87).

[3] Susanna Perceval (1667?–1703). Her name first appears in
casts in 1681 at the Theatre Royal. In July 1686 she married
the actor-dramatist, William Mountford (often misspelt
Mumford). Many of the best parts of the Restoration
comedies were assigned to her. Aston speaks of her as a fine
woman, plump, full-featured; her face of a smooth oval: 'Her
greatest charm was laughing, flirting her fan, and je ne sais
quoi with a kind of affected twitter' (*Brief Supplement*, pp. 18–19;
see also Cibber's *Apology*, Everyman ed., pp. 89–91).

Mrs. Barry[1] bears up as well as I myself have done. My poor Lord Rochester[2] could not weath[er] the cape and live under the line fatal to puling constitutions. Though I have given over writing plays I should be glad to read a good one, wherefore let Will. Richards send me Mr. Shadwell's[3] when it is printed, that I may know what follies are in fashion. The fops I knew are grown stale, and he is likely to pick up the best collections of new ones. I expect to see my Lord Carlingford[4] in his way to Vienna, then you may be sure all the remains of the Dog and Partridge[5] will be remembered. To make him more welcome I intend to have a minister or two of my acquaintance, who can swallow as well and are no less solid than his Lordship. Our carnival ends to-morrow, and I am just now agoing to a ball, where there will be a great many and some pretty young women, though, to tell you the truth, I have of late lived as chaste as my Lady Etherege. The best fortune I have had here has been a player, something handsomer, and as much a jilt, as Mrs. Barry. Nevertheless this is a country to satisfy Sir Robert Parker's vanity, for few foul their fingers with touching of a —— that does not belong to a countess. Do me all the good offices you can to keep me in the memory of my friends, and never let

[1] Elizabeth Barry (1658–1713) owed her introduction to the stage to Wilmot, Lord Rochester, whose mistress she subsequently became. She showed little promise at first, but lived to be one of the greatest actresses of her time. For her connexion with Etherege see Introduction, p. 15.

[2] John Wilmot, Earl of Rochester, worn out by debauchery and excess, died prematurely in 1680, aged 32.

[3] Thomas Shadwell's *The Squire of Alsatia* was produced at Drury Lane in the spring of 1688 and printed the same year. It ran for thirteen nights, and the author received £130 for his benefit, a large sum for those days.

[4] See *ante*, p. 320.

[5] See *ante*, p. 321, note 1.

me have the displeasure of suspecting you have forgot, Sir, &c.

Ratisbon, 1/11 March, 1687/8.

Sir (Marquis d'Albeville):

I have received your favour of the 2nd instant, new style, but being indisposed of a cold I got by being too careless of myself this carnival I cannot to-day return you my thanks for it with my own hand. This fault I know you will easily excuse in me, who has that real esteem for you which your merit does deserve.

I am mightily pleased with the two last memorials you delivered to the States; the matter is so closely couched, in terms so firm and expressive, the quotations of the articles of treaties and the precedents so proper to the business, that they have convinced all who are not prejudiced here of the injustice of their proceedings with his Majesty. I am sorry you were not capacitated at first according to your desire, and that you had not time given you before his Majesty demanded the brigades that you might have discoursed with the officers severally and have removed the evil impressions which malignant spirits have given them. For I doubt not but that among other things they were made believe his Majesty would take away their commissions and give them to Roman Catholics; besides, it would have been necessary to advance money to those that wanted it to pay their debts in Holland. I am sure you reflected on what was expedient and are troubled you had not an opportunity to execute it. With news from Rome and Altona.

Ditto.

My Lord (Middleton):

Yesterday I received a visit from the Swedish envoy, who told me he was come to execute the King his master's orders, which I found were something differing from what I had understood from him before: for he said that the King by the Count d'Oxenstern[1] had given his answer to Mr. Poley, and that a copy of it was sent to Monsieur Lionberg, to be communicated by him to all the ministers at the court of England, and he was commanded to do the like to me, and I believe to all the ministers here. He did it by word of mouth, which was the same in effect which, I was acquainted from Copenhagen, had been delivered to Mr. Poley. After some discourse of these matters I told him I believed, considering the present state of the Duke of Gottorp's affairs, it might agree with his interest to accept of an equivalent, but that he thought as well as I it agreed better with his master's interest that he should be restored; at which he laughed and answered I was in the right, but with all his master was in honour and gratitude obliged to do all he could to have the Duke restored to his patrimony; but the interest more than the other considerations make the Swedes animate the Duke in his firmity. The fortress the King of Denmark is building at Oldensloa[2] begins already to be talked of here, and I believe ere long it will be represented to the Diet as a grief of no less importance than the French fortifications. The Imperial towns Dortmund, Mühlhausen, and Nordhausen have delivered a memorial against the Elector of Brandenburg's demands,[3] and so has the minister of Ostfriese; the

[1] Gabriel Thureson, Count of Oxenstierna (1641–1707), served in the Swedish army and diplomatic service. It seems more likely that Etherege was referring to Bengt Oxenstierna (1623–1702), Swedish prime minister, who did much to restore prosperity to his country.

[2] Oldensloe, on Danish territory between Hamburg and Lübeck. Preparations were begun at the end of December, and the fort was designed to consist of eleven bastions and twelve ravelins.

[3] The three towns drew up a memorial stating the reasons

substance of them is in the paper I sent your Lordship in a letter of the 30th of January last.

The Abbot of St. James arrived here two days
since, and he has overjoyed me by assuring me I
have still the same place I had in your favour. I
shall endeavour to deserve it by being constantly,
&c.

AN IMPERFECT COPY OF THE MOST RENOWNED ORIGINAL S[IR] G[EORGE] E[THEREGE]:

Hudibras's surpassing worth
The manner how he sallyed forth &c.

A man of parts and learning much
That scarce in Europe there is such;
Nay Turks and heathens, I may say,
Had never yet a man of clay
That knew so many things at once
As knight Sir George had in his sconce.
He played oft the philosopher,
Altho' he was no strict liver;
And if his Latin had held out
He would have baffled all the rout.

which ought to exempt them from being made an accession
to any other prince: they were free cities immediately connected with the Empire; they had an original and inherent
right to a voice and seat in the Diet, territorial jurisdiction,
and power of levying money; by the constitution of the Empire
no state might usurp another; by the Treaty of Westphalia
the free towns were to have liberty of suffrage with the other
states of the Empire. No compensation was due to the Elector,
for he lost no towns nor territory that he was immediately
possessed of before the war; the Elector had even protested
when the Emperor desired some free towns as an equivalent
for his loss of Freyburg. The memorial stressed the importance of Dortmund as the only free town between the Weser
and the Rhine, and urged the other Imperial towns to reject
Brandenburg's pretences as an ill precedent.

To teach and preach he did not care,
But as for practice he was rare,
For all that ere went before him
Were of Sir G, not worth a limb.
For he, by force of magic might,
At pleasure turn the day to night.
Ramble, revel, caterwaul it,
And all to show his parts and wit.
His grammar was to name in Dutch
A whore, a bawd, a common bitch,
His rhetoric was of sing'lar use,
In brothel houses and in stews,
Whence 'tis impossible to stir
When cat Sir G. began to purr:
Then he thought him in his kingdom,
When any would commit whoredom
With sound of fiddle, pipe, or drum.
His learning yet went much higher
With Rhenish wine and a good fire,
For then, his animal spirits roused,
Decayed with pox, and soundly soused,[1]
He'd speak Dutch, Greek and Hebrew,
Though knew no more than I or you;
His Latin went at any rate,
But could not warrant Priscian's pate.
He could at once philosophize,
And play the fool with cards and dice.
Ethics and morals he knew not,
Nor who could love them but a sot.
He was above the silly ways
Of honour, virtue, credit, praise;
For all these he loved no better
Than salt, vinegar, and pepper.
His economy all men saw
Was not the best, but so and so;
He kept both men and women too,
The first to pimp, the last to woo.

[1] MS. 'souced'.

No kitchen wench could ere escape
Without the danger of a rape;
Hobgoblin-like, as soon as night,
He ranged in shirt the maids to fright;
And she that offered to resist
He broke her door with feet and fist;
Sometimes he got in at window,
A lepp'd his maids like buck and doe:
That such a house and such a spark
You scarce can find in Whetstone's Park.[1]
All such pranks he counted nothing
But pure effects of good living;
For none knew how to live but he,
So wise, so tame, from faults so free.
Being deeply skilled in politics
He played the wisest scurvy tricks;
Envoys and doctors him did fear
Just as children do a bugbear:
For he'd say (not to their faces)
Th'are all fools, coxcombs, and asses.
He knew two parts of physics well:
The nature of a beast could tell
By practice, and for medicament
You needs must know him by the scent.
He'd fart and piss, fas and nefas,
All to ease his rotten carcase.
Metaphysics spoiled his credo,
Like a faithless renegado.
He thought nothing of religion,
Took the very name in dudgeon,
And, Latitudinarian he,
Would fain par force a statesman be.
His mathematics who but knew
When Tory Sensheim[2] and his crew
Attacked his house vi et armis
To steal the carrion called his miss,

[1] An infamous neighbourhood.
[2] See *post*, pp. 390–2.

For them, by courage and by skill,
He forced the rebels to his will;
Gained a most triumphant battle,
Which made the street of Regens. rattle.
He fancied much arithmetic,
But took up all things upon tick;
Witness the bills of pock-Bader
Tailor, baker, band and butcher.
He held trinum est perfectum
Pimp, whore and he made up the sum.
Of music he was an admirer, ⎫
And loved a fiddler or a piper, ⎬
Far much better than his brother. ⎭
In geometry 'twas an angle
Cracks in corners to entangle.
Optics was to spy them coming,
Going, staying, turning, squatting;
And geography then was useful
To know which way to catch the trull.
If he succeeded well therein,
And found an alehouse or an inn
Fit to enter with his doxy,
He cried ho! landlord! with a pox t'you!
Let's in and show room that's fit
To practise astronomic wit;
For here's a scholar to my will
That fears no pox, and dreads no pill, &c., &c.

LETTERS RECEIVED.

Whitehall, Dec. the 7th, 1685.

Sir,

I was very glad to hear of your safe arrival at
Ratisbon. I thank you for your letters, by which
you approve yourself a very pretty proficient. I
hope in a little time we may hear something of your
diversions as well as your business, which would be
much pleasanter, and perhaps as instructive.

I can tell you for comfort that this place is as dull as your Diet; the young fellows you left here are so unlike you that they have not had vigour enough to afford scandal, nor will enough to invent any. For the little we have had we have been beholding to a Dutch tapster, which only begot a ballad below Humphrey Bell to the tune of fourpence halfpenny farthing.

Every week there are plays at court. The last time Sir Fopling[1] appeared with the usual applause, and the King was pleased to tell me that he expected you should put on your socks, which puts me in mind of Denham on Killigrew:[2]

> He has plotted and penned
> Six plays, to attend
> The farce of his negotiation.

This you are to consider as an instruction, and, as for advice, zagos is the best that can be given you by Sir,

Your most faithful servant,

Middleton.

Monsieur,

J'ai reçu la lettre que vous m'avez fait la faveur de m'écrire; elle a été lue en bonne compagnie et a été fort approuvée de quantité de Milord[s] qui ne don-

---

[1] Etherege's last and best play, *The Man of Mode, or Sir Fopling Flutter*. A warrant dated Dec. 28, 1685, in the Lord Chamberlain's department of the Public Record Office, contains the following entry, 'Nov. 30 Sᵣ Phoplyn att Whitehall £20' (Professor Nicoll's *Restoration Drama*, p. 312). This performance must have been the occasion of the King's remark.

[2] *On Mr. Killigrew's Return from Venice and Mr. William Murray's from Scotland.* The second stanza runs:

> 'But who says he was not
> A man of much plot
> May repent that false accusation,
> Having plotted and penn'd
> Six plays to attend
> The farce of his negociation.'

nent pas légèrement leur approbation. Votre description de traîneaux nous a fait regretter d'être ici dans
un climat si temperé que nous ne pouvons pas espérer
de semblables divertissements.

J'ai Monsieur une grand[e] joie d'avoir pu
contribuer à la liaison qui me parait être entre
Monsieur de Crécy et vous. Je suis assuré qu'elle
augmentera à proportion que vous vous connaîtrez
d'avantage.

Croyez je vous prie, Monsieur, que je suis avec
beaucoup d'estime et de vérité,

Monsieur,

Votre très humble et très obéissant serviteur

Barrillon.

A Londres ce 22e Janvier 1686.

To you who live in chill degree,[1]
(As map informs) of fifty three,
And do not much for cold atone
By bringing thither fifty-one,
Methinks all climes should be alike,
From tropic ev'n to pole arctic;
Since you have such a constitution
As nowhere suffers diminution.
You can be old in grave debate,
And young in love's affairs of state,
And both to wives and husbands show
The vigour of a plenipo.
Like mighty missioner you came:
Ad partes infidelium;
A work of wondrous merit sure
So far to go, so much endure;
And all to preach to German Dame
Where sound of Cupid never came.
Less had you done had you been sent
As far as Drake or Pinto went

[1] Printed in Dryden's *Miscellany Poems*, 1716, vol. ii, p. 281.

For cloves and nutmegs to the line a
Or ev'n for oranges to China:
That had indeed been charity, ⎫
Where lovesick ladies helpless lie: ⎬
Chapt[1] and for want of liquor dry. ⎭
But you have made your zeal appear
Within the circle of the Bear.
What region of the earth so dull
That is not of your labours full?
Triptolemus (so sing the nine)
Strew'd plenty from his cart divine;
But spite of all those fable makers
He never sowed on Almain acres:
No, that was left by fate's decree
To be perform'd and sung by thee.
Thou breakst through forms with as much ease
As the French King through articles.
In grand affairs thy days are spent ⎫
Of waging weighty compliment ⎬
With such as monarchs represent ⎭
They who such vast fatigues attend,
Want some soft minutes to unbend,
To show the world now and then
Great ministers are mortal men.
Then Rhenish rummers walk the round,
In bumpers every King is crown'd,
Besides three holy mitred hectors,
And the whole College of Electors.
No health of Potentate is sunk
That pays to make his Envoy drunk.
These Dutch delights I mention'd last,
Suit not I know your English taste.
For wine, to leave a whore or play
Was ne're your Excellence's way.
Nor need the title give offence;
For here you were his Excellence

---

[1] MS. 'chopt'.

For gaming, writing, speaking, keeping,
His Excellence for all but sleeping.
Now if you tope in form and treat
'Tis the sour sauce to your sweet meat,
The fine you pay for being great.
Nay, there is a harder imposition,
Which is indeed the Court's petition,
That setting worldly pomp aside,
(Which poet has at font defy'd),
You wou'd be pleas'd in humble way
To write a trifle call'd a play.
This truly is a degradation,
But wou'd oblige the crown and nation
Next to your wise negotiation.
If you pretend (as well as you may)
Your high degree, your friends will say
That Duke St. Aignan[1] made a play.
If Gallic poet convince you scarce,
His Grace of Bucks has writ a farce,[2]
And you, whose comic wit is terse all,
Can hardly fall below Rehearsal.
Then finish what here you began,
But scribble faster if you can:
Forget no George to our discerning
Has writ without a ten years' warning.[3]

Thought to be written by Mr. Dryden, sent to Sir G[eorge]
by my Lord Middleton.

[1] François de Beauvilliers, Duc de St. Aignan (1607–87),
distinguished French soldier and courtier, wrote a tragi-
comedy entitled *Bradamante.*
[2] *The Rehearsal,* in which Dryden was the principal scapegoat.
[3] Dryden taunts the Duke of Buckingham for having taken
ten years to write *The Rehearsal.* Cf.:

'I come to his farce, which must needs be well done,
For Troy was no longer, before it was won
Since 'tis more than ten years since this farce was begun.'

For regulating extraordinaries.

Whitehall, February the 11th, 1686/7.

Sir,

His Majesty having thought it necessary for his service to regulate the extraordinary allowances of his ministers employed abroad, and having thereupon passed an order under his royal signet and sign manual the 7th of this instant February, he hath been pleased thereby to declare that if your accounts of extraordinaries exceed the sum of fifty pounds every quarter of a year during your residence at Ratisbon in his Majesty's service, his Majesty will allow no more than fifty pounds a quarter, and that no other extraordinaries shall be allowed you from time to time upon any occasion, except for such extraordinary expenses as shall be made by you in pursuance of his Majesty's particular order to be signified by one of his principal secretaries of state; or for such expenses as shall appear absolutely necessary for his Majesty's service in case there be not time to send or receive his Majesty's directions in the matter. And his Majesty hath commanded me to signify this his pleasure unto you that you may govern yourself accordingly.

I am, Sir,
Your most humble servant,
Middleton.

Sir George Etherege.

Made by the Siam Ambassadors to the French King, 1686/7.[1]

Très grand Roi,

Nous venons ici pour demander à votre Majesté la permission de nous en retourner vers le Roi notre maître. L'impatience où nous savons qu'il est

---

[1] They left for Brest on January 15, 1687.

d'apprendre le succès de cette ambassade, les merveilles que nous avons à lui raconter, les gages précieux[1] que nous lui portons de l'estime singulière que Votre Majesté a pour lui, et surtout l'assurance que nous lui devons donner de la royale amitié qu'elle contracte pour jamais avec lui, tout cela, beaucoup plus encore que les vents et la saison, nous invite enfin à partir pendant que les bons traitements que nous recevons ici de toutes part[s] par les ordre[s] de Votre Majesté seraient capables de nous faire oublier notre patrie et, si nous l'osons dire, les ordres même de notre Prince. Mais sur le point de nous éloigner de votre présence royale nous n'avons point de paroles qui puissent exprimer les sentiments de respect, et d'admiration, et de reconnaissance dont nous sommes pénétrés. Nous nous étions bien attendus à trouver en Votre Majesté des grandeurs, et des qualities extraordinaires; l'effet y a pleinement répondu, et a même de beaucoup surpassé, notre attente. Mais nous sommes obligés de l'avouer, nous n'avions pas cru pouvoir y trouver tout l'accès, la douceur, l'affabilité que nous y avons rencontrés. Nous ne jugions pas même que des qualités qui paraissent si opposées pussent compatir dans une même personne, et qu'on put accorder ensemble tant de majesté et tant de bonté. Nous ne sommes pas surpris que vos peuples, trop heureux de vivre sous votre Empire, fassent paraître partout l'amour de la tendresse qu'ils ont pour Votre Royale personne. Pour nous, Grand Roi, comblés de vos bienfaits, charmés de vos vertus, touchés jusqu'au fond du cœur de vos bontés, saisis d'étonnement à la vue de votre haute sagesse, et de tous les miracles de votre règne, notre vie nous parait trop courte et le monde entier trop petit pour publier ce que nous en pensons.

[1] MS. 'pretieux'.

Notre mémoire aurait eu peine à retenir tant de choses. C'est ce qui nous a fait recueillir dans des registres fidèles tout ce que nous avons pu en ramasser, et nous les terminerons par cette protestation: que quoique nous en disions beaucoup il nous en a encore plus échappé. Ces mémoires seront consacrés à la posterité et mis en depôt entre les monuments les plus rares et les plus précieux de l'état. Le Roi notre maître les enverra pour présents aux princes ses alliés, et par là tout l'Orient saura bientôt, et tous les siècles à venir apprendront, les vertus incomparables de Louis le Grand. Nous porterons enfin l'heureuse nouvelle de la santé parfaite de Votre Majesté et du soin que le ciel a pris de continuer le cours d'une vie qui ne devrait jamais finir.

Harangue des Ambassadeurs de Siam en prenant congé du Roi.

Sir,

Mr. Skelton, being come to this place in quality of his Majesty's envoy extraordinary, and being as yet in such a hurry upon his first arrival that he has not time to write to you himself, has done me the honour to desire me to do it for him and make you a tender of the services of this station, which I am sure he will, with a great deal of sincerity, most readily give you.

Sir, I have had formerly thoughts of troubling you with a letter, out of the esteem I have for you, to give you an account of reports which we had in Holland: that in your discourses, where you are you frequently made reflections upon the conduct of Mr. Skelton in his negotiations abroad, and particularly that you have of late much condemned the seizing of Sir Robert Peyton[1] at Rotterdam and vindicated him from being a rebel. I am concerned

---

[1] See *ante*, p. 144, note 1.

for this for your sake, for, as for Mr. Skelton, he knew the grounds he went upon, and the King has very well approved of what he did, and you are under a great mistake if you do not think him as guilty as any man.

And I have also heard that you accuse Mr. Skelton with breach of faith for endeavouring to seize a man with whom he was in treaty for the obtaining his pardon. This is a great mistake too, for, though he received letters from Peyton entreating his solicitations in his behalf, to which he made no other returns than that we would send over his letters to the King as he did those he ever received from any other rebels, and made known to his Majesty all the offers that were made to him by this man or others; yet he never did or could make any promises of safety to him, and coming in his way was as liable to be apprehended as Ferguson[1] himself.

You will excuse me for endeavouring the rectifying your mistakes in this matter. I am sure I aim only at your service in it, and continue to be with great esteem, Sir,

Your most faithful, humble servant
Sol. Slater.[2]

Paris, 28 December, 1686.

Sir,

Your enclosed in one to Mr. Corbet I have received, and sorry I cannot say so much of another you mention to have sent me formerly. I hope my not answering of it in all this time is a sufficient demonstration to you that I never received it; for you cannot think I understand my advantage so little as not [to] embrace the first opportunity of holding so good a correspondence with one whose friendship I ever valued at too high a rate to venture

[1] See *ante*, p. 321, note 2.
[2] For Etherege's answer to this letter see pp. 143–6.

the losing of it by so unpardonable a neglect; and to tell you the truth I have been very often out of countenance, and somewhat out of humour, not to be able to give an account of Sir George Etherege, when inquired for amongst his friends, and have not drunk his health with that gusto I used to do, but have either spilt my wine or put on a sullen, grave face, thinking by that foolish means to be revenged on you. But now we are fully reconciled (and that is a word at this time of no small importance) I will confess to you that I am not so fond of my court employment as you imagine, because that either I grow old, or the set of maids do so, and consequently have not many charms to make any one sigh but poor Robin Sayers, who has blown (not in Sunderland's cant) Mrs. Yarburgh[1] into the north, there to lead apes in hell; for she has left the court, and her court portion is paid without any obligation of marrying. Her place is not ill supplied by Mrs. Fairefax, who was once married, and I doubt not as good a maid as any of the whole set, to Lord Abergavenny, who released her for a thousand pound. The widow Swan,[2] they say, is disposing of her person, whose place will not be ill filled by Mrs. Fragmorton, who has made Packe's eyes water a hundred times, even when Lady Dorset[3] sat governess of his unruly passion. Mrs. Frazier[4] will not declare herself till she knows whether Scarborough's[5] passion will keep alive a year and a

[1] Henrietta Yarburgh, Maid of Honour to the Queen Consort, was granted a royal bounty for her marriage on Dec. 9, 1686, £2,000 for her marriage portion, and £120 17s. 6d. for fees (Treasury Books, 1685–9, 8.2, p. 1054).

[2] See *ante*, p. 309, note 1.

[3] See *ante*, p. 303, note 3.

[4] Probably Sir Alexander Frazer's wife, a maid of honour.

[5] Sir Charles Scarborough had been sent as envoy extraordinary to Portugal in March 1685/6.

day at Lisbon. As for the Pr— maids I suppose you are not very solicitous to know what is become of them since Mrs. Nott's face was spoiled with the small-pox. However, I cannot forbear telling of you that Harry Wharton[1] is no more the constant, and that gives great alarms to Ginee Deer lest the disease should run in a blood and infect poor Tom,[2] for he has forsaken Mrs. Mary and makes violent love to Mrs. Drumar by the help of his friend Lord Scarsdale,[3] who is contented at present with an amusement with Mrs. Ogle.[4] The Lord you desire to be informed of deceives nobody's expectations, for ever since the first month of their marriage 'tis cross and pile,[5] but that before night they part and nothing hinders of his side but the two thousand per annum separate maintenance; but now the quarrels are so loud that bitch and rogue are words of very civil respect, so that very soon you will hear of an elopement which they say she did very lately for two or three days, and he, being very unwilling to part with any ready money, submitted and made peace; but it is no more expected to be kept than betwixt the Turks and Christians. I will now fill

[1] Probably Henry Wharton, brother of Thomas, who died, a colonel in the English army, in Ireland, 1687.

[2] Thomas Wharton, 1st Marquis of Wharton (1648–1715), had the reputation for being the greatest rake in England. 'He and Henry indulged themselves in all the Pleasures of Mirth and Gallantry' (*Memoirs of the Life of Thomas Marquis of Wharton*, 1715, p. 12).

[3] Robert Leke, 3rd Earl of Scarsdale.
 'Scarsdell tho' loath'd, still the fair Sex adores'
  (*A Faithful Catalogue of our Most Eminent Ninnies in* 1687, Harl. MS. 7317).

[4] Perhaps the sister of Jack Ogle, the notorious gamester, who was gentlewoman to the Countess of Inchiquin until 'her extraordinary beauty, genteel carriage, and graceful mien soon recommended her to be the Duke of York's mistress' (Lucas, *Lives of the Gamesters*, pp. 186–7).

[5] i.e. pitch and toss.

up my sheet and tell you that the King has taken away my Lord Shrewsbury's[1] and my Lord Lumley's[2] regiments for reasons best known to himself, though the town will have it because of their refusal to comply with the King's desires in taking off the Test. But of these matters of state I know you have a much better account, therefore will not further trouble you but to assure you I am,

Your most obedient and humble servant
T. Maule.

London, Jan. the 25th, 1686.

London, Feb. 16th, 87.

A guilty man you know, Sir, naturally avoids one who can convince him of his faults, and I acknowledge myself to be of that number; for which reason I have not dared in three weeks time since your last letter lay by me yet to open it, for my conscience tells me that, though you may express yourself with all imaginable civility, and I believe kindness too, yet there must be somewhat of upbraiding me for my neglect which I will not go about to excuse because I cannot. 'Tis a blot and you may enter, if you will not forgive, an oversight which you may safely do and win the game afterwards in good writing, for I will never enter the lists in prose with the undoubted best author of it which our nation has produced. Therefore, O thou immortal source of idleness (you see I am ready to make prayers to you and invoke you by your darling attribute), pardon a poor creature who is your image, and

[1] Charles Talbot, Earl, later Duke, of Shrewsbury (1660–1718), obtained a colonelcy of the horse under James II, which he retained until 1686/7. During Dykvelt's mission to England his house was a frequent place of meeting between the agent and friends of the Prince of Orange.

[2] See *ante*, p. 211, note 3. It is generally stated that dissatisfaction with James's policy caused Lumley to lay down his commission in January 1686/7.

whom no gratitude, no consideration of friendship, no letters, though never so elegantly written, can oblige to take up the pen, though it be but to manage it half an hour. For while I am writing this I have laid it down and almost concluded with an imperfect sentence. I am almost lazy enough to get a stamp for my name like the King of France; which indeed would be to be great in idleness. I have made my court to the King once in seven months, have seen my Lord Chamberlain[1] full as often. I believe, if they think of me at all, they imagine I am very proud, but I am gloriously lazy. I have a son,[2] whom I love entirely, with my Lord Middleton, but I never thank him for his kindness for fear of opening my mouth. I might probably get something at court, but my Lord Sunderland, I imagine, thinks me dead while I am silently wishing him all prosperity. For wishes cost me no more than thinking. In short, without apoplexy, Wycherley's long sickness,[3] I forget everything to enjoy nothing —that is myself. Can you expect news out of Covent Garden[4] from such a man? The coffee-house stands certainly where it did, and angry men meet in the square sometimes as Abercomy and Goodman[5] lately did where they say Alexander the Great was wounded in the arm, by which you may note he had better have been idle. I cannot help hearing that white sticks change their masters, and that officers

[1] Lord Mulgrave.

[2] This must have been the poet's eldest son, born in 1666 and educated at Trinity College, Cambridge.

[3] William Wycherley, the dramatist (1640–1716).

[4] Then a very fashionable quarter, especially famous for the Piazza.

[5] Cardell Goodman (1649?–99), an actor in the King's Company at Drury Lane. His first recorded appearance was in Lee's *Rival Queens, or the Death of Alexander the Great*, in 1677, in which he also made his greatest success. He was a paramour of the Duchess of Cleveland, and a highway robber.

of the army[1] are not immortal in their places, because the King finds they will not vote for him in the next sessions. Oh, that our monarch would encourage noble idleness[2] by his own example as he of blessed memory did before him, for my mind misgives me that he will not much advance his affairs by stirring. I was going on, but am glad to be admonished by the paper. Ask me not of love, for every man hates every man perfectly and women are still the same bitches; but after all I will contradict myself and come off with an exception as to my own particular, who am, as much as idleness will dispense with me, Sir, your most faithful servant,

John Dryden.

Whitehall, March 7, 1687.

I saw t'other day by chance a letter of yours to Mr. Dryden which put me in mind of one I received from you a good while ago, as well as of the Lady in the Garret. For the last memorandum I thank you with all my heart; the remembrance of her being very sweet, both as a pleasure enjoyed and a danger escaped. I am not so young now, but that I can chew the cud of lechery with some sort of satisfaction; you who are so amorous and vigorous may have your mind wholly taken up with the present but we grave, decayed people,[3] alas, are glad to steal a thought sometimes towards the past, and then are to ask God forgiveness for it too. This is a little revenge for your suspicion of my being altered, as well as a vindication of my innocency[4] in that particular. But to speak more seriously, you

[1] Alluding to the dismissal of Lord Rochester from the Treasury and Lords Lumley and Shrewsbury from their colonelcies.

[2] This sentence is quoted by Macaulay in a footnote (*op. cit.* ii, p. 123). He gives the date wrongly as Feb. *1688*.

[3] Lord Mulgrave was only thirty-nine years old!

[4] MS. 'inncency'.

shall never find me changed whenever there is any occasion of employing

Your humble servant
Mulgrave.

Vienna, 24 June, 1686.
Honoured Sir,

I could wish it were as easy for me to thank you, both upon Mr. Fitzjames' account and my own, as it has been for you to oblige us both in so particular a manner that, though he may, yet I despair of finding any other return than that of ever owning and remembering. I thank God he got safe to Vienna upon Saturday and is going post to the army, the camp being already before Buda. I know not whether I may not get a broken head at Buda, but I am sure I got a broken heart at Ratisbon, where there were neither bombs nor cannons to be apprehended. Whatever Mademoiselle de Regalle may think of the business, she has made a breach not easily to be repaired, and exercised a cruelty beyond the Turks' to take away my liberty and yet not keep me for her slave. Had I as much time as mind to complain I should tell you a dismal story and tire you, in revenge of the harm you have done me by being the first author of the mischief; but I will refer all things till I see you next, and live in hopes you are in the meantime perhaps no less uneasy than Sir;

Your most obliged, humble servant
E. Vaudrey.

From the camp before Buda.
July the 29th, 86.
Sir,

I willingly embrace this opportunity of acquitting myself of the debt I owe you for the honour of yours of the tenth instant; you may easily guess how acceptable it was to me, and I as easily believe the news of our good success upon Saturday will make mine not altogether ungrateful to you.

I doubt not but you have had already a plan of the town with both the attacks, and perhaps some other hand has before this given you the particulars of the general assault upon Saturday last. I have little to do therefore more than in general terms to confirm to you the success of that happy day which made us masters of the two towers and the whole breach betwixt them. Those few actions I had seen before were comedies if compared to what that bloody day presented to us. All that unthinking madness or the unruly rage of despairing men could oppose in their own defence was employed by the Turks with the utmost skill a losing gamester uses to play off his last stake. Musket shot, arrows, stones, bombs, grenadoes, &c., were poured down upon our mounting men with a rage not unbecoming such sturdy Turks. But of all other[s] the most bloody defence was that of their mines, which, having sprung no less than nine successively amongst us, had that cruel effect you might have seen whole heaps of our men blown up together, others swallowed in the earth, others burnt to an unshapen mass liker anything than to a man. But the devil himself and all his hell of fire was not able to repulse the jolly Germans, who mounted boldly over their companions' bodies and maintained the post in spite of Mahomet and all his myrmidons. The Bavarian attack upon their side has had an equal success with ours, being masters of the Tower and a small post in the castle. This morning we have sprung two mines[1] under the second wall with

---

[1] Jacob Richards in his *Journal of the Siege of Buda* reports that three mines were sprung without great success by the Imperialists, though they helped to fill the ditch between the lodgment and the second wall.

pretty good success. To-night we shall build a battery upon the breach, which I hope will soon dislodge them from a retrenchment they have made within the town. The army marches to their relief, this presses our proceedings.

I am malicious enough to wish I have tired you in revenge for having tired myself, but not ingrateful enough to forget you have obliged me too much to be otherwise than

Honoured Sir, your most faithful, humble servant
E. Vaudrey.

Mr. Fitzjames presents you his most humble service.

August the 11th, 1686.

Sir,

I am to thank you by this for the additional favour of yours of the 31st of July. I could sincerely wish I had in any wise deserved the esteem, which, if it be true you have of me, I must wholly owe to your goodness. One way at least I will endeavour to deserve it: by a discreet refusing you of the private remarks I may have made in this campaign till the honour of seeing you again affords me a fair liberty of speaking. Matters of fact may be committed to a letter, and I am sorry they have not been so successful as I could have wished. The third of this proved as unsuccessful to us as the 13th of the last.[1] I wish the general assault we are preparing for to-day may be more to the advantage of Christendom. The enemy's army is arrived near us and we have escarmouched[2] these three days

[1] For Lorraine's unsuccessful assault see p. 97, note 2. On August 3rd, owing to the ill success of a mine which the Imperialists had sprung, Lorraine desired to defer the attack, but the Bavarians had already begun the assault. Both they and the Imperialists were forced to retire with considerable losses.   [2] i. e. skirmished.

with his [a]vantgarde. My private thoughts give me leave to spare till a fitter time. I had not failed in my duty as often as I have done if the unlucky stroke with a stone you spoke of had not put me out of the posture of writing for some days.

Mr. Fitzjames, I thank God, is well, and all the reports false you have heard of him. I have delivered with care the enclosed to Mr. du Heron, who has been, as well as I, unluckily wounded with a stone. I am in all respect,

Yours ever to command in all submission,

E. Vaudrey.

From the camp before Buda,

Friday, the 16 of August, 87.

Honoured Sir,

I observe so little what I write that I forgot whether I gave you an account in my last of the Grand Vizier's arrival, since which, the first days having passed in pure skirmishes, there happened on Wednesday last an action not unworthy your knowledge.

At the break of day we saw him detach from his army a body of men which, falling down from the hills into the plain which separates his from ours, passed it without opposition and gained those which command our lines upon the right hand. Their number as we have since been informed by prisoners was[1] six thousand janizaries and four thousand horse, chosen men out of his whole army and the very flower of all his troops. Their design was either to force a way into the town upon our right whilst he drew his whole army into the plain to attack our left, or, if failing of that, to retrench themselves upon the hills and inconvenience by their cannon our camp, which lay at their foot.

The Duke of Lorraine, having penetrated their

<hr>

[1] MS. 'were'.

designs, kept the main body of his troops to oppose
those of the Grand Vizier's in the plain, and sent
seven regiments of horse, with some few Hungarians,
to make head against the detachment upon the
hills. 'Twas here they charged us with some salvoes
from their cannon, and so furious a fire from their
janizaries, that the Hungarians with the regiment of
Cravats,[1] which were drawn up at our head, fell
into disorder upon their first shock; upon which
the regiment of Taaffe (at the head of which Mr.
Fitzjames charged) advancing came timely up to
retrieve the business, and, by the help of the other
horse, forced the enemy headlong down the hills,
with that confusion that above two thousand of
their janizaries remained upon the place, and the
rest, as we have since been informed by fugitives,
thought fitter to return towards Constantinople than
join the army. We brought back eight pieces of
cannon, above fifty standards, and very near three
hundred prisoners. A more vigorous action was
perhaps never performed by horse alone with those
disadvantages, both of ground and number. Having
regained our first post after the pursuit of the enemy,
which we made the shorter by not knowing but
that the main body was engaged, the high hills
having separated us from the sight of what passed
at our left, we found the G[rand] V[izier] had drawn
his whole army into the plain, to which the Duke of
Lorraine had opposed his; but that they both stood
at a respectful distance from one another without
action. After that our victorious body of horse had
by a new order quitted its champ de bataille and
joined the right wing of our army, that of the enemy's
began to make several movements, which showed
more the uneasiness of his mind and the irresolution
of what he had to do than any design to attack us.
So that by degrees, having withdrawn all his infantry

[1] See *ante*, p. 277, note 2.

to the foot of his own hills, our right wing received orders [to advance] towards some bodies of horse which had taken a familiar liberty of approaching too near to us. Proportionably as we advanced they withdrew, till, finding themselves at the foot of their mountains, and seeing that our wing had by much outmarched the rest of our army, they charged a small body of Hungarians upon our left, who, yielding before them, had like to have discovered our flank and caused some disorder but by the fermeté of our troops and skill of our officers, who immediately fronted some squadrons that way and covered our flank. The Turks at their turn retired, and we at the same time, it being already late, received orders to withdraw.[1] The next morning, for what reason we yet know not, the enemy decamped and went some two or three hours' march further off. This is matter of fact and as near as I guess the truth. That which is doubtful is the report we have by fugitives of three bashas having been killed in this action; some say the seraskier[2] was likewise killed two days before in a skirmish. Certain it is we found letters in his pocket of that consequence which give just grounds for the suspicion.

As for the siege I own I was never so cheated in my life, not doubting we should have been masters of Buda long before this; where the fault lies I dare not judge much less commit to paper. Certain it is we advance but slowly since our lodgement upon the towers. The attack I told you in my last we prepared for was put off by the defect of our mines which sprung all to our disadvantage. I hope well of the success but we are neither yet in the town nor the G[rand] V[izier] out of the country.

E. Vaudrey.

[1] The Turks retired to the hills, which were difficult of access, so that Lorraine thought it advisable to return to his lines and prosecute the siege.   [2] A Turkish general.

1686

Honoured Sir,

Since you are pleased I should continue the same way of addressing my letters I did whilst Mr. Hughes was in your service,[1] be likewise pleased to pardon a trouble you have thus unwarily pulled upon yourself. If writing was never a pleasure to me in my life I am sure it was never a greater pain to me than now. This obliges me to write no other letters than what either domestic business or some other indispensable duty will not excuse me from. I therefore beg those few I shall trouble you withal may be careful[ly] sent forward towards their address.

There has little happened material since my last, except a party of 3,000 janizaries backed by another of spahis,[2] who at the rate of twelve crowns a head had hired themselves to enter into the town; these upon break of day on Thursday last endeavoured to pass our lines, but were forced back with the loss of about three or four hundred of the most pressing. Be pleased to pardon this and all other troubles I am likely to give you, and believe me in all sincerity
Yours ever to command,
E. Vaudrey.

O Rus quando te aspiciam? quandoque licebit
Nunc veterum scriptis nunc somno et inertibus horis
Ducere sollicita jucunda oblivia vitæ?

Paraphrased:

Upon the downs when shall I breathe at ease,
Have nothing else to do but what I please,
In a fresh cooling shade upon the brink
Of Arden's spring, have time to read and think,

[1] Perhaps Hughes had temporary leave, or had decided to quit his post and then changed his mind.
[2] Turkish cavalrymen.

And stretch, and sleep, when all my care shall be,
For health, and pleasure my philosophy?
When shall I rest from business, noise, and strife,
Lay down the soldier and the courtier's life,
And in some little, smiling, melancholy seat,
Begin for shame at last to live and to forget
The nonsense and the farce of what the fools call
　　great.

Colonel [1] Ashton's.

　　　　　　　　　　　　Paris, Aug. 29, 1687.
Sir,
　　I received the favour of yours of the 18th instant
whereby you give me an account of the Turks'
defeat[2] which we had here four days before your
letter came; and on Wednesday I rejoiced with the
Emperor's envoy here, who entertained all the
foreign ministers at dinner. However, I am obliged
to you for the care you took to inform me of this
welcome news, and when anything happens in
these parts as remarkable I shall not fail to impart
it to you. I am,
　　　　　Sir,
　　　Your most faithful, humble servant,
　　　　　　　　　　　　B. Skelton.

This bill was sent　　　[3] [Sir George Etherege employed by
for England the　　　　his Majesty at Ratisbon humbly
1/11 Feb., 85/6.　　　　desires allowance for these extra-
　　　　　　　　　　　ordinaries following, laid out by
　　　　　　　　　　　him from the 30th of August, 1685,
　　　　　　　　　　　to the 1st of February, 1685/6.

[1] MS. Coll. This is far better than other occasional poems
by Etherege. Probably it is by the 'Coll. Ashton' whose name
is so enigmatically appended to it. The reference to the
soldier's life does not apply to Etherege, but on the other
hand he may have written it for, or at the request of, Ashton.
[2] See *ante*, p. 249, note 1.
[3] The accounts enclosed in brackets are deleted in the MS.

The charge of passing a privy seal and receiving money out of the exchequer	29	00
For several journeys in Holland & money laid out on Mr. Dowglass there, in order to his Majesty's service	10	00
For postage of letters, stationer's ware, & intelligence	13	10
	52	10

Geo. Etherege.

This bill was sent for England the 21 Octob./3 Nov., 86.

Sir Geo. Etherege &c. From the 1st Feb., 85/6, to the 30th of Aug., 1686.

For postage, stationer's ware, copies & translations of memorials, recesses, &c.	16	00
For intelligence	24	00
	40	00

Geo: Etherege.

Sent by the packet of the 14/24 March, 86/7.

Sir Geo. Etherege &c. from the 30th of Aug., 86, to the 29th of Feb., 1686/7.

For fees in the Treasury of a year	24	10
For mourning for the Empress Dowager[1]	20	00
For postage and stationer's ware	7	10
For intelligence	20	00
	72	00

Geo. Eth.

These three bills of extraordinaries are made into one in the following page.]

[1] See *ante*, p. 123, note 3.

Sir Geo. Eth. &c. from the 30th
of Aug. to the 11th of Febr.,
1685/1686/7.[1]

	l	s
The charges of passing a Privy Seal & receiving money out of the exchequer	29	00
For several journeys in Holland & money laid out on Mr. Dowglass in order to his Majesty's service	10	00
For mourning for the Empress Dowager	20	00
For postage, stationer's ware, copies & translations of memorials, recesses, &c.	37	00
For intelligence	44	00
For fees in the Treasury & the charges of receiving more money out of the exchequer	—	
	—	

Geo. Eth.

These two bills were
sent by the ordinary[2]
of the 3/13 Octob., 87.

Sir Geo. Etherege &c. From
the 11th of Feb., 86/7 to the
30th of August, 1687.

For postage & stationer's ware	7	13
For intelligence	20	00
For mourning for the Duchess of Modena[3] by his Majesty's command for myself & my secretary, my family & coach.	80	00
	107	13

Geo. Etherege.

[1] It is interesting to compare these accounts with those finally sent in to Middleton. The item in the first bill for £44 was raised to £48, the postage, stationer's ware, and intelligence in the second bill, 'according to his Majesty's regulation of Feb. 7th for six months', was brought up to £100. Middleton took exception only to the items of the exchequer fees which he referred to the Lords of the Treasury.

[2] MS. 'ordre'.   [3] See *ante*, p. 247, note 1.

SIR GEORGE'S ACCOUNT OF THE FEAST ON THE B[IRTH] OF THE P[RINCE] OF W[ALES][1]

On Tuesday, the 6th of July, new style, I received the happy news of her Majesty's being safely brought to bed of a Prince,[2] which was long wished for, and impatiently expected, by all pious and honest people here, as being the only thing wanting to complete the felicity of his Majesty and to secure the peace and glory of his kingdoms. The great marks of satisfaction which appeared in me in reading of the letter, made those who were by me conclude there was something extraordinary in it; and I had not the power to conceal it one minute from them. This in a moment was spread all over the house, and the servants, transported as well as the master, opened the cellar before I had time to give them order, and every one abandoned himself to joy and good drinking. After a little recollection I sent my secretary to notify this blessing to the Imperial commission and to most of the[3] ministers, but in the first place to those I knew it would be most welcome to, who all returned me their compliments by their principal domestics, and many of them came themselves to testify the great part they took in what is for the common good of all Europe. In a word, never news was received here with so universal a concurrence of applause, and, though the ministers which compose this body are divided by several interests, they all agreed to rejoice in this

[1] This account was printed by Edward James in 1688. A copy of the printed version is in the Bodleian; I have noted the more important variations.

[2] James, the Old Pretender, was born on June 10, 1688, at St. James's Palace.

[3] Bod.: 'and to the other ministers who all returned me their compliments, &c.'

conjuncture. The Abbot of St. James, an ancient monastery founded in this town in the time of Charlemagne by William brother to Achaius, King of the Scots, came running hither filled with joy proportionable to the zeal he has always had for the glory and prosperity of his Majesty. He and I, after we had given way to the first motions of our passion, consulted together what was fit to be done by us in this place on so great an occasion. We considered we were at the general Diet of the Empire which is held in a manner in the heart of all Christendom, where feasts and public divertisements have been made for the coronation of Emperors and for choice of Kings of the Romans; where there is a greater confluence of ministers than at the courts of the greatest monarchs who hold intelligence all the world over, and that the plenipotentiary of France had but a few years since splendidly treated them and all the town on the birth of the Duke of Burgundy.[1] Wherefore we concluded it was necessary to do something which was answerable to his Majesty's greatness and the honour of the nation. Having taken this resolution I desired the Abbot to charge himself with what was convenient to be done in the Church; thanksgiving and praises to God being the first things by which all good Christians should acknowledge his mercies. He willingly accepted of that care, and I myself undertook to order and cause to be got ready all which might make the feasting part delightful and surprising. We pitched on Sunday, the 25th of the same month, being St. James's day, to begin the celebration of the feast at the monastery aforesaid. The Abbot having prepared and beautified his church, invited the Imperial commission to a Te Deum Laudamus in consideration of the holy day,

[1] Louis, Duke of Burgundy, son of the Dauphin, was born in 1682.

and I invited the Margrave of Baden, the Count de Windischgrätz, the French plenipotentiary, all the members of the Diet, and what other ministers are here, thither to celebrate the birth of our Prince, and after the Te Deum to a dinner at my house. The magistrates of the town were very civil and obliging to me; they lent me their cannon, which is not very usual, and in a greater number than ever they had done before. They sent me a company of foot to keep order and to hinder the rabble from crowding into my house, which is the most convenient in Ratisbon for such a purpose by reason of the largeness and number of apartments, and its being situated in the great place of St. James,[1] which will hold many thousands of people. The day being come, the first signal of the feast was given about four o'clock in the morning by the discharge of twenty-four great pieces of cannon; after which the great bells of the monastery rang and prayers began, which lasted till twelve o'clock. At eight was preached by the Reverend F. Laurence Beer of the Society of Jesus a sermon suitable to the occasion with general applause; that ended, the high mass was sung by the Count of Wartemberg of the house of Bavaria, suffragan bishop of this place and bishop of Laodicea *in partibus*. I having been with the Abbot to visit him and to invite him to do us this favour, he seemed overjoyed at our request, and, after having given the young Prince a thousand blessings, said nothing could be proposed to him so conformable to his wishes. After mass the Te Deum was sung, and during the whole service divers masses were said by all the orders of religious here for their Majesties' and the Prince's conservation, and for the preservation of the peace of their realms and victory over their enemies; the Margrave of Baden,

---

[1] Now the Bismarck Platz, into which the Gesandten Strasse leads.

the Count de Windischgrätz, the French plenipotentiary, the Director and all the members of the Diet, as well Roman Catholics as Reformed, being present. The Margrave and the Count sent their trumpets and tymbals, and the Abbot had taken care to have all the best consorts[1] the town could afford of instrumental and vocal music. Above eighty pieces of cannon were shot off while the High Mass and the Te Deum were singing. The report the day before in what manner this was to be performed made many ladies and cavaliers of different religions meet there. The church was thronged, and all the places without were filled with crowds of people, who were curious to see what passed at so great a solemnity (*seq. in Sir George's own hand*). In the place before my house were erected two large substantial buildings; the one a kitchen, where an ox was roasted whole, a thing which is usual here on the coronation of an Emperor and never otherwise; the other was a triumphal pyramid built triangular, the top being covered with an Imperial crown; beneath was an arbour wrought artificially with branches of trees in which a consort of hautbois played; below that was a rock out of which three fountains of wine sprung; in the hollow of this the men were place[d] which were to play the engines and direct the pipes. In the frontispiece were his Majesty's arms, on the side next the house the Prince's, and on the other the four banners of England, Scotland, France and Ireland. In the three corners were erected in carved work two lions and an unicorn as big as the life, as they are in the supporters of the arms, the wine pouring from the lions' mouths, and the unicorn's horn. The lower part was a representation of an antique palace, the pillars of the Doric order with corniches and festons. On the front was painted Bacchus presiding

[1] Bod. 'concerts'.

at the celebration of a bacchanal with the inscription:

Nunc est bibendum, nunc pede libero, pulsanda tellus.

On another side a cornucopia was drawn with beds below, on which the guests lay extended as in the feasts of the ancients, they and their goblets crowned with red and white roses mixed, handsome youths waiting on them and bringing in jars of wine with this writ:

Ante hac nefas depromere caecubum
Cellis avitis.

On the third side Mars appeared above, and the drunken combat between the Centaurs and Lapithes was described with these words, likewise out of Horace:

Natis in usum laetitiae scyphis
pugnare Thracum est.

The ministers coming I received them, as the ceremony is, at their coaches, with the sound of trumpets and kettle-drums, and conducted them into an upper apartment, where a band of violins was playing. The table had forty-five covers, and as soon as the meat was served up the signal was given by the discharge of six pieces of cannon. The dinner consisted of three several services, each of fifty-two dishes loaded with venison, and all manner of fowl which the country could yield for above thirty English miles in circumference. The shouts and acclamations of joy among the people made them rise from the table to be spectators, the wine ran,[1] and it was a pleasant sight to see the contests that arose, and the shift the rabble made, who should get the greatest share. Several workmen who were appointed for that purpose, broke down the sides of the kitchen and the ox and all the materials [were] exposed to be their spoil. While

[1] MS. 'run'.

this was doing twenty dozen of bread was thrown out among them. The ministers turning from the window, they saw the table covered anew with a banquet of sweetmeats and all manner of fruits in season. A large dish in the middle held three pyramids on each of which a flag was displayed. The first was his Majesty, represented by Neptune, with this writ above:

Summus moderator aquarum

beneath, her Majesty represented by a sea goddess bearing a royal infant in her arms environed with Nereids, with this verse out of Virgil (devised by Mr. H[ugh] H[ughes],

Felix et nato felix et conjure Peleus

and at the bottom

Halcyonei Dies.

The second was the Prince's arms; on the top was writ:

Spes Britanniae

and below

Deodatus tribus regnis die S.S^{mae} Trinitatis 1688.

The third was the Prince represented by an infant Neptune sleeping in a shell on a bed of moss and rocked by the waves. The inscription above was (by Mr. H[ugh] H[ughes])

Ingens pacis Europeae pignus.

Beneath were several river gods with their urns, from which several streams discharged themselves into the sea, and under that these word[s]:

Ad me confluunt omnes.

The entertainment lasted from two o'clock till between nine and ten, during which time above 100 pieces of cannon were shot off for the several healths that were drunk; and to conclude the day, after nine omers of wine were run out I caused two more to be given to the people with the ends knocked out bidding them drink the Prince of Wales his health. And at the same time I called for the biggest glass on the buffet and drank it to the ministers, it having been drunk in form before, who all pledged it, twelve cannons being discharged and the trumpets and tymbals sounding all the while.

On the second day I entertained all the ladies and cavaliers of the town and neighbourhood. When the company were all assembled I took 400 pieces of silver, each about the value of a shilling, and, having first flung two or three handfuls myself out of the window among the poor people, I gave a handful to every lady, beginning with them of the greatest quality and desired them to follow my example. While the crowd was scrambling and fighting for the money footmen, who were placed in the windows for that purpose, flung three or four hundred squibs to part them, who were most mutinous. This had an admirable effect and caused much laughter. As soon as this was over all the house from top to bottom was illuminated without with a great number of flambeaux of white wax, which were held by artificial arms, and all the lustres and sconces within were lighted. This day, I having a great many more guests, two large tables were prepared in two adjoining rooms with between eighty and hundred covers. The ladies sat at one, and such ministers who were gallant enough to come again for their sakes and the cavaliers sat at the other. The supper was an ambigu,[1] very handsomely served by the help of cooks and other officers, which were appointed by my friends to serve me.

The first day I had all sorts of good wines, which can be had here, with great plenty of ice, but this

[1] A feast consisting of a medley of dishes.

day I had over and above all sorts of waters, cream and fruit frozen. The trumpets sounded and the kettle-drums beat while the supper lasted; after which the ladies were led into another apartment, where they were invited to begin the ball by a consort of violins and flutes. About two o'clock in the morning I invited them into another room, where they were surprised with a new scene, being a banquet consisting of nine pyramids of dry sweetmeats, the spaces were filled with liquids, chocolates, comfits, and abundance of China oranges and lemons which were all given up to be plundered. The citizens' wives, their daughters, and all the chambermaids, were admitted to be spectators and to partake of the remainder of the spoil; so that I think no less than four hundred people ate and drank in my house this day.

The third day I entertained the chief magistrates and all the whole senate with so good a dinner that they owned they never saw the like. They had good wine and they spared it not. I gave them likewise the diversion of seeing three barrels of wine run among the people, and while they were entertaining themselves with that a banquet of sweetmeats was sent on the table and I proposed to them to send for their wives[1] to carry that away, as the ladies had done the other the day before, and the violins being there they might dance if they thought fit. Some were for it and others, who preferred drinking, excused themselves by pretending their wives would not be dressed in time. So the confitures were given them in basins, which they, like good husbands, sent home to their dear halves; and gammons of bacon, neats' tongues, Bologna sausages,[2] and cheese being set on the table in their stead, the glasses went round; and when I saw every one had

[1] Bod. 'wives and daughters'.
[2] MS. 'Bolognia sauceges'.

his load I desired the cannon might be drawn out of the arsenal which is near my house (and was the reason I could have no fireworks) to conclude the feast. While this was doing I caused a vessel of five omers of wine to be brought out of my cellar, which was immediately done by wine-coopers, and, the soldiers having kept off the crowd till the top was beat out, the people were told they were to drink their Majesties' and the Prince's health. At the same time I called for three of the biggest glasses and drank them to the chief magistrates, and thirty pieces of cannon were shot off. The senate was so pleased with their entertainment that they refused to take money for the powder I had put them to the expense of, and I had much ado, after a long contest of civility, to oblige them to accept of it.

F I N I S

A CATALOGUE OF SIR GEORGE'S BOOKS[1]

English Books:

The History of the Council of Trent.
Cowley's Works.
The Hind and Panther.
Shakespeare's Plays.
The State of the Empire.
Rymer's Tragedy of the Last Age.
An English Common Prayer Book.
Lovell's Indicus Universalis.
Reflections on Aristotle's Treaty of Poesy.

[1] An article in the *Edinburgh Review*, Jan. 1864 on the Scots religious houses states that Etherege 'had kindly relations with St. James, for he left them a library of valuable books'. A. W. Verity discovered in the monastery library eight volumes bearing the inscription 'left by Sir Geo. Etherege with Abbot Fleming 1689', among which was a copy of Voiture's works. A copy of Cowley without any name, which had been added to the library in 1689, was also probably left by Etherege.

Procopius' Secret History.
Mazarine's Memoires.
Plato Redivivus.
The Lady's New Year's Gift.[1]

French Books:
Dictionnaire de l'Abbé d'Anet.
Histoire de la Reformation, Burn[et].
Dictionnaire en 3 Langues, Es[pagnole], Fr[ançaise], It[alienne].
Les Œuvres de Voiture.
L'Ambassadeur par Wickfordt.
Lucrèce par Morralles.
Juvénal et Perse par M.D.M.
Properse.
Catulle.
Tibulle.
Tite-Live. 14 t. par Frenchemy.
Critiques sur Horace. 5 tomes.
Quinte Curse par Vaugelas et Ryer.
Tacite. 3 t. par d'Ablancourt.
Lucien. 2 t. par d'Ablancourt.
Commentaires de Caesar.
Com[mentaires] de Térence par Sibour.
Polybe et ses frag[ments] par du Ryer.
Erasme cum notis varior.
Histoire de François I, en 2 t. par Varil[las].
Histoire de Henry II par Varillas.
Histoire de Charles IX par Varillas.
Histoire de l'Empire. 2 t. par Heiss.
Decamaron de Bocace. 2 tomes.
La Vie du Vicomte de Turenne.
La Vie de Gustave Adolphe par de Prade.
Recherche de la Vérité.

[1] Sedley also possessed this book (de Sola Pinto *Sir Charles Sedley*, App. II, 341). It consists of advice given to his daughter by the Marquess of Halifax, and was published anonymously 1688.

Œuvres de Molière. 2 tomes.
Œuvres de Sarazin. 1 t.
Mémoires Gallans.
Histoires de Medicis par Varillas.
Histoire de M. de la Roche.
L'Homme de Cour.
Nouveaux Dialogues des Morts.
La Princesse de Monferrat.
Le Parlement Pacifique.
Les Comparaisons de Grands Hommes.
Mémoires de la Morée.
Voyage de Chardin en Perse.
5 Dialogues par Oratius Tubero.
Boileau L'Alcoran.
Histoire des Oracles. Duc de Monm[outh].
Education des Princes.
Histoire abrégé de l'Europe.
Histoire de la paix nouvelle.   Inter. de Princes.
Maximes des Princes.
Le Triomphe de l'Amour.
Lettres d'Ossat.
La Vie de Coligni.

Italian Books:
Oudin's Dizionario.
Machiavello 4 tomes.

AN ACCOUNT OF SIR G[EORGE]'S LIFE AND MANNER OF LIVING, WRIT IN SEVERAL LETTERS FROM RATISBON.

Sir,

I suppose you have been already informed (and therefore there is no need I should tell you) of what passed at the Hague either as to his losing £250 by play,[1] his haunting pitiful and mean houses contrary

---

[1] In a letter to Corbet, p. 163, Etherege says he won £200 in Holland but lost it again at Ratisbon.

to Mr. Skelton's advice, or as to his making love, for which he was sufficiently laughed at. And not to mention his caressing every dirty drab that came in his way from Holland to this place, I shall only begin with the manner of his life and conversation after his arrival.[1]

He had two letters of recommendation he brought with him from London, the one from Monsieur Barillon to the French plenipotentiary, the other from the Spanish ambassador[2] to Monsieur de Neuforge, the Burgundian minister. As for the first the letter was delivered him in two or three days, and thereupon Sir G[eorge] made him two or three visits, as he fancied, incognito. But as for the other Sir G[eorge] was here five months before he made him a visit or gave him any account of the letter sent by him. It is not to be known whether the French were more glad or the Burgundian more dissatisfied with this way of proceeding. This writ back to complain of it, the other returned thanks for so hopeful an acquaintance, and Sir G[eorge] himself writ to Monsieur Barillon complaining of the formality and gravity of the ministers, and letting him know how much he was obliged to him; for that, as he said, there was not a house in all the town besides the Count de Crécy's where he could go when he pleased without standing upon ceremonies and idle punctilios.[3]

And now, having laid the foundation of his future acquaintance at the French ambassador's, the next

---

[1] Mr. Dobrée (*op. cit.*) has implied, evidently from this passage and the fact that the Letterbook was not begun until March 1686/7, that Hughes did not arrive in Ratisbon until the spring of 1687, but it is quite clear from the Latin letter that the secretary accompanied Etherege on his journey: 'ad hæc responsum dedi mihi deliberatum esse una cum illo Ratisbonum petere, ita ut ad iter me paratum esse monuit.'

[2] Pedro de Ronquillos.

[3] See *ante*, p. 54, for this letter.

thing he judged necessary was to find out gamesters as such as would help him, as he called it, to pass away the time. Thus instead of making his visits and getting acquaintance with the ministers he presently fell to gaming, for there were in the town at that time several French sharpers who, hearing of his laudable designs, were not a little glad of such a guest, nor in the least wanting, you may be sure, to make the best use and advantage they could of so fair an opportunity. So then as soon as some of them were brought into acquaintance with him by the French ambassador's people, they never ceased to introduce one another, till the whole gang of them began to resort and haunt his house. They managed him so dexterously, and played their cards so well, that he could not either eat or drink without some of them; but not being content with living upon him, his house day and night being full of them, nor with winning his money at a slow rate they found him out, or, as others say, sent on purpose to Vienna for another gamester who went by the name of Count Purpurat. The Frenchmen were known to go partners with this rook, who played with him constantly night and day till he had won upwards of 10,000 florins, and thereupon would have left off playing till the money was paid, but Sir George quarrelling with him upon it forced him to play till it came only to 1,500 florins, in part whereof Sir G[eorge] paid 800 florins, and towards the other seven gave him a pair of pistols and a fusil which he had caused to be made just before he came from London. The spark finding there was no more money to be had and that Sir G[eorge] would not play with him any longer, having heard that they had bragged of their winnings and that they said to others of their friends *nous le déplumerons*, returned to Vienna, whence it was written afterwards in the public newspapers that he had shewed the pistol and fusil at the Emperor's court, boasting that he had won them at play, and making it appear where he had had them by Sir G[eorge's] coat of arms which remained upon them.

The next pickpocket they recommended to him was a shabby Count, fled from justice at Augsburg for several tricks and for stealing away his landlord's maid. This person was so notoriously scandalous that some of the ministers sent to Sir G[eorge] to dissuade him from having anything to do with him, but instead of taking advice he became so fond of his company that he thought every minute lost when the time called him from his presence. It was not above five or six in twenty-four hours that they used to be asunder, for either he came to Sir G[eorge] or Sir G[eorge] went to him at his lodgings in a paltry common alehouse, and, though all the town wondered he was not ashamed of such a camarade, yet he was so far from it that out of familiarity (and I know not what) he lent him a hundred florins, with which he won from Sir G[eorge] six hundred florins more, and, as it was thought, would have cheated him of his coach and horses if the magistrates of the town had not prevented it by threatening to clap him up in prison for former cheats, which made him sneak with his seven hundred florins out of town.

Though Sir G[eorge] found at last that he had been practised upon, yet he had not the power to leave off embracing his French acquaintance; however, finding his money grown short he resolved to look after their play a little more narrowly than hitherto he had done; but as their cheats and tricks became apparent so they did not fail to produce their known effects of constant quarrelling and wrangling, till the whole town began to ring of it. One while they should seem as fond as children of each other, and another time they would be daggers-drawing, calling names and challenging. But still all this ended amicably, Sir G[eorge] not being able to live without them, nor they much less without him. All the fine they used to impose upon themselves was only to forbear playing for two or three days, and in the meantime their trade was to drink till two or three o'clock in the morning, and, if they were able, to go and walk about the streets with clubs in their hands to guard themselves and their music. You will easily imagine, sir, how famous he must needs make himself by such an extravagant course of life; for one night they would make themselves so drunk that endeavouring to go home they should be found next morning to lie sleeping in the streets. Another night they would break windows, and a third attack indifferently all such persons, whether men or women, as had the misfortune to come in their way, though sometimes they returned all covered with blows and bruises the true recompense of such knight errantry, *et sic de ceteris*.

Thus passed the winter, and the campaign drawing on these sparks began to retire, which gave him leisure to bethink himself of making his first visits; wherein he went so slowly to work that he has not made them all to this day. The Elector of Bavaria's envoy[1] absolutely refused to admit him to the first visit, and all other ministers have either refused to receive him to a second visit or have not repaid it after they had accepted it. So that it is now near seven months since he received the last from any one whatsoever.

About the beginning of summer one Monsieur le Febure, forced to fly from Vienna for several extravagancies, was kindly entertained and received by Sir G[eorge]. This person had lately belonged to a company of foot in the quality of a player on the hautbois, which proved such an effectual recommen-

[1] Wampel.

dation that no person or profession could have been more welcome. The Frenchman, perceiving that his countrymen here were resolved to take no notice of him, had found a conveniency of sending his bundle by the Augsburg messenger in order to return for France, and was just ready to march after it when Sir G[eorge] hearing of it sent to invite him to his house, and, having gently prevailed with him to stay, a footman was dispatched away on horseback for Augsburg to fetch back his trumpery, and he, presently finding whom he had to deal with, became so predominant in a short time that the whole house was at his command. He seldom went abroad but in Sir G[eorge]'s coach, who would never stir without him; when it was generally observed and laughed at by all that he likewise gave him the hand. Le Febure, to requite these civilities brought him acquainted with all the cracks of the town, with whom they would pass whole nights at one scandalous alehouse or another. When this trade failed their manner was to torment the whole town with coaching, fiddling, piping and dancing till two, three and four o'clock in the morning. The whole town complained of the noise and stir they made night after night. Of all others the Countess de Windischgrätz was most angry with them, for by her jealous husband's instigation she threatened them publicly and laid an ambuscade of stout fellows to watch for them, whose clutches they escaped narrowly one night and so saved drubbing; therefore they durst not venture there any more, though the rest of the town could never be rid of them till cold weather began to keep them at home. What they did upon St. Louis's day was more famous than all the rest. For Sir G[eorge], not thinking it enough to have had two sisters in his chamber that night, where they all danced stark naked, went afterwards about the streets with Le

Febure having nothing on but their shirts. One of these sisters was a wench that Sir G[eorge] at his first coming hither had taken from drawing beer at a poor, miserable alehouse to make her his mistress. By his often going abroad he brought home a distemper which infected both his maid and his valet de chambre, and neither of them escaped much better than himself, who lay six weeks under a chirurgeon's hand. This was known over all the town, for the landlord, having quarrelled with Sir G[eorge] about the disorders he committed in his house was not wanting to complain both in public and in private that they had spoiled him three of his featherbeds. After he had kept this second sister about half a year he turned her away for her insolent behaviour and for bragging of his favours. As soon as she was gone her sister from another alehouse was taken in her stead, and I suppose she will ever repent it, for another disaster having befallen Sir G[eorge] about two months ago, of which he is not as yet well recovered, she likewise shared in it, which made her be sent out of the house about a fortnight since. The chirurgeon made a good deal of noise before he promised to take her to cure, having never received any money for his pains nor for any physic he administered. Here it may be seen what a paymaster he is to others who is not willing to pay his physician. He seldom rises out of bed before two or three o'clock in the afternoon, dines most commonly at five or six and then goes to the French ambassador's for three or four hours every night in the week. This gave one of the Austrians an occasion to say: on voudrait bien savoir si c'est par l'ordre du Roi qu'il donne tant d'ombrage à tous les ministres de l'Empire. He is so entirely for the French interest that meeting the Swedish envoy[1] at his

---

[1] Etherege had himself written to Lord Middleton about this incident. See *ante*, p. 138.

going from hence to the congress at Augsburg he made him a compliment and wished his fine coach might break on the way because he went to make an alliance against France. To justify his siding with the French he has always given it out for certain truth that his Majesty had made an alliance offensive and defensive with the French King.[1] His reporting of this alarmed all the ministers and gave them a worse opinion of him than before. When first he heard the news of the taking of Buda he said he neither believed it nor hoped it to be true; and some two or three days after the Jesuits' students happened to have a comedy where every minister but himself was particularly invited. However, he went thither and heard his very words repeated on the stage: *nec credo nec spero*. The Austrians upon this news sent to give notice of it to all the ministers, Sir G[eorge] only excepted, who was in the like manner neglected when they made their feasts.[2] He was very much offended to see himself not taken notice of, and therefore he began to exclaim heavily against the Bishop of Passau. In the next place he told the French ambassador that he had heard the Count de Windischgrätz say that the Emperor did not intend to treat in earnest of the execution of the armistice, and only made the French believe it till the end of another campaign.[3] Although this may be supposed

[1] James II had indeed renewed his brother's engagements to France. James and his ministers denied any alliance with Louis though the French ambassador in a memorial to the States General announced that the French King would regard any move against England as an invasion of his own lands. Burnet speaks of the French ambassador's visit to Trumbull in Constantinople: 'He told him, there was no ceremony to be between them any more, for their masters were now one' (*op. cit.* ii, 501–2).

[2] See *ante*, p. 219.

[3] For Etherege's version of this incident see *ante*, p. 142. The secretary insinuates that Etherege wilfully fabricated the statement and maliciously fathered it on Windischgrätz; he

to be their design, yet it is something hard to believe that the Count de Windischgrätz should tell it to Sir G[eorge], whom he knew to be so much a friend to the French as would be sure to tell them whatever he heard though it should prove the cause of an immediate war; and the want of treating of the execution of the peace is the likeliest thing I know to be the occasion of. The compliment he sent the Count de Lamberg was: that though he had heard nothing of the taking of Buda[1] either himself or from any of the Imperial ministers, yet he could not but let him know that he had heard it as a common report, and therefore desired an opportunity to make him a visit and to congratulate with him upon that occasion. Count Lamberg sent his steward before night to carry this message: that the Count had strangers to sup with him that night and if Sir George would bring his dancing master along with him he should be welcome. *Spesso vengono rebuttate le personne mordenti con morsi piu fieri.* Whatever ministers come hither or go away they always forget to give him notice of it, though they are very punctual with everybody but himself, and, though the Count de Crécy tells him to his face all his loose life and conversation, yet he is far from speaking well of him even behind his back: for one night that Sir G[eorge] happened not to go to his house his expressions next day at dinner were : 'je m'étonne où était Monsieur d'Etheridge hier au soir; peutêtre qu'il a resté au logis pour jouer comme il fait quelque fois pour des liards avec son valet de chambre et son maître d'hotel. Il ne sort jamais d'ici sans gagner quelques écus de Madame la Comtesse parce qu'autrement il n'aurait rien pour maintenir sa famille. Ce que je trouve de plus pire en lui que

forgets to mention that Windischgrätz by accusing Etherege of revealing a secret admitted that he had disclosed it himself.
[1] This letter must have been written in the autumn of 1686.

toutes ses débauches est, qu'il est profane et voudrait persuader tout le monde d'être de son sentiment'. He has disobliged the magistrates in
calling them all rascals for turning the whores out
of the town and saying that, if he were Elector of
Bavaria, he would raze the walls of the town and
build an hospital for decayed whores in the place
where the council-house stands. I must not forget
to give you an account of what passed on Monday,
the second day after your departure, but, before I
come to the story, it is necessary I should tell you
something by way of introduction.

Before it was known what distemper Sir G[eorge]
was sick of, the Countess de Crécy was pleased to
tell one of her women: 'J'entends que Monsieur
Etherege est malade pour l'amour de moi, s'il est
qu'il meurt.' It seems he pretended some such thing,
but, when he had heard what she said, it turned his
love into despair, as you will see by the verses
enclosed. This I can assure you caused a great deal
of laughter amongst all the ministers, who hate him
as well as the French, and are glad to hear of any
ridiculous thing. About ten days ago, one of the
ministers happened to give a collation to twenty or
thirty persons where Sir G[eorge] was present, it
being the first time of his appearing again in public,
but of all the whole company he was the only
person that sat by himself without being taken
notice of or asked to come to the table. On
Thursday last a great company of gentlemen and
ladies met to take their pleasure of riding through
the town in traîneaux according to the fashion of
this country, and, because Sir G[eorge] would be
of the number, they contrived it so that he was the
nineteenth and the last of all the gang, which the
meanest minister but himself would have been
ashamed of. Being come to the house where they
were to make merry he offered to salute the Countess

of Schalemberg, who gave him this reprimand in the hearing of all: 'Monsieur je vous prie ne faites pas tant de familiarité avec moi parce que je suis la Comtesse de Schalemberg et non pas une comédienne.' This was nothing to what followed, which seems to have been done by complot on purpose to affront him. One person being left to keep Sir G[eorge] in discourse the rest of the company sat down at table and reserved only a place for one. Sir G[eorge] approaching and thinking to sit down, the other without ceremony prepossessed the place, leaving Sir G[eorge] a noun substantive. To expose him the more the Anhalt minister whom he had formerly abused asked him faintly to sit down, but without any farther care of him they fell to it, all strutting and stretching to keep him out when otherwise they could have made place enough for half a dozen more. Sir G[eorge] seeing himself thus abandoned immediately sent for his coach and told them upbraidingly that he could find a supper at home. Some few nights ago one of his footmen was carried to prison for making noise in the streets, and another night the dancing-master, whom he admires for his debauches, being pursued by the watch was forced to fly to the French ambassador's, and, having got within the gate, he took up a stone and knocked down the foremost; but the rest would have paid him for it had not the Ambassador run down in his night-gown with his sword in hand to save him, as being come within his liberties.

Amongst a company of strollers lately come hither from Nuremberg under the name of comedians there happened to be one woman who seemed to have something of grace in her face though none in her manners. She had not been here many days before his Excellence, Sir G[eorge] E[therege], intending to forestall the rest of the ministers in paying the honour due to her character (of an errant whore), was civilly pleased to send his steward to make her a compliment and to desire audience (which is the only kind he has hitherto had). It is not to be doubted but so forward a zeal was well accepted, especially in such a place as this, where people stand so much upon the punctilios of honour that none certainly but himself would have done it. Having seen her credentials and finding her *plein pouvoir* conformable to his own, though not according to the style of the Empire, he gently proposed that, without any cavil or contestation, they should presently proceed to name a place *ad designandos limites* (as France and the Empire had done some days before). The Whalefish, a paltry little alehouse where she lodged, was pitched upon for one, and his Excellence's house for another. They lost no time in their negotiation, for either he sent his coach to fetch her or went himself to her lodgings, where he would make his coach wait on him for whole nights and most part of the day for fear as it were, that the town should not come to the knowledge of the scandal. She was so bare in clothes as his Excellence was of money and credit at that time, which made him pawn his watch to buy her a new suit. The Jew who had it was afraid of his bargain, and therefore showed it in so many places till at last the whole town came to ring of it. But he was so far from being concerned at what any one said that sometimes after the play was ended he has put her into his coach before all the company, notwithstanding all the giggling and hishing of the Austrian ladies and of the ministers' wives and daughters, himself humbly walking home on foot. These and other civilities made the damsel report at last that Sir G[eorge] had a design to marry her, if the magistrates had not hindered the match by turning her out of town.

Honoured Sir,

On Monday, the 15th of November,[1] about three o'clock, his Excellence Sir G[eorge] E[therege] sent his coach for the comedian to come and dine with him in private, according to his custom. Several young fellows hearing of this entertainment, though it was no news to them, resolved to show some feats for the honour of their country, and like so many London prentices, that now and then use to show their displeasure against Whetstone's Park,[2] they mustered up a good, handsome company. About seven o'clock several parties of them appeared in sight and posted themselves in several places about the house and garden, according to their orders. By eight o'clock they had formed the siege, and within less than half an hour after, they began to make their regular approaches, advancing within five or six yards of the very door. They continued to carry on their works with silence till nine; then they loudly proclaimed an open war and threatened, if this Helena was not delivered into their hands, they would presently let Paris see the dire effects of his obstinacy. In expectation of an answer, they lost no time in whetting their swords on the stone walls and pavements, in fixing their firearms, &c. A little before ten his Excellence began to parley with them out at the window, and desired they would grant him an hour's time to consider of their proposition. Having obtained it with some difficulty, he resolved to make the best use he could of it to prepare for his defence. This shows Mahomet was no true lover who brought

[1] 1686.
[2] An infamous neighbourhood. The apprentices' raids have been turned to account in Duffett's *Mock Tempest*. On Shrove Tuesday and during the Easter Holidays the apprentices gathered in large numbers assaulting and often destroying houses of ill fame. See Pepys, March 24, 1667/8.

out his fair Irene and sacrificed her with his own hand to the rage of the multitude; and, in spite of all his murmuring soldiers, Titus Vespasian had never banished Berenice out of Rome, if he had had but half the courage of this truly heroic and valiant knight. Much about eleven his Excellence, with a detachment of his three footmen, two French lackeys, his fencing, dancing, and hof masters[1] (the secretary not thinking fit to concern himself at all with their broils), sallied out upon seven or eight persons who were left to keep the trenches, and, being seconded by his French vice bassa who commanded the reserve (the cook, coachman, and kitchen wench), would have totally routed them but that his second thoughts proved better than his first. However, some blows happened; for a lute-player having clapped his Excellence two or three times on the back (pretending likely to take him prisoner) was answered with a slap on the face, and the dancing-master, more accustomed to a capriole[2] than the use of the sabre, gave another of the enemies a slight cut in the neck, for which the vice bassa knocked him down for fear of farther mischief. The ringleader seemed to be the Baron de Sensheim disguised in a footman's habit; his janizaries were his valet de chambre, his two footmen, two or three lackeys belonging to the Count de Lamberg, &c. As soon as they saw his Excellence retreat they took it for a sign of victory and began again to play the Rabshakehs,[3] so that their language was so opprobrious and scurrilous as none but those who have been at Billingsgate ever heard the like. Notwithstanding all their outrages her ladyship resolved

[1] Ger. Hofmeister = steward.   [2] Caper.
[3] Rabshakeh was one of the officers sent by Sennacherib, King of Assyria, to demand the surrender of Jerusalem. He derided King Hezekiah in loud and insolent language (2 Kings xviii. 19 ff.).

rather to venture home with a good convoy than to suffer things to come to extremity and run the risk of a general assault. The order of the procession was as follows: two footmen marching before with pistols ready cocked in one hand and flambeaux in the other; the damsel with a man and a musketoon followed after in the coach which was guarded on each side by two persons, and behind by three more all well furnished with swords and pistols. Baron de Sensheim and his company pursued them closely, but, fearing by their appearance they might make too great an opposition, they were forced to content themselves with hooting and hollowing; except only one action that happened on this manner: the fencing-master, perceiving that some of the enemy were like to fall in upon them in the flank by the favour of a defile where they annoyed them with stones, betook himself to pursue them with all his might, till by running he happened to stumble over a turnstile, which was like to cost him his neck, but, having escaped this ambuscade, he returned to the main body, and so they continued on, some crying one thing and some another, but all with one voice agreed in this: *that great was the Diana of the English envoy*. Thus attended she arrived at her lodgings, having passed along three of the principal streets and two of the most public places of the town. It is not known which was greater, the show and the music that went along with it, or the noise it made in the town the next morning. The fame of this expedition was not a little increased by a letter which his Excellency writ to Baron de Sensheim *en termes piquants* whereof a copy goes herewith. The comedian, being privately warned by the magistrates to leave the town, trooped immediately away for Nuremberg, where, as soon as ever she arrived, the council gave order to take her into custody and carry her to the Zuchthaus or Bridewell, where Sir

G[eorge]'s fine clothes are like to maintain her for some years on bread and water. Count Lamberg cashiered one of his footmen, and the chamberlain of this town made the lute-player be put in prison for two or three days upon a promise Sir G[eorge] gave him of living more regular for the future. Very many doubt of it since he designs already to visit Nuremberg and to plague that town, as well as this, if his mistress be not released. Nobody knows where the business between him and Monsieur Sensheim is like to end, but for fear of the worst[1] Sir G[eorge] carries a musketoon in his coach, and each footman has always since a pair of pocket pistols ready charged.

The letter above mentioned.[2]
Monsieur,

J'étais surpris d'apprendre que ce joli gentil-homme travesti en Italien hier au soir était le Baron de Sensheim. Je ne savais pas que les honnêtes gens se mêlaient avec des laquais ramassés pour faire les fanfarons et les batteurs de pavés. Si vous avez quelque chose à me dire faites la moi savoir comme vous devez, et ne vous amusez plus à venir insulter mes domestiques ni ma maison. Soyez content que vous l'avez échappe belle et ne retournez plus chercher les récompenses des telles folies. Pour vos beaux compagnons j'ai des autres mesures à garder avec eux.

Geo. Etheridge.

Honoured Sir,

How fast soever we thought the comedian, it is now but too apparent we all lay under a mistake; for if ever Hannibal and Alaricus made the Roman senators tremble, the patricians of Nuremberg, as they say, were no less frightened when they heard that Sir G[eorge] designed them a visit. It shows

[1] MS. 'worse'.   [2] A copy of the letter on p. 119.

how much they were alarmed at the report of his coming when, for fear of drawing judgement on their own heads, they were glad to turn loose his atoning mistress for a scapegoat; and rather than not be able to stop his journey, his approach, we may safely conclude, might have been sufficient to procure a general gaol delivery. But why I should trouble you with probabilities I know not since matter of fact is more than I can tell you. As soon as she had got her liberty she gave notice of it by a letter, and, within [a] few days after, arrived in person in the suburbs of Bayrischenhof,[1] where she took a lodging at a famous alehouse called the Golden Lion. It is true some few visits were made her, but they were looked upon to be merely out of formality and for fashion's sake, since Sir G[eorge] would neither procure her leave to enter within the gates, nor vindicate his own honour and authority so far as to coach her into the town triumphantly in spite of all the magistrates, as he would often propose to himself. One would think it somewhat strange that a person of her public note and character should pretend to get into the town incognito when the guards were doubled on purpose to keep her out. However, as we are most likely and subject to be deceived by our own selves, so she made use of a soldier's habit, and by that means got in, though she finds after all that Sir G[eorge] is run out of all his money and therefore trading is like to be broke.

[You see, sir, I cannot forbear to write to you for fear of neglecting my promise which you may call duty, for, though I be but one of the meanest of his Sacred Majesty's subjects, yet I can frame to myself such an idea of his honour as will not suffer me without grief and shame to see it abused.][2]

[1] Stadt-am-Hof, on the opposite side of the Danube, was the property of the Dukes of Bavaria.
[2] The lines in brackets are deleted in the MS.

Honoured Sir,

According to the liberty you were pleased to grant me I made bold to send you by the last post what I could not well resolve upon before I heard of your safe arrival in England, the news whereof did very much alleviate my heart, for otherwise I should scarce have been able to write of such things as would infallibly be taken for fabulous knight errantries if all that live in this town did not know them to be real truths. Sir G[eorge], who has not as yet ten words of Dutch,[1] being forced not only to make use of a truchman,[2] but also to entrust one or another of his lackeys with all his intrigues, was discovered in everything as soon as it was done, for whatever any one has a mind to publish he need not but let a Dutch servant know it for a secret and he shall be sure to tell it wherever he goes. And whereas one would think that Sir G[eorge] in particular should be kind to his servants, as the only means to engage them to silence, yet it has always been observed on the contrary that his footmen of all others have the hardest service and the worst usage: for when others sup they dine; when it is time to be abed and asleep they are forced to wander up and down the streets, &c., which has been the cause that Sir G[eorge] has had about twenty-two different Dutch servants within this twelvemonth, and never above five or six at a time, as a cook and a kitchen wench, a coachman, and two or three lackeys. Although Sir G[eorge]'s own servants had been never so silent, yet the stragglers that constantly live upon him, and generally such as have the name of idle fellows, were enough to disclose all his concerns. I believe there has passed [a] great many things which I have not heard, for at his first coming hither I thought I could do no less than

---

[1] German.　　　　　　[2] Interpreter.

inform him of such stories as I had heard reported of him, but, finding he was far from taking it in good part, by asking how I was concerned, if I was sent with him for his governor, &c., I resolved to say nothing, and being left to follow his own course he did all his endeavours to keep things from my hearing, lest it should be told him again that such a night he had been visiting all the alehouses of the town accompanied with his servants, his valets de chambre, his hofmaster and his dancing and fighting master, all with their coats turned inside outwards.

Sir George having promised me in England three score pound a year, with my own and my man's diet, would have flinched from his bargain when he came to Ratisbon, but, money being sent him to Ratisbon, after he had left his post and was retired to France, I laid an arrest upon it till I should be paid what he owed me by his note in writing. After all my fair proposals to be satisfied, he would have shuffled me off and writ to the magistrate against me, calling me his domestic with other harsh terms, which gave occasion to the following letter sent him to Paris.

Nobilissimis, amplissimis, prudentissimis sacri Romani Imperii liberae civitatis Ratisbonensis dominis camerariis ut et reliquis senatoribus spectatissimis dominis meis maxime devenerandis:

Sub initio literarum suarum Dominus Etherege judicium suum fert de actionibus ignominiosis; omnibus agnoscendum et vero verius est quod ille optimo jure de his possit decernere cum sit homo vulgatae nequitiae, et ad usum omnium facinorum peritissimus. Impii mores et vitae ipsius vitia satis superque omnibus sunt nota. Et hinc aliis persuasum habere vellet, quod labe contagionis (uti pestis proprium est) me inquinaverit, sed deum ter optimum maximum qui intactum me hucusque conservavit pro bonitate sua divinâ spero me semper conservatarum! Videtur quod sit Dominus Etheregius qui maximam prorsus infamiam subiit eo magis quod, propter lenocinia et effusas in omni intemperantia libidines, illi non suppeditebat unde mihi aliisque creditoribus satisfaceret quando hinc abiit ad asylum apud Gallis quaerendum. Hisce literis suis singulatim narrare[1] simulat res omnes, quae mihi cum illo intercessêre. Sed non satis possum admirari, quod ille audeat dicere se cum fratre me pactum fecisse. Nemone cui meliori debeamus jure fidem adhibere quam Domino Etheregio? Quid! illumne latet, quod male audit, et quod omnes qui plane boni sunt et cum primis honesti, hominem illum ducunt sine existimatione necnon honoris et virtutis expertum? putatne titulum illum equitis curati sufficere, quo minus de fide[2] et probitate suâ dubitandum sit? audetne sub hoc titulo veritati facere injuriam? et speratne legationem suam Ratisbonnensem unquam efficere, ut probra quaeque et dedecorosae ipsius vitae actiones in oblivionem veniant? paucis dicam si tantillum honoris vel honestatis Domino Etheregio reliquum est, set non denegaret veritatem rei quam cum illo habui; bene ac pro certo scit quod fratri meo promisit, antequam cum illo unquam alloquutus sum, se mihi sexagintas libras angliae quotannis daturum, si illi negotiis suis Ratisbonae exequendis adesse vellem. Ibi me frater enixe petiit ut dictum Dominum Etheregium viserem, et cum illum invenerim apud chryrurgum quendam gallum nomine Fucadium. Ipse Etheregius jamtum mihimet ipsi etiam atque etiam, non solum 60 libras sed et pedissequuum meum victu pascere pollicitus est, ubi antea fratri meo promiserat. Ad haec responsum dedi mihi deliberatum esse una cum illo Ratisbonam petere ita ut ad iter me paratum esse monuit.

[1] MS. 'ennarrare'.   [2] MS. 'fine'.

Tantam abfuit quando huc venissem ut *liberalitate* et *beneficiis* me prosequeretur ut contra justitiam et honestos mores ne promissis ipsis stare voluit: subjiciendo non plus habuisse secretarium domini Polei quam 40 libras per annum. Ex quo evenit ut mihi opus fuit cum illo contendere atque ante oculos ponere quanto dedecoris sensu illum afficere deberet me viginti libris defraudare. His verbis commotus de novo se pactione devinxit has mihi 20 libras e sumptibus extraordinariis daturum; et id responsum a me tulit, quod non multum curarem ex quo argento mihi persolveret, dummodo summa rationum in 60 libras quadraret, ubi prius promiserat; si regem rationibus suis in fraudem inducere illi potius fuit, quam ut ex proprio mihi numeraret argento. Queritur in literis quod viginti fere millia florenorum illi debentur ex aerario publico sed quod hoc ad me? ullamne cum illo pactionem feci, me pro libitu suo stipendium accepturum? ullamne inter se proportionem habent trecenti thaleri, et quinque millia thalerorum quos quotannis habuit Dominus Etheregius praeter sumptos extraordinarios? Legationis suae munus per tres annos, et sex menses administravit, et nulla ratio est quod ego ducentos et quinquaginta thaleros illi condonarem quia viginta, millia florenos ex aerario regio non accepit, quorum fere dimidium, falso et graeca fide rationibus suis addidit, contra juramentum et sub praetextu sumptuum extraordinariorum; uti manifestum faciam, si opus fuerit porro literis suis addit, illum non plus extraordinariorum accepisse quam ad annum unum et novem menses nihilominus fatetur, quod ex his quidem debitum 40 librarum mihi numeravit pro duobus annis, nonne restat ergo, ut mihi altero sesquianno satisfaceret? et quando quidem mihi trimestris spatii stipendium absolvit etsi non accepisset, satis constat, illum pecunias mihi debitas non dedisse secundum quantitatem acceptam, sed secundum suam nummositatem aut nummariam difficultatem. Mentionem facit de scripto quodam cui chirographum meum est appositum, persuadere vellet me illi acceptilationem dedisse, hinc insignem se deceptorem praebet; nonne ille ipse scit bene aeque ac omnes eius domestici, quam magnam cum illo controversiam, et altercationem mihi habere necesse fuit antequam ab illo hoc scriptum extorquere potui, quod nihil aliud est quam apographum scripti, quod mihi coactus fuit dare, quasi per vim et post multas minas praesentibus et audientibus suis domesticis cum nonnullis aliis, quia animadvertebam illum mihi debitum solvere non curare et abeundi solummodo occasionem quaerere, ut me aeque ac famulum suum cubicularem defraudaret. Haeccine ergo in me domini Etheregii liberalitas! qui cum vidisset se non abiturum nisi prius mihi solvendi promissum faceret (quod et propria manu se attestatus est facturum quamprimum ille pecuniam acciperet) autoramentum seu obligationem hanc mihi aegre tradidit et necesse illi fuit me obtestari patienter ferre, praetendendo pecuniam illi ad iter faciendum non suppeditare. Forte fortuito procurator domini Etheregii post ipsius decessum huc ex Anglia quingentos misit thaleros sed ut mihi fucum faciat pro solutione debiti. Falso persuadere vellet quod sunt ex amicis suis intimis, qui praeter expectationem hanc illi pecuniam misêre. Bene notum est quod dominus Etheregius ne minimum habet redditum annualem nec vitae nec cultus subsidia praeter pensionem quam rex illi quotannis pendebat. Erat dominus Robsonius et postea dominus Richardus qui pensionem hanc ex serario regio cepêre. Eratque etiam dictus Richardus qui hos quingentos thaleros huic misit more solito et per literas cambii Domino Martino Dalas. Praeterea cum domino Etheregio et non cum rege pactionem hanc feci; est ergo dictus Etheregius qui mihi conditiones et promissa praestare debet; et ad hoc jure tenetur. Magistratus haud dubio justitiam colunt et spero quod id re comprobaturi sunt, adjudicando mihi debitum; et Dominum Etheregium ad solutionem condemnando. Magnis quidem laudibus, et encomiis rationem suam videndi celebrat, et valde apud illos se gratiosum esse ambitiose sibi pollicetur. Sed de his penitus inquirendi alia mihi vice occasionem expecto, quod quidem pensum in me libenter accipiam. Caeteroquin quomodo possumus magni id aestimare, quod per Deum, et per honorem asserit, quandoquidem omnibus bene notum est, quod laudem effectat et gloriatur de eo, quod non credit esse Deum quoad honorem attinet, nemo arte omnino non scit, quod ille nunquam honoris famam sibi conciliavit, sed e contra susque deque semper habuit. Jam vestrum, viri praestantissimi, judicium appello, si sua in me liberalitas et quam jactat largitio non jure potiori fraudis et mali doli titulum mercantur. Quod ita res se habet Dei hominumque fidem imploro, et pro justitia et virtute qua omnes ad recte agendum inclinantur senatum vestrum, egregii viri, quam primum de hac se decreturum spero &c.

APPENDIX

TRANSLATION OF LATIN LETTERS

Copy of the Imperial transcript delivered to the Apostolic Nuncio in the cause of the Palatinate.

In the name of the sacred Imperial Majesty to the very eminent Lord Cardinal Bonvisi, Nuncio, to his question and instance whether, according to the Imperial laws, [a man] claiming the succession and not grasping possession of the same within a year and a day forfeit the benefit of possessing it. With all kindness answer must be made that the laws of the Empire under this head do not differ from the common and feudal Roman law, and therefore [a man] claiming the succession in fiefs of the Empire or other good [fiefs] in a competent way, is able to act against him who has forestalled him in taking possession, and enjoy, even after the lapse of a year and a day, all benefits appointed by the common law in the matter of possession and candidature; but if, neglecting the way of law and competent judgement, he presume to declare the law for himself, and by his own authority and deed to seize the possession grasped by another, he forfeits his right and also incurs other penalties, according to the nature of the circumstances. In conclusion His Sacred Imperial Majesty willingly embraces the very Eminent Lord Cardinal with his favour and good will.

To the very noble, great and wise Lord Chamberlains of the free state of Ratisbon of the Sacred Roman Empire, as also to the rest of the Senators, my most approved and venerable Lords.

At the beginning of his letter Sir [G.] Etherege gives his judgement concerning shameful actions; all must acknowledge, and it is truer than the truth, that he has the best right to decide concerning them since he is a man of notorious villainy and very skilful in the practice of all evil deeds. He is of a wicked character, and the vices of his life are enough, and more than enough, known to all. And hence he would wish to have persuaded others that

401   D d

he has polluted me with the stain of infection (in the manner that is peculiar to the disease), but I hope that God, thrice best and greatest, who has hitherto preserved me uninjured, by His divine goodness will ever preserve me! It seems that it is Sir [G.] Etherege who has incurred the greatest infamy, the more because, on account of pandering, and lusts indulged in every kind of intemperance, he had not sufficient wherewith to satisfy me and his other creditors when he departed hence to seek a refuge with the French. In these letters of his he pretends that he relates one by one all the transactions which took place between us. But I cannot marvel enough that he should dare to say that he made an agreement with my brother; is there nobody to whom we ought to give credence by better right than to Sir [G.] Etherege? What! does it escape his notice that he is of bad reputation, and that all who are wholly good and especially honourable will deem him a man of no reputation, devoid also of honour and virtue? does he think that title of gilded Knight is sufficient that there be no doubt of his faith and integrity? does he dare, under this title, to do injury to truth? does he hope that his embassy at Ratisbon will ever bring it about that all the shameful deeds and disgraceful actions of his life pass into oblivion? In a few words I will say, if ever so little honour or probity is left to Sir [G.] Etherege he will not deny the truth of the matter between us; he knows well and for certain that he promised my brother before ever I spoke with him that he would give me £60 every year if I would agree to help him in the execution of his affairs at Ratisbon. There my brother earnestly besought me to visit the said Sir [G.] Etherege, and when I found him at the house of a certain French surgeon, Fucadius by name, Etherege himself at once promised me not only £60 but also to keep my footman in victuals as before he had promised my brother, to which I gave answer that I had decided to go to Ratisbon in his company, so that he warned me to be prepared for the journey. When I had come hither so far was he from treating me with generosity and benefits, that contrary to justice and good morals he would not even abide by his promises, alleging that the secretary of Mr. Poley had not more than £40 a year, from which it happened that I must needs contend with him and put before his eyes with what a great sense of disgrace it should affect him to defraud me of £20; moved by these words he bound himself anew by an agreement to give me these £20 from his extraordinary expenses; and he got this answer from me that I would not much care in what money he paid me so long as the total should square with £60 as he had before promised; if it was better for him to deceive the King by his reckonings than that he should pay me out of his own private money. He complains in his letter that nearly 20,000 florins are owing to him out of the public Treasury; but what is this to me? Did I make any agreement with him that I would accept payment according to his whim? What proportion is there between 300 thalers and 5,000 thalers which Sir [G.] Etherege had yearly besides his extraordinary expenses? He administered the office of his embassy for three years and six months, and there is no reason that I should excuse him 250 thalers because he has not received 20,000 florins from the Royal Treasury, more than half of which he added to his accounts by false and Greek faith, contrary to his oath, and under pretext of extraordinary expenses; that I may make it manifest if need shall be he adds further in his letter that he has not received more extraordinary expenses than for one year and nine months, nevertheless he confesses that out of these he paid me a debt of £40 for two years. Does it not remain, then, that he should satisfy me for the other year and a half? and since he paid me the salary for three months, although he had not received it, it is evident that he had not given me the money owing according to the accepted quantity, but according to his supply of money, or pecuniary difficulties. He makes mention of a certain deed to which my autograph is annexed, would like to persuade people that I had given him a bill of discharge for the debt; herein he shows himself an illustrious deceiver; does not he himself know well, just as all his servants know, what a great controversy and altercation I needs must have with him before I was able to extort that deed from him, which is nothing other than the copy of a deed which he was compelled to give me, as it were, by force and after many threats, his servants and some others being present and listening, because I perceived that he did not care to pay me that debt and only sought an opportunity for departing that he might defraud me as well as his groom of the chamber. Is this then the liberality of Sir [G.] Etherege towards me? who, when he saw that he could not depart unless he had first fulfilled his promise of payment to me (which too with his own hand he attested that he would do as soon as he received the money), reluctantly handed over to me this contract or bond, and he needs must implore me to endure patiently, pretending that he had not sufficient money to make the journey. By chance the proctor of Sir [G.] Etherege in England, after his departure, sent hither 500 thalers, but that he might make excuse to me for payment of the debt, wished untruly to persuade me that they are from his intimate friends, who, contrary to expectation, have sent him this money. It is well known that Sir [G.] Etherege has not the smallest annual income, nor means of livelihood or attire, beyond the pension which the King paid him yearly. It was Mr. Robson, and afterwards Mr. Richards, who took this pension from the Royal Treasury. It was too the said Richards who sent hither these 500 thalers in the accustomed fashion, and by letter of exchange to Mr. Martin Dalas. Moreover, I made this agreement with Sir [G.] Etherege, who ought to make good to me the conditions and promises, and to this he is bound by law. The magistrates, doubtless, regard justice, and I hope that they will prove this in fact by adjudicating the debt to me and by condemning Sir [G.] Etherege to payment. Great indeed are the praises and encomiums with which he celebrated his mode of life, and he promises himself ostentatiously that he is in great favour amongst those people. But concerning this I expect an opportunity of inquiring more closely another time, what indeed is paid to me I will gladly accept. However, in so far as we are able [we will] esteem it of great value that he makes his declaration by God and by honour, since it is well known to all that he aims at praise and makes his boast in this, that he does not believe in the existence of God, and as to honour, certainly no one at all is ignorant, that he has never won for himself the reputation of honour but has always had it both up and down. Now, most excellent sirs, I appeal to your judgement, whether his liberality towards me and the largesse which he boasts of do not by better right deserve the title of fraud and evil treachery. And that this is so I call upon the faith of God and men, and I hope, noble sirs, that your Senate will, as soon as possible, decide concerning this matter in accordance with justice and virtue, by which all are inclined to right action.

OTHER LETTERS OF SIR GEORGE ETHEREGE.

PUBLIC RECORD OFFICE. S.P. TURKEY 19

Sr

Were you acquainted with this place you wou'd not condemne mee much for not giving you before this time any account of ye affaires of Turky. During ye Warr of Candia the News wee had from thence was sent us from Smyrna, where you hold a correspondence wth Consul Ricaut, so that ye advices wch I should have given you wou'd have bin stale and insignificant; besides ye remotenes of ye Court (which has bin ever since our arrivall in Thessaly and Macedon) has made this citty as barren of intelligence as a Village: here seldome happens anything worthy remarke and when there does it is so uncertainly reported to us by our Druggermen[1] who are our only Intelligencers, that experience makes us very incredulous; what wee heare one day is commonly contradicted ye next, and shou'd I give you a dayly account of things according to your desire my busines would bee almost every other Letter to disabuse you in what I had writt to you before.

My Lord is lately return'd from Salonica, where hee has had audience. Hee arriv'd there some days before ye Court and had notice given him that hee shou'd expect ye Grand Signor's coming from Larissa. The Grand Signor arriv'd upon Thursday 25°. Nov. in ye evening, came in incognito to visit his Hasachi or Sultana, and ye next morning went out againe to make a publique entry. His

---

[1] i.e. dragomans.

405

traine consisted of ffootemen and pages, Faulconers and Huntsmen who were in all about two thousand: He was attended by no men of note but ye mufti, ye Kaimakam[1] of ye port, and his favourite commonly called Culogli. His ffootmen were all clothed in cloth of gold and silver, and his Pages who are his Guard were clad in coates of Male with olive colour'd Sattin vests over them, all Young men pick'd out for their strength and beauty: Severall doggs were lead cover'd with vests of cloth of gold and silver. Doubtless this Entry wanted much of that magnificence hee appeares in when hee enters Adrianople or Constantinople, Yet it made a very handsome showe, and was a very splendid hunting equipage, for such it was accounted. The Munday following, My Lord visited ye Chimacam, and ye next day had audience of ye Grand Signor, who treated him with extraordinary markes of respect and civility. The Grand Signor is about thirty years of age, of a middle stature, leane, and long visag'd, hee has lately let ye haire grow on his chin, his complexion is a darke browne, his aspect is not disagreeable, however hee is generally accounted very ugly. Hee is a Bigot in his Religion, and a most extravagant lover of hunting, the fatigue hee undergoes in it is almost incredible, great numbers of poore people are summon'd in to attend him and many of them perish in ye ffield through hunger and cold. This has chiefly got him ye hatred of his subjects. In all other recreations hee is moderate, hee is very constant to his Hasachi and not given to that unnaturall vice with wch he has bin slander'd. The Sultana is a Candiot, and though women here are not so polite and refin'd as in Christendome, yet shee wants not her little arts to secure her Sultan's affections, shee can dissemble fondnes and jealousy and can swoone at pleasure. The Grand Sig[r] has had two children by her, a son and a daughter, the son is called Sultan Mustapha, hee is about six yeares old and design'd by his father to bee circumciz'd when hee comes to Constantinople to make ye allaigresse ye greater. The Daughter is not much more than a year old, and is already marryed to the ffavorite Culogli, a man of seaven and twenty yeares, well featur'd,

---

[1] Governor of Constantinople and deputy of the Grand Vizier.

modest and wise, he avoids busines and by that meanes makes himselfe less lyable to ye envy of ye Ministers of State. His equipage is not much inferior to his Master's, his footmen and pages weare ye same Livery, Hee is allow'd six hundred thousand Dollers a yeare besides all necessaries for his retinue, and yet this vast income is not able to keepe him out of debt, but whether that bee an effect of his generosity or prudence is uncertaine, for there is nothing here more dangerous than to be rich. The Grand Signor's Privy Councell consisted here but of five persons, ye favorite, ye Chimacam of the port, ye Mufti, Vani Effendi a famous Arab preacher, and one of ye Pashas of ye Bench; most of the great men being with ye Vizir who is imploy'd in Candia in fortefying and setling the affaires of that Kingdome. He is to come to Court in the Spring as it is reported, and then ye Grand Signor intends to begin his journey hither. This Chima-cam's name is Mustapha Pasha, hee was formerly Capt pasha or Admirall of ye Gallies, and has married ye Vizier's sister, yet this allyance keeps them not from secret emula-tions and hatreds, and it is thought ye Chimacam will dis-pute ye Grand Signor's favour with him at his returne. The Vizier they say exceeds not ye age of two and thirty yeares, hee is of a middle stature and has a good Mine, hee is prudent and just, not to bee corrupted by money the generall vice of this country, nor inclin'd to cruelty, as his father was. The Chimacam is about ye age of forty five, well spoken, subtill, corrupt and a great dissembler, hee flatters ye Grand Signor in his inclinations, and ever accompanies him in his hunting, a toyle which nothing but excessive ambition and interest cou'd make him undergoe. All conclude ye Vizier will commence another Warr, but who will fall under ye [pai]ne of it is unknowne. The Chimacam of this place Ibrahim Pasha has a particu-lar respect for my Lord, and is exceeding courteous and obliging whensoever hee treats with him about any busi-nes; hee is a man of great resolution, wisdome and honesty, hee is neere sixty yeares old but very vigorous of his age, he was bred a souldier and by his courage and other merits has raised him selfe to this eminent degree. Hee was Kiabeigh or Lieuetennant of ye Janizaries at ye battel of Rab, where hee was shot through ye shoulder, and upon ye death of his Captaine was there made Aga, hee serv'd in that charge at Candia till he was this yeare sent hither to bee Chimacam in the stead of Useph pasha a timorous doting old man who was remoov'd for multiplying ye danger and giving a dreadfull account to ye Court of some little stirrs that hapned here some months since upon a report that ye Grand Signor had sent to cutt off his brothers Sultan Soliman and Sultan Achmet; 'tis thought these princes will bee in great danger when ye Grand Sig^r arrives here. My busines was at ye beginning to excuse my not writing to you, and now I ought to begg your pardon for having writt soe much, but I hope you will let mee know you have forgiven mee ye impertinencies of this Letter, and that will incourage mee to give you notice of whatsoever I shall bee inform'd of here worthy of your knowledge.

I am, S^r,

Your very humble servant,

Geo. Etherege.

These ffor Joseph Williamson Esqr
Whitehall.

The 3^d May, 1670.

S.P. GERMAN STATES 86

Ratisbonne, 23 Nov./3 Dec., 1685.

My Lord,

I have taken the House Mr. Pooley liv'd in, and am very well setl'd allready considering the shortnes of the time and how hard it is to find Conveniencies here. I am just now goeing to make my first visit to the Prince of Passau. I will dispatch all the rest as fast as I can, that I may have more Liberty to informe myselfe about affaires. I have inclos'd a paper of wt newes is currant here. This day the post comes from Vienna and if I can get intelligence of wt it brings time enough I will inclose it in this likewise. I am not well enough acquainted wth this Towne yet to give you an account how people spend there idle houres here, and whether it is like to make any

one of the unknowne[.] ... the Governoure of this Place[.] Ibrahim Patha
... a particular respect for my Port, and ... exceeding courteous & obliging notwithstanding
hee treats with him about any busines. Hee is a man of great resolution, wisdome, and
honesty, hee is aged sixty yeares old, but very vigorous of his age, hee was bred a
souldier and by his courage & other merits hay raisd himselfe to this eminent degree
hee was through ... or advancement of the Janisaries at ... battaill of ... before hee
was first through .... and ... wast of his Captaine was there made
Aga, hee hath in that charge at ... till hee was this yeare sent hither to be
Governoure ... the head of Stept Pasha, a generous doting old man who was somewhat
... neglecting ... or giving ... account to the Port of some little thing that
happened here ... monthly since upon a report that ... was sent to cut off his
head was Sultan salmon a Sultan .... he thought this prince would have ne great
danger ... by ... here ....
My ... not only acquainting me
secure my not writing to you, & now sought to begg or pardon for troubling with so
trivall ... But hope you will but now know you have forgiven ... & importunning
of this letter, and will not discourage me, & give upon better of whatsoever I shall bee
... of hope worthy yo: knowledge. I am

Sir
Yo: very humble servant
Geo. Pharoe.

amends for wt I have lost in London; but I can assure yor
Lo^p that I find I can live wthout play, a thing my best
ffriends will hardly believe. I have really no more con-
cerne for Basset then I us'd to have for an old Mistres in
her absence, nor am I troubl'd at the loss of any thing but
the opportunitys I had of being neare yor Lo^p and the
rest of my ffriends; this touches me so nearly that nothing
but now and then an assurance of the continuance of yor
Lo^{ps} favour is able to bring any comfort to My Lord,

Yo^r Lo^{ps} most faithfull & most obedient

servant

Geo. Etherege.

Ratisbonne, 14/24 Dec., 1685.[1]

My Lord,

Since my coming hither I have had a little Fever, w^{ch}
has been the reason I have not payd my Duty so regularly
as I ought to do, to yor Lo^p. I am now pretty well recover'd, and hope I am quit at a reasonable price for wt
I was to pay on the change of Climats, and a greater
change in my manner of Living. Is it not enough to breed
an ill habit of body in a man who was us'd to sit up till
morning to be forc'd for want of knowing wt to do with
himselfe to go bed in the Evening; one who has been
us'd to Live with all freedom, never to approach any body
but with Ceremonie; one who has been us'd to run up
and down to find out variety of Company to sit at home,
and entertaine himselfe in solitude. Play and women are
not so much as talk'd of, and one wou'd think the Diett
had made a Reichsguttachten to banish those pastimes the
Citty. Here was ye Countess of Nostitz but malice wou'd
not let her live in quiet and she is lately remov'd to
Prague; good company met at her howse and she had a
little ombre to entertaine 'em; a more comode Lady by
wt I heare never kept a Bassett in London. If I do well
after all this you must allow me to be a great Philosopher,
and I dare afirme Cato left not the world with more
firmenes of soule then I did England.

The disputes that happen about Ceremonials in the
Diett I shall onely torment my Lo: Middleton wth being

[1] See Letterbook, p. 58.

409

properly appartenances of his Province, when anything of moment is debated I shall acquaint you wth it, but that wch I shall be most carefull to informe you of, is wt is done when the Campagne opens, knowing the king loves to heare of those matters.

The best acknowledgement I can make to yor Lo^p for all I owe you, wch is indeed all I have, is to be industrious in my Station, you prefer'd me to his Ma^{ttes} Service, and in gratitude I shall daily studdy to acquit myselfe well in it. I know no better way here to make yor Lo^p see how truly sensible I am of yor favour whereever I am hereafter, all the actions of my life shall still show wth how much sinserity, and humility I am, My Lord,

Yo^r Lo^{ps} most faithfull and most obedient serv^t,
G. Etherege.
Lo: Sunderland.

Ratisbonne, 1/11 Jan., 1686/7.
My Lord,
I doubt but yor Lo^p knows all I am able to say of matters in agitation here. Wthin these few dayes the Diet will open again, and then there may happen something, wch may excuse my troubling you wth it; all that I have to doe now, according to the good breeding of this place, is to wish yor Lo^p a happy new yeare: this piece of formallity is far from satisfieing me who have allways yor benefits in my mind, and can never enough acknowledge them, tho my wholle life were employd in yor Lo^{ps} service. You may think this a time of Leisure, but I assure you I never had so much busines since I left England. The Countess of Zinzendorffe, and two of her Daughters are come from Neurenberg to pass the Holydayes here. I cannot think you have a good opinion enough of my Judgement in beauty to believe me when I say these two young Ladys have in full perfection all that three or fower of our Country women (wch I need not name) have in a manner lost. Germanie has no good name in this matter, but it is no new thing for Countrys who have no reputation in the general to produce something very extraordinary in particular. All the false Catos of this place say by their sower looks, and put on smiling faces; neg-

lect their ceremonies, forget their Excellencies and vieu in making of their Court. I leave your Lo^p to think whether I am idle. I knowe nothing can make this Letter be pardon'd but your considering it has taken up some minutes of that time wch shoul'd be wholly employ'd in so important a busines by, my Lord,

Yo^r Lo^{ps} most faithfull and most humble servant,
Geo: Etherege.

Earle of Sunderland.

FROM THE *MISCELLANEOUS WORKS* OF GEORGE VILLIERS, DUKE OF BUCKINGHAM, 1704

A Letter from Sir George Etherege to the Duke of Buckingham.
Ratisbon, Nov. 12, 1686, N.S.

My Lord,

I Received the News of your Grace's retiring into Yorkshire, and leading a sedate contemplative Life there, with no less Astonishment than I should hear of his Christian Majesty's turning Benedictine Monk, or the Pope's wearing a long Perriwig, and setting up for a flaming Beau in the seventy fourth Year of his Age. We have a Picture here in our Town-hall, which I never look upon but it makes me think on your Grace; and I dare swear you'll say there is no Dishonour done you, when you hear whose it is. In short, 'tis that of the famous Charles the V Who amidst all the Magnificence that this foolish World affords, amidst all his African Lawrels and Gallic Triumphs, freely divested himself of the Empire of Europe, and his hereditary Kingdoms, to pass the Remainder of his Life in Solitude and Retirement.

Is it possible that your Grace (who has seen ten times more Luxury than the Emperor ever knew, convers'd with finer Women, kept politer Company, possess'd as much too of the true real Greatness of the World as ever he enjoyed) should in age still capable of Pleasure, and under a Fortune whose very Ruins would make up a comfortable Electorate here in Germany, Is it possible, I say, that your Grace should leave the Play at the Beginning of the fourth Act, when all the Spectators are in

Pain to know what will become of the Hero, and what mighty Matters he is reserv'd for, that set out so advantageously in the first? That a Person of your exquisite Taste, that has breathed the Air of Courts ever from your Infancy, should be content, in that Part of Life, which is most difficult to be pleased and most easie to be disgusted, to take up with the Conversation of country Parsons, a sort of People, whom to my knowledge, your Grace never much admir'd, and do penance in the nauseous Company of Lawyers, whom I am certain you abominate.

To raise our Astonishment higher, Who could ever have prophecy'd (though he had a double Gift of Nostradamus's Spirit) that the Duke of Buckingham who never vouchsafed his Embraces to any ordinary Beauty, wou'd ever condescend to sigh and languish for the Heiress apparent of a thatch'd Cottage, in a straw Hat, flannen Petticoat, Stockings of as gross a thrum as the Blew-Coat Boy's Caps at the Hospital, and a Smock (the Lord defend me from the wicked Idea of it!) of as course a Canvas as ever serv'd an Apprenticeship to a Mackarel Boat? Who could have believed, till Matter of Fact had confirmed the Belief of it, (and your Grace knows that Matter of Fact is not to be disputed) that the most polished, refined Epicure of his Age, that had regaled himself in the most exquisite Wines of Italy, Greece, and Spain, would in the last Scene of his Life, debauch his Constitution in execrable Yorkshire ale? And that He who all his Life Time had either seen Princes his Playfellows or Companions, would submit to the nonsensical Chat and barbarous Language of Farmers and Higlers?

This, I confess, so much shocks me that I cannot tell what to make on't, and unless the news came to me confirmed from so many Authentic Hands, that I have no room left to suspect the Veracity of it, I should still look upon it to be Apocryphal. Is your Grace then in earnest, and really pleased with so prodigious an Alteration of Persons and Things? For my Part, I believe it; for I am certain that your Grace can act any Person better than that of a Hypocrite. But I humbly beg your Grace's pardon for this Familiarity I have taken with you: Give me leave therefore, if you please, to tell you something of my self. I presume that an Account of what passes in this busie Part of the World, will not come unacceptable to you, since all my Correspondents from England assure me, your Grace does me the Honour to inquire often after me, and has express'd some sort of a Desire to know how my new Character sits upon me.

Ten years agoe I as little thought that my Stars designed to make a Politician of me, and that it would come to my share to debate in public Assemblies, and regulate the Affairs of Christendom, as the grand Signior dream'd of losing Hungary. But my royal Master having the Charity to believe me Master of some Qualities, of which I never suspected my self, I find that the Zeal and Alacrity I discover in my self, to support a Dignity which he has thought fit to confer upon me, has supply'd all other Defects, and given me a Talent, for which (till now) I justly fancied myself uncapable.

I live in one of the finest, and best manner'd Cities in Germany, where tis true we have not Pleasure, in that Perfection as we see it in London and Paris, yet to make us amends, we enjoy a noble serene Air, that makes us hungry as Hawks; and though Business, and even the worst Sort of Business, wicked Politics, is the distinguishing Commodity of the Place, yet I will say that for the Germans, that they manage it the best of any People in the World; they cut off and retrench all those idle Preliminaries and useless Ceremonies that clog the Wheels of it everywhere else. And I find, that, to this Day, they make good the Observation that Tacitus made of their Ancestors; I mean, That their Affairs (let them be never so serious and pressing) never put a stop to good Eating and Drinking, and that they debate their weightiest Negotiations over their Cups.

'Tis true, they carry this Humor by much too far for one of my Complexion, for which Reason I decline appearing among them, but when my Master's Concerns make it necessary for me to come to their Assemblies. They are, indeed, a free hearted, open sort of Gentlemen that compose the Diet, without Reserve, Affectation, and Artifice; but they are such unmerciful Plyers of the

413

Bottle, so wholy given up to what our Sots call Good-fellowship, that 'tis as great a Constraint upon my Nature to sit out a Night's Entertainment with them, as it would be to hear half a score long-winded Presbyterian Divines Cant successively one after another.

To unbosome my self frankly and freely to your Grace, I always looked upon Drunkenness to be an unpardonable Crime in a young fellow, who without any of these foreign Helps, has Fire enough in his Veins to enable him to do Justice to Caelia whenever she demands a Tribute from him. In a middle-aged Man, I consider the Bottle only as subservient to the nobler Pleasure of Love, and he that would suffer himself to be so far infatuated by it, as to neglect the Pursuit of a more agreeable Game, I think deserves no Quarter from the Ladies: In old Age, indeed, when 'tis convenient very often to forget and steal from our selves, I am of Opinion that a little Drunkenness, discreetly used, may as well contribute to our Health of Body as Tranquillity of Soul.

Thus I have given your Grace a short System of my Morals and Belief in these Affairs. But the Gentlemen of this Country go upon a quite different Scheme of Pleasure; the best Furniture of their Parlours (instead of innocent China) are tall overgrown Rummers, and they take more care to enlarge their Cellars than their patrimonial Estates. In short, Drinking is the Hereditary Sin of this Country, and that Heroe of a Deputy here, that can demolish (at one Sitting) the rest of his Brother Envoys, is mentioned with as much Applause as the Duke of Lorain for his noble Exploits against the Turks and may claim a Statue erected at the public Expence in any Town in Germany.

Judge then, my Lord, whether a Person of my sober Principles, and one that only uses Wine (as the wiser sort of Roman Catholics do Images) to raise up my Imagination to something more exalted, and not to terminate my Worship upon it, must not be reduced to very mortifying Circumstances in this Place; where I cannot pretend to enjoy Conversation, without practicing that Vice that directly ruines it.

And as I have just Reason to complain of the men for laying so unreasonable a Tax upon Pleasure, so I have no less Occasion to complain of the Women for wholy denying it.

Could a Man find out the Secret to take as long a Lease for his Life as Methuselah and the rest of the Antidiluvian Gentlemen, who were three hundred Years in growing up to the Perfection of Vigour, enjoy'd it the same Number of Years, and were as long a decaying, something might be said for the two crying sins of both Sexes here; I mean Drunkenness in the Men, and Reservedness in the Ladies.

What would it signify to throw away a Week's, nay a Month's Enjoyment upon one Night's Debauch, if a Man could promise himself the Age of a Patriarch?

Or where wou'd be the mighty Penance in dancing a dozen Years Attendance after a coy Female, watching her most favourable Moments, and most accessible Intervals, at last to enjoy her, if Infirmities and Old Age were to come so late upon us?

But since Fate has given us so short a Period to tast Pleasure with Satisfaction, three or four Days Sickness is too great a Rent-charge upon humane Nature, and Drunkenness cannot pretend (out of its own Fund) to acquit the Debt.

And, my Lord, since our Gayety and Vigour leaves us so soon in the lurch, since Feebleness attacks us without giving us fair Warning, and we no sooner pass the Meridian of Life but begin to decline, its hardly worth a Lover's while to stay as long for compassing a Mistress, as Jacob did for obtaining a Wife; and without this tedious Drudgery and Application, I can assure your Grace that an Amour is not to be managed here.

But, my Lord, I forget that while I take upon me to play the Moralist, and to enlarge so Rhetorically upon the Preciousness of Time, I have already made bold with too much of your Grace's: For which reason, I here put a stop to my Discourse, and will endeavour the next Pacquet that goes from this Place, to entertain your Grace with some thing more agreeable.   I am,

My Lord,

Your Grace's most obedient Servant,

G. Etherege.

Ratisbonne, October 21, 1689 [*sic*]

My Lord,

I Never enjoy my self so much, as when I can steal a few Moments, from the Hurry of public Business, to write to my Friends in England; and as there is none there to whom I can pay a profounder Respect than to your Grace, wonder not if I afford my self the Satisfaction of conversing with you by way of Letters (the only Relief I have left me to support your Absence at this distance) as often as I can find an opportunity.

You may guess by my last, whether I don't pass my Time very comfortably here; forc'd as I am by my Character, to spend the better part of my time in Squabling and Deliberating with Persons of Beard and Gravity, how to preserve the Ballance of Christendome, which would go well enough of its self, if the Divines and Ministers of Princes would let it alone: And when I come home, spent and weary from the Diet, I have no Lord D—ts or Sir Charles S—ys to sport away the Evening with; no Madame I—, or my Lady A—s; in short, none of those kind charming Creatures London affords, in whose Embraces I might make my self amends for so many Hours murdered in impertinent Debates; so that not to magnifie my sufferings to your Grace, they really want a greater stock of Christian Patience to support them, than I can pretend to be Master of.

I have been long enough in this Town (one would think) to have made Acquaintance enough with Persons of both Sexes, so as never to be at a loss how to pass the few vacant Hours I can allow my self: But the terrible Drinking that accompanies all our Visits, hinders me from Conversing with the Men so often as I would otherwise doe; and the German Ladies are so intollerably reserv'd and virtuous (with Tears in my eyes I speak it to your Grace) that 'tis next to an impossibility to carry on an Intrigue with them: A man has so many Scruples to conquer, and so many Difficulties to surmount, before he can promise himself the least Success, that for my part I have given over all Pursuits of this Nature: Besides,

416

there is so universal a Spirit of Censoriousness reigns in this Town, that a Man and a Woman cannot be seen at Ombre or Piquet together, but 'tis immediately concluded some other Game has been played between them; and as this renders all manner of Access to the Ladies most impracticable, for fear of exposing their Reputation to the Mercy of their ill-natur'd Neighbours, so it makes an innocent Piece of Gallantry often pass for a criminal Correspondence.

So that to deal freely with your Grace among so many noble and wealthy Families as we have in this Town, I can only pretend to be truly acquainted but with one: The Gentleman's Name was Monsieur Hoffman, a frank, hearty, jolly Companion; his Father, one of the most eminent Wine-Merchants of the City, left him a considerable Fortune, which he improved by marrying a French Jeweller's Daughter of Lyons: To give you his character in short, he was a sensible ingenious Man, and had none of his Country's Vices, which I impute to his having travelled abroad and seen Italy, France and England. His Lady is a most accomplish'd ingenious Person, and not-with-standing she is come into a Place where so much Formality and Stiffness are practiced, keeps up all the Vivacity, and Air, and good Humor of France.

I had been happy in my Acquaintance with this Family for some Months, when an ill favour'd Accident rob'd me of the greatest Happiness I had hitherto enjoy'd in Germany, the loss of which I can never sufficiently regret. Monsieur Hoffman, about three Weeks ago, going to make merry with some Friends (at a Village some three Leagues from this Place) upon the Danube, by the Unskilfulness or Negligence of the Watermen, the Boat, wherein he was, unfortunately chanced to over-set, and of some twenty Persons, not one escaped to bring home the News but a Boy that miraculously saved himself by holding fast to the Rudder, and so by the Rapidity of the Current was cast upon the other Shore.

I was sensibly afflicted at the Destiny of my worthy Friend, and so indeed were all that had the Honor of knowing him; but his Wife took on so extravagantly, that she (in a short Time) was the only talk both of City and

Country; she refus'd to admit any Visits from her nearest Relations, her Chamber, her Antichamber, and Pro-anti-chamber were hung with Black, nay the very Candles, her Fans and Tea-table wore the Livery of Grief; she refus'd all manner of Sustenance, and was so averse to the Thoughts of Living, that she talk'd of nothing but Death; in short, you may tell your injenious French Monsieur de Saint Evremond, that Petronius's Ephesian Matron, to whose Story he has done so much Justice in his noble Translation, was only a Type of our more obstinate, as well as unhappy German Widow.

About a Fortnight after this cruel Loss (for I thought it would be Labour lost to attack her Grief in its first Vehemence) I thought my self obliged, in Point of Honour, and Gratitude to the Memory of my deceased Friend, to make her a small Visit, and condole her Ladyship upon this unhappy Occasion: And tho' I had been told that she had refused to see several Persons who had gon to wait on her with the same Errand, yet I presumed so much upon the Friendship her late Husband had always express'd for me, (not to mention the particular Civilities I had received from her self) as to think I should be admitted to have a sight of her. Accordingly I came to her House, sent up my Name, and word was immediately brought me, that if I pleas'd I might go up to her.

When I came into the Room, I fancy'd my self in the Territories of Death, every thing looked so gloomy, so dismal, and so melancholly. There was a grave Lutheran Minister with her, that omitted no Arguments to bring her to a more composed and more Christian Disposition of Mind. Madam (says he) you don't consider that by abandoning your self thus to Despair, you actually rebel against Providence. I cann't help it, (says she) Providence may e'en thank it self, for laying so insupportable a Load upon me: O fye, Madam (cries the other) this is down right impiety: What would you say now, if Heaven should punish it by some more exemplary Visitation? That is impossible, replies the Lady sighing, and since it has rob'd me of the onely Delight I had in this World, the only Favour it can do me is to level a Thunderbolt at my Head and put an end to all my Sufferings. The Parson finding her in this extravagant Strain, and seeing no likelihood of Perswading her to come to a better Temper, got up from his Seat and took his leave of her.

It came to my turn now to try whether I was not capable of comforting her, and being convinced by so late an Instance that Arguments brought from Religion were not like to work any extraordinary Effects upon her, I resolved to attack her Ladyship in a more sensible part, and represent to her the great inconveniences not which her Soul, but her Body received from this inordinate Sorrow.

Madam, saies I to her, next to my Concern for your worthy Husband's untimely Death, I am griev'd to see what an Alteration the Bemoaning of his Loss has occasion'd in you: These Words raising her Curiosity to know what this Alteration was, I thus continu'd my discourse; In endeavouring, Madam, to extinguish, or at least to alleviate your Grief, than which nothing can be more prejudicial to a beautiful Woman, I intend a publick Benefit, for if the Public is interested, as most certainly it is, in the preserving of a beautiful Face, that Man does the Public no little Service who contributes most to its Preservation.

This odd Beginning operated so wonderfully upon her, that she desired me to leave this general Road of Complements, and explain my self more particularly to her. Upon this (delivering my self with an unusual Air of Gravity, which your Grace knows I seldom carry about me in the Company of Ladies) I told her, that Grief ruines the finest Faces sooner than any thing whatever, and that as envy it self could not deny her Face to be the most charming in the Universe, so if she did not suffer her self to be comforted, she must soon expect to take her Farewel of it. I confirm'd this Assertion, by telling her of one of the finest Women we ever had in England who did her self more injury in a Fortnight's time by lamenting her only Brother's Death, than ten Years could possibly have done; that I had heard an eminent Physician at Leyden say, That Tears (having abundance of saline Particles in them) not only spoild the Complexion, but hastned Wrinkles. But, Madam, concluded I, why should I give my self the trouble to confirm this by foreign instances, and by the Testimonies of our most knowing Doctors, when alas! your own Face so fully justifies the Truth of what I have said to you.

How! reply'd our disconsolate Widow, with a Sigh that came from the Bottom of her Heart, And is it possible that my just concern for my dear Husband, has wrought so cruel an Effect upon me in so short a Time? With that she order'd her Gentlewoman to bring the Lookinglass to her, and having survey'd her self a few Minutes in it, she told me she was perfectly convinced that my Notions were true; but, cries she, what would you have us poor Women do in these Cases? For something, continues she, we owe to the Memory of the Deceased, and something too to the World, which expects at least the common Appearances of Grief from us.

By your leave, Madam, saies I, all this is a Mistake, no better; you owe nothing to your Husband, since he is dead, and knows nothing of your Lamentation; besides, cou'd you shed an Ocean of Tears upon his Hearse, it would not do him the least Service; much less do you lye under any such Obligations to the World, as to spoil a good Face only to comply with its tyrannic Customs: No, Madam, take care to preserve your Beauty, and then let the World say what it pleases, your Ladyship may be revenged upon the World whene'er you see fit. I am resolved, answers she, to be entirely govern'd by you, therefore tell me frankly what sort of a Course you'd have me steer? Why, Madam saies I, in the first place forget the Defunct; and in order to bring that about, relieve Nature, to which you have been so long unmerciful, with the most exquisit Meats and the most generous Wines. Upon Condition you'll sup with me, cries our afflicted Lady, I will submit to your prescription. But why should I trouble your Grace with a Narration of every Particular? In short, we had a noble Regale that Evening in her Bedchamber, and our good Widow push'd the Glass so strenuously about, that her Comforter (meaning my self) could hardly find the way to his Coach. To conclude this Farce (which I am afraid begins now to be too tedious to your Grace) this Phoenix of her Sex, this Pattern of Conjugal Fidelity, two Mornings ago was marry'd to a smooth chin'd Ensign of Count Trautmandorf's Regiment, that had not a farthing in the World but his Pay to depend upon: I assisted at the Ceremony, tho' I little imagin'd the Lady would take the Matrimonial Receit so soon.

I was the easier perswaded to give your Grace a large Account of this Tragi-comedy, not only because I wanted better Matter to entertain you with at this Lazy Conjuncture, but also to show your Grace, that not only Ephesus in ancient, and England in later Times have afforded such fantastical Widows, but even Germany it self, where, if the Ladies have not more Virtue than those of their Sex in other Countries, yet they pretend at least a greater Management of the outside of it!

By my last Pacquet from England, among a heap of nauseous Trash, I received the Three Dukes of Dunstable,[1] which is really so monstrous and insipid, that I am sorry Lapland or Livonia had not the Honour of producing it; but if I did Penance in reading it, I rejoyced to hear that it was so solemnly interr'd to the Tune of Catcalls.[2] The Squire of Alsatia however, which came by the following Post, made me some amends for the cursed impertinence of the Three Dukes; and my witty Friend Sir C— S—y's Bellamira gave me that intire Satisfaction that I cannot read it over too often.

They tell me my old Acquaintance Mr. Dryden has left off the Theatre, and wholly applies him self to the Study of the Controversies between the two Churches. Pray Heaven! this strange alteration in him portends nothing disastrous to the State; but I have all along observed, That Poets do Religion as little Service by drawing their Pens for it, as the Divines do Poetry by pretending to Versification.

But I forget how troublesome I have been to your Grace, I shall therefore conclude with assuring you that I am, and to the last Moment of my Life shall be ambitious of being, My Lord,

Your Grace's most obedient,
and most obliged Servant,
G. Etherege.

---

[1] *A Fool's Preferment, or The Three Dukes of Dunstable*, by Thomas D'Urfey, was printed in 1688 and acted at Dorset Garden, *c.* April, 1688.
[2] The letter was reprinted up to this point in *The Matrons*, 1762.

To his Friend in London.

Dear Sir,

My Letters from England tell me, that this Summer my Lord-Chamberlain has won the Mony at Bowels, and my Lord Devonshire at Dice; I hope neither of 'em have been lucky at your cost. Before you receive this, I reckon you will be in your Winter-quarters, where you may have leisure to give me a short Account of what pass'd at the Campaign at Tunbridge. I cannot but remember Mr. M. tho' he seems to have quite forgot me; he is a very extraordinary Person, I find he had rather lend a Friend a hundred Pounds, than take the pains to write to him. I'm sensible his many Imployments afford him little leisure, and I shou'd pity his Mistress, but that I am perswaded his Prudence has made him chuse her in the Family. The Women here are not generally Handsome; yet there is a File of young Ladies in this Town, whose arms wou'd glitter were they drawn up against the Maids of Honour; but the Devil's in 't, Marriage is so much their Business, that they cannot satisfie a Lover that has Desires more fervent than Frank Villers. 'Tis a fine thing for a Man, who has been nourish'd so many Years with good substantial Flesh and Blood, to be reduc'd to Sighs and Wishes, and all those airy Courses which are serv'd up to feast a belle Passion; but, to comfort my self, in my Misfortune, I have learn'd to Ogle and Languish, in publick, like any Walcup; and to content my self, in private, with a piece of Houshold-bread, as well as some of my Friends. However unkind Fortune has been to you, don't revenge yourself on me; force the Sullenness of your Temper, and let me hear from you; it is not reasonable I should lose a Friend, because you have lost your Mony. Yours,

G. Etheridge.

From Ratisbon,
Aug. 23rd, 88.

PAPERS OF SIR WILLIAM TRUMBULL

Historical Manuscripts Commission. *Report on the MSS. of the Marquess of Downshire preserved at Easthampstead Park, Berks, Vol. I.*

Sir George Etherege to Sir William Trumbull.

1685, Dec. 8/18, Ratisbon.
I was going about making of legs and muttering of compliments and had wished a merry Christmas to half the Ministers here when I was stopped by a small fever... The Diet never does anything in holidays, and breaks up as formally as a great school before Christmas. I doubt not but my Lady Trumbull likes Paris as well as London with .... your good company, and I should like Ratisbon as well as Knightrider Street, were not the chief charm wanting, for here silence, solitude and good hours are in as great perfection as there, and keeping at home is the greatest pastime, for no visits can be made without sending a herald before to agree upon the entertaine. [3 pp., holograph. XXIII. 117.]

Sir George Etherege to Sir William Trumbull.

1685/6, Jan. 5/15, Ratisbon.
His Christian Majesty is ill satisfied of the Elector Palatine for not delivering up the accomplices of Cardel whom he has caused to be seized for some designs against him; this was the occasion of his recalling the Abbé Morel from that Court as appears in a letter the King wrote to the Elector from Versailles the 19th of December last, a copy of which I have seen. Monsieur de Crécy assures me that his Master has writ him a word that his displeasure against that Elector shall not make him undertake anything that may disturb the peace of the Empire: nevertheless the Empire is jealous of it as I find by the Count of Windisgratz, one of his Commissioners and Ambassador Extraordinary for foreign affairs here. [3 pp. holograph. XXIII. 6.]

Sir George Etherege to Sir William Trumbull.

1685/6, Jan. 5/15, Ratisbon.
Letters from Vienna say that the late Serasquier Seytan Basha has been strangled at Belgrade by the G. Signior's

orders, (1) for not relieving Neuheusal, (2) for not retaking Gran, (3) for hazarding battle.

Generals Mercy and Heusler understanding that the Turks had prepared a convoy in Transylvania to be sent to Temesvar and Lippa, sent 2,000 horse out of Szolnok, with some Dragoons and 3,000 Hungarians under Le Betnehazi to surprise the convoy, but the Turks fled to Arad. The two Generals marched thither with all their force and took the Town and burnt it to the ground. Six kettledrums and ten colours were sent to the Emperor.

The Castle of Mongatz is still in the Princess Ragotsky's possession, the marshy ground making it inaccessible to General Caprara except in hard frost.

Complaints are made that the troops of Brunswick and Luneberg coming from Hungary entered Mulhausen and Nordhausen by force and took up winter quarters there. [2½ pp. XXIV. 23.]

Sir George Etherege to Sir William Trumbull.

1685/6, Feb. 2/12, Ratisbon.

Your Memorial was printed here and made a great noise all over the Empire. It came to me at a time when the Elector Palatine's Minister had given in one to the Diet and the Emperor had caused another to be dictated there on behalf of the Knights of the Teutonic Order for grievances done them by his Christian Majesty against the *Armestitia* but now they begin to wonder they hear no more of it. The King of Poland's Envoyé in Persia has sent a courier to inform his Master that the Persian is marching with 30,000 men towards the Ottoman frontiers and intends next spring to fall on the Turk in those parts; by reason of the badness of the season and the danger the couriers run who are sent from Upper Hungary, our news is very uncertain. Teckeli is this post at liberty and is to command a body of Turks and Tartars, is made by the Grand Signor Prince of Transylvania in the place of Prince Abaffi who is to be driven out of that country. It may be the next will tell us he is close prisoner again, for it has gone alternatively so for some weeks. [2½ pp. holograph. XXIV. 66.]

Sir George Etherege to Sir William Trumbull.

1685/6, Feb. 23/March 5, Ratisbon.

The Carnival was this year pleasanter than ordinary, for Monsieur de Torsie (Mr. Colbert's son) being here has been the occasion of balls and masquerades. The Diet has done nothing this great while and the news from Vienna is not considerable.

The Duke of Zell at the time of the invasion of Hamburg sent two letters, one to the King of Denmark, the other to the Elector of Brandenburg, to acquaint them with his reasons for it; first as the Emperor's Commissioner he had sent to them several times to restore Mr. Meurer, a Burgomaster, to his office and possessions from which he was expelled about three years since, for having a design to betray the privileges of the town, as a contrary faction pretended. Meurer is now at the Court of Zell, but the Emperor has lately made him *Consiliarius Imperii Aulicus*. Secondly, that the town has behaved itself insolently towards him, having prohibited all commerce with his subjects, and refused to annul the Act at his instance. The King of Denmark has marched all his troops to the banks of the Elbe in to Holstein Gottorf, and sent the Duke word he has no other intent but to secure his frontiers from the incursions of ungovernable soldiers; he has sent copies of the Duke's letter and his answer to a Deputy of the Electoral College here and has desired him to assure the Diet he will undertake nothing against the *Armistitia* concluded. Nevertheless we hear the Lunenburgers keep close together since the approach of these troops and will draw off when they have gotten what money they can of the Hamburghers for sparing their gardens, which are very extraordinary for their beauty and number. The Elector of Brandenburg offered the town 2,000 men to assist them, but they refused the offer. They are jealous of all their neighbours, and not without cause; they all strive to have them in their protection, and they wisely refuse all, and find the number of pretenders is their best security.

I do not doubt your intimation concerning the Elector of Cologne; the Bishop of Strasburg, who governs all, knows how to be grateful for being named in the next promotion. [3½ pp. holograph. XXIV. 90.]

425

Sir George Etherege to Sir William Trumbull.

1685/6, March 2/12, Ratisbon.

The relation the Emperor has to the Elector Palatine is that the Prince his son has married a sister of the Emperor's. How far that will engage him against the King of France's pretensions is not discoursed of here, but the great preparations for the next campaign against the Turks and the zeal with which he carries on that war make me believe he will be very unwillingly diverted from it.

To-morrow the Count de Crécy delivers a memorial to the Diet by instruction from his master; the substance of it is that he will accept the Pope's mediation, which is what the Elector has offered as to the differences between them. The King insisted upon an arbitration, which the Elector waived, pretending he could not consent to it without the approbation of the Emperor and the whole Estates of the Empire. The difference between a mediation and an arbitration, together with the whole state of the case, I will send you by the next post. But the acceptance of this mediation is limited with these conditions, that the Estates of the Empire are to engage (that is make a decree) that Madame d'Orleans is not to suffer in her right by the elapsing the year during which time the Elector has possession of the lands she pretends to. [3 pp. holograph. XXIV. 101.]

Sir George Etherege to Sir William Trumbull.

1685/6, March 9/19, Ratisbon.

Monsieur de Crécy delivered last week to the Diet the French King's demands that the Estates of the Empire would assure him that the Elector Palatine shall not receive any damage by the possession of the lands in dispute, to the prejudice of Madame d'Orleans, though the year elapses, and that upon this caution he will yield to the Pope's mediation, which is what the Elector offered, when he would not submit to his arbitration without the Emperor's and the Estates of the Empire's consent. The King, it is supposed here, has been brought to this by the Nuncio's solicitation at Paris and some of the

Princes of the Empire have been privy to it, since many of their Deputies owned they had already received instructions in this matter upon the delivery of the Memorial. What the King will accept of, and what the Diet will offer, is not discoursed of; many of the Deputies say it is but reasonable they should do something towards satisfying his M.C. Majesty. The law here differs not much in this point from ours in England, and Madame d'Orleans will receive no other damage by the elapsing of the year than what she receives at present in being kept out of possession and being forced to be plaintiff. If by a suit she recovers the lands, she will discover the mean profits too: besides Monsieur de Crécy in a former Memorial has made claim in Madame's name, which secures her right. This being so, many imagine anything will satisfy his M.C. Majesty but the putting Madame into possession, and makes them apprehend that this Memorial is but a manifest that he will undertake nothing against the common peace of the Empire, and if the Diet does not do it, he will take possession in her name, and make the Elector plaintiff in his turn. The most prudent here are of opinion the Elector has done himself an injury by taking possession of the personal estate before it was inventoried and praised; though he promises to be responsible (that undoubtedly belonging to Madame) it gives his adversaries occasion to say (most of it consisting in corn and wine) that there is a daily consumption of it, and that the true value can never be known; I find the opinion of the moderate Ministers here is that the County of Spanheim, which came into the family by the marriage of an heiress is allodial; but that Zimeren and Lautren, which some ages since came by purchase are fiefs-male. It is certain the Duchy of Zimeren was not a member of the Electorship, since the branch of Charles the late Elector were Dukes of Zimeren when by the failure of another line the Electoral Dignity fell to them; whether it is now annexed to the Electorship is very disputable, since it has been often bequeathed to younger brothers of the family; and after a contest Edward, the younger brother of Charles Lewis, was put into possession of it in 1653, and enjoyed it till his death not many years since,

427

but it is certain also that this Duchy upon the wanting of issue male has still returned to the family, but not gone to the daughters of those younger brothers. The Diet have given the Emperor fifty Roman months. There is some difference among the Colleges about the form of the conclusion but it is thought it will be adjusted to-morrow. [3pp. holograph. XXIV. 96.]

Sir George Etherege to Sir William Trumbull.

1686, April 20/30, Ratisbon.
The Imperial decree was concluded by the Diet a week ago. It is what was desired by Monsieur de Crécy in his memorial; the three Colleges, having deliberated on that and on one of the Elector Palatine's, resolved that they ought to give the French Plenipotentiary the declaration on behalf of the Empire that not only the annual possession could not be alleged to the advantage of the Elector but that it could not bring any prejudice to Madame d'Orleans.

The Council of War at Vienna are ordering the next campaign. I know not whether the Emperor's envoy will own to you that Caprara had abandoned the siege of Mongatz. [3pp. holograph. XXIV. 176.]

Sir George Etherege to Sir William Trumbull.

1686, June 1/11, Ratisbon.
Refers to death of his friend, Sir William Clifton, a hopeful young gentleman. Has not yet heard of Mr. Fitz James. The Diet have admitted the Princes of D[i]etrickstien and Waldeck into the College of Princes. The Conference at Augsburg begins about the middle of the month; the business is an alliance projected, since that of Luxemburg and Franconia are [*sic*] expired for the defence of the Empire till the *Punctum securitatis publicae* be settled here: that which will chiefly obstruct this matter is the difficulty the Circle of Swabe makes in admitting the Spaniard and Swede and indeed any strangers into the Alliance. The Circle of Franconia is willing to admit them, only the Duke of Wurtemburg, it is said, intends to protest against the instruction of the

428

Deputies of the Directory of that Circle, this being a league against the French. They are very industrious to hinder the keeping of 60,000 men in arms to watch their motions, and I am apt to believe they have possessed some of the parties with such prejudices that it will not have the good success the Emperor expects.

I heard from the camp by Kaab on the 2nd instant, new style, that Prince Louis of Baden came thither the night before and that the Elector of Bavaria arrived there that day. There are many factions in the army which occasions the so often changing their resolutions; it was then agreed the Elector with the Army he is to command a part should besiege Alba Regalis and the Duke of Lorraine with his army was to cover the siege towards Buda: that which delays the campaign is the Brandenburg troops, who are not yet arrived but expected in 8 days from the date of my letter. I hear since from Vienna that the Duke of Lorraine is come to the camp and that Major-General Ralerta Taff and Palfy with many other officers have left that town to hasten thither, that their counsels are changed again and that Buda is to be besieged with both the armies joined. The factions and punctilios among the officers will make them do the Turk more service than the Emperor. [4pp. holograph. XXV. 14.]

Sir George Etherege to Sir William Trumbull.

1686, July 20/30, Ratisbon.
Understands that Sir William receives news from Hungary by the Emperor's minister. Mr. Fitz-James was named in the Gazette as among the dead, but is well. Vaudrey was wounded with a stone in the assault [of Buda]. [2½pp. holograph. XXV. 70.]

Sir George Etherege to Sir William Trumbull.

1686, August 24/Sept. 3, Ratisbon.
The succour which got into Buda some days after the victory against the 10,000 which were detached on the 14th August by the Grand Vizier, is not considerable, as appears from letters captured of the Governor to the

429

Vizier—of 150 Janissaries who got in not 50 were un-wounded; he cannot defend himself long. The Vizier had drawn his army some hours further from the Imperialist camp, but now appears again, and it is thought he resolves whatever it cost him to succour the place. The German infantry is in a manner ruined; the Duke of Lorraine and the Elector of Bavaria have had to dismount their cavalry to supply their wants in the trenches. The Brandenburgers and Saxons have lost half their numbers. No advance has been made towards taking the place since they lodged themselves on the breach on 27 July. Their pioneers are worth nothing, almost all their mines have a contrary effect. Disease prevails. A Saxon officer writes that he has not been in bed for eighteen days; bread is scarce and rotten. The Turks might starve all their horses: if they made a bridge and stopped their foragers. The Bavarians got into the second story of the castle, and disputed it chamber by chamber with the Turks, making holes in the walls, and flinging *grenados* at one another. The Imperialists are not strong enough to guard their trenches and force the Turks to a battle. The 1,200 Swedes are at Cormoren, and General Scharfenberg is daily expected with 9,000 men from Transilvania. Mr. Forbes died at Vienna of his wounds. [5pp. holograph. XXV. 118.]

Sir George Etherege to Sir William Trumbull.[1]

1686, Aug. 31/Sept. 10, Ratisbon.
It was designed to take the Governor of Buda alive, but he was killed in his own house. The Grand Vizier, who saw the town taken is endeavouring his retreat. The Turks set fire to the town. The army, except twenty regiments, is marching after the Vizier to ease him of his baggage.

Lord Chandos, not deserving the favour of the Court, serves the Turkey Company at a cheaper rate than ordinarily. Find for how many years he agreed with them, how near his time is out, and how much yearly they allow him. Lord Winchelsey had 10,000 rix dollars

[1] Cf. Letterbook, p. 101.

per annum and 2,000 gratuity. Sir Da. Harvey the same allowance, but the Company disputed the gratuity. Lord Chandos as a disaffected person serves them at an under rate. The King's having no good opinion of him, was the reason he was intended to be recalled. The charge, if looked into, is not so great as the Company will pretend in setting out Sir W. Soames: the same presents will serve and it is no more than what they gave for equipage, which I think was £600, and I am sure not more than £800. If your friends press hard at Court, you may get over this rub. [4pp. holograph. XXV. 128.]

Sir George Etherege to Sir William Trumbull.[1]

1686, November 8/18, Ratisbon.
The Secretary of this Embassy at Constantinople ' is allowed 600 Lion Dollars a year which is paid by the merchants, the Company esteem him their servant and pretend a right to choose him; if you think fit to have a private secretary, you must pay him yourself, but you may endeavour to get the Company to approve one whom you shall recommend; the man who enjoys the place at present is one Mr. Cook;' his principles and his countenance ' are both very odd .... he is of a humour that agrees with that people, is a man of good .... parts, but I fear you will not find them turned to your liking.... As for other matters I recommend you to Sir Dudley North, who is the best able of any I know to inform you; he is a kinsman of my dead friend, Sir Wm. Soames, and can tell you what agreement he made; he has been Treasurer to the Company at Constantinople, and knows what things you will find there and what will be necessary for you to carry with you; .... he is very much a gentleman, and will not be wanting to oblige one who has deserved his Majesty's favour.' [3pp. XXV. 170.]

[1] Cf., Letterbook, pp. 115–16.

EXTRACTS FROM VISCOUNT PRESTON'S PAPERS.

B. M. Add. MS. 34517.[1]

Ratisbon, 24 Dec./3 Jan., 1688/9.

My Lord:

The Prince Lewis of Baden has been here three days with the Margrave his uncle; and this morning is gone past for Munich from whence he goes to the Elector of Saxony and other chief Princes of the Empire, to execute a secret commission which he has from the Emperor. I believe it is nothing else than to assure them, that he will jointly with them make a vigorous war against the French the next spring and to take such measures with them as are necessary for the beginning of the campaign. The French have so enraged the Germans with the many outrages they have committed in the country that the several States were never so united and animated to revenge them. This makes me hope but little success from any endeavours which may be used to prevent the bloody war which is threatened.

His Majesty has been so shamefully betrayed at home that our nation has justly lost the little reputation it had recovered. Honour and honesty are looked upon by foreigners to be no more of the growth of our unhappy island. A Parliament is called I hear. I wish it could be such a one as would sincerely labour to establish a healing peace among us by having a due regard to his Majesty's prerogative as well as to the privilege of the subject. I must confess the greatest good I expect from it, is that it will open the eyes of many well meaning men who have been grossly imposed upon.

God preserve his Majesty from the hands of his enemies; while his person is not in their power it will mark the place where all his faithful subjects may rally. Whose numbers cannot but be considerable though the perfidious and ungrateful have seduced many with them. The most considerable thing in this conjuncture is to gain

[1] The originals of the following letters are in possession of Sir Richard Graham, Bart., at Netherby Hall, Cumberland. Extracts have been printed by the Historical Manuscripts Commission, Report 7, p. 428 seq.

time, impostures cannot be long concealed, mankind is unconstant especially the humour of a whole nation, the face of affairs cannot be long the same in Christendom so that a powerful assistance may be had in case it be requisite. I hope your Lordship will pardon me the confidence I have taken in communicating to you a few of my sentiments on this matter; the zeal I have to serve his Majesty makes me very uneasy in a place where I cannot shew it as I would do wherefore I think of coming into England.

Pray my Lord if this should happen prepare his Majesty to forgive me my not waiting till I was recalled. I am so useless here that I hope you will think it a lawful ambition to desire[1] to be where I may venture my life in performing my duty. My allegiance and my gratitude tell me it is base to be unactive when my King and Master's crown and person are in danger. I am, My Lord,
Your Lordship's most faithful and most humble servant,
Geo. Etherege.

My Lord, [1688/9 Jan. 28th.][2]
On Saturday last a certain paper came to my hands which I find was read a day or two before in the hall of re et correlatione to most of the members of the Diet, by Danckleman, the Elector of Brandenburg's deputy. I send it your Lordship translated into French. I believe you will be very much surprised at the insolence of this deputy, who durst publish in so august an assembly so infamous a libel against his Majesty. To vex me the more, I cannot prudently at this time take so much notice of it as I should, but must wait for a more favourable conjuncture. In the meantime all I can do is to expose the weakness and deceitfulness of his arguments in such places as are proper. The States of Holland and the Protestant Princes who are engaged in the Prince of Orange's design, recollecting themselves that a war begun by them on the account of religion may be of dangerous consequence, should it be taken notice of by

---

[1] MS. 'sesire'.
[2] Date supplied from Hist. MSS. Com. Report.

F f

the Roman Catholic Princes before they have proceeded so far as to fix the foundation of that vast building which seems to be projected by them, have ordered their ministers, especially those who are employed in the Empire, to insinuate and declare that the invasion of our country by the Prince of Orange is not so much to establish the affairs of the Church as to regulate the affairs of State, in order to lessen the greatness of France, and is purely grounded on a politic interest. They hope with this to amuse the Roman Catholics, while they carry on their own business; but to make this theme take, the Prince of Orange should have made another manifest. I wish all our countrymen who are misled by an apprehension that their religion is in danger were well informed of these practices, that they may be no longer cheated by any tinsel pretexts. The foolish and impudent author of the enclosed is so confident of the success of his party that he already places the Prince of Orange on the throne, regulating the affairs of England. The house of Austria can do nothing without the help of this Almanzor.[1] He will do them justice against the French, and fight for all the Princes who will favour his ambition; no wonder, since it is to make way for so general a blessing that his Majesty is unjustly attacked under the name of evil counsellors, and the Prince of Wales presumed to be supposed. Notwithstanding the pains he takes to dissemble he is not able to hold out to the end of the chapter, his praising a notable pamphlet called *L'Europe Esclave si L'Angleterre ne rompt ses fers*, which was written by the same foolish zealot who made *Le Croisade des Protestants ou projet sur l'institution des Chevaliers de St. Paul*, discovers what his principals are at bottom.

My Lord,

Yo^r Lo^{ps} most humble and most obedient servant,

Geo. Etherege.

[1] See Dryden's heroic tragedy *The Conquest of Granada*, in which the hero Almanzor wins battles single-handed.

MSS. OF SIR FREDERICK GRAHAM BART. AT NETHERBY HALL, CO. CUMBERLAND.

Historical Manuscripts Commission, Report 7, pp. 428.

[*Sir*] *George Etherege to Mr. Tempest.*

1688/9, Dec. 24/Jan. 3, Ratisbon.

While things go so ill in England I imagine you are not very curious to know what passes in the Empire . . . . . . I have received your letter of the 4th instant, which is so obliging that I am impatient to be personally acquainted with you.

EXTRACT FROM WIGMORE'S LETTER TO ETHEREGE.

European Magazine, June 1795, p. 397. See Introduction, p. 43, note.

Last night was buried Mad. Ellen Gwyn, the D. of St. Albans' mother. She has made a very formal will, and died richer than she seemed to be whilst she lived. She is said to have died piously and penitently; and as she dispensed several charities in her lifetime, so she left several such legacies at her death; but what is much admired is she died worth and left to D. of St. Albans, vivis et modis, about 1,000,000l. stirling, a great many say more, few less.

APPENDIX

The two following letters should have appeared on page 125.

Ratisbon, 27 Dec./6 Jan. 86/7.

To my Lord Middleton of Count Lamberg's being checked for saying things might be heard etc. Of Monsieur de Crécy's orders to tell the Diet, that in case they come not speedily to treat of the execution of the armistice, his master will take such measures etc. :

Ditto.

To Mr. Robson presenting him 20 guineas to buy his wife a plate (for soliciting in the Treasury).

INDEX

437

438

CENTRAL EUROPE
IN THE XVIIᵗʰ CENTURY

PR. = Principalities   D. = Duchy   EL. = Electorate
The Boundary of the German Empire shown thus ‑·‑·‑